Aaron Pinnix, Axel Volmar, Fernando Esposito, Nora Binder (eds.)
Rethinking Infrastructure Across the Humanities

I0616424

Aaron Pinnix is a postdoctoral researcher in American studies at Universität Konstanz in Germany. His research is on ocean-focused poetry that conjoins ecological and social justice.

Axel Volmar is currently a guest professor at the Institute for Music and Media at Humboldt-Universität zu Berlin. His research is on media history, media theory, and the praxeology of media, intersecting with the history of science, infrastructure studies, and disability studies.

Fernando Esposito is assistant professor at the Department of Modern History at the Universität Konstanz. His book *Fascism, Aviation and Mythical Modernity* (2015) scrutinizes the aviation discourse in Italy and Germany, reading it as a blueprint for a fascist mythical modernity. His second book (habilitation) deals with the transformation of European understandings of time and history and the chronopolitics that arose from modern temporality.

Nora Binder is a postdoctoral researcher in the history of the human and social sciences at Universität Konstanz. Her current project investigates the epistemology of human interrelations within applied psychology and its ties with the concept of social competence (1930-1970). In her doctoral thesis *Kurt Lewin und die Psychologie des Feldes* (2023) she scrutinizes early experimental social psychology and the beginnings of group dynamics.

Aaron Pinnix, Axel Volmar, Fernando Esposito, Nora Binder (eds.)

Rethinking Infrastructure
Across the Humanities

[transcript]

Bibliographic information published by the Deutsche Nationalbibliothek
The Deutsche Nationalbibliothek lists this publication in the Deutsche Nationalbibliografie; detailed bibliographic data are available in the Internet at http://dnb.d-nb.de

First published in 2023 by transcript Verlag, Bielefeld
© **Aaron Pinnix, Axel Volmar, Fernando Esposito, Nora Binder (eds.)**

Cover layout: Maria Arndt, Bielefeld
Cover illustration: Berlin Tempelhof Airport, former airport of Berlin, Germany. Photo: katatonia / Adobe Stock

https://doi.org/10.14361/9783839469835
Print-ISBN: 978-3-8376-6983-1
PDF-ISBN: 978-3-8394-6983-5
ISSN of series: 2702-8968
eISSN of series: 2702-8976

Contents

Section III: Infrastructures and Sociality

Section IV: Infrastructures and Religion

Section V: Infrastructures and Genre

Section VI: Infrastructures and the Environment

Section VII: Infrastructures and Colonialism

Section I: Setting Out Some Definitions

Introduction

Aaron Pinnix, Axel Volmar, Fernando Esposito, and Nora Binder

Looking back on a fascinating life between New York and Berlin, recently deceased cultural historian Wolfgang Schivelbusch recalled his first train journey in the United States in the 1970s. To his great surprise, the train car had no compartments at all. Rather, it was an open coach—a single continuous space divided by a centre aisle and seats arranged in rows—an arrangement Europeans have since become accustomed to. On the other hand, "The space in which people travelled in Europe, at least over long distances, was actually a small intimate cabinet. Easily recognizable as the successor to the stagecoach, where travellers sat facing each other."[1] This "fundamentally different shaping of the same technical apparatus" prompted Schivelbusch to trace the origins of this difference.[2] Whereas the horse-drawn carriage was the starting point of the European train car, the American open coach was, according to Schivelbusch, inspired by the steamboat. In fact, "it is a ship set on land."[3] However, the reasons for the differences between the railroad cars extend beyond that and concern not only divergent settlement histories of the two continents, but also the very different "superstructures" of each continent, an observation he presented in his 1977 book *Geschichte der Eisenbahnreise*, translated 2 years later as *The Railway Journey: The Industrialization of Time and Space in the Nineteenth Century*.[4] Drawing on Leo Marx's 1964 classic text *The Machine in the Garden*, Schivelbusch argues that,

> In the United States the industrial revolution was seen as a natural development, not only because it appeared right at the beginning of American history, but also because it happened first in agriculture and transportation, and was thus related

---

1   Wolfgang Schivelbusch, *Die andere Seite: Leben und Forschen zwischen New York und Berlin* (Hamburg: Rowohlt, 2021), 120. Translation by Fernando Esposito, 2023.

2   Schivelbusch, *Die andere Seite*, 121.

3   Schivelbusch, *Die andere Seite*, 123.

4   Wolfgang Schivelbusch, *Geschichte der Eisenbahnreise* (Munich: Carl Hanser Verlag, 1977); Wolfgang Schivelbusch, *The Railway Journey: The Industrialization of Time and Space in the Nineteenth Century* (Berkeley: University of California Press, 1977).

directly to nature. [...] This immediate relation with (or embedding in) nature provided the material base for the American notion, classically described by Leo Marx,
of machinery and industry as forces that do not destroy nature but actually realize
its potential by cultivating it. Paraphrasing Emerson, Marx says that the industrial
revolution appeared as a "railway journey in the direction of nature."[5]

Whereas people in Europe, by and large, perceived technology as destructive, public
discourse in North America often perceived technology as creative. This interpretation may lack nuance, but it draws attention to *infrastructures* as multifaceted and
multilayered phenomena that serve as a means of moving people, goods, and signs
across physical spaces, act as topics of public debate and political struggle, as sites
of individual experience, and as catalysts for collective meaning making. Infrastructure is commonly understood in ways that emphasize its material and organizational characteristics, for instance, in the form of transport, energy, or communication infrastructures or as public institutions and services. However, as *The Railway
Journey* reminds us, a crucial yet frequently neglected aspect of infrastructure are its
cultural dimensions. Railroads in the nineteenth century, as Schivelbusch argues, not
only sped up the pace of material and cultural flows between distant places, they also
fundamentally changed perceptions of time and space. However, this radical transformation was not caused by steel rails or the steam engine alone. Rather, it was the
practices and discourses that accompanied the railroad which directed its meanings, and in turn even influenced how train cars were constructed. Drawing on Karl
Marx, these different kinds of "superstructure" affected how the railroad became an
infrastructure—of transportation, of economic exchange, of sense perception, and of
political/imperialist ideology—in the first place. In a similar vein, the contributions
to *Rethinking Infrastructure Across the Humanities* approach diverse types of infrastructures as the support systems of human sociality, as well as fundamentally shaped by
cultural aspects like public imaginaries, social practices, and historical transformations.

Our understanding of infrastructure builds on a growing body of scholarly
works which have contributed to the formation of *infrastructure studies* as an interdisciplinary research field. Infrastructure is commonly understood in ways that
emphasize its material characteristics, but as recent theoretical developments in a
range of fields, including science and technology studies (STS), history, anthropology, urban studies, literary studies, and media studies have argued, infrastructure
comprises far more than just the roads, bridges, pipelines, dams, subways, airports,
electrical grids, and other material structures people often associate with the term.
Rather, as infrastructure studies has shown, the seemingly immaterial structures

---

5   Schivelbusch, *The Railway Journey*, 91; et seq. See also Leo Marx, *The Machine in the Garden:
     Technology and the Pastoral Ideal in America* (New York: Oxford University Press, 1964), 238.

and cultural configurations that undergird and direct life across the globe today are just as important. In his influential 2013 article, "The Politics and Poetics of Infrastructure," anthropologist Brian Larkin adopts a traditional definition of infrastructure as "built networks that facilitate the flow of goods, people, or ideas and allow for their exchange over space,"[6] while also equally calling attention to the fact that infrastructures "exist as forms separate from their purely technical functioning, and they need to be analyzed as concrete semiotic and aesthetic vehicles oriented to addressees."[7] Infrastructures, then, "are things and also the relation between things."[8] Such an approach raises questions regarding infrastructures' symbolic and cultural values, their hidden social biases and exclusions, the normativity of their assumed use practices, and the ways in which infrastructural systems are "embedded"[9] or "grounded"[10] in various physical, socio-political, and cultural environments. As humanities scholars have grappled with the notion of infrastructure, an earlier focus on the vast "underlying structures" of societies and economies has shifted toward examining infrastructural configurations on smaller scales and orders of magnitude, as well as to infrastructures of a less material and more abstract nature. By asking what it means to take such reinterpretations of infrastructure seriously, the contributions to this volume consider infrastructures as foundational parts of diverse phenomena ranging from clan structures to couple apps, as well as understanding language, concepts, ideology, religion, and genre as symbolic infrastructures.

Transformations of "Infrastructure" as a Concept

Understanding infrastructure to mean such diverse things might make the term feel rather diluted—and indeed some scholars have criticized such uses of infrastructure as a concept because of this.[11] Germany's most prominent infrastructure scholar,

---

6   Brian Larkin, "The Politics and Poetics of Infrastructure," *Annual Review of Anthropology* 42, no.1 (2013): 327–343, 328.

7   Larkin, "The Politics and Poetics of Infrastructure," 329.

8   Larkin, "The Politics and Poetics of Infrastructure," 329.

9   Susan Leigh Star and Karen Ruhleder, "Steps Toward an Ecology of Infrastructure: Design and Access for Large Information Spaces," *Information Systems Research* 7, no. 1 (1996): 111–134.

10   Nicole Starosielski, *The Undersea Network* (Durham: Duke University Press, 2015), 19.

11   Charlotte P. Lee and Kjeld Schmidt, "A Bridge Too Far? Critical Remarks on the Concept of 'Infrastructure' in Computer-Supported Cooperative Work and Information Systems," *Socio-Informatics: A Practice-Based Perspective on the Design and Use of IT Artifacts*, eds. Volker Wulf et al. (Oxford: Oxford University Press, 2018), 177–217; David Hesmondhalgh, "The Infrastructural Turn in Media and Internet Research," in *The Routledge Companion to Media Industries*, ed. Paul McDonald (London: Routledge, 2021), 132–142.

Dirk van Laak, for instance, has recently argued against the expansion of the term, as "in the broadest sense, it describes everything that enables societal activities of any kind," and thus "runs the risk of becoming a 'diffuse all-purpose metaphor for almost any form of system,' robbing the term of analytical sharpness."[12] However, we maintain that the reason why so many different phenomena have been referred to as infrastructures in the past years has to do with the transformation—some would rightly speak of decay—of the centralized nation state model of large scale industrial technical systems and the rise of a new plurality of infrastructural regimes that we have yet to fathom.[13] Thus the shift in how infrastructure is understood—away from meaning only the technical-material arteries of "solid" modernity and toward the seemingly immaterial support systems, formal structures, and cultural forms of our "liquefied" and digitalized present—was triggered by a fundamental structural change that in the past five decades has radically altered the world and our societies.[14] At the same time, infrastructure's semantic expansion reflects a waning focus on "structure" in the wake of poststructuralism and the decline of Marxism. The concept of infrastructure has thus entered a gap left by the exhaustion of Marxist debates regarding the relationship between superstructure and base—a term rendered as infrastructure by French Marxists and 'structuralists' such as Louis Althusser for example—and poststructuralism's as well as others' critiques of the concept of structure.[15] For more on these developments, please see the second chapter in this volume, which features a detailed history of the relation between "structure" and "infrastructure" (*Christian Meyer*). In the following, we review some of the discursive shifts that contributed to this recent and expanded understanding of the "infrastructure" concept before introducing the individual contributions in greater detail.

Materially, infrastructure has existed since the oldest human-created roads, canals, and bridges. Conceptually, however, the term is far more recent. Combining the prefix "*infra*," meaning below or beneath, with "*structura*," meaning the form or arrangement and relation of the essential parts of an object, the word "infrastructure" was seemingly first used as a French railroad engineering term in 1875 to refer to the literal understructure of railways, meaning the land, embankments, and

12   Dirk van Laak, "Infrastructures," *Docupedia* (May 20, 2021), https://doi.org/10.14765/zzf.dok-2 215.

13   See Eva Barlösius, *Infrastrukturen als soziale Ordnungsdienste. Ein Beitrag zur Gesellschaftsdiagnose* (Frankfurt a.M.: Campus 2019), 194–198.

14   Zygmunt Bauman, *Liquid Modernity* (Malden: Polity Press, 2000). See also Manuel Castells, *The Rise of the Network Society* (Cambridge: Blackwell 1996); and Anselm Doering-Manteuffel and Lutz Raphael, *Nach dem Boom. Perspektiven auf die Zeitgeschichte seit 1970* (Göttingen: Vandenhoeck & Ruprecht, 2008).

15   See François Dosse, *History of Structuralism*, Two Vols. (Minneapolis: University of Minnesota Press, 1997); and Johannes Angermüller, *Nach dem Strukturalismus. Theoriediskurs und intellektuelles Feld in Frankreich* (Bielefeld: transcript, 2007).

bridges over which the railway ran, as distinct from the railway's superstructures of rails, trains, and stations.[16] The term entered the English language in 1927 as a means of referring to underground military constructions like tunnels or culverts, before being used to describe the larger network of civilian networks like roadways, waterways, airports, and communication systems that could be mobilized for national self-defence.[17] In the late 1950s, the term infrastructure began to be used within the NATO—the point of entry, for instance, into German—replacing the earlier phrase of "social overhead capital," which had itself referred to much of what we might still understand today as infrastructure, including transportation and power systems, as well as amorphous large-scale systems like educational and governmental services.[18] Expanding outward from its roots in the French railway system, and greatly fuelled by its NATO-related uses in post-WWII Europe, the term "infrastructure" came to be understood as referring to the shared public (or quasi-public) installations and services that provide resources to citizens, ranging from transportation networks, electricity grids, and water and sewage systems, to services in health care, education, and commerce that continue to underlie much of contemporary existence.

In the 1970s, infrastructures began to spark the interest of scholars from within the social and human sciences, including economic sociologists, political economists, and historians of science and technology. Through the end of the 20th century, numerous studies on large-scale energy, transportation, and communication systems appeared, such as works on the emergence and development of railroads, highways, electric power, the telegraph, the telephone, the radio, and the internet.[19] Moreover, a group of European and American researchers of technol-

---

16   Dirk van Laak, "Der Begriff der 'Infrastruktur' und was er vor seiner Erfindung besagte," *Archiv für Begriffsgeschichte* 41 (1999): 280–299. See also, Ashley Carse, "Keyword: Infrastructure. How a Humble French Engineering Term Shaped the Modern World," in *Infrastructures and Social Complexity: A Companion*, eds. Penelope Harvey, Casper Bruun Jensen, and Atsuro Morita (London: Routledge, 2016), 27–39; Ara Wilson, "The Infrastructure of Intimacy," *Signs: Journal of Women in Culture and Society* 41, no. 2 (January 2016): 247–280, 267.

17   Wilson, "The Infrastructure of Intimacy," 267, and Geoffrey Bowker, "Sustainable Knowledge Infrastructures," in *The Promise of Infrastructure*, eds. Nikhil Anand, Akhil Gupta, and Hannah Appel (Durham: Duke University Press, 2018), 203–222, 212.

18   William Rankin, "Infrastructure and the International Governance of Economic Development, 1950–1965," in *Internationalization of Infrastructures: Proceedings of the 12th Annual Conference on the Economics of Infrastructures*, eds. Jean-Francois Auger, Jan Jaap Bouma, and Rolfe Künneke (Delft: Delft University of Technology, 2009): 61–75, 64–65. See also Dirk van Laak, *Alles im Fluss: Die Lebensadern unserer Gesellschaft – Geschichte und Zukunft der Infrastruktur* (Frankfurt am Main: S. Fischer, 2018), 15.

19   Alfred D. Chandler, *The Visible Hand: The Managerial Revolution in American Business* (Cambridge, Harvard University Press: 1977); JoAnne Yates, *Control through Communication: The Rise of System in American Management* (Baltimore: Johns Hopkins University Press, 1989); Tom

ogy began to systematically examine the formation and evolvement of large-scale infrastructures, which they termed "large technical systems" (LTS).[20] Following the lead of Thomas Parke Hughes, LTS researchers argued that large technical systems unfolded according to distinct patterns or evolutionary steps. Taking the dissemination of power grids as an exemplary case, in his monograph *Networks of Power* Hughes proposes a "model of systems evolution" for infrastructure formation that consists of an invention and development phase, followed by stages of technology transfer, system growth, and system momentum.[21] More generally, as Paul Edwards points out, the LTS researchers argued that "individual infrastructures follow a life cycle, a developmental pattern visible only on historical time scales," and that "infrastructures consist not only of hardware, but also of legal, corporate, and political-economic elements."[22] The general lesson was that technological systems are "not only socially shaped," but rather "social through and through."[23]

Although the perspectives taken in LTS studies changed over time—for instance, while Hughes focused on what he called "system builders," i.e. inventor-entrepreneurs, managers, and financiers, Claude Fischer applied a "user heuristic" to emphasize how user practices contribute to further developments in technical systems[24]—the studies were nonetheless united by a common focus on infrastructures

---

Lewis, *Divided Highways: Building the Interstate Highways, Transforming American Life* (New York: Viking, 1997); Stephen Goddard, *Getting There: The Epic Struggle between Road and Rail in the American Century* (New York: Basic Books, 1994); Bruce E. Seely, *Building the American Highway System: Engineers as Policy Makers* (Philadelphia: Temple University Press, 1987); Thomas Hughes, *Networks of Power: Electrification in Western Society, 1880–1930* (Baltimore: Johns Hopkins University Press, 1983); Menahem Blondheim, *News Over the Wires: The Telegraph and the Flow of Public Information in America, 1844–1897* (Cambridge: Harvard University Press, 1994); Tom Standage, *The Victorian Internet: The Remarkable Story of the Telegraph and the Nineteenth Century's On-Line Pioneers* (New York: Walker; 1998); Susan Douglas, *Listening In: Radio and the American Imagination* (New York: Times Books, 1999); Janet Abbate, *Inventing the Internet* (Cambridge: MIT Press, 1999); Michael Hauben and Ronda Hauben, *Netizens: On the History and Impact of Usenet and the Internet* (Los Alamitos: IEEE Computer Society Press, 1997).

20   Wiebe E. Bijker, Thomas P. Hughes, and Trevor Pinch, eds., *The Social Construction of Technological Systems: New Directions in the Sociology and History of Technology* (Cambridge: MIT Press, 1987); Renate Mayntz and Thomas P. Hughes, eds., *The Development of Large Technical Systems* (Boulder: Westview Press, 1988); Todd R. La Porte, ed. *Social Responses to Large Technical Systems: Control or Adaptation* (Dordrecht: Kluwer Academic Publishers, 1991); Jane Summerton, ed., *Changing Large Technical Systems* (Boulder: Westview Press, 1994).

21   Hughes, *Networks of Power*, 14.

22   Paul N. Edwards, "Infrastructure and Modernity: Force, Time, and Social Organization in the History of Sociotechnical Systems," in *Modernity and Technology*, eds. Thomas J. Misa, Philip Brey, and Andrew Feenberg (Cambridge: MIT Press, 2003), 187–225, 199.

23   Edwards, "Infrastructure and Modernity," 199–200.

24   Hughes, *Networks of Power*; Claude S. Fischer, *America Calling: A Social History of the Telephone to 1940* (Berkeley: University of California Press, 1992), 17.

as socio-technical systems of large proportions. With the growing dissemination of digital information and communication technologies brought about by networked computing, the 1990s gave rise to rather different approaches to conceptualizing and studying "infrastructure." During an ethnographic study accompanying the development of a distributed digital information system for biologists, sociologists Susan Leigh Star and Karen Ruhleder (1996) observed that programmers ("designers") and scientists ("users") held importantly differing views regarding the purposes, and hence functionality, of the information system under construction. Based on their ethnographic work, Star and Ruhleder reframed infrastructure as "a fundamentally relational concept" based on a number of features that link infrastructures to different actors and their respective experiences, interests, and social status.[25] For more on this shift from a material, system-oriented perspective on infrastructure to a relational, actor-oriented, and praxeological understanding as well as some of its methodological implications, please see the third chapter in this collection (*Axel Volmar*).

In their co-authored book *Sorting Things Out*, Star and Geoffrey Bowker extend this relational concept of infrastructure to include *symbolic* entities, such as labels, categories, and classification systems, thereby highlighting the political dimensions and implications of such seemingly insignificant structures.[26] Several chapters in this book build upon the idea of symbolic or abstract infrastructures, exploring, for instance, how different groups maintain and shape language (in both oral and written form) as a basic infrastructure of human communication (*Bettina Braun* and *Bernhard Brehmer*), and how the intentional "engineering" of concepts and conventions of language use may affect how people perceive reality (*Jochen Briesen* and *Steffen Koch*). Other contributors understand symbolic infrastructures as comprising customs and rituals (*Rudolf Schlögl*), intepret Kurt Lewin's experimental practice as well as concept of "group dynamics" as an infrastructure of democractic change management (*Nora Binder*), or consider the hashtag as an infrastructural medium that allows for organizing online discourses and supporting the formation of collective "voices" (*Steffen Krämer* and *Isabell Otto*).

This relational understanding of infrastructure developed by Star and her collaborators not only reverberated within STS, it also impacted scholars of other academic disciplines, including historians, anthropologists, literary scholars, and me-

---

25   Star and Ruhleder defined eight features to capture the relationality of infrastructure: (1) embeddedness, (2) transparency, (3) reach or scope, (4) learned as part of membership, (5) links with conventions of practice, (6) embodiment of standards, (7) built on an installed base, and (8) becomes visible upon breakdown. Star and Ruhleder, "Steps Toward an Ecology of Infrastructure", 113.

26   Geoffrey C. Bowker and Susan Leigh Star, *Sorting Things Out: Classification and Its Consequences* (Cambridge: MIT Press, 1999).

dia scholars. Additionally, as more and more scholars from the humanities started to grapple with the notion of infrastructure, new understandings of the term, as well as new infrastructural approaches, emerged.

Surprisingly, it was not until about the year 2000 that historiography devoted itself to systematic infrastructure research. As the aforementioned Schivelbusch demonstrates, there had of course been (cultural) historical studies on large scale infrastructures like railroads or the development of municipal supply systems, but these works were not based on theoretically-supported concepts of infrastructure.[27] In fact, historical scholarship has, by and large, utilized a narrow concept of infrastructure as "fixed facilities," or as "everything stable that is necessary to enable mobility and an exchange of people, goods and ideas."[28] Often, historiography has concentrated "on the practices of negotiating, building, maintaining and using" large-scale infrastructures, as well as on the nexus between infrastructures, power, and sovereignty.[29] Whether imperial or national, infrastructures served as a means of politics: they penetrated space, integrated even the most remote territories, and helped to extract resources.[30] For instance, in the Imperium Romanum infrastructures served as monumental symbols of power that underpinned the legitimacy of rule, with the building of infrastructures legitimating the state.[31] The complementarity of state and infrastructure has led Jo Guldi to speak of the "infrastructure state."[32] As recent studies show, practices regarding provision of the public good (*Daseinsvorsorge*) are by no means limited to the modern state—such practices were already commonplace in late medieval Italian city-states.[33] Historical scholarship

---

27   See Dirk van Laak, "Infra-Strukturgeschichte," *Geschichte und Gesellschaft* 27, no. 3 (2001): 367–393, 387.

28   Edwards, "Infrastructure and Modernity," 186; and Laak, *Alles im Fluss*, 13.

29   Christian Henrich-Franke, "Historical Infrastructure Research: A (Sub-)Discipline in the Making?," in *Infrastructuring Publics*, eds. Matthias Korn et al. (Wiesbaden: Springer Fachmedien, 2019), 49–68, 50. See also: Keller Easterling, *Extrastatecraft: The Power of Infrastructure Space* (London: Verso, 2016) and Jens Ivo Engels, "Machtfragen. Aktuelle Entwicklungen und Perspektiven der Infrastrukturgeschichte," *Neue Politische Literatur* 55, no. 1 (2010): 51–70.

30   Dirk van Laak, *Imperiale Infrastruktur: Deutsche Planungen für eine Erschließung Afrikas 1880 bis 1960* (Paderborn: Schöningh, 2004), 404–409.

31   On infrastructures in antiquity, see for example: Clifford Ando and Seth Francis Corning Richardson, eds., *Ancient States and Infrastructural Power: Europe, Asia, and America* (Philadelphia: University of Pennsylvania Press, 2017); and Anne Kolb, ed., *Infrastruktur und Herrschaftsorganisation im Imperium Romanum: Herrschaftsstrukturen und Herrschaftspraxis III* (Berlin: De Gruyter, 2014). See also, in this collection Ulrich Gotter's "Command and Consilium: On Infrastructures of Decision-making in Roman Culture."

32   Jo Guldi, *Roads to Power: Britain Invents the Infrastructure State* (Cambridge: Harvard University Press, 2012).

33   See Guy Geltner, *Roads to Health: Infrastructure and Urban Wellbeing in Later Medieval Italy* (Philadelphia: University of Pennsylvania Press, 2019).

has also concentrated on infrastructures as "the connective tissues and the circulatory systems of modernity."[34] Accordingly, within the field of history there is a wide variety of works on the development and expansion of canals, roads, railroads, electricity networks, systems for supplying water, as well as communication systems.[35]

More recently, an expanded concept of infrastructure has begun gaining a foothold in historical scholarship—there too infrastructure is being transformed from an object of study to an approach. For instance, Mary Bridges has recently argued that historians should not only move away from a narrow, materialist understanding of infrastructure and adopt a function-oriented approach, but they should also focus their attention on infrastructure's latent potential or dispositions, as well as to the hidden power dynamics infrastructures set in motion.[36] In line with such debates, contributions in this book argue for an expanded understanding of infrastructure in relation to power, such as approaching Roman *consilia* as infrastructures of decision-making (*Ulrich Gotter*), and exploring the medieval parish church as a meeting ground and form of connection between the church and local communities (*Gabriela Signori*). Other chapters trace the interplay and conflicts between co-existent material, ideological, or cultural infrastructures, for instance in medieval transmediterranean relations between Christians and Muslims (*Daniel G. König*), between transportation systems and clan structures in southern France (*Manuel Borutta*), in relation to imagined infrastructure projects as expressing eurocentrist visions of "Eurafrica" (*Martin Rempe*), and in relation to imperialist road building as being driven by fascist Italy's culture of "total mobilization" (*Fernando Esposito*).

In urban studies, the idea that infrastructure can be used as a means of uncovering how power and people interrelate (or are divided) through infrastructure has become quite influential. In 2001, the collected volume *Splintering Urbanism: Networked Infrastructures, Technological Mobilities and the Urban Condition*, co-edited by Stephen Graham and Simon Marvin, introduced sociologists and geographers

---

34   Edwards, "Infrastructure and Modernity," 185 et seq. See Birte Förster and Martin Bauch, eds., *Wasserinfrastrukturen und Macht von der Antike bis zur Gegenwart* (Berlin: De Gruyter, 2015); and Abigail Agresta, *The Keys to Bread and Wine: Faith, Nature, and Infrastructure in Late Medieval Valencia* (Ithaca: Cornell University Press, 2022).

35   Seminal studies on the respective infrastructures are, for example: Chandra Mukerji, *Impossible Engineering. Technology and Territoriality on the Canal du Midi* (Princeton: Princeton University Press, 2009); Schivelbusch, *Railway Journey*; Hughes, *Networks of Power*; Susanne Frank and Matthew Gandy, eds., *Hydropolis: Wasser und die Stadt der Moderne* (Frankfurt am Main: Campus, 2006); Roland Wenzlhuemer, *Connecting the Nineteenth-Century World the Telegraph and Globalization* (Cambridge: Cambridge University Press, 2015).

36   Mary Bridges, "The Infrastructural Turn in Historical Scholarship," *Modern American History* (April 18, 2023): 1–18, 10 et seq.

to understanding urban environments and urban experiences through the lens of infrastructure. Within the last two decades, the goal of studying the distribution of structural inequalities through infrastructures has led to the development of various infrastructural approaches. By "plac[ing] infrastructure at the heart of understanding the social and political composition of cities worldwide,"[37] urban studies has sought to address the inequalities brought about by the design and execution of urban infrastructures, in turn pioneering understanding infrastructure as an indirect means of rule and governance.[38] Recent studies have moved toward identifying the social and political impacts of less visible infrastructures, such as how "municipal debt has proven to be a durable means of structuring racial privileges, entrenching spatial neglect, and distributing wealth and power."[39]

In a similar vein, anthropologists have mobilized infrastructural approaches as a means of observing infrastructure's political implications. Drawing on previous works, the collection *The Promise of Infrastructure* considers how infrastructure functions as a "technology of liberal rule," reminding us that "this form of governance known as liberalism must always be understood, from its inception, as guaranteeing the liberties of some through the subordination, colonization, and racialization of others,"[40] activities which are themselves enabled through infrastructures. Locally, access to infrastructures and infrastructural needs often spark debates and may lead to informal political constellations.[41] For instance, in relation to the "economic collaboration among residents seemingly marginalized from and immiser-

---

37   Alan Wiig et al., "From the Guest Editors: Splintering Urbanism at 20: Mapping Trajectories of Research on Urban Infrastructures," *Journal of Urban Technology* 29, no. 1 (2022): 1–11, 2.

38   For more on this topic, see, for instance, Adrienne Brown, *The Black Skyscraper: Architecture and the Perception of Race* (Baltimore: Johns Hopkins University Press, 2017); Stephen Graham, *Disrupted Cities: When Infrastructure Fails* (New York: Routledge, 2010). For related topics that move beyond the urban, strictly defined, to include rural and contested spaces, see Ashley Carse, *Beyond the Big Ditch: Politics, Ecology, and Infrastructure at the Panama Canal* (Cambridge: MIT Press, 2014); Huub Dijstelbloem, *Borders as Infrastructure: The Technopolitics of Border Control* (Cambridge: MIT Press, 2021).

39   Destin Jenkins, *The Bonds of Inequality: Debt and the Making of the American City* (Chicago: University of Chicago Press, 2021), 1.

40   Nikhil Anand, Akhil Gupta, and Hannah Appel, eds. *The Promise of Infrastructure* (Durham: Duke University Press, 2018), 4, 5.

41   One such example for the emergence of nonofficial social infrastructures is Nikhil Anand's study on the water system in Mumbai, where slum-dwellers engage powerful patrons to negotiate access to the water system by promising electoral support. Nikhil Anand, "Pressure: The Politechnics of Water Supply in Mumbai," *Cultural Anthropology* 26, no. 4 (2011): 542–564. Another example is Antina von Schnitzler's investigation of biopolitical subject formation through an infrastructural lens by linking the introduction of water meters in South Africa with a campaign that seeks to educate people in how to monitor and moderate their water consumption. Antina von Schnitzler, "Citizenship Prepaid: Water, Calculability, and Techno-Politics in South Africa," *Journal of Southern African Studies* 34, no. 4 (2008): 899–917.

ated by urban life" in Johannesburg, AbdouMaliq Simone suggests considering "people as infrastructure."[42] As Hannah Appel, Nikhil Anand, and Akhil Gupta emphasize, anthropological approaches have rightly stressed the fact that infrastructures are "critical locations through which sociality, governance and politics, accumulation and dispossession, and institutions and aspirations are formed, reformed, and performed," and therefore deserve our utmost attention.[43] Adding to this line of infrastructure research, the contributions to this volume trace the interplay and co-dependency of transportation infrastructures and infrastructures of spirit in Zambia (*Thomas G. Kirsch*), and highlight the power of metrics as a narrative infrastructure that guides the development of the solar off grid energy sector in Kenya (*Eva Riedke*).

In the last decade, media scholars have turned to infrastructure studies to complement traditional approaches to studying media infrastructures, question common narratives of technological progress, or reconsider widespread conceptions of "media." In their collection *Signal Traffic: Critical Studies of Media Infrastructures*, Lisa Parks and Nicole Starosielski draw on insights from previous scholarship on infrastructure to suggest attending to today's "contradictory global mediascapes and multiple *media infrastructures*" by considering their interrelatedness on multiple scales, their relationality and interconnectedness with other systems, as well as their environmental conditions and affective relations.[44] In *The Undersea Network*, Nicole Starosielski uses site-specific histories of distinctive "nodes" of the Pacific undersea cable network to trace how cable infrastructure intersects with, and is embedded within, physical, socio-political, and cultural environments. Based on this topographic approach, Starosielski suggests an understanding of the global cable infrastructure that is rather counterintuitive to popular narratives of networking: "wired rather than wireless; semicentralized rather than distributed; territorially entrenched rather than deterritorialized; precarious rather than resilient; and rural and aquatic rather than urban."[45] In turn, by bringing together infrastructural thinking with cultural techniques research and emphasizing the logistical and infrastructural role of media, John Durham Peters attempts to reconceptualize "media" in his book *The Marvelous Clouds* as less a means of conveying information and unifying society than more generally as "devices of tracking and orientation"

---

42   AbdouMaliq Simone, "People as Infrastructure: Intersecting Fragments in Johannesburg," *Public Culture* 16, no. 3 (2004): 407–29, 408, 410.

43   Hannah Appel, Nikhil Anand, and Akhil Gupta, "Introduction: Temporality, Politics, and the Promise of Infrastructure," in *The Promise of Infrastructure*, eds. Nikhil Anand, Akhil Gupta, and Hannah Appel (Durham: Duke University Press, 2018), 1–38, 3.

44   Lisa Parks and Nicole Starosielski, eds., *Signal Traffic: Critical Studies of Media Infrastructures* (Urbana: University of Illinois Press, 2015), 1, 7. Italics original.

45   Nicole Starosielski, *The Undersea Network* (Durham: Duke University Press, 2015), 10, 19.

or, in other words, as "media that stand under."[46] Following Star and Bowker's attention toward the infrastructuredness of symbolic objects, media scholars have addressed seemingly immaterial and mundane phenomena, such as the sociotechnical patterning of time as an infrastructure comprised of artifacts, technical standards, human labor, social norms and conventions.[47] Adding to these works, contributions in this volume consider couple apps as mobile infrastructures of "relationship work" (*Anne Ganzert*), and the hashtag as an important infrastructure of the internet's public sphere (*Steffen Krämer* and *Isabell Otto*).

In the realm of literary studies, the concept of "infrastructure" has gained traction as a means of analysing and understanding literary forms, as well as a means of considering how material and social infrastructures affect our lives. In 2010, Caroline Levine proposed "infrastructuralism" as a new formalist mode for analysing texts, an approach that takes seriously the institutions that lie beneath social life in order to discover the abstract patterns that are repeated across time and space, and in turn identifying social and literary structures as themselves forms of infrastructure.[48] For instance, Levine considers the television show *The Wire* as "demand[ing] that we read multiple institutions for their discrepant temporalities, their multiple speeds, their replication over long stretches, and their unpredictable shifts and disruptions of one another's power." [49] Competing infrastructural traits are expressed in a range of jostling and competing institutions that get depicted both within the show's narrative and in viewers' experience of the show. The term "infrastructuralism" was picked up again five years later by Michael Rubenstein, Bruce Robbins, and Sophia Beal in their introduction to a special issue of *MFS: Modern Fiction Studies* on infrastructure, in which they argue for the importance of attending to infrastructure as a means of engaging with the assumptions and ambiguities that mark individuals' encounters with infrastructures, including the "'planned violence' of infrastructures of control and coercion."[50] Similarly, the scholar Dominic Davies has pub-

---

46   John Durham Peters, *The Marvelous Clouds: Toward a Philosophy of Elemental Media* (Chicago: University of Chicago Press, 2015), 7.

47   See, for instance, Sarah Sharma, *In the Meantime: Temporality and Cultural Politics* (Durham: Duke University Press, 2014); Axel Volmar and Kyle Stine, *Media Infrastructures and the Politics of Digital Time. Essays on Hardwired Temporalities* (Amsterdam: Amsterdam University Press, 2021): 9–38, 11–12, 15. https://library.oapen.org/handle/20.500.12657/50573.

48   Caroline Levine, "Infrastructuralism, or the Tempo of Institutions," in *On Periodization: Selected Essays from the English Institute*, ed. Virginia Jackson (Cambridge: The English Institute, 2010), para. 53–96, 65.

49   Levine, "Infrastructuralism," para. 95.

50   Michael Rubenstein, Bruce Robbins, and Sophia Beal, "Infrastructuralism: An Introduction," *MSF Modern Fiction Studies* 61, no. 4 (2015): 575–586, 581, 585. This understanding of infrastructure as a form of "planned violence" is further explored in the collected volume *Planned Violence: Post/Colonial Urban Infrastructure, Literature and Culture*, edited by Elleke Boehmer and Dominic Davies (Cham: Springer, 2018).

lished two books on colonial and postcolonial literature and media that focus on how infrastructures can function as structural forms of violence.[51] For instance, *Urban Comics: Infrastructure and the Global City in Contemporary Graphic Narratives* considers how graphic narratives produced by artistic collectives in cities across the globe subvert genre norms in order to express anti-colonial sentiments.[52] Here, infrastructure includes the formal aspects of graphic narratives, such as comics' "grids, gutters and panels," as well as material infrastructures (or the lack thereof) that are represented in these texts, such as roads, electrical wiring, or security cameras.[53] As these examples show, in literary studies infrastructure can be understood as referring to genre norms and literary forms, as well as referring to material infrastructures, how such material infrastructures are represented in texts, and infrastructures' effects of people's lives, with special attention paid to how such effects are represented within literature.[54] In line with such studies, the contributions of literary scholars in this volume explore such topics as how the formation of infrastructural systems in the 19th and 20th century shaped the modern novel and expectations of literature (*Timo Müller*), how infrastructures can themselves be used as allegories for understanding abstract concepts like sustainability (*Katalin Schober*), how romance functions as genre infrastructure and how such genre norms can be subverted, especially in relation to contemporary queerings (*Anja Hartl, Jonas Kellermann*, and *Christina Wald*), how 17th century South American Indigenous water infrastructures are represented in Indigenous documents in ways that argue for the benefit of Indigenous models for organizing society (*Kirsten Mahlke*), how written correspondence among religious actors in early Christianity functioned as infrastructures of knowledge production and circulation (*Barbara Feichtinger*), and how poetry can guide us in attending to, and accounting for, the life-disrupting byproducts of infrastructures (*Aaron Pinnix*).

In the central studies discussed above very different aspects of infrastructure, both as a topic and a concept, have been brought to the forefront. What unites these different studies, both within the humanities and STS, is that they consider infrastructure as complex and multi-layered cultural phenomenon. Moreover, the heightened scholarly interest on infrastructure as a topic and concept has inspired re-

---

51   In addition to *Urban Comics*, discussed next, Davies also published *Imperial Infrastructure and Spatial Resistance in Colonial Literature, 1880–1930: Race and Resistance across Borders in the Long Twentieth Century* (New York: Peter Lang, 2017).

52   Dominic Davies, *Urban Comics: Infrastructure and the Global City in Contemporary Graphic Narratives* (New York: Routledge, 2019).

53   Davies, *Urban Comics*, 6.

54   See, for instance, Michael Rubenstein, *Public Works: Infrastructure, Irish Modernism, and the Postcolonial* (Notre Dame: University of Notre Dame Press, 2010); Manu Karuka, *Empire's Tracks: Indigenous Nations, Chinese Workers, and the Transcontinental Railroad* (Oakland: University of California Press, 2019); Lauren Berlant, "The Commons: Infrastructures for Troubling Times," *Environment and Planning D: Society and Space* 34, no. 3 (2016): 393–419.

searchers to develop and apply what could be called infrastructural approaches or methodologies. The notion of "infrastructuralism" that has emerged from these different interests is an exciting concept that we believe will guide future research and allow us to rethink infrastructure across the humanities.[55] What exact features may constitute infrastructuralism as a broad set of theoretical and methodological approaches shared across the humanities, and whether such an approach may be able to take up the legacy of older paradigms, such as structuralism and poststructuralism, remains an open, yet alluring possibility. What insights might we gain if we consider our disciplines' phenomena using infrastructure as an analytical tool? And how best might an infrastructural methodology, especially one that traverses disciplinary boundaries, proceed? These questions are far-reaching, certainly too far-reaching to be answered here, and yet they came to the fore as we—an interdisciplinary group of scholars at the University of Konstanz—began discussing the concept of "infrastructure" as an object of study, an analytical term, and a methodology. *Rethinking Infrastructure Across the Humanities* in part documents these conversations and is intended as an exploration of the possibilities of infrastructure research within the humanities.

Rethinking Infrastructure Across the Humanities

Rather than organizing this collection's chapters according to strictly academic fields, we have grouped the chapters into six unique thematic arrangements that invite the possibility of transdisciplinary conversations and connections. Taking seriously the idea that infrastructures can be understood as foundational support structures of human sociality, the following sections are organized around unique, and perhaps surprising, conceptual foci: "Setting out Some Definitions," "Infrastructures and Communication," "Infrastructures and Sociality," "Infrastructures and Religion," "Infrastructures and Genre," "Infrastructures and the Environment," and "Infrastructures and Colonialism." This organizational approach emphasizes how infrastructural research within the humanities can traverse and conjoin a wide range of academic fields, while also articulating aspects of infrastructure that often remain underexplored and underarticulated. Overall, we hope that this collection

---

55   See the above conversation regarding literary scholars Caroline Levine and Michael Rubenstein, Bruce Robbins, and Sophia Beal. In his 2010 memorial for Claude Lévi-Strauss, anthropologist Marshall Sahlins also proposes "infrastructuralism" as a means of conjoining concepts and the material within social anthropology (Sahlins, "Infrastructuralism," 374–375). In 2015, John Durham Peters suggests "infrastructuralism" as "a way of understanding the work of media as fundamentally logistical" (Peters, *The Marvelous Clouds*, 37–38). Clearly, the relevance of infrastructuralism as a conceptual tool is growing.

will help to foster a robust conversation within the humanities about infrastructure as both topic and methodological tool.

Section I, "Setting Out Some Definitions," extends the work begun in this introduction by further clarifying and defining infrastructure in regard to its historical development and growth as a concept today. In addition to this introduction, this section features chapters drawn from the fields of sociology and media studies to articulate infrastructure's conceptual development and explore how infrastructure can offers us unique conceptual insights. Following the introduction, sociologist *Christian Meyer*'s "From Structure to Infrastructure: Some Glimpses on a Theoretical Movement in the Social Sciences and Humanities" clarifies and historicizes the concept of infrastructure, including the shift from structure to infrastructure. As Meyer shows, while today's understanding of infrastructure was originally subsumed under the concept of structure, there remain important ontological differences between both. In the next chapter, "From Systems to 'Infrastructuring': Infrastructure Theory and Its Impact on Writing the History of Media," Axel Volmar revisits how the notion of infrastructure became an analytical tool in the social and human sciences since the 1990s and how the rise of infrastructural thinking is tied to a conceptional shift from a systemic to a praxeological understanding of infrastructure. Volmar exemplifies the impact of this shift with regards to theoretical and methodological changes within media studies and more particularly, the historiography of media.

Drawing from the fields of linguistics, philosophy, media studies, and history, Section II, "Infrastructures and Communication," explores how communication, which is often understood as foundational for human experience, can itself function as a form of infrastructure. First, in "Language as Infrastructure," linguistic scholars *Bettina Braun* and *Bernhard Brehmer* explore how language is a basic means of information exchange, how language is routinized, and also undergoes change. Braun and Brehmer present specific examples proving their claims, including how speech sounds are produced by the body, the differences between oral and written language, and how communities maintain and navigate language, including in relation to material infrastructures like public signs. In the next chapter, "Conceptual Infrastructure and Conceptual Engineering," philosophers *Jochen Briesen* and *Steffen Koch* consider conceptual systems and languages as a form of abstract infrastructure that could be purposefully engineered to help certain terms and concepts stand out favourably, with the overall goal of improving our social, political, and personal lives. As Briesen and Koch show, since language and concepts are maintained they can also be purposefully guided. In the following chapter, "Practices of Classification: The Hashtag as Infrastructure for Interaction," media scholars *Steffen Krämer* and *Isabell Otto* consider the hashtag as infrastructural media that mediates between platform technologies and cultural processes, while also being generative and relational in its own right, as the #metoo movement shows. Krämer and Otto persuasively use the hashtag to argue for understanding infrastructures, practices, and cultural formations as both recursively interrelated and able to produce new narratives and social movements. This section concludes with historian *Rudolf Schlögl*'s "On the Symbolic Infrastructure of Communication Among Those Present in Early Modern Society: Simple Successful Media," which explores how communication mechanisms in Early Modern European society served as infrastructures for differentiating and reproducing social systems. Drawing on sociologist Niklas Luhmann's concept of the interplay of Alter and Ego, Schlögl demonstrates how forms of communication like gifts and rituals functioned as infrastructures by providing local opportunities for reinforcing large-scale social hierarchies and processing social problems.

With research drawn from the fields of history, media studies, and history of the humanities, the chapters in Section III, "Infrastructures and Sociality," argue for considering how interpersonal relations themselves function as infrastructures, revealing important outcomes for how socialization and relationships occur within society. As historian *Ulrich Gotter* shows in "Command and Consilium: On Infrastructures of Decision-Making in Roman Culture," decision-making processes in middle and late republican Rome (4th–1st century BCE) functioned as infrastructures of political space. Gotter first considers the example of the elevation of a victorious army commander to imperator before discussing the more historically common, though thus-far-undertheorized, *consilia*, which were advisory councils that often consisted of people from a range of cultural backgrounds. *Consilia* enabled channels of communication between lower- and upper-ranking individuals, while also influencing other structures, such as the social distribution of roles. Moving to the digital age, media studies scholar *Anne Ganzert*'s "Couple Apps as Relationship Infrastructures" considers couple apps as infrastructures that both emerge within media practices and mediate human relationships. Arguing for the importance of understanding apps as infrastructures, this chapter shows how apps shape the user's behaviour, value perceptions, and social interactions. In "Infrastructures of Democracy: Lewinian Group Dynamics and the Managment of Social Change (1930s-1940s)," historian of science *Nora Binder* considers the invention of group dynamics by social psychologist Kurt Lewin and his student Ronald Lippitt in the 1930s and 1940s, in order to argue that in Lewinian group dynamics the interplay of the group's relational features and its generative capacity account for its exploitation as a powerful infrastructure of democratic re-education. This section concludes with historian *Daniel G. König*'s "Conflicting Infrastructures: Ideological vs Social Infrastructures in Transmediterranean Communications of the Twelfth and Thirteenth Centuries," which explores how an ideological infrastructure, namely European-Christian crusading ideology, interrelated with a social infrastructure, as expressed in the *fondaco-*system in which a separate quarter in a Muslim-ruled port city was populated by European-Christian foreigners, mostly traders. Considering Genoa between 1250 and 1270, Koenig's chapter shows how the ideological and social infrastructures of crusading zeal and long-standing commercial interests coexisted.

Religion, marked as it is by an emphasis on belief and an engagement with the spiritual, may initially seem like an odd choice for being understood in infrastructural terms, but as the chapters in Section IV, "Infrastructures and Religion," show, religion can have profoundly infrastructural roles. Including research from the fields of anthropology, classical philology, and medieval history, in this section authors argue that expressions of faith codify and cultivate larger social structures. First, in "Spiritual Infrastructures," anthropologist *Thomas G. Kirsch* considers Pentecostalist practices in Zambia's Gwembe Valley as a spiritualist infrastructure that forges relationships among religious practitioners and with the spiritual realm. Drawing on Kirsch's ethnographic fieldwork, the chapter first considers how the expansion of Zambia's road infrastructure contributed to the evangelizing mission of Bishop Rabson of the Spirit Apostolic Church (SAC), before considering how a spiritual entity like the Holy Spirit can organize and influence adherents who might otherwise have little connection with each other. Next, in "Infrastructure of Faith: Some Considerations on Correspondence in Late Antique Christianity," classical philologist *Barbara Feichtinger* explores how long-distance written correspondences among bishops, clerics, and Christian ascetic movements were constitutive for the historical spread of Christianity in the Mediterranean region. Feichtinger argues that the circulation of letters functioned as an infrastructure of knowledge production and dissemination that fostered a common understanding of Christianity, and she presents the writings of Saint Jerome as a prime example of how text migration shaped early Christianity. This section concludes with medieval historian *Gabriela Signori*'s "Religious Infrastructure: The Parish Church," which considers the 13th century parish church as the basic ecclesiastical administrative unit of the German Christian church. Late medieval churches were both embedded within and influenced the local community, a relationship that was in turn developed by community members through altar and mass endowments that expressed their appreciation of the liturgy of the Mass, thus allowing the laity to influence the church.

Drawing on literary scholarship and anthropology, the following section, "Infrastructure and Genre," considers how the stories we tell and are told are themselves infrastructured in ways that have specific, locatable effects. In "Infrastructural Poetics," literary scholar *Timo Müller* compares Charles Dickens's *Bleak House* (1852–53) and James Joyce's *Ulysses* (1922) as a means of tracking how the increased infrastructuration of modern society influenced the modern novel. As Müller shows, the increasingly complex and intertwined world caused by the growth of new systems of mobility, communication, and mass media profoundly shaped the modern novel, including the internal organization of texts, as well as shaping the idea of what literature is and does. Next, in "Queering Infrastructures of Romance," literary scholars

Anja Hartl, *Jonas Kellermann*, and *Christina Wald* argue that romantic love is a mental, social, and cultural infrastructure that informs and guides experiences of love, and which in turn has been built and rebuilt over centuries. Showing how infrastructures of romance can be subversively repurposed, Hartl, Kellermann, and Wald consider William Shakespeare's *Romeo and Juliet* (1597) and its queer adaptation in Douglas Stuart's novel *Young Mungo* (2022) as one example of how modelled forms of love undergo change in response to diversifying sexualities and gender identities. This section concludes with anthropologist *Eva Riedke*'s "Counting the Impacts in the Solar Off Grid Sector," which addresses how the metrics used to measure off grid solar energy production attract investment. While metrics incentivize relations between solar off grid companies and investors, they are also future-oriented in ways that affect their function. For instance, companies use measurements that reflect the number of people in a household who could *potentially* use a lantern. This anticipatory praxis is a narrative embedded within the metrics of off grid energy production that affects which projects become realized.

Infrastructures are always specifically *located*, and as such affect and influence the people and the environments around them. Drawing on the fields of the literary and film studies, the chapters of Section VI, "Infrastructures and the Environment," explore infrastructures' substantial ecological and political effects. Literary studies scholar *Kirsten Mahlke*'s "Water for a Good Government: Andean Infrastructures in Guaman Poma de Ayala's Chronicle (1615)" focuses on Indigenous scholar Guaman Poma's arguments made to the Spanish king regarding the importance of valuing existing Indigenous water infrastructures. Challenging Spaniards failure to respect water, Guaman Poma advocated for a holistic Indigenous understanding of infrastructure in which Andean irrigation knowledge is understood as simultaneously material, cultural, and spiritual. Next, in "The Dangers of Infrastructure Byproducts and What We Can Learn From Muriel Rukeyser's 'The Book of the Dead,'" literary studies scholar *Aaron Pinnix* argues that we should attend to how even miniscule material byproducts of infrastructures affect the operations of life. Considering the high mortality rates of miners from silica poisoning, as discussed in Muriel Rukeyser's documentary poem series "The Book of the Dead" (1938), Pinnix connects this avoidable tragedy to the contemporary, but relatively underexamined, poisoning of salmon from tire wear and road runoff to argue that both intentional and unintentional byproducts of infrastructures should be accounted for, especially in relation to how such byproducts disrupt the operations of life. This section concludes with literary studies scholar *Katalin Schober*'s "Afrofuturist Infrastructure as Allegory: Picturing Sustainability in Wanuri Kahiu's *Pumzi* (2009)," which considers how infrastructures are allegorized can both conceal and reveal alternatives. Considering the titular short Afrofuturist film *Pumzi*, Schober argues that the film functions as an extended allegory that reflects infrastructures' capacities and shortcomings by helping to shift viewer's understanding of infrastructure away from overexploiting natural resources and toward alternative infrastructures of sustainability.

Rethinking Infrastructure Across the Humanities concludes with a focused consideration of how infrastructure has been utilized in transmediterranean colonial relationships and projects. Fully drawn from the field of history, the chapters of Section VII, "Infrastructures and Colonialism," explore how infrastructures, both real and imagined, have organized relationships between Europe and Africa. The section begins with historian *Manuel Borutta*'s "Canals & Clans: Mediterranean Infrastructures," which focuses on the idea of an integrated "Eurafrica." Beginning with Michel Chevalier's 1832 concept for a Euro-Mediterranean system of canals, railways, steam ships and telegraph lines, Borutta next focuses on Marseille as an exemplar city of Chevalier's plan before concluding with a consideration of the influence of Corsican mobsters on Marseille, pointing toward an alternative form of transmediterranean social infrastructure. Next, in "Imagined Infrastructures: Eurafrica and Worldmaking in the Mid-Twentieth Century," historian *Martin Rempe* explores unrealized infrastructure projects that sought to physically connect Europe and Africa. These include architect Herman Sörgel's *Atlantropa* project (1932), which proposed constructing a gigantic dam at the Strait of Gibraltar in order to lower the level of the Mediterranean and gain territorial connectivity to Africa, as well as subsequent imagined infrastructures envisioned a world spatially arranged and demarcated according to European imaginaries. Finally, in "Imperial Roads and the Fascist Culture of Total Mobilization," historian *Fernando Esposito* considers the Fascist invasion of Ethiopia from an infrastructural perspective, paying particular attention to the concept of movement and its relationship to imperial roads and total mobilization. Overall, Esposito shows how Fascist attempts to conquer Ethiopia relied on a massive road building project fuelled by a culture of total mobilization.

Acknowledgements

The editors would like to thank Daniel G. König and Kirsten Mahlke for being interlocutors and readers. We would also like to express our gratitude to Scott Walkinshaw and Rachel Ham for their invaluable work as assistants.

From Structure to Infrastructure: Some Glimpses on a Theoretical Movement in the Social Sciences and Humanities

Christian Meyer

Programmatic endeavours such as the "infrastructural turn"[1] or "infrastructuralism"[2] are not restricted to a new interest in technical systems but propose an entirely new axiom for the study of culture and society. In these endeavours, infrastructures are ascribed a new paradigmatic status far beyond technical installations that provide specific services for mankind. In other words, they are applied to immaterial—practical, symbolic, and ideational—phenomena. In doing so, infrastructuralist approaches put a particular focus on dimensions that have been overlooked by traditional approaches to the study of culture: materialities and proliferations, conditions and generative accomplishments, relations and regular operations, which are, often invisible and taken for granted, warranting the status quo of culture and society. Part of the concept "infrastructure" is the term "structure," literally meaning *setup*, *layout*, or *construction*, which is then qualified by the prefix "infra-," signifying *beneath* or *below (the ground)*. And yet, infrastructuralist endeavours critically distance themselves from ideas of structure that they view as overly static and overly metaphysical (i.e., transcendental in the sense of being latent and hidden as well as accessible only by scientific or otherwise sophisticated methods that are superior to everyday reason).

---

1   Explicitly: Stephen Graham, *Disrupted Cities: When Infrastructure Fails* (New York: Routledge, 2010), 10–16. Also see Susan Leigh Star and Karen Ruhleder, "Steps Towards an Ecology of Infrastructure: Complex Problems in Design and Access for Large-Scale Collaborative Systems," in *Proceedings of the Computer Supported Cooperative Work* (Association for Computing Machinery, 1994): 253–264.

2   E.g., Marshall Sahlins, "Infrastructuralism," *Critical Inquiry* 36 (2010): 371–385; John Durham Peters, *The Marvelous Clouds: Toward a Philosophy of Elemental Media* (Chicago: The University of Chicago Press, 2015).

In the Occident[3] the term "structure" has a colourful and consequential conceptual history. Originating in Latin Antiquity, it helped establishing the modern sciences in the 15th and 16th centuries by allowing them to conceptualize the interplay of different recurrent factors, or forces of nature, that are needed to initiate, constitute, produce, or causally determine, a phenomenon accessible to the human senses. In the 19th century, the term was transferred with quite some discussion to social, cultural, and mental phenomena. Here, the hopes were concentrating on the identification of long-term historical structures and their relation to events as well as on functions of structural elements that are required for a societal whole to continue existing. In this process, similarities, and differences between the sciences, that focus on nature, and the humanities, that address culture and society, were claimed, discussed, and reflected, and ever since, the well-known battles about the unity of the sciences versus the delimitation of the "two" or "three cultures," respectively, have become permanent.[4] These battles are partly about the concept of "structure" and its ontology.

It is the aim of this text to identify some of the theoretical potentials of the concept "infrastructure" by contrasting it to "structure" as it was used for centuries. I will therefore review in the following chapter some aspects the conceptual history of "structure." This necessarily broad-brushed review will enable me to consider some prospects and problems of the introduction of "infrastructure" as a social and cultural theoretical term in the subsequent chapter, before, in the conclusion, I will identify the main profits of a move forward from structure to infrastructure.

---

3   While there are some studies on the local particularity or on equivalents of the term "structure" in Non-Western regions, I will focus on the European and North American history of the originally Latin notion. Cf., e.g., Jana S. Rošker, "The Concept of Structure as a Basic Epistemological Paradigm of Traditional Chinese Thought," *Asian Philosophy* 20, no. 1 (2010): 79–96; Eni P. Orlandi, "On the Notion of Structure and Structuralism in Brazil," in *History of Linguistics*, eds. Eduardo Guimarães and Diana Luz Pessoa de Barros (Amsterdam: Benjamins, 2002): 207–222.

4   See e.g., Rudolph Carnap, *The Unity of Science* (London: Routledge, 1934); Eduard Spranger, "Die Einheit der Wissenschaft, ein Problem," *Archiv für Rechts-und Sozialphilosophie* 40, no. 1 (1952): 1–37; Otto Neurath, "Einheit der Wissenschaft als Aufgabe," *Erkenntnis* 5 (1935): 16–22; C.P. Snow, *The Two Cultures*, (Cambridge: Cambridge University Press, 2002); F.R. Leavis, *Two Cultures?* (Cambridge: Cambridge University Press, 2013); Wolf Lepenies, *Die drei Kulturen. Soziologie zwischen Literatur und Wissenschaft* (Munich: Hanser, 1985).

A Short and Selective History of "Structure"

The notion of structure has a long history as both a descriptive and analytical category.[5] The word "structure" originated from architecture in Roman antiquity. In addition, it was used in the fields of anatomy, botany, and geology. From Cicero on, the term was increasingly applied in rhetoric, denoting the interconnection of vocal sounds, or of the parts of a word, a phrase, or a performed or written text. Early Christian authors then put it into theological contexts and used it for further "immaterial" or imaginary phenomena. Classical conceptions of structure emphasize the connections, or relations, of individual parts to an encompassing, functional whole. This whole is thought of, mostly, as a passive, stable construction such as, prominently, a defence wall.[6]

From early to late modernity, the concept of structure adopted a more abstract meaning designating in philosophy and the emerging sciences the inner nature and arrangement of complex things and beings as well as hidden causal relations and invariant forces behind the visible which could only be discovered by experimentation.[7] According to Francis Bacon, for example, man would be able to explain the processes of nature if he fully understood the hidden structure and secret functioning of matter.[8]

From now on, the concept of structure was increasingly connected to an ambition to identifying "structures" in general as "real" causal forces "behind" perceivable appearances. Later, scholars such as Kant or Goethe dealt with the question whether

---

5   For overviews, cf. Matthias Kross et al., "Struktur," in *Historisches Wörterbuch der Philosophie*, eds. Joachim Ritter and Karlfried Gründer Bd. 10 (Basel: Schwabe, 1998), 303–335; Roger Bastide, ed., *Sens et usages du terme structure dans les sciences humaines et sociales* (The Hague: Mouton, 1962); Raymond Boudon, *The Uses of Structuralism* (London: Heinemann, 1971); Nicholas J. Allen, "On the Notion of Structure," *Journal of the Anthropological Society of Oxford* 21, no. 3 (1990): 279–282; François Dosse, *History of Structuralism*, Two Vols., (Minneapolis: University of Minnesota Press, 1997); Thomas G. Pavel, *The Feud of Language: A History of Structuralist Thought* (Oxford: Blackwell, 1990).

6   Godo Lieberg, "Der Begriff 'Structura' in der Lateinischen Literatur," *Hermes* 84, no. 4 (1956): 455–477.

7   Donald W. Mertz, "The Concept of Structure in Galileo: Its Role in the Methods of Proportionality and *Ex Suppositione* as Applied to the Tides," *Studies in History and Philosophy of Science* 13, no. 2 (1982.): 111–131; Nicholas Rescher, *Leibniz's Metaphysics of Nature: A Group of Essays* (Dordrecht: Springer, 1981); François Duchesneau, "Leibniz et Stahl: divergences sur le concept d'organisme," *Studia Leibnitiana* 27, no. 2 (1995): 185–212; John Earman, "Was Leibniz a Relationist?" *Midwest Studies in Philosophy* 4 (1979): 263–276.

8   Antonio Pérez-Ramos, *Francis Bacon's Idea of Science and the Maker's Knowledge Tradition* (Oxford: Oxford University Press, 1988).

events, or actions, are caused by these kinds of "structures" or by intentional subjects, as well as how causation can be related to structural part-whole relations.[9]

This also induced an increased interest in methodological questions. Some questions concerned the methodic discoverability and reducibility of manifest phenomena to other, structural factors hidden in some way.[10] "Structures" of cognition and knowledge (reasoning and understanding)—as being different to structures of the physical world—came into focus.[11] In the panlogical concept of structure, the structure of the mind, or of logic, is conceived of as corresponding to the structure of the world.[12] Another point of interest concerned the epistemological status of structure as actor's or observer's concept as well as its ontological status as, alternatively, "model of" or "model for" the external reality it represents.[13] This, in turn, entailed questions about the ontological status of causal, yet latent and hidden structures: are structures *behind*, *below*, or *between* events and manifestations?[14]

---

9   Immanuel Kant, *Metaphysical Foundations of Natural Science* (1786); Hannah Ginsborg, "Kant on Understanding Organisms as Natural Purposes," in *Kant and the Sciences*, ed. Eric Watkins (Oxford: Oxford University Press, 2001), 231–258; Ronald H. Brady, "The Causal Dimension of Goethe's Morphology," *Journal of Social and Biological Structures* 7 (1984) 325–344; Jean Petitot "Morphology and Structural Aesthetics: From Goethe to Lévi-Strauss," in *The Cambridge Companion to Lévi-Strauss*, ed. Boris Wiseman (Cambridge: Cambridge University Press, 2009), 275–295; Charles Darwin, *On the Origin of Species* (London: J. Murray, 1859).

10   Jakub Dziadkowiec, "The Layered Structure of the World in N. Hartmann's Ontology and a Processual View," in *The Philosophy of Nicolai Hartmann*, eds. Roberto Poli, Carlo Scognamiglio, and Frederic Tremblay (Berlin: de Gruyter, 2011): 95–123; John E. Smith, "Hartmann's New Ontology," *The Review of Metaphysics* 7, no. 4 (1954): 583–601.

11   E.g., in Wilhelm Dilthey (who used the German word "Aufbau" for "structure"), see Frithjof Rodi, "Dilthey's Concept of 'Structure' within the Context of 19th Century Science and Philosophy," in *Dilthey and Phenomenology*, eds. Rudolf A. Makkreel and John D. Scanlon (Lanham: Center for Advanced Research in Phenomenology, 1987): 107–121; in Husserl, cf. Giulio C. Lepschy, "Osservazioni sul termine Struttura," in *Mutamenti di prospettiva nella linguistica*, Giulio C. Lepschy (Bologna: Il Mulino, 1981), 37–73; or in Dewey, cf. John Dewey, *The Later Works, 1925–1953, Volume I: Experience and Nature*, ed. Jo Ann Boydston (Carbondale: Southern Illinois University Press, 2008).

12   An example for this model is Bertrand Russell, cf. William Demopoulos and Michael Friedman, "The Concept of Structure in *The Analysis of Matter*," *Minnesota Studies in the Philosophy of Science* 12 (1989): 183–199; The early Wittgenstein of the *Tractatus* also assumed an isomorphic relation between the structure of the "things" in the world, connected in facts, and their representation in the mind of people. Wittgenstein's concept of structure found its way into analytic philosophy through representatives of the Vienna Circle.

13   Clifford Geertz, *The Interpretation of Culture* (New York: Basic Books, 1973), 93.

14   A consequential example of this metaphor is Marx's "base and superstructure" model of society that assumes hidden causal forces behind the visible appearances, dividing social reality into an economic-technological "base" which conditions, if not determines, the political-ideological "superstructure." Cf. Karl Marx, Preface to *A Contribution to the Critique of Political Econ-*

In the 19th century, along with epistemic and semantic structures, the emphasis was laid on the idea, and discovery, of long-term historical structures and their relation to events.[15] This was carried further in the 20th century by social scientists who analyzed the social functions of structural elements that are required for a societal whole to continue existing (structural functionalism), as well as by Saussure and Jakobson who formalized linguistic structures.[16] Drawing on this newly emergent tradition, Maurice Merleau-Ponty attempted to combine theoretical elements of phenomenology and structuralism,[17] which influenced later theoretical endeavours such as Lévi-Straussian structuralism in which the trend towards an ever more sophisticated systematization of empirically certifiable structural elements and wholes, relations, and derivations culminated.[18] Lévi-Strauss assumes the historically endless recombination of individual elements that integrate to the wholes of culturally and symbolically structured social groups for which human individuals serve as mere media. The assumed universal anthropological basis for all variant forms is an ultimately unbridgeable opposition between nature and culture grounded in the precarious human existence. Lévi-Straussian structuralism is intended to solve the question of how to conceptualize social stability over time and across generations. In doing so, however, Lévi-Straussian structuralism admits transformations and substitutions, but not mere additions and subtractions (since they would destroy the balance of the structure). Furthermore, structures, in Lévi-

---

omy (German original: 1859). The English translation of 1904 preserves the "base" metaphor, while the French translation of 1899 translates the German "Basis" as "infrastructure."

15   Leonilla Krol, "Spencer's Meaning of Structure," *Organon* 3 (1966): 201–218; F. Braudel, "Histoire et sciences sociales: La longue durée," *Annales Économies, sociétés, civilisations* 13, no. 4 (1958): 725–753; Michael Pickering, "Experience as Horizon: Koselleck, Expectation, and Historical Time," *Cultural Studies* 18, no. 2–3 (2004): 271–289.

16   Ernst A. Cassirer, "Structuralism in Modern Linguistics," *Word* 1, no.2 (1945): 99–120; Lewis A. Coser, ed., *The Idea of Social Structure* (New York: Routledge 1975).

17   James M. Edie, "The Meaning and Development of Merleau-Ponty's Concept of Structure," *Research in Phenomenology* X (1980): 39–57; Elmar Holenstein, *Linguistik, Semiotik, Hermeneutik. Plädoyers für eine strukturale Phänomenologie* (Frankfurt: Suhrkamp, 1976); James Daly IV, "Merleau-Ponty: A Bridge Between Phenomenology and Structuralism," *Journal of the British Society for Phenomenology* 2, no. 3 (1971): 53–58; William C. Gay, "Merleau-Ponty on Language and Social Science: The Dialectic of Phenomenology and Structuralism," *Man and World* 12 (1979): 322–338; James Schmidt, *Maurice Merleau-Ponty: Between Phenomenology and Structuralism* (New York: St. Martin's Press 1985); John Kultgen, "Phenomenology and Structuralism," *Annual Review of Anthropology* 4 (1975): 371–387.

18   Claude Lévi-Strauss, "Social Structure," in *Structural Anthropology* (New York: Basic Books, 1963), 277–323; Claude Lévi-Strauss, *Wild Thought: A New Translation of "La Pensée sauvage,"* trans. Jefferey Mehlman, Jeffrey and John Leavitt (Chicago: University of Chicago Press, 2021); Nathan Rotenstreich, "On Lévi-Strauss' Concept of Structure," *The Review of Metaphysics* 25, no. 3 (1972): 489–526; John B. Fisher, "The Concept of Structure in Freud, Levi Strauss, and Chomsky," *Philosophy Research Archives* 1 (1975): 88–108.

Strauss' conception, are not changed by mere external influences, but obey a law of self-regulation or self-organization. Its culminated obsession with structural combinations of meaningful entities was terminated by variants of neo- and post-structuralism (e.g., Althusser, Foucault, Bourdieu, Derrida) that were interested in the ongoing dynamics of structure formation, in vagueness of meaning, existential imponderabilities, and questions of embodiment and materiality.[19] However, it is certainly true that by voluntary opposition to structuralism, misrepresentations were created, and strawmen were built up, to the distortion of Lévi-Strauss' original aims.[20]

In sociology, in a renewed Galilean gesture of reducing all observations, even those of human beings concerned with meaning, to primary properties expressible in exact mathematical descriptions of the true, objective, and real world (mathesis universalis),[21] strong versions of 20th century (non-Lévi-Straussian) sociological structuralism conceptualize social structure exclusively in terms of measurable physical variables such as size, density, and propinquity.[22] Accordingly, strong

---

19   Caroline Williams, "Structure and Subject," in *The Edinburgh Companion to Poststructuralism*, eds. Benoit Dillet, Iain MacKenzie, and Robert Porter (Edinburgh: Edinburgh University Press, 2013), 189–206; Rodolphe Gasché, *The Tain of the Mirror: Derrida and the Philosophy of Reflection* (Cambridge: Harvard University Press, 1986).

20   See David R. Howarth, *Poststructuralism and After: Structure, Subjectivity and Power* (Basingstoke: Palgrave Macmillan, 2013); Edith Kurzweil, *The Age of Structuralism: Levi-Strauss to Foucault* (New York: Columbia University Press, 1980); John Sturrock, ed., *Structuralism and Since: From Levi-Strauss to Derrida* (New York: Oxford University Press, 1979); Sunil Manghani, ed., *Theory, Culture & Society* 39, no. 7–8, Special Section: *Notes on Structuralism* (2022); Iain Campbell, "Structuralist Heroes and Points of Heresy: Recognizing Gilles Deleuze's (Anti-) Structuralism," *Continental Philosophy Review* 55, no. 5–6 (2022): 215–234; Christopher Bryant and David Jary, eds., *Giddens' Theory of Structuration: A Critical Appreciation* (London: Routledge 1991), especially pp. 52–73; Derek Robbins, "Phenomenology and Poststructuralism," in *The Edinburgh Companion to Critical Theory*, ed. Stuart Sim (Edinburgh: Edinburgh University Press, 2016), 91–108.

21   In a way, this strong sociological structuralism manifests the ongoing desire to identify a "primum movens" (Aristotle) even for social and cultural phenomena. This endeavor was, sure enough, criticized from Vico (and his "verum factum principle") via Dilthey to Husserl (and his "Crisis") and others.

22   Peter M. Blau, ed., *Approaches to the Study of Social Structure* (New York: Wiley, 1976); Peter M. Blau, "A Macrosociological Theory of Social Structure," *American Journal of Sociology* 83 (1977): 26–54; Harrison White, S.A. Boorman, and Ronald Breiger, "Social Structure from Multiple Networks: Parts I and II," *American Journal of Sociology*, 81, no. 4, 6 (1976): 730–781, 468–498; Bruce Mayhew, "Structuralism vs. Individualism: Parts I and II" *Social Forces* 59, no. 2, 3 (1980): 335–375, 627–648; Charles Warriner, "Levels in the Study of Social Structure," in P. Blau & R. Merton (Eds.), *Continuities in Structural Inquiry*, eds. P. Blau and R. Merton (London: Sage, 1981), 179–190; David Rubenstein, "The Concept of Structure in Sociology," in *Sociological Theory in Transition*, eds. Mark L. Wardell and Stephen P. Turner (Boston: Allen & Unwin, 1986), 80–94.

structuralist sociologists insist on explaining action entirely by these types of structural factors and reject altogether explanations framed in terms of cultural orientation, intention, and purpose. It was partly this overly fossilized concept of structure that was addressed by poststructuralists as well as, in sociology, by the "interpretive paradigm"[23] and related movements such as symbolic interactionism and ethnomethodology. Some scholars, such as Bourdieu and Giddens, attempted to reconcile with their theoretical programs the antagonistic forces of "structure" and "agency."[24]

As we have seen, the notion of structure, in an abstract sense, denotes *the totality of relatively constant relationships between the parts of a whole*. The term "relatively constant relationships" mostly concerns relations of spatial arrangement or of temporal sequence. With the emergence of modern science and humanities in early modern times and, in particular, the course of the 19th century, it is also applied to relations of cause and effect (or power and powerlessness, or subject and object), of exchange or interaction, of reality, knowledge, and (linguistic) representation, or of social stability and continuity, as well as change and transformation. Once transferred from architecture to other realms of human activity, it is by no means limited to recurrent problems of "construction." However, the assessment of the concept of "structure" by the different scholarly traditions in the late 20th and early 21st century is anything but unanimous.

A first discussion concerns the relationships between the individual components and the whole of the structure. The basic question here is: Are these relationships, and if so, in what way, patterned in such a manner that the whole is more than the sum of its parts (emergence)? Or does the whole merely consist in an aggregation of the individual elements? Are structures subject to a gradation "upwards and downwards?" If so, how far does upward or downward causation occur? Do superordinate

---

23   Thomas P. Wilson, "Normative and Interpretive Paradigms in Sociology," in *Understanding Everyday Life: Toward the Reconstruction of Sociological Knowledge*, ed. Jack D. Douglas (Chicago: Aldine, 1970), 57–79; Thomas P. Wilson, "Conceptions of Interaction and Forms of Sociological Explanation," *American Sociological Review* 35, no. 4 (1970): 697–710; Thomas Luckmann, "Philosophy, Science, and Everyday Life," in *Phenomenology and the Social Sciences*, ed. Maurice Natanson (Evanston: Northwestern University Press, 1973), 143–185.

24   See, e.g., Alex Dennis and Peter J. Martin "Symbolic Interactionism and the Concept of Social Structure," *Sociological Focus* 40, no. 3 (2007): 287–305; Wes Sharrock and Graham Button, "The Structure Problem in the Context of Structure and Agency Controversies," in *Human Agents and Social Structures*, eds. Peter J. Martin and Alex Dennis (Manchester: Manchester University Press, 2010), 17–33; Omar Lizardo, "Beyond the Antinomies of Structure: Levi-Strauss, Giddens, Bourdieu, and Sewell," *Theoretical Sociology* 39 (2010): 651–688; J. D. Mendoza, "Structuralism and the Concept of Structure," in *Anthony Giddens: Critical Assessments*, eds. Christopher Bryant and David Jary, vol. 1 (London: Taylor and Francis, 1997), 234–256.

structures determine subordinate structures (supervenience)?[25] Are only transformations and substitutions admitted, as in Lévi-Strauss, or are additions and subtractions equally possible? Do structures obey laws of self-regulation and self-organization?

A second discussion concerns causality: Are structures principally causal? Do they essentially engender effects, or are they merely observed and inferred primarily or even exclusively through their effects?[26]

Thirdly, there are controversies about what structures are actually constituted of: individual entities as components or relations between components. Do they necessarily possess individual elements as components, or are relations the defining factors?[27]

Further debates concern the relationship of structures as either opposed to or inclusive of dimensions such as (a) dynamic phenomena, (b) time, (c) culture, (d) action and intention, and (e) manifestation.

(a) Drawing on the analogy with invariant natural laws, structures are sometimes viewed as opposed to dynamic phenomena. They are viewed as representing the static pole of the *stasis/dynamis* binarity (Auguste Comte) by some. Others—Lévi-Strauss among them—claim that structures as relational wholes are actually constantly adapting to changes of individual components, according to different timescales.

(b) For the same reasons, structures are often seen as atemporal. Again, Lévi-Strauss insisted that they are anything but super-temporal, but rather subject to time and transformation. If one element changes, systemic consequences

---

25   Cf. Jens Greve and Annette Schnabel, eds., *Emergenz. Zur Analyse und Erklärung komplexer Strukturen* (Berlin: Suhrkamp, 2011); Paul Hoyningen-Huene, "Zu Emergenz, Mikro- und Makrodetermination" in *Kausalität und Zurechnung*, ed. W. Lübbe (Berlin: de Gruyter, 1994), 165–195; Niklas Luhmann, *Die Gesellschaft der Gesellschaft* (Frankfurt: Suhrkamp, 1997); Marta Bertolaso, "Uncoupling Mereology and Supervenience: A Dual Framework for Emergence and Downward Causation," *Axiomathes* 27 (2017): 705–720.

26   See, e.g., Judea Pearl Causality, *Models, Reasoning, and Inference* (Cambridge: Cambridge University Press, 2000); Paul Lewis, "Realism, Causality and the Problem of Social Structure," *Journal for the Theory of Social Behaviour* 30, no. 3 (2001): 249–268; Philip Kitcher, "Explanatory Unification and the Causal Structure of the World," in *Scientific Explanation*, eds. Philip Kitcher and Wesley Salmon (Minneapolis: University of Minnesota Press, 1989), 410–505.

27   The concepts of structure advocated ever since Lévi-Strauss tend to the second answer that relations are defining. This argument might come from Gestalt theory. Cf. Talia Welsh, "From Gestalt to Structure: Maurice Merleau-Ponty's Early Analysis of the Human Sciences" *Theory & Psychology* 16, no. 4 (2006): 527–551; Sara Heinämaa, "Phenomenological Responses to Gestalt Psychology," in *Psychology and Philosophy*, eds. S. Heinämaa and M. Reuter (New York: Springer, 2009), 263–284; Also cf. Hans Buffart and Haike Jacobs, "A Gestalt Theory Approach to Structure in Language," *Frontiers in Psychology* 12 (2021).

are engendered for the structure as a whole. However, the temporalities and durabilities of (long-term) structures and of their (short-term) "effects" (manifestations, events) differ from each other in different ways and with different consequences.

(c) A much-disputed topic is the translatability and transferability of the concept of structure to matters of culture. The first question is whether culture possesses structures at all or whether it is "non-structural." Then, the question comes up whether structures are reducible in the same way to physical variables such as size, density, and propinquity as natural object, i.e., in accordance with the Galilean project of science. Alternatively, culture (or society, or life-world) might be conceptualized as possessing a "structure" that is entirely different, and yet analogous, to the physical world, as in Schütz and Luckmann's conception of "structures of the life-world," and that needs to be methodically dealt with in entirely different ways than physical objects.[28] Closely connected to this question is whether it is possible to speak of mental structures.

(d) Another controversy concerns the question of both the epistemology and the objectivity or subjectivity of structures. Many conceptions of structure (Lévi-Strauss and Foucault among them, as well as strong programs of sociological structuralism) view them as objectively determining subjective phenomena, as producing subjects, and as super-subjective. From this perspective, subjects are mere media of structures, incapable of free will and spontaneous action and intention. The alternative view, advocated in phenomenology, puts that structures are produced by subjects, thus not lying latently *behind* events but (temporally) *between* situations (thus Merleau-Ponty).

(e) This relates to the last dispute I want to mention here: differences among scholars also refer to the question of how structure relates to manifestation. Strong structuralisms claim that structures are hidden powers that produce and determine manifestations. Others would object that structures are mere regularities observed in the statistical aggregation of manifestations in the world. In regard to epistemology, structures are often viewed as epistemologically inaccessible for everyday actors and only identifiable by scientists who use specific instruments and methodologies. Others would say, in turn, that structures are part of our everyday assumptions that help us understand other persons and find our way in the world.

---

28   Alfred Schutz and Thomas Luckmann, *The Structures of the Life-World*, trans. Richard M. Zaner and H. Tristram Engelhardt, Jr., vols. 1–2 (Evanston: Northwestern University Press, 1973, 1989).

We are now in a position to reflect upon the concept of "infrastructure" against the foil of both the genealogy and basic features of the concept of "structure" and its variation in current scholarly discourse.

Two Stories of the Conceptual Past of "Infrastructure"

As a term, "infrastructure" has a much shorter history than "structure." As a phenomenon, however, some current schools of thought go as far as positioning the activity of "infrastructuring" as having been crucial for the emergence of homo sapiens. The cognitive equipment of homo sapiens is viewed as an evolutionary outcome of their constant active infrastructuring of their natural environment. Some types of environmentally coupled infrastructure are considered conditions for the sustained human existence from its earliest stages on (especially by the "ecological niche hypothesis"[29]). However, the materialization of these cognitive infrastructures has long left the genetic realm and part of the *conditio humana* are more or less preliminary and volatile social, communicative, transport, or protective infrastructures that become crucial for all kinds of social organization in human history.

As topic of systematic reflection, what today is called "infrastructure" came up relatively late in history, again partly in terms of "structure," with the emergence of the modern nation state in the context of market economy and industrialization.[30] The emergence of modern national economy depended upon infrastructures, and accordingly classical liberalist economists were theoretically attentive to them. Interestingly, they usually dealt right from the start with different types of infrastructure, such as traffic systems, general compulsory education, or a uniform school system in terms of "public" or "common good." Right from the start, they did not distinguish between material and immaterial, or "hard" and "soft" infrastructure.[31] This has its origins in the writings of liberalist writers of the 19th century and is most ex-

---

29   Kim Sterelny, "Social Intelligence, Human Intelligence and Niche Construction," *Philosophical Transactions of the Royal Society B* 362 (2007): 719–730; Kim Sterelny, *The Evolved Apprentice: How Evolution Made Humans Unique* (Cambridge: MIT Press, 2012); Emanuel A. Schegloff, "Interaction: The Infrastructure for Social Institutions, the Natural Ecological Niche for Language, and the Arena in which Culture is Enacted," in *Roots of Human Sociality: Culture, Cognition, and Interaction*, eds. N. J. Enfield and S. C. Levinson (Oxford: Berg, 2006): 70–96.

30   Ashley Carse, "Keyword: Infrastructure: How a Humble French Engineering Term Shaped the Modern World," in *Infrastructures and Social Complexity: A Companion*, eds. Penelope Harvey, Casper Bruun Jensen, and Atsuro Morita (London: Routledge, 2016): 27–39. Also cf. the introduction to the present volume.

31   John Durham Peters, *The Marvelous Clouds: Toward a Philosophy of Elemental Media* (Chicago: The University of Chicago Press, 2015), 32.

plicitly represented by John Stuart Mill.[32] For these systemic, mostly material, and often social establishments for the public good, the term "infrastructure" has found general usage only since, or better, during, the Second World War.[33] In today's public, it is mostly used in the narrow sense of technical pipes and lines *under the ground* or roads, railroads, electric and fibreoptic cables *on the ground* that offer specific service to society.

However, there is a second, parallel story of the emergence of the concept of "infrastructure," which starts in the French Third Republic and which is much less considered in the literature. Here, "infrastructure" is used in additional ways to "technical installation."

The story begins with that fact that, right after the publication of Marx's writings in German and English, "infrastructure" was used as the French translation of Marx's concept of "basis" or "real foundation" as opposed to "superstructure" in the sense explained above (n. 14). This translation makes perfect sense. Marx, in his intent to turn Hegel from his head to his feet, intended to identify the "material and more" foundations on which symbolic systems are grounded: "the ideas of the ruling class are in every epoch the ruling ideas, i.e., the class which is the ruling material force of society, is at the same time its ruling intellectual force."[34] For him, these bases, as infrastructures, are partly material, but also include other phenomena such as property rights or knowledge. Furthermore, the bases, as infrastructures, are, in a routinized way, productive of social reality, insofar as they constantly produce *forces* that make specific symbolic systems methodically plausible and unquestionable and at the same time produce societal contradictions that ultimately lead to conflicts and turn-overs.[35]

---

32 Mill approves various restrictions on individual liberty if this serves to benefit others (and not only prevents harm). By this, he justifies enforceable duties to contribute one's fair share to the provision of various kinds of public goods, especially infrastructures of public safety (lighting, police, courts, correctional facilities), market regulation, common defence, transport (roads, docks, harbors, canals), public health (cleansing, sanitation, hospitals), mandatory education (schools, colleges), works of irrigation and drainage, printing-presses, banks, as well as support and encouragement of arts, letters, and science. Cf. John Stuart Mill, *The Principles of Political Economy: With Some of Their Applications to Social Philosophy* (1848), I.viii.6, 130, I.xii.3, 181, II.xiii.3, V.vii.1, V.xi.8, V.xi.15-16; *On Liberty* (1859), V 12–14; *Considerations on Representative Government* (1861), 467–470.

33 "*Infrastructure* was first a military term." John Durham Peters, *The Marvelous Clouds: Toward a Philosophy of Elemental Media* (Chicago: The University of Chicago Press, 2015), 30.

34 Karl Marx and Friedrich Engels, *The German Ideology*, ed. C. J. Arthur, (New York: International Press, 1947), 64

35 Karl Marx, *Critique de l'économie politique* (Paris: Schleicher frères, 1899); cf. Guillaume Fondu and Jean Quétier, "Comment traduire Marx en français?" in *Marx, une passion française*, eds. Jean-Numa Ducange and Antony Burlaud (Paris: La Découverte, 2018), 111–123.

Inspired by the translation of Marx' basis as *infrastructure*, in French vitalist philosophy around 1900 infrastructure is also referred to as "primordial vital needs, which the conscience notices, which it can to a certain extent counteract and direct, but of which it is not the author, and which resound in the consciousness in the form of sensations and emotions."[36] Morality, from this perspective, is but the rational legislation of these primitively irrational tendencies, the "suprastructure" raised by the intelligence on the organic "infrastructure." In this context, the term "infraconsciousness" is invented to precisely refer to these vital impulses forming the invisible basis of consciousness.

Henri Bergson has used in theoretically interesting ways the idea of an infralogical structure, applying it to the functioning of human existence and social phenomena in terms of consciousness and intellect. Georges Gurvitch[37] has summarized Bergson's approach in his book on *Laughter*[38] quite succinctly. Bergson, Gurvitch reports, explains the phenomenon of laughter by the conflict between spontaneous social life and its external symbolism. The conflict becomes grotesque, and laughable, when the external symbolism ceases to be appropriate to the phenomenon and is transformed into a kind of ready-to-wear garment, poorly matched to the social spontaneity it was intended to express. On this basis, Bergson develops an "extremely suggestive and fruitful theory of the deeper layers of social reality."[39] The layers of social reality are the organized and conventionalized *superstructures* and the spontaneous *infrastructures* that underlie any organization.

> As we are both in and of [society], we cannot help treating it as a living being. Any image, then, suggestive of the notion of a society disguising itself, or of a social masquerade, so to speak, will be laughable. Now, such a notion is formed when we perceive anything inert or stereotyped, or simply readymade, on the surface of living society.[40]

This ready-made is the organized, schematic, static superstructure, insofar as it closes itself to the vivifying penetration of the spontaneous social life that infrastructures it. In this case, "we have rigidity over again, clashing with the inner

36   Alfred Fouillée, "La Question Morale: Est-Elle Une Question Sociale?" *Revue des Deux Mondes* 160, no 3 (1900): 481–512, 503.

37   Georges Gurvitch, "La Philosophie Sociale de Bergson," *Revue de Métaphysique et de Morale* 53, no. 3 (1948): 294–306.

38   Henri Bergson, *Laughter: An Essay on the Meaning of the Comic*, trans. Cloudesley Brereton and Fred Rothwell (New York: Macmillan, 1913 [1900]).

39   Gurvitch, "La Philosphie," 298.

40   Bergson, *Laughter*, 44.

suppleness of life. [...] It might be said that ceremonies are to the social body what clothing is to the individual body."[41]

The ceremonies, the organized superstructures, Bergson tells us in a metaphor, in which the hot interior of the earth represents the infrastructure, are like a "a cool and solid crust [covering over] the fiery mass of seething metals"[42] of the living social spontaneity. For Bergson, says Gurvitch, in every social organization "there is an element of artificial mechanization requiring that social mobility be regulated by the immutability of a formula."[43] If the organization is entirely detached from the underlying spontaneous social infrastructure, it becomes "something mechanical encrusted upon the living."[44] Then, as Gurvitch paraphrases Bergson, social explosions occur, revolutions, as similar to "volcanic eruptions."[45]

Furthermore, Bergson has also applied the idea of an infra-versus supralogical structure to knowledge, specifically to the relation between representations and intuitions. He distinguishes between what he calls the *infra-intellectual* and what, as he says, he would call the *supra-intellectual*, "if the word did not immediately and exclusively evoke the idea of superiority of value: it is just as much a question of priority in time, and of the relation between that which generates and that which is generated."[46] In the case of the infra-intellectual, the intuition is a consequence of, and stirred by, an idea or mental picture independent of it, while in the case of the supra-intellectual, the intuition is not produced by a representation but is itself *productive* of ideas and representations. It is, "in relation to the intellectual states which are to supervene, a cause and not an effect."[47] Therefore, "it is pregnant with representations, not one of which is actually formed, but which it draws or might draw from its own substance by an organic development."[48]

Bergson does not establish a hierarchy of value between infra-intellectual and supra -intellectual processes of intuition and knowledge, which ultimately represent the two "sources of morality" of which speaks in the title of his book. Instead, he seeks to show that there is a continuity and reciprocity between the two.

French vitalist philosophy is not the only example for the application of the notion of infrastructure to ideational matters. Even in the discussions during and after the second world war, the concept of infrastructure was anything but restricted to material supply lines and pipes under the ground. Instead, it was explicitly, and

41   Bergson, *Laughter*, 44–45.
42   Bergson, *Laughter*, 159.
43   Gurvitch, "La Philosphie," 298; referring to Bergson, *Laughter*, 48 and 46.
44   Bergson, *Laughter*, 37, emphasis left out.
45   Gurvitch, "La Philosophie," 298; referring to Bergson, *Laughter*, 159.
46   Henri Bergson, *The Two Sources of Morality and Religion*, trans. R. Ashley Audra and Cloudesley Brereton (Westport: Greenwood, 1935), 36.
47   Bergson, *Two Sources*, 35.
48   Bergson, *Two Sources*, 35.

non-metaphorically, applied to imaginary, immaterial phenomena as well, e.g. to the religious foundations of belief systems.[49]

Most relevant for the French usage of the term "infrastructure" in a non-technical sense in the 20th century was probably the phenomenological philosopher Maurice Merleau-Ponty. In his early work, *The Structure of Behavior*, Merleau-Ponty develops a concept of structure that shows the formal characteristics identified above: a structure is a totality whose elements are not individually determined for themselves, but by their position in relation to each other in the whole; which admits transformations and substitutions, but not mere additions and subtractions; which is not changed by mere external influences, but obeys a law of self-regulation or self-organization. For Merleau-Ponty, structure is neither thing nor idea, it belongs neither to a pure external world nor to a pure internal world, and it subverts classical oppositions such as empiricism and rationalism, materialism and idealism, and the epistemological duality of subject and object. However, Merleau-Ponty also has a number of reservations against the term which result from the fact that the concept is used within a polarity between two extremes: in a volatile way, as mere forms of consciousness, and in a reifying and naturalizing manner. This is why Merleau-Ponty—drawing on different theoretical resources provided by Edmund Husserl[50]—introduces a hierarchical and yet integrative gradation of structure into infrastructure and superstructure.[51]

In particular, Merleau-Ponty uses the concept of infrastructure to denote the bodily grounded conditions of perception that adopt qualities of media but are themselves invisible to our perception and reflection. He thus speaks of a "humoral"[52] and "bodily infrastructure."[53] His interest is to identify existential,

---

49   Charles Harold Dodd, *According to the Scriptures: The Sub-structure of New Testament Theology* (Digswell Place: Nisbet, 1952); translated as: *Conformément aux Écritures. L'infrastructure de la théologie du Nouveau Testament* (Paris: Éditions du Seuil, 1968).

50   These theoretical resources are too complex to be depicted here. They encompass Husserl's distinction between "theme" and "horizon," his ideas of "sedimentation," "passive synthesis," "appresentation," and "anonymity," as well as his concept of "operative intentionality" which Merleau-Ponty uses in specific ways informed by Gestalt theory and the philosophy of Aron Gurwitsch. See, e.g., Richard McCleary, "Introduction," in *Signs*, Maurice Merleau-Ponty (Evanston: Northwestern University Press 1964), ix–xxxiii.

51   Maurice Merleau-Ponty, *Signs* (Evanston: Northwestern University Press 1964), 165; Bernhard Waldenfels, "Die Offenheit sprachlicher Strukturen bei Merleau-Ponty" in *Maurice Merleau-Ponty und das Problem der Struktur in den Sozialwissenschaften*, eds. Richard Grathoff and Walter Sprondel (Stuttgart: Enke, 1976), 17–28, 18–19.

52   Maurice Merleau-Ponty, *The Primacy of Perception* (Evanston: Northwestern University Press, 1964), 5.

53   Maurice Merleau-Ponty, *Phenomenology of Perception* (London: Routledge, 2012), 455; Maurice Merleau-Ponty, *In Praise of Philosophy and Other Essays* (Evanston: Northwestern University Press, 1963), 174.

intellectual, and social functions which are tied to this bodily infrastructure.[54] The importance of the bodily infrastructure cannot be overestimated, it is a "living infrastructure without which reason and freedom are emptied or break down."[55] Human action, subjectivity, and intersubjectivity, human temporality and sociality, and the human relations to the world are grounded in, and produced by, it as well as our everyday consciousness, "for which the world is 'self-evident,' that finds the world 'already constituted' and present even within consciousness itself."[56]

In his later work, Merleau-Ponty has particularly focused on the relevance of the visual senses for our everyday consciousness that assumes self-evidence, stability and continuity: Through vision, "this superstructure," as he calls it, "gains a relative independence with respect to praxical infrastructures."[57] It is our visual sense that, as part of our bodily infrastructure, suggests the stable objectivity of the external world—physical, social, and historical.[58] However, "the visible," which continuously tricks us into believing in the sheer "thereness" of the external world is, Merleau-Ponty says, "pregnant with the invisible."[59] It is based on its own invisible "infrastructure of vision."[60] Dreyfus and Dreyfus[61] give an example of this "infrastructure of vision:"

> For example, when I perceive an object, such as a house from the front, the back is involved in this perception not merely as a possible perception which I judge could be produced if I walked around the house, nor as a necessary implication of the concept 'house.' Instead, the back is experienced as actually co-present—concealed but suggested by the appearance of the front. Philosophers of ordinary language such as Gilbert Ryle have made a similar point by noting that under ordinary conditions we do not say that we see the front of a house but say that we see a house from the front. Both Merleau-Ponty and the Oxford philosophers would go on from such considerations to suggest there is something wrong with the traditional view that we experience 'sense data'—isolated units of experience, which must then be organized by the mind.

---

54 Merleau-Ponty, *Phenomenology of Perception*, 9; Maurice Merleau-Ponty, *The Visible and the Invisible* (Evanston: Northwestern University Press, 1968), 120; Merleau-Ponty, *Signs*, 118–119; Maurice Merleau-Ponty, *The Sensible World and the World of Expression: Course Notes from the Collège de France, 1953* (Evanston: Northwestern University Press, 2020), 112.

55 Merleau-Ponty, *Phenomenology of Perception*, 57.

56 Merleau-Ponty, *Phenomenology of Perception*, 479–480.

57 Merleau-Ponty, *The Sensible World*, 107.

58 Merleau-Ponty, *The Visible and the Invisible*, 144–145.

59 Merleau-Ponty, *The Visible and the Invisible*, 216.

60 Merleau-Ponty, *The Visible and the Invisible*, 145.

61 Hubert L. Dreyfus and Patricia A. Dreyfus, "Translators' introduction," in *Sense and Non-Sense*, Maurice Merleau-Ponty (Evanston: Northwestern University Press, 1964), ix-xxvii, xi.

With his conception of infrastructure, Merleau-Ponty has added a further chapter to the French usage of the concept of infrastructure which was started by the translation of Marx "basis" and "real foundation," by its application to immaterial phenomena by vitalist philosophy, and its usage for processes of knowledge by Bergson.

Merleau-Ponty's doubts about the concept of structure have influenced Jacques Derrida's infrastructural conception of structure. It states that infrastructure must be understood as difference between "the ground" and "what is grounded," as generative condition of both "possibility" and "impossibility."[62] In this model, different infrastructures (in Merleau-Ponty's sense) are able to coexist equiprimordially.

This second, parallel story of the concept of infrastructure indicates that their dominant conception as primarily material and technical and only secondarily, and only in a figurative sense, applicable to immaterial, imaginary, or practical phenomena is not accurate. The parallel story shows that material and immaterial infrastructures must be understood right from the start as equiprimordial, since it turns the (Marxian) ideology of the primordiality of the material-technical aspect of infrastructure into an empirical question: how do ideational, or symbolic, infrastructures, interact with material and technical ones?

This is where the greatest prospects of "infrastructuralism" and the "infrastructural turn" are located. One example of this new programmatic endeavour is provided by Marshall Sahlins. He used the term "infrastructuralism"[63] to designate his position vis-à-vis Lévi-Straussian structuralism. As Sahlins recalls, Lévi-Strauss once said that he was not interested in "the exchange of women or words" but in "infrastructure," i.e., "the exchange of vital goods and the specializations of production this entails."[64] Thus, Lévi-Strauss was interested in the basic—elementary—structures of the social—i.e., its infrastructures—which, in Lévi-Strauss, however, culturally laden and symbolic as they are, are not part of what Marx called superstructure. Rather the economic base, as Marx calls it, is for Sahlins itself an objectification of culture—mediated by "values."[65]

Thus, Sahlins' concept of "infrastructuralism" is intended to resolve "the longstanding opposition between praxis and culture by encompassing the former in the latter."[66] This allows, he says, to reconcile Lévi-Strauss' structuralist approach with techno-determinism, which assumes that the cultural order is a reflex of real-practical activity.[67] Sahlins' idea is that "rather than a discontinuity, temporal as well

---

62   Gasché, *The Tain of the Mirror*, 155–156.

63   Marshall Sahlins, "Infrastructuralism," *Critical Inquiry* 36 (2010): 371–385.

64   Quoted in Sahlins, "Infrastructuralism," 372.

65   Sahlins, "Infrastructuralism," 375ff.

66   Sahlins, "Infrastructuralism," 373.

67   Sahlins himself refers to Leslie White, *The Evolution of Culture* (New York: McGraw-Hill, 1959), 21–26. Other theories of media and technology determinism could be mentioned as well. See Sally Wyatt, "Technological Determinism Is Dead: Long Live Technological Determin-

as ontological, wherein culture appears as the symbolic afterthought of a material practice that has its own rationality, what is entailed in infrastructuralism is the realization of encompassing conceptual schemes in the particular material function of provisioning the society. Economy, one might even say, is the objectification of cosmology."[68] Thus, the notion of infrastructure helps Sahlins' to preserve his focus on material practice while abandoning its traditional (Marxist) emphasis. More precisely, Sahlins assumes a cultural infrastructure underlying the economic and technological infrastructures of social practice which is mediated by values and orients its materializations. With his argument, Sahlins emphasizes that theories of practice, which are even more relevant today in anthropology and sociology than when he wrote his text, need an answer to the question how practices are regulated and oriented, and the idea of cultural infrastructure is his answer to that question.

The second theorist of infrastructuralism is John Durham Peters[69] (followed by Rubinstein, Robbins, and Beal[70]). Theoretically most relevant for his approach are phenomenology (in particular Edmund Husserl and Martin Heidegger) as well as media theory (especially Marshall McLuhan and Harold Innis). On this basis, Peters advocates a media theoretic conception of infrastructure in a broad sense. For him, media must be understood as material processes extended in, and themselves extending, the world. Aligning to this tradition, he states: "Infrastructure was pushed beyond large, heavy systems to be a question of how basic categories and standards are formed, and how they are formed as ordinary. How the taken-for-granted gets constructed in the first place is a classic phenomenological question: how did the water ever become invisible to the fish?"[71] Since infrastructure is often defined by being "off the radar, below notice, or off stage," his basic theoretical question is: What is it that the structure is *infra* to?[72] The question is: what is generated when the process of generating itself is hidden in such way that the product appears naturally given? Peters, in his conception of infrastructuralism, emphasizes, like the phenomenological

ism," in *The Handbook of Science and Technology Studies*, 3rd Ed., ed. Edward J. Hackett et al. (Cambridge: MIT Press, 2008), 165–180; Allan Dafoe, "On Technological Determinism: A Typology, Scope Conditions, and a Mechanism," *Science, Technology, and Human Values* 40, no. 6 (2015): 1047–1076; Robert Heilbroner, "Technological Determinism Revisited," in *Does Technology Have History?*, eds. M. R. Smith and L. Marx (Cambridge: MIT Press, 1994), 67–78; Bruce Bimbe, "Karl Marx and the Three Faces of Technological Determinism," *Social Studies of Science* 20 (1990): 333–351.

68   Sahlins, "Infrastructuralism," 374–375.

69   Peters, *The Marvelous Clouds*.

70   Michael Rubenstein, Bruce Robbins, and Sophia Beal, "Infrastructuralism: An Introduction," *Modern Fiction Studies* 61, no. 4 (2015): 575–586

71   Peters, *The Marvelous Clouds*, 35.

72   Peters, *the Marvelous Clouds*, 36.

traditions, the aspect of the hidden, taken-for-granted nature of infrastructures as well as their generative capacities.

Conclusion

As we have seen in the review of the concept of "structure," what today is called "infrastructure" was in former times termed "structure," especially related to buildings for transport and the military. Especially in modernity, the concept of structure took on a life of its own and, with the identification and formulation of natural laws, assumed transcendental qualities when transferred to the realm of the social and cultural. More and more, "structure" replaced the idea of an unmoved *primum movens* that causally determines manifest phenomena.

The notion of infrastructure, though not fully developed theoretically, as we have seen, is partly intended to turn back to non-metaphysical conceptions of structure. These conceptions imply that all notions of sharedness, commonality, and jointness (e.g., shared knowledge, joint action, common meaning) must be abandoned and a logic of ongoing constitution is defended. Thinking in terms of infrastructure (i.e. asking for the systems and operations that are generative for the phenomena under study) allows us to study cultural and social phenomena systematically as achieved and not as given.

Another difference concerns the ontological status of infrastructure: infrastructures, different to structures, are not observed in regard to being either "models for" or "models of" and of being either latent or manifest. Rather, they are observed in regard to their materialities and materializations as well as practices in time. In particular, practices of "infrastructuring"[73] are viewed as constitutive of precisely those dimensions that are taken for granted and reified by, in, and through, the concept of structure. These dimensions include, for example, collectivities, or assumptions of shared, common, and joint phenomena (shared knowledge, joint action, common meaning). Rather, the concept of infrastructure, as we have seen in our second story, focuses on the conditions of possibility of these phenomena, in terms of their *production*, and do not rely on the assumption of pre-established meanings, or entities, as putatively given.

While the concept of structure assumes a causal chain between structures, which are latent, and appearances (or events), which are manifest, the concept of infrastructure, drawing in the phenomenological tradition, posits infrastructures as di-

---

73   Cristina Alaimo and Jannis Kallinikos, "Social Media and the Infrastructuring of Sociality," in *Thinking Infrastructures*, eds. Martin Kornberger et al. (Bingley: Emerald, 2019), 289–306; Volkmar Pipek, Helena Karasti, and Geoffrey Bowker, eds., *Infrastructuring and Collaborative Design*, special issue of *Computer Supported Cooperative Work (CSCW)* 26, no. 1–2 (2017).

alectic, in an epistemological twist: Focusing on one infrastructure invisibilizes others, upon which it is dependent. Moreover, the process of focusing itself is dependent upon an embedded (epistemic, cognitive) infrastructure that when focused on becomes its own object. This is where the greatest potentials of the concept of infrastructure—as contrasted to a concept of structure that is beyond remedy—are located.

From Systems to "Infrastructuring": Infrastructure Theory and Its Impact on Writing the History of Media

Axel Volmar

Since the early 1990s, "infrastructure" as both an object and analytical concept has been a growing research interest in the social and human sciences. In the last ten years or so, the study of infrastructure has also experienced a lively boom in my own discipline, media studies. One reason for this heightened interest is the increasing interconnectedness of digital and data-driven media, which since the popularization of the Internet in the 1990s came to determine the everyday lives of many people. Moreover, the ubiquity of digitally networked media has increasingly directed the theoretical interest of media studies away from the computer as a "universal solvent"[1] to "the stuff beneath, beyond, and behind the boxes our media come in."[2] In recent years, the notion of "media infrastructure" has been taken up, for instance, in research on data-driven media (such as social media, digital platforms, and mobile applications), digital signal traffic, and media history.[3]

Recently, however, objections have been raised against the increased use of the infrastructure concept, warning that the term is being watered down or accusing its boom to be merely a fad. Charlotte P. Lee and Kjeld Schmidt, for instance, have complained that "the concept of 'infrastructure' has become increasingly muddled over time. Disparities in use of the concept have become an immense source of confusion [...]. The unquestioned and seemingly unnoticed use of the term 'infrastructure' in

---

1   Paul E. Ceruzzi, *A History of Modern Computing* (Cambridge: MIT press, 2003), 346.

2   Johnathan Sterne, *MP3: The Meaning of a Format* (Durham: Duke University Press, 2012), 11.

3   See, for instance, Jean-Christophe Plantin and Aswin Punathambekar, eds., "Digital Media Infrastructures: Pipes, Platforms, and Politics," *Media, Culture & Society* 41, no. 2 (2019): 163–74, https://doi.org/10.1177/0163443718818376; Lisa Parks and Nicole Starosielski, eds., *Signal Traffic: Critical Studies of Media Infrastructures* (Urbana: University of Illinois Press, 2015), https://www.press.uillinois.edu/books/catalog/26bxm4qd9780252039362.html; Axel Volmar and Kyle Stine, eds., *Media Infrastructures and the Politics of Digital Time: Essays on Hardwired Temporalities*, Recursions (Amsterdam: Amsterdam University Press, 2021), https://www.degruyter.com/document/doi/10.1515/9789048550753/html.

myriad ways is hobbling the development of the area."[4] Similarly, David Hesmondhalgh criticizes "a tendency in media and internet studies to use the term 'infrastructure' in such a variety of ways that the term risks losing its analytical value; an
uncertain engagement with ideas of materiality and 'relationality'; and a tendency
towards banality and vagueness."[5] Despite the legitimate objections, however, the
critics generally fail to solve the confusion they bemoan. For example, neither Lee
and Schmidt nor Hesmondhalgh fully acknowledge the different scholarly motivations for extending the concept of infrastructure and for using it in the context of
research in the humanities and especially in media studies.

The critical assessments, however, raise the legitimate question of what can actually be gained in theoretical-methodological terms by resorting to the concept of
"infrastructure" as opposed to similar notions, such as "system," "network," "platform," or simply "technology." Or in Hesmondhalgh's words, it seems "worth asking
why the concept of infrastructure is so seemingly fashionable *now*."[6] This essay attempts to trace the history of the concept of infrastructure and its fortune as an analytical concept in the social sciences and humanities. It aims to show what the fundamental fascination or promise of the concept of infrastructure is, what it means
or implies, and why it can be useful to engage with materiality, relationality, and,
yes, even banalities. I am particularly interested in outlining how an engagement
with the concept of infrastructure can inform theoretical perspectives and research
methods in the humanities. I will argue that infrastructural or even infrastructuralist ways of thinking emerged from a critical reinterpretation of the concept of infrastructure within the sociology of technology in the late 1990s and early 2000s, which
since provided important impulses for the humanities.

What seems characteristic of this interest in infrastructures is not primarily the
fact that humanities scholars turn to infrastructures as new research objects but that
they developed the term "infrastructure" into an analytical lens, resulting in major
reinterpretations of its meaning and methodological reorientations. My main argument is that a key feature of this shift is a move from a systemic understanding
of infrastructure to a praxeological one, and this fact is also the reason why the different meanings of the infrastructure concept in current research discourses often
seem so incommensurable. To clear up some of this confusion, I aim to show why

---

4   Charlotte P. Lee and Kjeld Schmidt, "A Bridge Too Far?: Critical Remarks on the Concept of
     'Infrastructure' in Computer-Supported Cooperative Work and Information Systems," *Socio-
     Informatics: A Practice-Based Perspective on the Design and Use of IT Artifacts*, eds. Volker Wulf et
     al. (Oxford: Oxford University Press, 2018), 177–217, 178.

5   David Hesmondhalgh, "The Infrastructural Turn in Media and Internet Research," in *The Rout-
     ledge Companion to Media Industries*, ed. Paul McDonald (London: Routledge, 2021), 132–142,
     132, https://doi.org/10.4324/9780429275340-13.

6   Hesmondhalgh, "The Infrastructural Turn in Media and Internet Research," 140.

infrastructural thinking involves a strong focus on practices and how this has influenced methodological approaches. In the first section, I will look into how scholars from the social and human sciences first became interested in the notion of 'infrastructure' in the 1970s and 80s. I will then trace how, starting in the 1990s, the term underwent major reconceptualizations within the sociology of technology. In the last section, I will discuss some more recent examples that show how this conceptual shift has shaped—and can continue to inspire—new research topics and methodological approaches. While these examples stem from my own discipline, my hope is, however, that the general implications and the potential of infrastructural or infrastructuralist thinking that are shown in them might equally provide inspiration for scholars from other disciplines in the humanities.

1. From Systems to Infrastructures

In a way, of course, research in media studies and media history, especially those focusing on mass media, have in principle always been *infrastructure* studies. Hesmondhalgh, for example, accuses the rise of infrastructure theory in media studies of "seeming to have led to a neglect of other traditions of research, such as political economy of media, that might provide insights into the workings of media infrastructures as traditionally understood."[7] However justified this objection may be, it is important to note that the term "infrastructure" as such was rarely used in the early discourses of media studies research. Instead, the notion of "system" was much more common. In Harold Innis's foundational text *Empire and Communications*, for example, the term "infrastructure" does not appear once, while "system" is mentioned nearly a hundred times.[8] For Marshall McLuhan, too, for example in *Understanding Media*, media systems formed one class of systems among many others.[9] Similarly, in his standard work on the history of television, *Television: Technology and Cultural Form*, Raymond Williams refers to individual media as distinct systems that may follow each other in time or coexist.[10] In a similar but different vein, scholars of

---

7   Hesmondhalgh, "The Infrastructural Turn in Media and Internet Research," 132.

8   Innis mentions, among others, numerical, economic, administrative, agricultural, political, sign, and epistemic systems and even refers to customs and rituals as systems. Harold A. Innis, *Empire and Communications*, ed. David Godfrey (Oxford: Clarendon Press, 1950).

9   McLuhan talks, among others, about the railway system, the electric grid system, information systems and communication systems, though the term "infrastructure" does not appear in the book. Marshall McLuhan, *Understanding Media: The Extensions of Man* (New York: McGraw-Hill, 1964).

10   Williams mentions the general system of electric telegraphy, the telephone system, the system of television, the broadcasting system, and the North American communications system. Raymond Williams, *Television: Technology and Cultural Form* (London: Fontana 1974).

science and technology have addressed, since the late 1970s, the histories of transportation, energy, and communication infrastructures as "large technical systems" (LTS).[11] Moreover, in the 1980s and 1990s, German-language media cultural studies in particular liked to speak of "media compounds" (*Medienverbünde*), in which the entanglement of individual media were understood to provide the content for new compound systems.[12]

The concept of infrastructure as such remained primarily an actors' category for the first century after its emergence. The term first appeared in the French discourse of railroad engineering, where it literally referred to the built substructure of the rails, such as bridges, land cuts, or tunnels. From the 1920s onward, the term came to refer to military installations needed for combat operations and the general logistics of conflict. It was not until the second half of the twentieth century, however, that the concept of infrastructure came into general use, as it increasingly became part of public policy and political economy discourses, beginning with NATO position papers. There, the term was used to describe technical facilities as well as government institutions and services of national scope thought to support national economies and democracy.[13] This brief look at the history of the infrastructure concept already suggests that it does not merge with that of system. While a system can be an infrastructure or function as such, an infrastructure does not necessarily have to take the shape of a system. Infrastructure is first of all, a foundation, which, in the original sense of the term in railroading, compensates for the unevenness of nature (here, the territory) or, in a figurative sense, for the contingencies of everyday life. Infrastructures, both as resources in material form or in the form of labor and services, therefore, can be thought of more generally as exerting a levelling effect, allowing them to appear as something that can repeatedly be relied on and built upon to pursue even more far-reaching goals.

As a substructure or supporting structure, the term thus tends to draw attention to mediated relations between actors and environments and to evoke the presence of goal-oriented practices, for infrastructures are always infrastructures *of* something and *for* someone. Applied to the military's ability to act or to the development of national economies, the concept refers to facilities and precautions that have a supporting or catalytic effect intended to making processes run as smoothly as possible. Infrastructures in this classical sense can therefore be technical in nature (e.g.,

---

11   See Wiebe Bijker, Trevor Pinch, and Thomas Hughes, eds., *The Social Construction of Technological Systems: New Directions in the Sociology and History of Technology* (Cambridge: MIT Press, 1987); Renate Mayntz and Thomas P. Hughes, eds., *The Development of Large Technical Systems* (Boulder: Westview, 1988); Jane Summerton, ed., *Changing Large Technical Systems* (Boulder: Westview Press, 1994).

12   See, for instance, Friedrich A. Kittler, *Grammophon, Film, Typewriter* (Berlin: Brinkmann & Bose, 1986), 8.

13   See also the introduction to this volume.

in the form of energy or water supply systems, or information and data infrastructures), in the form of public institutions (e.g., education or health care), or in the form of services and legal or regulatory frameworks. For example, the Internet is not only a distribution network for digital data, but also provides a base for the development of individual subsystems, such as websites, mobile applications etc. Because of this openness of purpose, infrastructure research has emphasized the *generative potential* of infrastructures.[14]

By pointing to what lies beneath, the notion of infrastructure further implies a vertical logic, which suggests the potential development of higher-order infrastructures. In this regard, Ingo Braun and Bernward Joerges studied how large technical systems can be interconnected to form "second-order systems," such as the systems of organ transplantation and hazardous waste disposal.[15] Applied to the history and present of digitally networked media, digital platforms, and mobile apps—and, ultimately, any development activity in the web that provides new functions and services—can be conceived as higher-order systems. This layered understanding of systems as infrastructures is important because it points to the fact that without the existing substructure, these systems would not exist (be it because they would not be feasible at all or because they would not be economically sustainable). Infrastructures are therefore usually linked to other infrastructures. Just as the track bed is the literal substructure for railroad tracks, the tracks are the substructure for railroads, and railroads are a general transportation infrastructure. Infrastructures, unlike closed systems or rhizomatic networks, are always already infrastructures of something and for someone.

2. Infrastructure as an Analytic Lens

The emergence of a suprisingly different theoretical interpretation of the concept of infrastructure has its origins in the early 1990s, when the term "information infrastructure" was coined in the field of public infrastructure policy.[16] As a catch-

14   See, for instance, Cymene Howe et al., "Paradoxical Infrastructures: Ruins, Retrofit, and Risk," *Science, Technology, & Human Values* 41, no. 3 (May 1, 2016): 547–65, https://doi.org/10.1177/01 62243915620017; Kalle Lyytinen, Carsten Sørensen, and David Tilson, "Generativity in Digital Infrastructures: A Research Note," in *The Routledge Companion to Management Information Systems*, ed. Robert D. Galliers and Mari-Klara Stein (London: Routledge, 2017), 253–75.

15   Ingo Braun and Bernward Joerges, "How to Recombine Large Technical Systems: The Case of European Organ Transplantation," in *Changing Large Technical Systems*, ed. Jane Summerton (Boulder: Westview Press, 1994), 25–51.

16   See, for instance, Al Gore, "The National Information Infrastructure: Agenda for Action" (1993), 58 Fed. Reg. 49025–01, 1993 WL 365171 (Sept. 21, 1993); the National Information Infrastructure Act (1993); and the Bangemann Report on *Europe and the Global Information Society* (1994).

phrase put out by policymakers and research funders, the term was taken up and theorized primarily in the context of sociological research accompanying software development projects in the area of distributed computing. The research of sociologists of technology Susan Leigh Star and Karen Ruhleder has proven foundational for what is now known as infrastructure theory. In the 1990s, Star and Ruhleder conducted an ethnographic study about the construction of a digitally networked information system for biologists (a.k.a. the worm study). In the course of their research, they observed that the ideas about how the system should be conceived and what it should be able to do diverged quite sharply between the designers and the intended users. Star and Ruhleder took these conflicting views and experiences as a prompt to think about infrastructure "relationally," that is, not as technologies as such but as resources in relation to concrete actors' groups and "communities of practice."[17] Just as Bruno Latour claimed that a network is local at all its points, Star and Ruhleder's account of infrastructure and its meaning appeared as fundamentally situated and actor-related.[18] From the material collected in their ethnography, Star and Ruhleder distilled eight features that they believed illustrated such a relational understanding of infrastructure. As Christine L. Borgman synthesizes in an article,

> Star and Ruhleder are among the first to describe infrastructure as a social and technical construct. Their eight dimensions can be paraphrased as follows: An infrastructure is *embedded* in other structures, social arrangements, and technologies. It is *transparent*, in that it invisibly supports tasks. Its *reach or scope* may be spatial or temporal, in that it reaches beyond a single event or a single site of practice. Infrastructure is *learned as part of membership* of an organization or group. It is *linked with conventions of practice* of day–to–day work. Infrastructure is the *embodiment of standards*, so that other tools and infrastructures can interconnect in a standardized way. It *builds upon an installed base*, inheriting both strengths and limitations from that base. And infrastructure *becomes visible upon breakdown*, in that we are most aware of it when it fails to work—when the server is down, the electrical power grid fails, or the highway bridge collapses.[19]

To say that Star and Ruhleder were "among the first to describe infrastructure as a social and technical construct" may seem a bit misleading, if not unfair, given, for instance, the rich history of research on large technical systems and especially the fact

17   Susan Leigh Star and Karen Ruhleder, "Steps Toward an Ecology of Infrastructure: Design and Access for Large Information Spaces," *Information Systems Research* 7, no. 1 (1996): 111–134, 112, https://doi.org/10.1287/isre.7.1.111.

18   See Bruno Latour, *We Have Never Been Modern*, trans. Cathrine Porter (Cambridge: Harvard University Press, 2012), 117–119.

19   Christine L. Borgman, *From Gutenberg to the Global Information Infrastructure: Access to Information in the Networked World* (Cambridge, Mass: MIT Press, 2000), 19. Italics original.

that the major take-away of LTS research had already been the assertion that "'technology' is not only socially shaped [but] social through and through."[20] What distinguishes the approach of Star and Ruhleder, as well as subsequent scholars, from LTS research, however, is a strong focus on the micro-level of social interaction and, relatedly, a heightened attention to the local contexts of infrastructure development and the lived experience of diverse social groups.

As a sociologist of technology whose thinking was strongly influenced by feminist and critical theory, Star was particularly driven by the question of how technologies and the design choices that went into them affected people's concrete everyday lives and what kinds of inequalities they produced among different populations. By referring, for example, to Langdon Winner's seminal article "Do Artifacts Have Politics?," Star repeatedly pointed out that while infrastructures may act as helpful "bridges" for many, they might equally present obstructive "barriers" for some.[21] It is on this sensitivity to social and cultural difference that Star and Ruhleder argue that in studying infrastructure one must ask *when* (i.e., under which conditions)—not *what*—is an infrastructure?"[22] Throughout her career, Star would repeatedly emphasize the relational nature of infrastructure, developing it into a form of infrastructural critique, for example, by addressing how mobility infrastructures such as steps and stairs can be both embraced and overlooked by many people, but "for the person in a wheelchair, the stairs and doorjamb in front of a building are not seamless subtenders of use, but barriers. One person's infrastructure is another's topic, or difficulty."[23] Star and Ruhleder's understanding of infrastructure thus unfolds less as a meso-level perspective on infrastructural systems, as has typically been pursued in media history and LTS research (among others), but more on the micro-level of ethnographic observation with a focus on diverse social actors and their contexts of practice related to the infrastructure in question. Consequently, this perspective led to a shift of focus from the development and "success" of individual infrastructural systems to different communities of practice and their respective relations to and within a system, such as the incompatibilities between the assumptions and practices of various stakeholders involved in the system (such as developers' assumptions about future users versus the actual needs and interests of different user groups).

Important contributions to this praxeologically oriented understanding of infrastructure were made not least by Star's partner Geoffrey Bowker. In fact,

---

20   Paul N. Edwards, "Infrastructure and Modernity: Force, Time, and Social Organization in the History of Sociotechnical Systems," in *Modernity and Technology*, eds. Thomas J. Misa, Philip Brey, and Andrew Feenberg (Cambridge, MA: MIT Press, 2003), 185–225, 199–200.

21   Susan Leigh Star, "The Ethnography of Infrastructure," *American Behavioral Scientist* 43, no. 3 (December 1999): 377–391.

22   Star and Ruhleder, "Steps Toward an Ecology of Infrastructure," 113. Italics original.

23   Star, "The Ethnography of Infrastructure," 380.

Bowker had already used the term infrastructure to explain his historiographic approach in his book *Science on the Run* (1994) about the history of Schlumberger Corporation (SLB), which became the world's largest oil exploration company and offshore drilling contractor. In his book, Bowker advances the argument that it was not the supposed scientific and technical superiority of the oil exploration technology developed and marketed by Schlumberger that contributed to the company's sustained success, but rather the skillful and intensive personal networking of the company's founders and the acquisition of detailed information about local conditions:

> Schlumberger's chief means of strategic consolidation and scientific development was infrastructural work. By this I mean the set of techniques (administrative, social, and technical) that the company marshaled in order to get to work in the vicinity of an oil field. I will develop the position that this set of techniques preceded, created the conditions for, and determined the form of Schlumberger's science.[24]

This "infrastructural work" performed by actors to secure influence in a particular local environment and thus create or develop their own "infrastructure," takes place primarily behind the scenes and serves to put the actors in a better position to achieve their goals.[25] Bowker articulates his approach in the methodological concept of "infrastructural inversion," which encourages us to examine less the visible or exhibited practices of actors, and more the practices and circumstances in the background that enable actors to do or achieve what they do in the first place.[26] Bowker's use of the term infrastructure to mark resources for personal action and the practices of acquiring them thus contributed significantly to the rather radical, actor-centered reinterpretation of the concept. In the co-authored article "How to Infrastructure" from 2002, Bowker and Star further developed this new understanding of the term by conceptualizing it in its verb form "to infrastructure" as a *practice of in-*

---

24   Geoffrey C. Bowker, *Science on the Run: Information Management and Industrial Geophysics at Schlumberger, 1920–1940*, Inside Technology (Cambridge: MIT Press, 1994), 10.

25   The concept of "infrastructural work" here is thus somewhat different from that of, for example, Schabacher, who uses the notion "infrastructure work" (*Infrastruktur-Arbeit*) to consider the work *of* and *on* infrastructures (in a more classical understanding of the term). Rather, it seems to transfer Michael Mann's concept of "infrastructural power" from the macro scale of nation states to the meso scale of corporate actors. See Gabriele Schabacher, *Infrastruktur-Arbeit: Kulturtechniken und Zeitlichkeit der Erhaltung* (Berlin: Kulturverlag Kadmos, 2022), 9; Michael Mann, "The Autonomous Power of the State: Its Origins, Mechanisms and Results," *European Journal of Sociology / Archives Européennes de Sociologie* 25, no. 2 (November 1984): 185–213, https://doi.org/10.1017/S0003975600004239.

26   Bowker, *Science on the Run*, 10.

frastructuring that emanates from both individual and collective actors.[27] Infrastructuring, then, represents a rather fundamental everyday practice: Since all humans pursue goals in one way or another and often encounter obstacles along the way, in principle each of us—consciously or unconsciously—is "infrastructuring" everywhere and all the time. This conceptualization, as well as the approach of "infrastructural inversion," thus encourages writing historical developments as histories of "infrastructuring."

Star and Ruhleder's observation that the work of software development performed in the context of IT projects often consisted of the modular assembly of already existing elements and components, such as hardware, software, technical standards and protocols etc., further led to the realization that the users of these already existing "installed bases" were not only provided with practical advantages, but also with restrictions or path dependencies. In addition, the developers' assumptions about later users were reflected in the digital objects, for example, through preliminary decisions and classifications made in the context of the pre-structuring of databases, which were usually adopted unquestioningly or without reflection. As a rule, these anticipations have had and continue to have normative effects that interfere with the user experience of non-normative users, simply because developers tend to assume tech-savvy, able-bodied, middle-class users as a default.

In their co-authored book *Sorting Things Out* (1999), Star and Bowker continued this line of research by critically examining mundane categorizations and rubrics found in, for instance, medical history forms, the gender assignments of public toilets, or the table of contents of the Yellow Pages. Not only are classifications ubiquitous, but the "categorical saturation furthermore forms a complex web"—a symbolic infrastructure that both supports and governs processes and practices through the indirect exercise of power and normativity.[28] Because of these political implications of supposedly banal everyday categories, Star and Bowker's infrastructure theory emphasizes the need to address the agency of the mundane and seemingly taken-for-granted.[29] Due to their consisting of data structures, the relevance and

---

27 Susan Leigh Star and Geoffrey C. Bowker, "How to Infrastructure," in *Handbook of New Media: Social Shaping and Social Consequences of ICTs*, eds. Leah A. Lievrouw and Sonia Livingstone (London: Sage, 2002), 151–162. The notion was later taken up in the field of socio-informatics. See Volkmar Pipek and Volker Wulf, "Infrastructuring: Towards an Integrated Perspective on the Design and Use of Information Technology," *Journal of the Association of Information Systems* (JAIS) 10, no. 5 (2009): 306–32.

28 Geoffrey C. Bowker and Susan Leigh Star, *Sorting Things Out: Classification and Its Consequences* (Cambridge: The MIT Press, 2000), 38.

29 In 1997, Star half-jokingly co-founded "The Society of People Interested in Boring Things" in Palo Alto. Her interest in the politics encapsulated in seemingly dull and mundane objects later led to a collective volume co-edited together with Martha Lampland on standards,

consequences of "classification work" are particularly relevant with regard to digital objects and processes.[30] Applied to the development of networked applications and services on the Internet, this perspective thus prompts us to scrutinize not only the functionality but the socio-cultural dimension and cultural-political implications of technological objects and applications, and in particular the dynamics of normalization and marginalization that emanate from them.

3. Some Methodological Implications of Infrastructural Thinking in Media Studies

The concept of infrastructure coined by Star, Ruhleder, and Bowker—with its consideration of actors groups, its interest in the everyday and the taken-for-granted, and its sensitivity to the normalizing and marginalizing effects of technological configurations—has been taken up and further developed in various disciplines within the social and human sciences, including STS, urban studies, anthropology, and literary studies (some of these developments have been touched on in the introduction to this volume). Since a detailed account of them would exceed the scope of this paper, I would like to end by focusing on a central aspect of infrastructural thinking to discuss some of the methodological implications it has had for the study and historiography of media. This aspect consists primarily in the paradoxical fact that the preoccupation with infrastructural theory has drawn scholarly attention away from technical *systems* and operations to the importance and variety of human (and non-human) *practice*. This praxeological shift has equally affected both the study of contemporary media and the writing of its history and seems to yield new methodological possibilities for future research in other humanities disciplines too.

Drawing on earlier STS work, for instance, Steven J. Jackson suggested in his 2014 article "Rethinking Repair" that media studies should not only focus on technological innovation, but also consider more closely the labor of maintenance and repair, a call that was echoed shortly thereafter in studies of media infrastructure and the history of computing.[31] In *The Undersea Network*, Nicole Starosielski uses a

---

which in turn inspired media scholars to interrogate the assumed neutrality of technical norms and specifications, such as color cards used in photography or the MP3 format, within the history of media. Martha Lampland and Susan Leigh Star, *Standards and Their Stories: How Quantifying, Classifying, and Formalizing Practices Shape Everyday Life* (Ithaca: Cornell University Press, 2009); Lorna Roth, "Looking at Shirley, the Ultimate Norm: Colour Balance, Image Technologies, and Cognitive Equity," *Canadian Journal of Communication* 34, no. 1 (2009); Sterne, *MP3*.

30   Bowker and Star, *Sorting Things Out*, 1.

31   See, for instance, Tarleton Gillespie, Pablo J. Boczkowski, and Kirsten A. Foot, eds., *Media Technologies: Essays on Communication, Materiality, and Society* (MIT Press, 2014); Andrew Rus-

similar focus on site-specific labor and everyday practices to tell the story—or rather stories—of the Pacific submarine cable network in a different way. Focusing on the diverse practices of managers, cable workers, local residents, politicians, and researchers at distinct sites or "nodes" (such as cable stations, cable landings, or islands), Starosielski shows where cable infrastructure intersects with and how it is "grounded" in physical, sociopolitical, and cultural environments through strategies of "insulation" and "interconnection."[32] Based on this praxeological perspective, Starosielski argues that global signal traffic is as much rooted in people (in terms of "human labor and embodied experience"[33]) and their respective practices of "infrastructuring" as it is in the material and technological components of the cable network.

A similar focus on practices is mobilized by John Durham Peters in his book *The Marvelous Clouds*, in which he pairs infrastructure theory with German and French cultural techniques research to forge a doctrine of "infrastructuralism." According to Peters, "infrastructuralism suggests a way of understanding the work of media as fundamentally logistical."[34] In particular, present-day digital media do not only integrate aspects of the "old" mass media, but also "resurrect old media such as writing, addresses, numbers, names, calendars, timekeepers, maps, and money [and] give new life to age-old practices such as navigating, cultivating, stargazing, weather forecasting, documenting, and fishing."[35] By centering the "logistical" and cooperative role of media and the history of their invention and development within the scope of quotidian practices and cultural techniques of "recording, transmitting, and processing culture; of managing subjects, objects, and data; [and] of organizing time, space, and power," Peters ultimately argues that "media serve more as devices of tracking and orientation than in providing unifying stories to the society at large" and that we should therefore understand them more generally as "infrastructural media" in the sense of "media that stand under."[36]

Attention to everyday strategies of "infrastructuring" also foregrounds new practice-oriented stories of media change and technological transformation. The recent boom in video conferencing applications at the onset of the global Covid-19 pandemic is a particularly striking example: Rather than being fuelled by the potential of new media practices based on technological innovation, billions of people affected by lockdowns and measures of "social distancing" turned to remote

sell and Lee Vinsel, "Hail the Maintainers," *Aeon*, 2016, https://aeon.co/essays/innovation-is-overvalued-maintenance-often-matters-more; Parks and Starosielski, *Signal Traffic*.

32   Nicole Starosielski, *The Undersea Network* (Durham: Duke University Press, 2015).

33   Starosielsk, *The Undersea Network*, 98.

34   John Durham Peters, *The Marvelous Clouds: Toward a Philosophy of Elemental Media* (Chicago: University of Chicago Press, 2015), 37.

35   Peters, *The Marvelous Clouds*, 8.

36   Peters, *The Marvelous Clouds*, 7, 19, 33.

technologies, and particularly video conferencing, to "re-infrastructure" collapsed routines of everyday cooperation that had previously taken place in shared spaces such as offices, classrooms, or gyms.[37] A significant part of this re-infrastructuring work involved processes of appropriating video conferencing tools and adapting them to one's own needs, existing contexts of practice, and related social expectations, for example by redecorating or otherwise staging the domestic space visible to the camera during video calls, by acquiring new technological devices such as ring lights, or by reading (or even writing) one of the numerous "guides" aimed at teaching (and thereby normalizing) user behaviour for "successful" Zoom calls. In this light, infrastructuring appears as a two-way process: On the one hand, the new users of remote technologies and video conferencing applications had to adapt to the functionalities of the existing solutions; on the other hand, the providers of products, such as Zoom, also reacted to the specific needs of the new user groups, by, for instance, incorporating new functionalities or different workflows.[38] The general practice of quotidian infrastructuring can thus be understood as a process of mutual adaptation and harmonization of media (including technologies and other elements related to their use) and sets of already existing practices, a dynamic which can complement provider-oriented accounts of traditional media history.

Moreover, the public discourse that accompanied the mainstreaming of video-conferencing applications also revealed on-site practices as the social norm prior to the pandemic. To give an example, many people with disabilities used the hashtag #AccessibilityForAbleds created by Canadian disability activist Kate McWilliams to express their frustration about the fact that the shift to remote practices at the beginning of the pandemic was accomplished in just a few weeks when it affected the abled-bodied majority, while the demands for opportunities to participate remotely in work or educational activities often voiced by people with disabilities had not been heard for years. The example of videoconferencing thus points to the normativity inherent in the general development of technology, which tends to neglect—and thereby potentially exclude—user groups outside the boundaries of the implicit norm that is both consciously and unconsciously considered to be the default. This inherent bias extends to the historiography of media, too. It is striking, for instance, that Deaf people are rarely featured in the history of video telephony and video conferencing, even though their use of sign language makes them an ideal

---

37   Axel Volmar, Charline Kindervater, Sebastian Randerath, and Aikaterini Mniestri, "Mainstreaming Zoom: Covid-19, Social Distancing, and the Rise of Video-Mediated Remote Cooperation," in *Varieties of Cooperation: Mutually Making the Conditions of Mutual Making*, eds. Clemens Eisenmann, Kathrin Englert, Cornelius Schubert, and Ehler Voss, Media of Cooperation (Wiesbaden: Springer VS, 2023), 99–133.

38   See Volmar et al., "Mainstreaming Zoom"; Axel Volmar, Olga Moskatova, and Jan Distelmeyer, eds., *Video Conferencing: Infrastructures, Practices, Aesthetics* (Bielefeld: transcript, 2023).

demographic for visual communications technologies. A closer look at the history of media use from the perspective of non-normative user groups reveals that the normalizing effects inscribed in media technologies cause further marginalization in terms of lesser options for use and participation when compared to standard users because the technologies are simply not conceived *for* them but for people with other bodies and abilities. The insights into the significance of practices of non-normative infrastructuring has led, for example, to new alliances and academic exchanges between media studies and disability studies, as evidenced, for example, by the academic network "Dis-/Abilities and Digital Media," funded by the German Research Foundation.[39] An actor-centered focus on infrastructure that critically engages with the normativity of the supposedly universal *standard user* can thus help us to both produce richer and more diverse histories of media and the people who use them, and to advocate for a more inclusive media infrastructure in the future.

Conclusion

As I attempted to show in this brief conceptual history, the term "infrastructure" is much more than just another synonym for a technological system, network, or platform. Rather, the nuanced notion of infrastructure developed within the sociology of technology invites us to ask what kinds of normalized preconceptions and uses are inscribed in technological, institutional, symbolic, and other everyday resources, and thus which user groups are implicitly supported in carrying out their everyday practices and which are not. The term thus encourages us to reconsider traditional objects of humanities research in relation to the lived experience of different actor groups in order to unveil their inherent politics.

In terms of methodology, an infrastructural or infrastructuralist perspective suggests that we no longer look at only existing infrastructural systems but take different actors groups and their respective infrastructural needs and practices as a starting point for scholarly investigations. Obtaining a praxeological and situated understanding of infrastructure, which centers actors first before determining what may or may not count as an infrastructure in relation to these actors, is not least a politically motivated shift of the analyst's attention used to identify infrastructurally underserved and disadvantaged populations and to understand practices of "infrastructuring." This fact seems to escape some of the current critics of the infrastructure concept, whose understanding often still assumes infrastructures to be existing and clearly defined objects or services of some kind.

---

39   See "Scientific Network Dis-/Abilities and Digital Media," accessed August 29, 2023, https://dis-abilities-and-digital-media.org/index.php/en/project.

This shift in the focus of scholarly attention from infrastructures in the common sense of the term to actor-centric support infrastructures, however, often remains implicit in the discourse of current infrastructure research. Thus, the danger of "vagueness" that can accompany the use of the concept of infrastructure, as criticized by Hesmondhalgh for example, is certainly present. In the context of one's own work, it is therefore advisable, of course, to clearly indicate what understanding of infrastructure one is relying on. Rather than overstress the necessity for clarity when defining the notion of infrastructure, we should, however, focus more on emphasizing the *purpose* of using the concept in the first place. Or, put differently: the pressing question today seems to be not so much how exactly we define infrastructure but how an infrastructural perspective can change the ways scholars in the humanities actually work and how they present their research. Of course, studies of infrastructures within the humanities can continue to start from technical systems and other geographically distributed installations. The shift from an systemic to a praxeological understanding of infrastructure invites us, however, to account for infrastructure's relationality due to the social, cultural, spatial, and other differences among its various stakeholders, the politics and cultural-historical significance of the taken-for-granted, and the everyday practices of "infrastructuring." At the very best, an infrastructural perspective could help us to look at familiar themes with fresh eyes and ultimately to create more context-sensitive and diverse stories.

Section II: Infrastructures and Communication

Language as Infrastructure

Bettina Braun and Bernhard Brehmer

Starting from a general working definition of infrastructure as "matter that enable the movement of other matter,"[1] the relationship between language and infrastructure can be approached from several perspectives: First, language in its spoken or written form is the basic means for exchanging information. As such, it enables individuals among many other things to pass on knowledge to others or to organize collaborative action which would be hard to achieve without language. Thus, language itself represents an infrastructure par excellence that paves the way for communication among human beings. Second, as any other form of infrastructure, languages are to a certain extent consciously constructed by the members of respective communities. Communities undertake numerous actions to take care of their language or to maintain it. These efforts manifest themselves in language planning or other forms of language policy. Third, languages interact dynamically with their environment, be it other languages or their own speakers coming from various social or regional backgrounds. This leads to language change or the emergence of social ("slang") and regional varieties ("dialects") of a language. However, language change may be driven not only by external sources, but also stipulated by internal processes like analogical levelling of irregular forms or other types of language-internal developmental dynamics related to language typology (e.g. the development of definite and indefinite articles in languages from demonstrative pronouns or numerals). Fourth, language overlaps with classically understood material infrastructures: Information signs indicating directions of travel, place/street names, names of institutions, warnings or advertisements crucially build on language. Visible language on public signs does not only facilitate perception of material infrastructures, but can also function as an index of representation and power of different parts of the inhabitants of this city/district etc.

In this essay we elaborate more on three of the above-mentioned aspects of language as infrastructure. We start from language as a basic infrastructure for communication itself and the relationship between its different forms of existence (oral

---

1   Brian Larkin, "The Politics and Poetics of Infrastructure," *Annual Review of Anthropology* 42, no. 1 (2013): 329, https://doi.org/10.1146/annurev-anthro-092412-155522.

vs. written language), then turn to a discussion of measures undertaken by the respective communities to develop and maintain languages as common infrastructure, and close with issues regarding the role of language on material infrastructures in contexts of marginalization and struggles of representation by linguistic minorities. By doing so, we try to apply the notion of "infrastructure" as an analytical tool and organizing concept that provides a way for crossing disciplinary boundaries within linguistics and to counterbalance tendencies towards a separate analysis of systemic and social aspects of language.

From Biology to Oral and Written Forms of Language

The production of language as the most widely used medium of communication and information exchange crucially depends on the physiological infrastructure of the human body: Speech sounds are produced through the manipulation of the pulmonal airflow by means of articulators in the larynx (vocal folds), the velum, the tongue and the lips.[2] The resulting acoustic signals are in turn perceptually and cognitively decoded by the listener through the perceptual apparatus (organs of the outer, middle and inner ear) organ and neuronal processes in the brain[3]: "Language processing consists of a complex and nested set of subroutines to get from sound to meaning (in comprehension) or meaning to sound (in production), with remarkable speed and accuracy."[4] While oral forms of language fulfil the basic function of an infrastructure for exchanging information and represent the basis of natural language transmission from one generation to the next, many communities have developed a special infrastructure to fix the elusive nature of oral language use by inventing writing systems.

Building on a system of written signs that either iconically represent the concepts denoted (cf. Egyptian hieroglyphics) or symbolically map units of sound (syllables, individual phonemes) onto graphical units (letters), the invention of writing systems has made it possible to extend the infrastructural potential of language by allowing communication across distances and times. Further, a writing system lends power to the oral language that is encoded. Not surprisingly, one typical distinction between a dialect and a standard language is that the latter has a codified writing system. Writing systems not only allow communication across space and time, but they are also able to reach a large range of people (pupils) that are initiated

---

2   Bernd Pompino-Marschall, *Einführung in die Phonetik* (Berlin: Walter de Gruyter, 2009).

3   Anne Cutler, *Native Listening* (Cambridge: MIT Press, 2012).

4   Peter Hagoort and David Poeppel, "The Infrastructure of the Language-Ready Brain," in *Language, Music, and the Brain*, ed. Michael A. Arbib (Cambridge: MIT Press, 2013), 233, https://doi.org/10.7551/mitpress/9780262018104.003.0009.

in its use. Germany is a country with a diverse set of historically derived dialects, but the Standard German writing system is quite distinct from the oral systems used in different dialectal areas. Due to its high prestige, its use in media (radio, TV), and possibly the availability of natural language processing devices (translation, automatic speech recognition, dictation systems), Standard German is on its way to replace the dialectal variants. Pröll even argues that "Standard German is in the process of becoming a nativized variety of German after centuries without native speakers."[5] If this was the case, then the tension between Standard and regional varieties is predicted to decrease. However, from our research on the development of children's lexical representations, we know that parents do speak regional varieties, in particular in more rural areas.[6] Once the standard is acquired, the standard becomes an infrastructure as self-evident to the language user as the regional variants in the generation before. The situation in Germany is not unique and is found in many European countries (e.g. Italy, the Czech Republic).

Language Policy and the Struggle for a Unified vs. Diversified Linguistic Infrastructure

Standard varieties are taught in schools, by authorities that enforce it.[7] This power differential can lead to defiant reactions and to the formation of groups that violate the rules on purpose. Examples are the development of youth language, sociolects (e.g. Kiezdeutsch) or the resurrection of dialects (e.g. "Förderverein bairische Sprache und Dialekte e. V.," http://fbsd.de). This goes together with an increase in heterogeneity and individualism and more identification with the local community or region than with the wider society of a country. The discrepancy is even more obvious in areas, in which local community languages were systematically disfavoured. There are many examples in the literature, the most recent being the reduction of

---

5   Simon Pröll, "Die Nativierung Des Standarddeutschen. Mikrotypologische Evidenz für supra-segmentalen Wandel," *Zeitschrift für Angewandte Linguistik* 2021, no. 75 (2021): 305–29, https://doi.org/10.1515/zfal-2021-2068, 305.

6   Bettina Braun et al., "Remote Testing of the Familiar Word Effect with Non-Dialectal and Dialectal German-Learning 1–2-Year-Olds," *Frontiers in Psychology: Empirical Research at a Distance: New Methods for Developmental Science* 12 (2022): 714363, https://doi.org/10.3389/fpsyg.2021.714363.

7   Lisa Fairbrother, "A Language Management Approach to Language Problems," *A Language Management Approach to Language Problems*, 2020, 1–283, https://doi.org/10.1075/wlp.7.01fai; Vít Dovalil, "Processes of Destandardization and Demotization in the Micro-Macro Perspective," in *A Language Management Approach to Language Problems: Integrating Macro and Micro Dimensions*, eds. Goro Christoph Kimura and Lisa Fairbrother (Amsterdam: John Benjamins Publishing Company, 2020), 177–96.

formal education in Basque or Catalan in Spain or the abandonment of Russian language-based education in Estonia or Latvia.[8]

The current debate about gender sensitive language makes the power struggle immediately obvious: on the one hand, there are conservative language users that learnt a particular standard grammatical system during their school time and point out its efficiency, on the other hand, there are more progressive language users that interpret the male forms as exclusive. That this debate is a power struggle is evident from the emotionality with which the debate is conducted and from the suspicion with which arguments from the other side are met. For supporters of gender sensitive language, language is either seen as a means to change reality (a more inclusive language leading to a more inclusive society) or as a means to reflect the change in reality (from a binary gender image to less binary concepts). Critics of gender sensitive language argue that the linguistic forms become more complicated, making the language less inclusive. No matter which side one takes, it is clear that there is a fight about a new standard, which will have winners and losers.

Inclusion is, however, not restricted to debates about gender sensitive language. It also applies to attempts for making linguistic diversity more visible. Due to the influx of several immigration waves after World War II, including the recent waves of refugees fleeing wars in different parts of the world (Syria, Afghanistan, Ukraine, to mention only a few), Germany has become a linguistically diverse country. According to recent surveys, 27% of all inhabitants of Germany have a "migration background," i.e., they immigrated from other countries to Germany themselves or have at least one parent who did so.[9] Thus, they normally speak other languages than German. While the debate regarding the integration (or rather linguistic assimilation) of guest workers (Gastarbeiter) in Germany in the second half of the 20th century centred around issues concerning the acquisition of German as a prerequisite for integration into the host society and individual success on the labor market, recent discussions also underline the benefit of being bi- or multilingual not only for the individual, but also for the host society.[10] This calls for measures to secure that the following generations can also benefit from their early acquisition of another language. The benefits include, but are not limited to, being an asset on the job market, having access and being part of the culture of their ancestors, thus fostering intercul-

8   Monika Wingender, "Russisch als neue Minderheitensprache im östlichen Europa. Die ECRM und die Diskussion um das Russische in Nachfolgestaaten der UdSSR," in *Die Sprachpolitik des Europarats*, eds. Franz Lebsanft and Monika Wingender (Berlin: De Gruyter, 2012), 165–90, https://doi.org/10.1515/9783110276695.165.

9   Statistisches Bundesamt, "Bevölkerung nach Migrationshintergrund und Geschlecht," Statistisches Bundesamt, 2022, https://www.destatis.de/DE/Themen/Gesellschaft-Umwelt/Bevoelkerung/Migration-Integration/Tabellen/liste-migrationshintergrund-geschlecht.html.

10   Cf. contributions in Ingrid Gogolin and Ursula Neumann, eds., *Streitfall Zweisprachigkeit – The Bilingualism Controversy* (Wiesbaden: VS Verlag für Sozialwissenschaften, 2009).

tural sensitivity. Maintaining individual bilingualism that arises from growing up in families where another language than German is commonly used, requires specific efforts from the individual, their parents and close relatives, i.e., by engaging in joint reading of books or consumption of media in the home language (especially in early childhood), by attending community schools offering additional instruction in the home language and aspects of the home culture etc. Language minority groups face the problem that "their" language is mostly restricted to communication within the family domain which serves only restricted functions. From a longitudinal perspective, the likelihood that the language is kept, and maybe even passed over to the following generations, depends on the possibility to use it outside of the family domain, i.e. it requires a certain infrastructure supporting the use of the minority language for special purposes.[11] Research on the concept of ethnolinguistic vitality of minority languages stresses the importance of several extralinguistic factors that facilitate the maintenance of home (or "heritage") languages, including the number of speakers of the minority language in the host country, its prestige in the host society, institutional support for the acquisition of these languages (community schools, heritage language instruction in public schools), the range of sociolinguistic domains where the minority language can be used (workplace, shops, church services, leisure activities etc.), contacts to people residing in the countries of origin etc.[12] The degree to which minority communities manage to establish a certain infrastructure differs considerably among the individual minority communities. Russian can be seen as an example of a linguistic minority group in Germany which succeeded in establishing an extensive infrastructure in Germany (mostly in bigger cities, but even in Konstanz) that facilitates Russian language maintenance to a remarkable extent.[13] This infrastructure includes Russian-speaking lawyers, doctors, grocery stores offering typical food and other items from Eastern Europe, community schools and bilingual nursery schools, clubs organizing cultural and sport activities, church communities etc. It remains to be seen how the current war in Ukraine and the subsequent damage of the international prestige of Russian will affect the future development of this infrastructure, although Russian is the dominant language for most of the refugees coming from Eastern and Southern Ukraine, which leads to a replenishment of the Russian-speaking community in Germany.

---

11   Such usage extends beyond just family small-talk, cf. Monika S. Schmid and Elise Dusseldorp, "Quantitative Analyses in a Multivariate Study of Language Attrition: The Impact of Extralinguistic Factors," *Second Language Research* 26, no. 1 (2010): 125–60, https://doi.org/10.1177/026 7658309337641.

12   Jörn Achterberg, *Zur Vitalität slavischer Idiome in Deutschland* (Munich: Peter Lang International Academic Publishers, 2005), https://doi.org/10.3726/b12748.

13   Bernhard Brehmer, "Maintenance of Russian as Heritage Language in Germany: A Longitudinal Approach," *Russian Journal of Linguistics* 25, no. 4 (2021): 855–85.

Material Infrastructures and Language Use

In the introductory section, we already stressed the importance of visible language for classically understood material infrastructure. Apart from language being the key to understanding public signs, the presence of language in the visual landscape of all kinds of settlements also gains additional symbolic value, especially in case of linguistically diverse populations (cf. debates about bilingual place name signs in areas where minorities live, e.g., in the Sorbian settlements in Brandenburg and Saxony). This is the subject matter of linguistic studies dealing with so-called "linguistic landscapes." Research on linguistic landscapes is nowadays a well-established branch of sociolinguistics that deals with language usage in public space and how language constructs public space mostly in urban areas.[14] For the purpose of the current paper, this adds another dimension to the topic of language and infrastructure, where infrastructure is meant to denote classically understood material infrastructure: the significance of material infrastructure for making (diverse) languages visible. While in its earlier stages the focus of linguistic landscape studies has been on areas where language use on public signs is a socially and politically controversial issue[15] it has now turned into the most influential paradigm in the study of visible language in urban areas.[16] The relation between the linguistic landscape of a city or urban area and minority communities is a classical topic in linguistic landscape research, but in earlier studies the main focus was on the quantitative presence of minority languages on public signage and whether the use of these minority languages

---

14   Rodrigue Landry and Richard Y. Bourhis, "Linguistic Landscape and Ethnolinguistic Vitality: An Empirical Study," *Journal of Language and Social Psychology* 16, no. 1 (1997): 23–49, https://doi.org/10.1177/0261927X970161002, 25.

15   E.g., Quebec: Rodrigue Landry and Richard Y. Bourhis, "Linguistic Landscape and Ethnolinguistic Vitality: An Empirical Study," *Journal of Language and Social Psychology* 16, no. 1 (1997): 23–49, https://doi.org/10.1177/0261927X970161002; the Basque region: Jasone Cenoz and Durk Gorter, "Linguistic Landscape and Minority Languages," *International Journal of Multilingualism* 3, no. 1 (2006): 67–80, https://doi.org/10.1080/14790710608668386; Ukraine: A. Pavlenko, "Linguistic Landscape of Kyiv, Ukraine: A Diachronic Study," in *Linguistic Landscape in The City*, ed. Elana Shohamy, Eliezer Ben-Rafael, and Monica Barni (Bristol: Multilingual Matters, 2010), 133–54; Israel: Bernard Spolsky and Robert L. Cooper, *The Languages of Jerusalem* (Oxford: Clarendon Press, 1991).

16   Elana Shohamy and D. Gorter, eds., *Linguistic Landscape: Expanding the Scenery*, 1st ed. (New York: Routledge, 2009); Adam Jaworski and Crispin Thurlow, *Semiotic Landscapes: Language, Image, Space* (A&C Black, 2010); Elana Shohamy, Eliezer Ben-Rafael, and Monica Barni, *Linguistic Landscape in the City.* (Bristol: Multilingual Matters, 2010); Peter Backhaus, *Linguistic Landscapes: A Comparative Study of Urban Multilingualism in Tokyo* (Clevedon: Multilingual Matters, 2007); Elana Shohamy, "Linguistic Landscapes and Multilingualism," in *The Routledge Handbook of Multilingualism*, ed. Marilyn Martin-Jones et al. (New York: Routledge, 2012), 538–551.

served communicative purposes or symbolic functions.[17] Contemporary research on linguistic landscapes has started to incorporate aspects of the visual, material, and spatial properties of signs into the analysis. Thus, questions like where the sign is fixed (its indexical relations to the shops, objects etc. it is referring to), how it is designed (including aspects of granularity, i.e. the visibility of a sign from different viewing distances, and, thus, the range of potential recipients it is addressed to), and how the material it is made of indexes types of institutional authority are increasingly taken into account.[18] Quantitative research on the linguistic landscape of several German cities has shown that while some minority languages (e.g. Turkish or Arabic) are rather well-represented on public signs, especially in districts where the respective communities form a considerable part of the inhabitants, other minority language communities (e.g. Polish), despite their high representation in the local districts, are almost absent from public signage, both with regard to official ("top-down," e.g. signposts, prohibition signs, commemorative plaques) and unofficial ("bottom up," e.g. shop names, advertisements, posters, graffiti) signs.[19] The visibility of their language in urban landscapes certainly has an impact on the perception of the respective communities by other groups, e.g. whether the presence and diversity of languages on public signs reflects the real diversity of the urban population, whether this distribution and presence of languages is treated as an indication of linguistic segregation (or ghettoization) or as a positive outcome of multicultural (and multilingual) urban settings and what arguments are used in favour or against the existence of multilingual infrastructures (which go beyond the classical linguae francae in the tourism sector like English or French) by representatives of different social groups. It comes as a surprise that these issues have been addressed only very recently, adding a new dimension to classical linguistic landscape research by focusing on the agency of readers in reinterpreting the cultural, historical, political, and social background of the linguistic landscape.[20]

---

17   Eliezer Ben-Rafael et al., "Linguistic Landscape as Symbolic Construction of the Public Space: The Case of Israel," *International Journal of Multilingualism* 3, no. 1 (2006): 7–30, https://doi.org/10.1080/14790710608668383.

18   Peter Auer, "Sprachliche Landschaften. Die Strukturierung des öffentlichen Raums durch die geschriebene Sprache," in *Sprache intermedial. Stimme und Schrift, Bild und Ton*, eds. Arnulf Deppermann and Angelika Linke (Berlin: De Gruyter, 2010), 271–298.

19   For Hamburg: Claudio Scarvaglieri et al., "Capturing Diversity: Linguistic Land-and-Soundscaping," in *Linguistic Superdiversity in Urban Areas: Research Approaches*, ed. Joana Duarte and Ingrid Gogolin (Amsterdam: John Benjamins, 2013), 45–73; for the Ruhr area: Tirza Mühlan-Meyer, "Mehrsprachigkeit in der Linguistic Landscape der Metropole Ruhr mit besonderer Berücksichtigung des Polnischen," in *Sprachbildung und Sprachkontakt im deutsch-polnischen Kontext*, eds. Britta Hufeisen et al. (Berlin: Peter Lang, 2018), 259–295.

20   See Evelyn Ziegler, Ulrich Schmitz, and Haci-Halil Uslucan, "Attitudes towards Visual Multilingualism in the Linguistic Landscape of the Ruhr Area," in *Expanding the Linguistic Landscape*, ed. Martin Pütz and Neele Mundt (Bristol: Multilingual Matters, 2018), 264–99, https://doi.

Conclusion

In this chapter, we argued that the term "infrastructure" can be applied to language on very different levels and that language shows all typical defining features of infrastructures: (1) Language serves as the basic means for information exchange among human beings, thus it functions as a basic infrastructure that enables human beings to get their messages across; (2) Production and perception of spoken and written language makes use of certain routines which are tied either to universal physiological processes (sound production and perception) or cultural practices that have to be acquired by every individual (e.g. spelling rules); (3) Language as an infrastructure interacts dynamically with its speakers and their social environment (resulting in different varieties of a language) or other types of infrastructures, especially classically understood material infrastructures (cf. language use on public signs); (4) Languages are characterized by external and internal dynamics leading to language change, but they are also subjected to external manipulations that regulate which changes make their way into the standard variety and which fail in getting accepted by the respective authorities (language policy).

The concept of "infrastructure" has not received much attention in linguistic research yet. The term might be used as an overarching framework allowing to combine different subfields of linguistics that are normally treated in isolation (e.g. sociolinguistics and the systematic description of individual language levels like phonology, morphology or syntax). Furthermore, conceptualizing language as infrastructure would make activities regarding language planning and language policies less emotional because they may be seen as investment in the infrastructure, rather than as unruly intrusion into our human lives. Finally, seeing the body as an infrastructure may help to evaluate regional and foreign accent as an issue of the external (body) system, rather than a cognitive deficit.

org/10.21832/9781788922166-015; Jakob R. E. Leimgruber and Víctor Fernández-Mallat, "Language Attitudes and Identity Building in the Linguistic Landscape of Montreal," *Open Linguistics* 7, no. 1 (2021): 406–22, https://doi.org/10.1515/opli-2021-0021.

Conceptual Infrastructure and Conceptual Engineering

Jochen Briesen and Steffen Koch

> "Concepts are the tracks our minds prefer to travel on [...] Unfortunately, sometimes concepts lead us astray."[1]

Section 1. Introduction

This paper introduces and analyses the method of conceptual engineering as a particular infrastructural practice. Although conceptual engineering is applied in various philosophical traditions, in this text the method is discussed primarily within the so-called analytic tradition of philosophy. It is this tradition that coined the term "conceptual engineering," and it is within this tradition that the structure as well as the problems of the method are explicitly investigated. The emphasized infrastructural perspective on conceptual engineering serves two purposes. First, the infrastructural perspective highlights the relevance and urgency of the method. Second, the infrastructural perspective allows us to understand why the method is of central importance not only to philosophy and science, but also with respect to the social and political domain.

In section 2, we introduce the infrastructural perspective on conceptual engineering. In section 3, we give various examples of conceptual engineering and emphasize its importance as a form of infrastructural maintenance. In section 4, we will give a (simplified) systematic analysis of the options within projects of conceptual engineering and highlight some of its main problems as well as topics for future research.

---

1   Edouard Machery, *Philosophy Within its Proper Bounds* (Oxford: Oxford University Press, 2017), 222.

Section 2. An Infrastructural Perspective on Conceptual Engineering

An infrastructure is a set of organizational units, rules, or facilities that are accidentally or deliberately designed and arranged to enable or facilitate the achievement of certain societal goals. An example of such a goal is the need to transport goods and people over long distances. A necessary means to achieve this goal is a certain *physical infrastructure* consisting of roads, bridges, tunnels, harbours, railways, etc., as well as an *institutional infrastructure* consisting of traffic regulations, engineering offices, freight forwarding companies, driving schools, etc. Other needs and goals such as safety, health, knowledge, or education require different infrastructures consisting (in part) of different units, rules, and facilities.

Infrastructures often face various challenges. For example, the aforementioned physical infrastructure directed at transporting goods and people is confronted with time-related deterioration, impairment due to more frequent weather extremes, the duty to be more responsive to the needs of underrepresented groups, and central ecological demands. In general terms, infrastructures of all kinds face a variety of functional, social, political, economic, and ecological challenges.

Faced with those challenges, the following questions are of central importance: What changes and improvements to a specific infrastructure are needed to adequately respond to the challenges in question? How can the necessary changes be implemented as effectively as possible? Is it possible to respond to all challenges simultaneously, or do we need to prioritize when responding to one challenge makes responding to another impossible or at least somewhat difficult?

Although these questions are of central importance, often they are raised too late. A central feature of infrastructure is that it is usually removed from our conscious attention. Only when the functioning of infrastructure is massively impaired does it attract our attention. However, by this point it is often too late to adequately respond to the multiple challenges—such as responding to the ecological challenges with regard to the physical infrastructures mentioned above. This is one of the reasons why it is so important to address and study in detail different variants of infrastructures and the various challenges they face.

Everything said so far not only applies to physical and institutional infrastructures, but also to infrastructure of a more abstract nature. One such abstract infrastructure is language (i.e., the words available to us; the syntactic, semantic, and pragmatic rules governing the use of those words; and the conceptual system related to them). The system of our representational devices (words and concepts) can be understood as the basic infrastructure that enables us to communicate and think—i.e., to classify things and thereby draw inductive, deductive, and abductive inferences which in turn enables us to act in coordinated, planned, and goal-oriented ways. Specifying the system of words and concepts as a conceptual infrastructure has the advantage of highlighting how our system of representational devices, just like any infrastructure, faces various challenges—challenges that are easily overlooked. Thus, the suggested perspective emphasizes that the system of words and concepts can (or even should) be changed and improved to fulfil its various functions in the face of multiple challenges.

The project of assessing and, when necessary, improving our system of representational devices has always been a central part of philosophy. Today, this method is known as *conceptual engineering*. What is conceptual engineering? What exactly is assessed and improved in such a project, and what kind of improvements are suggested? What are the main issues and problems of conceptual engineering, and what is its role in our scientific, social, political, and personal lives?

Section 3. Variants of Conceptual Engineering: What are the Goals? Why is it Important?

The view that our thinking and perception of reality are shaped by our language as well as the corresponding conceptual system can be found in various philosophical traditions. Immanuel Kant's transcendental idealism, for example, is in large part devoted to the analysis of conceptual conditions of our mental representation of reality.[2] Kant accepted certain conceptual preconditions of our cognitive life as fixed and considered it a central task of philosophy to discover and analyse them. In contrast, Friedrich Nietzsche declared that the central task of philosophy is not *analysis* but a profound *critique* of our conceptual repertoire. This critique resulted in the demand that philosophers "must no longer accept concepts as a gift, nor merely purify and polish them, but first make and create them."[3] This is a demand for a form of conceptual engineering in which philosophers improve or even create concepts so that they meet certain particularly important requirements. Traces of this Nietzschean attitude can be found in phenomenological (e.g., Heidegger) as well as (post-)structuralist traditions (e.g., Foucault).[4]

---

2   Immanuel Kant, *Kritik der reinen Vernunft* (Hamburg: Meiner, 1954).

3   Friedrich Nietzsche, *The Will to Power*, trans. by W. Kaufmann (New York: Random House, 1968), 221.

4   See, for example: Martin Heidegger, "Die onto-theo-logische Verfassung der Metaphysik," in *Identität und Differenz* (1955–1957), ed. Friedrich-Wilhelm von Herrmann (Frankfurt a. M.: Klostermann, 2006), 51–79; Martin Heidegger, "Zeit und Sein," in *Zur Sache des Denkens* (1962–1964), ed. Friedrich-Wilhelm von Herrmann (Frankfurt a. M.: Klostermann, 2007), 3–30; Michel Foucault, *Les mots et lex choses* (Paris: Gallimard, 1966); Michel Foucault, *L'archéology du savoir* (Paris: Gallimard, 1969).

Likely the most explicit examples of conceptual engineering, however, can be found in the analytic tradition of philosophy.[5] Within this tradition, the method of assessing and improving representational devices is closely linked to the seminal work of Rudolf Carnap and his method of *explication*.[6] This method is best introduced in comparison to the widely used philosophical method of *conceptual analysis*.

In applying conceptual analysis, philosophers seek to formulate application conditions of a term (for example, "knowledge," "truth," or "freedom"). The guiding question within such a project is the following: What are the conditions that actually govern the correct use of the term in question, and under which conditions is the term correctly applied? The aim is to reconstruct the meaning of a term by providing a definition that specifies conditions that are individually necessary and jointly sufficient for its correct application. As these definitions are considered ways of specifying the meaning of a term, and the meaning of a term is often taken to be the concept associated with it, this method is called "conceptual analysis."

In contrast to conceptual analysis, Carnap's method of *explication* is not an attempt to analyse the meaning of a term but to improve and reengineer it. The goal is not to formulate the conditions that govern the actual use of a term but to establish conditions of application that make the reengineered term stand out favourably with respect to certain scientific goals. Thus, the guiding question is not what are the conditions that actually govern the correct use of the term but how can the application conditions of a term be improved so that the term becomes more conducive to scientific aims? Within this project, deviations from the pre-theoretic use of a term are explicitly allowed.

Carnap illustrates the details of his account by considering the examples "warm" (understood roughly as "property that causes a certain sensation in subjects") and "fish" (understood roughly as "animals that live in water"). In his view, in relevant contexts the first term has been substituted by the quantitative term "temperature," and the second has been replaced by the biologically defined term "piscis" (understood roughly as "cold-blooded aquatic vertebrate").[7]

According to Carnap, these substitutions can be considered successful acts of explication because the new and reengineered terms meet the following conditions of adequacy. First, the reengineered terms are *similar* to the pre-theoretic ones in the

---

5   It is this tradition that coined the term "conceptual engineering." For early usages of the term, see Simon Blackburn, *Think: A Compelling Introduction to Philosophy* (Oxford: Oxford University Press, 1999); Robert Brandom, "Modality, Normativity, and Intentionality," *Philosophy and Phenomenological Research* 63 (2001): 611–623.

6   Rudolf Carnap, *Logical Foundations of Probability* (Chicago: University of Chicago Press, 1962). For an interesting and detailed discussion of Carnap's method of explication, see: Georg Brun, "Explication as a Method of Conceptual Re-Engineering," *Erkenntnis* 81, no. 6 (2016): 1211–1241.

7   Carnap, *Logical Foundations*, §§ 3–5.

sense that they can be used in many contexts in which the old terms are used. Despite their similarity, however, they also exhibit differences and even call for acts of reclassification; for example, in contrast to the pre-theoretic term "fish," "piscis" excludes whales. Second, the new terms are more *exact* in the sense that their application conditions are clearer and less vague than the application conditions of the pre-theoretic terms. Third, they are more *fruitful* in the sense that in contrast to the pre-theoretic terms, they are systematically embedded in established scientific theories, allowing for the formulation of more general laws as well as finer discriminations. Fourth, they are *relatively simple* and easy to grasp.[8] The second and third conditions of adequacy, exactness, and fruitfulness, are of central importance to Carnap. Only if these conditions are satisfied can a reengineered term or concept be considered an improvement with respect to scientific aims such as clarity, verifiability, systematicity, and explanatory power.

Carnap's method of explication can be applied to a wide range of terms and concepts, but the corresponding revisions are always concerned with improvements regarding scientific aims. Other analytic philosophers, however, have suggested projects of conceptual engineering that are supposed to be conducive to other aims, most importantly social and political ones. For example, for more than twenty years, Sally Haslanger has proposed a project of conceptual engineering (in her terminology, an "ameliorative project") for gender and race terms.[9] In line with critical theory, she proposes definitions of gender and race terms that clearly identify them as socially constructed and highlight certain power structures as constituents of their meaning.[10] The definitions are revisionary because they involve a change in the terms' meanings and call for acts of reclassification.

Haslanger argues that these revisions are an improvement because they force us to acknowledge (tacit) beliefs and inference patterns that are widespread in our society and that reinforce certain forms of social injustice. Why, for example, do we (tacitly) believe it more likely that a person has a certain profession once we know whether the person is a man or woman? By building oppressive structures into the meaning of "woman," we can answer this question in a way that helps us acknowledge and understand the flaws in our social practice. Understanding these flaws and acknowledging the force of oppressive systems is the first step in overcoming them

---

8   Carnap, *Logical Foundations*, 5–13.

9   Sally Haslanger, "Gender and Race: (What) Are They? (What) Do We Want Them to Be?" *Nous* 34, no. 1 (2000): 31–55; Sally Haslanger, "Language, Politics, and 'The Folk': Looking for the Meaning of 'Race,'" *The Monist* 93, no. 2 (2010): 169–87; Sally Haslanger, *Resisting Reality: Social Construction and Social Critique* (Oxford: Oxford University Press 2012); Sally Haslanger, "Going On, Not in the Same Way," in *Conceptual Engineering and Conceptual Analysis*, eds. Alexis Burgess, Hermann Cappelen, and David Plunkett (Oxford: Oxford University Press, 2020), 230–260.

10   Haslanger, "Gender and Race," 38–39.

and has, according to Haslanger, the additional positive consequence of reframing "our personal and political identities."[11]

Sarah-Jane Leslie proposed another form of conceptual engineering that also aims at being conducive to social justice.[12] Consider the generic use of the nouns "tiger" and "tick" in "Tigers are striped" and "Ticks carry Lyme disease." These generic expressions are correct even though not all tigers are striped and not all ticks (not even most of them) carry Lyme disease.[13] Sometimes we refer to social groups with a generic use of a noun (e.g., "Muslim," "African American," "refugee," "European"). Leslie points to empirical data showing that hearing a member of a social group being described with a noun rather than an adjective increases the extent to which people expect the person to conform to a stereotype. Thus, empirical data seem to suggest the generic use of nouns leads to something that Leslie calls acts of "essentializing." We form the false (tacit) belief that there is some hidden property or underlying essence shared by members of that group, which causally grounds common properties and dispositions.[14] Leslie suggests the risk of falling prey to the mistake of essentializing, which can reinforce social injustice, would be reduced by avoiding the use of social-kind nouns. Instead of describing someone as a Muslim, we could describe them as a person who practices the religion of Islam. This way of speaking would emphasize that "person" is the relevant sortal and that *practicing Islam* is a particular property they happen to possess. Given the aforementioned empirical data, it is reasonable to assume that as a result of avoiding social-kind nouns, the amount of essentializing is reduced, which in turn is conducive to overcoming certain forms of social injustice.[15]

The examples of conceptual engineering introduced so far have all been examples from philosophy.[16] It is important to note, however, that philosophy is not the only discipline in which conceptual engineering takes place. In law, for example, the meanings (extensions) of "murder," "intention," and "war" are matters of widespread

---

11   Haslanger, "Gender and Race," 47. See also: Haslanger "Going On," 237.

12   Sarah-Jane Leslie, "The Original Sin of Cognition: Fear, Prejudice, and Generalization," *Journal of Philosophy* 114, no. 8 (2017): 393–421.

13   For a useful introduction to generics, see Sarah-Jane Leslie and Adam Lerner, "Generic Generalization," in *The Stanford Encyclopedia of Philosophy* (Winter 2016 edition), ed. Edward Zalta, available at: https://plato.stanford.edu/archives/win2016/entries/generics/.

14   Sarah-Jane Leslie, "Carving up the Social World with Generics," *Oxford Studies in Experimental Philosophy* (forthcoming).

15   Sarah-Jane Leslie, "Carving."

16   For more examples, see: Herman Cappelen, *Fixing Language: An Essay on Conceptual Engineering* (Oxford: Oxford University Press, 2018), 9–27. For a more detailed discussion of the role of conceptual engineering in philosophy, see: Herman Cappelen and David Plunkett, "Introduction: A Guided Tour of Conceptual Engineering and Conceptual Ethics," in *Conceptual Engineering and Conceptual Analysis*, ed. Alexis Burgess, Hermann Cappelen, David Plunkett (Oxford: Oxford University Press, 2020), 18–23.

controversy, and in psychiatry, the question of how mental disorders should be classified is intensely discussed. Moreover, various public controversies are also related
to conceptual engineering. Clear examples are the debates over whether we should
use gender-neutral expressions and whether we should erase racial slurs from novels written in the past. Furthermore, the public debates over whether same-sex couples should be able to marry and whether a family can be constituted differently from
a husband, wife, and their biological offspring. These debates can also be understood as projects of conceptual engineering in that they seem to involve proposals to
reengineer the meanings of "marriage" and "family."[17]

At least with regards to these examples, the following general thought as well as
the infrastructural perspective plausibly establishes the importance of conceptual
engineering: If it is true that our social reality is at least in part constituted by the
words we use to describe social categories,[18] then debates over what those words
mean and how we should use them are of central importance. Revising and improving these terms and their use may help improve our social reality.[19] But even if we do
not want to subscribe to the ontological thesis that our social reality is constituted
by our use of words, the suggested infrastructural perspective still emphasizes the
importance of conceptual engineering in various domains. Since the system of our
representational devices (words and concepts) can be considered as the infrastructure that enables us to classify things and thereby draw inductive, deductive, and
abductive inferences—which in turn enables us to act in coordinated, planned, and
goal-oriented ways—considering possible challenges and improvements of that infrastructure becomes mandatory. This is true not only with respect to the achievement of our scientific goals, but with regard to our social and political interactions
as well.

Section 4. Systematic Options and Open Questions

The examples of conceptual engineering introduced in the previous section illustrated how important this form of maintenance of our conceptual infrastructure
is—not only for our scientific endeavours but also for our social, political, and personal lives. In this section, we will give a (simplified) systematic analysis of the options within projects of conceptual engineering and highlight some of its main problems as well as topics for future research. The goal is thus to illustrate the kinds of

---

17   For a defence of the view that such controversies can be construed as debates about the
      meaning of words, see: Peter Ludlow, *Living Words: Meaning Underdetermination and the Dy-
      namic Lexicon* (Oxford: Oxford University Press, 2014).

18   Cf. John Searle, *The Construction of Social Reality* (New York: Free Press, 1995).

19   Cappelen, *Fixing Language*, 44.

questions and problems that arise for those who aim to maintain conceptual infrastructures. We leave an assessment of the similarity and differences of conceptual engineering and other types of infrastructural practices for future work.

The first and most fundamental pair of questions that any conceptual engineer will have to answer is this: What exactly do they strive to engineer, and how can it be done? Note that answering these questions is more difficult than it may seem at first. For while it is (perhaps trivially) true that conceptual engineering does, in some sense, target *concepts*, the very term "concept" belongs to the most unclear and contested terms in theoretical philosophy and psychology.[20] Whereas many analytic philosophers construe concepts as abstract entities such as Fregean senses or modes of presentations,[21] philosophers of psychology typically construe them as bodies of information or mental representations that underwrite cognitive capacities such as categorization and inference-making.[22] These different approaches to the ontology of concepts yield radically different views of how they can be engineered. In a Fregean view, to engineer a concept is, roughly, to propose a set of necessary and jointly sufficient application conditions (see Carnap's method of explication introduced in section 3); in a psychological view, it is to change our (typically subconscious) ways of categorizing and making inferences.[23]

Some philosophers argue that unless one makes an explicit choice as to how one understands concepts, one does not really have an account of the nature and practice of conceptual engineering.[24] By now, various proposals about the target entities of conceptual engineering projects have been made, and there is a vibrant discussion about how such target entities can be engineered. A position that we deem particularly promising is pluralism: the view that conceptual engineering can potentially have many different targets, ranging from purely linguistic to more mental ones, that can be engineered by a great variety of different implementation strategies.[25]

---

20   Cf. Edouard Machery, *Doing Without Concepts* (Oxford: Oxford University Press, 2009).

21   Cf. Gottlob Frege, "Über Sinn und Bedeutung," *Zeitschrift für Philosophie und philosophische Kritik*, 100 (1892): 25–50; Christopher Peacocke, "Rationale and Maxims in the Study of Concepts," *Nous* 39, no. 1 (2005): 167–178.

22   Cf. Edouard Machery, *Philosophy Within its Proper Bounds* (Oxford, Oxford University Press, 2017); Guido Löhr, "Concepts and Categorization: Do Philosophers and Psychologists Theorize about Different Things?" *Synthese* 197, no. 5 (2020): 2171–2191.

23   See for more details: Steffen Koch, "Engineering What? On Concepts in Conceptual Engineering," *Synthese* 199, no. 1–2 (2021): 1955–1975.

24   Cappelen, *Fixing Language*, 141.

25   Cf. Manuel Gustavo Isaac, Steffen Koch, and Ryan Neftd, "Conceptual Engineering: A Roadmap to Practice," *Philosophy Compass* (2022), doi 10.1111/phc3.12879; Steffen Koch, Guido Löhr, and Mark Pinder, "Recent Work in the Theory of Conceptual Engineering," *Analysis* (forthcoming).

But how exactly to flesh out this sort of pluralism and the corresponding variety of implementation strategies remains a question for future research.

A related issue concerns the interplay between linguistic and more cognitive dimensions of concept application. Assume, as many other philosophers do, that conceptual engineering targets language: Does the relevant change conceptual engineers envisage concern the *meaning properties* of linguistic items such as words or how we go about *using them in practice?*[26] Both options give rise to tricky questions. If it concerns *use* rather than meaning, then what, if anything, distinguishes conceptual engineering from other forms of theorizing? For example, paleontologists' discovery and public declaration that birds are dinosaurs has normative linguistic consequences: people should no longer say that dinosaurs are extinct or that birds are not dinosaurs, for example. But did these paleontologists thereby *engineer* the concept of a dinosaur (or a bird)? It would seem that this is a case of a scientific discovery rather than a case of conceptual engineering. But then what exactly is it that sets the two apart? Or is "conceptual engineering" just a fancy new label for ordinary theorizing?[27]

On the other hand, if conceptual engineering primarily targets *linguistic meaning*, it is unclear how it could have the effects that advocates of conceptual engineering typically suggest it does. For example, conceptual engineers often claim that engineering concepts can be a means to increase social justice.[28] But how exactly can changes at the level of what certain words mean have such worldly consequences? Does this idea not rely, at least implicitly, on the truth of a controversial form of linguistic determinism, of which Steven Pinker famously said, "it is wrong, all wrong?"[29] Developing an empirically plausible rationale for how exactly language-centred versions of conceptual engineering may yield improvements in our reasoning patterns that translate into worldly consequences such as social justice remains an important desideratum for future research that ought to be approached from an interdisciplinary perspective.

A further set of questions concerns the normativity involved in conceptual engineering. As shown in section 3, conceptual engineering is not about the actual ap-

---

26   Cf. Cappelen, *Fixing Language*; Mark Pinder, "Conceptual Engineering, Metasemantic Externalism, and Speaker Meaning," *Mind* 130, no. 517 (2021): 141–163.

27   Something similar can be asked with respect to Carnap's examples of supposedly successful explications mentioned above: Should we take it as a scientific discovery or as a consequence of an act of conceptual reengineering that whales are not fish? What exactly is the difference between these two options?

28   Haslanger, "Gender and Race," 31–55. Leslie, "The Original Sin," 393–421. Paul-Mikhail C. Podosky, "Can Conceptual Engineering Actually Promote Social Justice?" *Synthese* 200, no. 160: //doi.org/10.1007/ s11229-022-03469-5

29   Steven Pinker, *The Language Instinct: How the Mind Creates Language* (New York: Harper Perennial, 1995), 57.

plication conditions of concepts but about what application conditions they should have. But what kind of normativity does "should" refer to here?[30] There is a plethora of views one could take, ranging from epistemic to moral or prudential normativity to what is *all-things-considered* best. The Carnapian tradition introduced in section 3 puts the greatest emphasis on epistemic considerations, such as furthering exactness or scientific fruitfulness. Contemporary approaches to conceptual engineering, by contrast, typically emphasize its utility for the attainment of nonscientific goals, including moral or political ones.

Broadening the normative basis on which concepts may legitimately be engineered from purely epistemic to moral and political considerations raises important questions about how to handle conflicting cases. For example, can it be legitimate to sacrifice exactness or scientific fruitfulness in the attainment of a political good? Can it be justified to render our concepts less morally good for the sake of increasing their purely epistemic qualities? These questions are hotly debated in current discussions of conceptual engineering. Mona Simion argues that a concept's primary function is epistemic, and that conceptual engineering should thus be bound by what she calls the "epistemic limiting procedure." A concept should be engineered if and only if there is an all-things-considered reason to do so and when doing so does not translate into epistemic loss.[31]

Contra Simion, Paul-Mikhail Podosky, and Robin McKenna argue it is sometimes legitimate to engineer a concept even when this results in temporary epistemic disadvantages. As we already indicated at the end of section 3, this is particularly plausible for so-called social-kind concepts such as "family," "husband," "wife," "parent," or, according to many philosophers, "woman" and "man." McKenna explicitly claims social-kind concepts are special in that they "serve to shape the world, not (merely) to represent it."[32] In other words, "[i]f we decided to apply these terms in different ways, then—perhaps over a long period of time—the social roles themselves might change."[33]

Plausibly, then, epistemic considerations do not always have the last word in decisions to reengineer concepts. But how epistemic and non-epistemic considerations can be weighed against each other is a difficult issue. What complicates things further is that even epistemic constraints can pull us in different directions. The

---

30   Note that a similar question arises also for practices that are concerned with other types of infrastructures, such as physical or institutional ones.

31   Mona Simion, "The 'Should' in Conceptual Engineering," *Inquiry: An Interdisciplinary Journal of Philosophy* 61, no. 8 (2018): 924.

32   Robin McKenna, "No Epistemic Trouble for Engineering 'Woman,'" *Logos and Episteme* 9, no. 3 (2018): 336.

33   McKenna, "No Epistemic Trouble," 340. See also Paul-Mikhail C. Podosky, "Ideology and Normativity: Constraints on Conceptual Engineering," *Inquiry: An Interdisciplinary Journal of Philosophy* (2018), //doi.org/10.1080/0020174X.2018.1562374.

ideal version of a concept for one scientific project might not be ideal for another one; more generally, the demand to have maximally specific concepts often contrasts with the demand to have concepts that can be used in general explanations of coarse-grained types of phenomena. All in all, it seems clear that resolving these various tensions and conflicts requires a comprehensive, multi-perspective approach that must be developed through intensive interdisciplinary collaborations among a wide variety of scientific disciplines and sociopolitical stakeholders.

We hope to have shown how theoretically fruitful it is to conceive of conceptual systems and languages as a kind of abstract infrastructure. Just as our transport system predetermines our travelling options, so do conceptual systems and languages predetermine our thought and speech patterns. Infrastructures are artifact kinds that serve the changing needs of their users. For this reason, infrastructures must be maintained. The philosophical project of conceptual maintenance work is conceptual engineering. We have also shown that the project of conceptual engineering faces numerous challenges, some of which can only be met through interdisciplinary collaborations.

Practices of Classification: The Hashtag as Infrastructure for Interaction

Steffen Krämer and Isabell Otto

When social media infrastructures are considered from a classic understanding of material, technical things, the cables, data centres, and routers are the focus of observation. Those with a technical understanding of infrastructures are concerned to emphasize the processes that take place 'underneath' the interface of social media platforms that make user interactions possible in the first place.[1] For our research perspective, following a rethinking of infrastructures in this context means not only attributing dynamics of 'infrastructuring'[2] to these basic material structures, but also looking for infrastructures in social media interactions themselves and to ask how infrastructures emerge from practices and vice versa. Instead of making a dualistic separation between interface and infrastructure, between what is visible or ready-at-hand to the human operator and what lies beyond reach, we would rather draw attention to the interconnectedness between infrastructures and practices. In what follows, we refer to the hashtag as a case study to ask about the interplay between infrastructures, practices, and cultural formations in ways that are overarching and transferable to other contexts. The aim of the paper is to show how an understanding of infrastructures that is not solely focused on the 'hard' materiality of technical things can clarify the relation between media *practices* (in our example: of users in social media) and social and cultural movements. The dynamics of infrastructuring are thus understood as processes that produce and structure interactions and make these interactions in their sociality relevant for and connectable to cultural discourses and narratives. From a media studies perspective, hashtags

---

1   Jason Farman, "Infrastructures of Mobile Social Media," *Social Media + Society* 1, no. 1 (2015), h ttps://doi.org/10.1177/2056305115580343.

2   We refer here to the implications of the concept of 'infrastructuring' by Susan Leigh Star and Geoffrey C. Bowker, for whom infrastructures are not immutable objects, but mobile structures that are constantly 'at work' and also offer the necessity as well as the possibility of being continuously redesigned: This work can be described as 'infrastructuring.' Susan Leigh Star and Geoffrey C. Bowker, "How to Infrastructure," in *The Handbook of New Media*, eds. Leah Lievrouw and Sonia Livingstone (London: SAGE, 2002): 151–162, https://doi.org/10.4135/9781 446206904.n12.

can be approached as media in their own right with various mediating functions. For example, they can also be understood as 'infrastructural media' insofar as they mediate the relation between platform technologies and cultural or social processes. Yet, research would have to further discern how this aspect of the hashtag's mediating capacity qualifies as 'infrastructural.' The fact that we refer to hashtags in this open sense as infrastructures and media is due to our non-essentialist understanding of both concepts. The goal is not to answer what infrastructures and what media are, but when and under what conditions they become media/infrastructures[3] and to what extent their observation as media and/or infrastructure can be productive for cultural studies research.

The 'origin' of the hashtag, as Johannes Paßmann shows, is part of a popular narrative of bottom-up-innovation: It is said to have originated on Twitter and not to have been implemented as a platform feature, but rather to have grown out of user practices.[4] U.S. blogger Chris Messina is credited with the 'invention' of the hashtag when he suggested in a tweet in 2007 to use the hash character to group multiple tweets under one keyword. However, according to Paßmann, # was already used in older Internet Relay Chats (IRC) to form groups and has been translated and transformed into a new context on Twitter. Twitter has turned it into a clickable feature, which in turn made other tweets findable that use the same hashtag. The classification system spread quickly from Twitter to other platforms, what enables Paul Dawson to describe it as a "folksonomy, a bottom-up, user-generated system of classification."[5] Others have argued that the hashtag, standardized in the use of the hash character in combination with a word or phrase written without spaces, facilitates not only the sortability and searchability of content on websites, but also becomes a way of (meta)-commenting and an indicator of affiliation to communities or social movements.[6] Zizi Papacharissi claimed that it can lead to a feeling of connectiveness in the sense of a social bonding in an 'affective public.'[7] Overall, the use of hashtags is not controlled or regulated by the platforms in the first place, but it makes platform

3   Joseph Vogl, "Medien-Werden. Galileos Fernrohr," *Archiv für Mediengeschichte*, no. 1 (2001): 115–123.

4   Johannes Paßmann, "Mediengeschichte des Followers," in *Following: Ein Kompendium zu Medien der Gefolgschaft und Prozessen des Folgens*, eds. Anne Ganzert, Philip Hauser, and Isabell Otto (Berlin: De Gruyter, 2023, in press).

5   Paul Dawson, "Hashtag Narrative: Emergent Storytelling and Affective Publics in the Digital Age," *International Journal of Cultural Studies* 23, no. 6 (2020): 968–983, 974, https://doi.org/10.1177/1367877920921417.

6   Maik Fielitz and Daniel Staemmler, "Hashtags, Tweets, Protest? Varianten des digitalen Aktivismus," *Forschungsjournal Soziale Bewegungen* 33, no. 2 (2020): 425–441, https://doi.org/10.1515/fjsb-2020-0037.

7   Zizi Papacharissi, *Affective Publics: Sentiment, Technology, and Politics* (New York: Oxford University Press, 2015).

interaction accountable. Keywords for specific topics and events emerge from user practices, as do recommendations to limit the number of hashtags used to classify a post.[8]

As this brief history of hashtags and their theorization illustrates, the hashtag has emerged from a specifically situated and vaguely organized media practice into a general infrastructure for social media interaction.[9] In the short time of the hashtag's infrastructuralization, it has formalized existing practices and, equally, spawned new practices. Hashtags exemplify that infrastructures do not only have to be large technical-material constellations, but that small signs can also have an infrastructural effect. In other words, the characteristic of **generativity** applies to hashtags, because they produce practices that would not exist without them or would not exist in this arrangement. On a most general level, hashtags have structured social media interaction by *organizing relations*. They provide a simple scheme of relating topics, accounts, and events. They enable an ongoing connecting and relatability in social media interaction. Hashtags are relations that enable relations. Even though the terms and phrases that attach themselves to the hash character can be fleeting and fast-moving, the relational structure itself remains stable and enduring.

The **relationality** of hashtag infrastructures is also reflected in the interaction of hashtags with other infrastructures in their environment. In this context, the question arises, which elements are part of the hashtag infrastructure, and which lie beyond it but affect the infrastructural operations and materiality and are affected by them. The silicon and transistors of the computers and the database operations of writing, storing, and retrieving the hashtag symbol do not only belong to the infrastructure of the hashtag but underlie its functioning. The same applies to the different representational forms that the hashtag may take, be it the octothorpe on the level of graphical user interfaces or its binary representation on the levels of computer instructions (1000011). The possibility and necessity of being represented in this way is not what defines the infrastructure of the hashtag, but it belongs to the infrastructure of standardized ASCI code. As has been claimed for infrastructures in general, the infrastructure of the hashtag is built upon existing infrastructures, and it might become the context in which new ones will be embedded. However, different from 'hard infrastructures' such as power plants and undersea cables, the

---

8   Ágnes Veszelszki, "#time, #truth, #tradition: An Image-Text Relationship on Instagram: Photo and Hashtag," in *In the Beginning Was the Image: The Omnipresence of Pictures: Time, Truth, Tradition*, eds. Benedek András and Ágnes Veszelszki (Frankfurt am Main: Peter Lang, 2016), 139–150; Michele Zappavigna, "Searchable Talk: The Linguistic Functions of Hashtags," *Social Semiotics* 25, no. 3 (2015): 274–291, https://doi.org/10.1080/10350330.2014.996948.

9   Cf. Christine Gerber, "Community Building on Crowdwork Platforms: Autonomy and Control of Online Workers?" *Competition & Change* 25, no. 2 (2021): 190–211, https://doi.org/10.1177/10 24529420914472.

hashtag's materiality appears to be more difficult to pin down. Here, the often scrutinized 'ideal type' of infrastructure—transportation and transmission infrastructure—might help as a first heuristic analogy. With infrastructures such as streets,
cables and pipelines, hashtag infrastructure seems to share the function to organize
movement. As a classification system the hashtag infrastructure allows its user to
move through database records and to inscribe something into the database records
and thereby increase its potential reach. In this analogy, the hashtag is an infrastructure of mobility, navigation, and reach. Moreover, the hashtag infrastructure builds
clusters of linkages, or as Yarimar Bonilla and Jonathan Rosa call it in comparison
to the classification system of a library: hashtags 'lasso' certain entries, making connections between accompanying texts.[10] We get a glimpse of the materiality of this
infrastructure where the reach and the clustering are not silently performed but debated, negotiated, and accounted for in practice. For example, social media users
regularly comment about other users' deployment of hashtags or outspokenly criti-
cize or even call to avoid specific ones.

This connects to the *practical* durability of hashtags, which stems from their integration into routinized behaviour. What hashtags accomplish is taken for granted
in their use. As media of relational dynamics and the designation of relations, they
are used as a matter of course and casually. Infrastructures and practices mutually
sustain each other as latent structures. But on the spectrum of latent structures,
they differ in their stability. Infrastructures are more conservative to change than
practices, yet both of them are generative. With the increasingly familiarized use
of hashtags, however, their meta-discursive function recedes in favour of the respective content or topic, and the medial function of networking is delegated to the
background. One can even say that the emergence of a social meaning of hashtags
(e.g., their use as a form of political expression or affiliation) is only possible when
the media operations of networking fade into the background. Yet, this background
function of networking remains essential part of the practical reality of the hashtag;
in the same sense that the associated milieu of technical objects affect their individ-
uation as Gilbert Simondon has described it.[11] For interrogating the infrastructural
function of a 'technical ensemble'—to further use Simondon's terminology—with
the hashtag at its centre and from the perspective of its practical realization, we

---

10   Yarimar Bonilla and Jonathan Rosa, "#ferguson: Digital Protest, Hashtag Ethnography, and
      the Racial Politics of Social Media in the United States," *American Ethnologist* 42, no. 1 (2015):
      4–17, 6, https://doi.org/10.1111/amet.12112.

11   Gilbert Simondon, *Die Existenzweise technischer Objekte* (Zürich: diaphanes, 2012), 56–60. Si-
      mondon understands the individual and its milieu as an inseparable unit. A technical object
      (or a digital object like the hashtag) is thus not produced in a technical environment in the
      sense that it could exist detached from it at some point. Rather, the environment accom-
      panies the ongoing ontogenesis of an object. Thus, a hashtag can never be understood as
      'finished' or separable from its technical milieu.

must then follow how this background relationality is accounted for by its users and how it is materially manifested. The habitual use of a hashtag is thus never detached from the hardware and software operations that make that use possible in the first place.

The general interest for the operative locus of infrastructures as 'being in the background,' often emphasized by infrastructure theory,[12] bears an interesting resonance with the theorization of the surface in the media theories of writing and diagrams.[13] The surface recedes and simultaneously enables and supports the inscription of graphical signs. By analogy, the materialization of the hashtag as a text token is premised on the surface of the screen. However, its background operationality goes beyond the surface of graphical user interfaces as indicated before. The writing of hashtags brings into being not only text but 'searchable' text,[14] which requires database operations of machinic writing and retrieval, and the possibility for users to access and perform search. This has two consequences: First, the background operationality of the hashtag as infrastructure and of the practices that revolve around it must thus be thought of as thoroughly sociotechnical. Secondly, the practice of searching is one of the key ways in which the background operationality of the hashtag infrastructure is accounted for.

Put differently, **regularity** or **routine** as a central characteristic of infrastructures can be found in the case of hashtags both on the level of platform features and on the level of user practices. Hashtags are only effective if they are repeated and used over a longer period. Moreover, because of their ability to be machine-readable and searchable, hashtags also enable and stabilize the algorithmic capture of social media interaction on the platform for subsequent analytical purposes. They can be easily integrated into recommendation engines and exploited to visualize trends. Hashtags are thus also important anchors of social media research. However, the prominence of the hashtag in attempts to analyse 'public discourse,' be it academic or commercial, also has its obvious shortcomings. On the one hand, the reliance on hashtags tends to be reductive, painting discursive dynamics as "chaotic" that await ordering through the hashtag, and overshadowing the structuration of discourse on other cultural levels.[15] On the other hand, the orientation at a limited set of popular hashtags comes at the price of invisibilizing other thematic anchors or sidelining

12   Susan Leigh Star and Karen Ruhleder, "Steps Toward an Ecology of Infrastructure: Design and Access for Large Information Spaces," *Information Systems Research* 7, no. 1 (1996): 111–134, 112, https://doi.org/10.1287/isre.7.1.111.

13   Sybille Krämer, *Figuration, Anschauung, Erkenntnis. Grundlinien einer Diagrammatologie* (Berlin: Suhrkamp, 1996), 65–70.

14   Zappvigna, "Searchable Talk: The Linguistic Functions of Hashtags."

15   Tommaso Venturini, Liliana Bounegru, Jonathan Gray and Richard Rogers, "A Reality Check(list) for Digital Methods," *New Media & Society* 20, no. 11 (2018): 4195–4217, 4210, https://doi.org/10.1177/1461444818769236.

perspectives on the issues not represented in the posts around the respective hash-tags. The ranking and competition of hashtags has been further stabilized by the design of social media platforms, which prominently display popular hashtags as trend markers or entry points for exploration or provide automatized recommendations which hashtags to use for a post. On the level of user strategies, this has led to organized attempts to get certain hashtags into the trends, to strategically combine different hashtags in order to alter the "framing" or "hijack" hashtags that are currently trending.[16] Besides search, discursive observation is a second key practice that 'sits on top' of the infrastructure of hashtags.

Hashtags are particularly relevant from a cultural perspective because they organize more than just internal platform interactions: they can give rise to specific metadata tagging that generate overarching discourses, debates, narratives, and movements. We would like to briefly illustrate this narrative generativity of hashtags using the example of #metoo. The case of #metoo is particularly interesting from a cultural perspective because a latent narrativity is already inscribed in every single post tagged with the hashtag through the phrase 'me too,' which calls for the sharing of personal stories and thus connects to the technological affordances of hash relationality. Dawson has called this "emergent storytelling."[17] First formulated in 2017, the call 'metoo' elicited a widespread response in the form of personal stories about sexual abuse, which, tied to the hashtag, created an extensive phenomenon that could in turn be expressed in a large amount of data via the countability of tagged posts, and then in a next step could be narrativized as a social phenomenon based on the multitude of individual posts. Storytelling took place at the micro-level of user practices and platform technicity as much as it did at the macro-level of cultural narratives enabled via the indexicality of the hashtag.[18]

The case of #metoo and other hashtags that started social movements in the recent years point to a social generativity of hashtags and the necessity of their maintenance. Hashtags facilitate discursive coordination and provide a symbolic address for practices of attachment and identification. They publicly coordinate a loose assembly of speakers that over time becomes recognizable as a collective project, transforming the act of hashtagging into one of possible affiliation or identification.[19] This socio-generative function of hashtags is premised on some degree of semantic

---

16   Moa Eriksson Krutrök and Simon Lindgren, "Continued Contexts of Terror: Analyzing Temporal Patterns of Hashtag Co-Occurence as Discursive Articulations," *Social Media + Society* 4, no. 4 (2018): 1–11, https://doi.org/10.1177/2056305118813649; Venturini et al., "A Reality Check(list) for Digital Methods."

17   Dawson, "Hashtag Narrative."

18   Dawson, "Hashtag Narrative."

19   Michele Zappavigna, "Ambient Affiliation: A Linguistic Perspective on Twitter," *New Media & Society* 13, no. 5 (2011): 788–806, https://doi.org/10.1177/1461444810385097; Summer Harlow and Anna Benbrook, "How #blacklivesmatter: Exploring the Role of Hip-Hop Celebrities in

plasticity of the hashtag, where the meaning of a hashtag is only stabilized over time and in whose course positions can be differentiated and claimed. Moreover, it is in the larger cultural narratives that the use of the hashtag becomes meta-reflexive, for it is precisely the mass use of #metoo on Twitter and Instagram that becomes the subject of (net)feminist narratives about the meaning of the social movement. Different formations within the spectrum of (post-/pop-/neoliberal-/anti-) feminist activism could emerge from the relationalizations that the hashtag or its counter concepts (like #notallmen or #mentoo) enabled. This clearly shows that hashtags as infrastructures also depend on **propellants** and **maintenance**. In our example, 'propellants' refer to the need to keep publishing new posts and images with the hashtag and thus keep the interactions going. 'Maintenance' in turn refers to ensuring the technical functioning, but also to the critical analysis and reflection of hashtag use at the level of practices, allowing for course corrections and adjustments of interaction dynamics if necessary. Only if hashtags are maintained and transformed in a constant "infrastructure work"[20] can they unfold their cultural dynamics. Conversely and especially in the manifold commercial uses of #metoo, this also raises the question of whether hashtags can wear out.[21]

To take stock: we have touched upon a wide panorama of different activities that have revolved around hashtags. This raises the question about the relationship between the universality of these activities and their particular role in the technical ensemble that defines hashtag infrastructures. Two perspectives might be followed to describe this relationship: Firstly, observed activities may be grouped into mid-range categories in order to identify 'fields' of pragmatic continuity and innovation shaped through the generative and organizing work of hashtags. From this perspective it appears that hashtags continued and transformed epistemic practices (classifying, sorting, searching), membership practices (affiliating, identifying), communicational practices (commenting, recommending, calling to connect), practices of publication (increasing reach) as well as observational practices (visualizing, counting, narrativizing). In their capacity to provide the infrastructural background for these practices to be performed, hashtags mediate long-established cultural techniques but also transform and reconfigure their relation. Most notably this can be seen in the intertwining of counting and narrativizing for collective self-observation. Secondly, we can move to a more abstract level of categorization and attempt

---

Constructing Racial Identity on Black Twitter," *Information, Communication & Society* 22, no. 3 (2019): 352–368, https://doi.org/10.1080/1369118X.2017.1386705.

20   Gabriele Schabacher, *Infrastruktur-Arbeit. Kulturtechniken und Zeitlichkeit der Erhaltung* (Berlin: Kadmos, 2022).

21   Tanisha Afnan, Hsiao-Ying Huang, Maria Sciafani, and Masooda Bashir, "Putting a Price on Social Movements: A Case Study of #metoo on Instagram," *Proceedings of the Association for Information Science and Technology* 56, no. 1 (2019): 1–9, https://doi.org/10.1002/pra2.2.

to identify activities that are particularly typical for infrastructures. For example, in their research on infrastructures of making public, Matthias Korn and his co-authors have proposed a heuristic of three basic activities to follow when studying infrastructures,[22] picking up a heuristic originally developed by Sebastian Gießmann for the study of 'media practices'[23]: activities of registration/identification, of delegation and of coordination. It must be added that these are metapragmatic categories for a very abstract level of description and largely inspired by work in Actor Network Theory and Science and Technology Studies. Despite this level of abstraction, especially the two metapragmatic categories of registration and coordination are useful reference points for a study of hashtags. While coordination has already been described above in the context of social movements, registration/identification translates into the provision of machine-readability and algorithmic capturing on the one hand, and into the registration of a relational structure as a meaningful token for potentially intensive affective attachment on the other hand.

With these different layers and scopes of practice in mind, we can now return to the tentative question from the beginning about the possibility of understanding hashtags as 'infrastructural media' that mediate between platform technologies and user practices. Rather than generalizing or essentializing this functional relationship, we would emphasize that it needs particular practice contexts, in which the hashtag can obtain the status of an infrastructural medium. For example, hashtags may obtain the status of an infrastructural medium for the above-mentioned relation between user and platform in the context of search operations, which are both relevant for user practices and the algorithmic operations of the platform; or they do so in the context of classification processes that are valuable to the economic procedures of the platform owners and the affiliation practices of users. In other words, whether we can attribute to hashtags the function of an 'infrastructural medium' depends on their role and recognition in particular practice networks.

In summary, hashtags function as infrastructures because they stabilize and organize existing practices and because they set social and cultural processes in motion. The study of hashtags clearly emphasizes the relevance of a cultural perspective on infrastructures for interaction in the following four points: First, infrastructures and practices are recursively interrelated. Infrastructures can emerge as stabilizations or materializers from practices and in turn give rise to new practices. Second: Infrastructures enable and process socio-technical relations. They can link technical connectivity with affective ties and combine matters of organization with those

---

22   Matthias Korn, Wolfgang Reißmann, Tobias Röhl, and David Sittler, "Infrastructuring Publics: A Research Perspective," in *Infrastructuring Publics*, eds. Matthias Korn, Wolfgang Reißmann, Tobias Röhl, and David Sittler (Wiesbaden: Springer VS, 2019), 11–47.

23   Sebastian Gießmann, "Elemente einer Praxistheorie der Medien," *Zeitschrift für Medienwissenschaft* 10, no. 2 (2018): 95–109, https://doi.org/10.25969/mediarep/1228.

of identification. Third, infrastructures can encompass different levels and scales of narrativization and discourse. They thus mediate between the level of micro-practices and the macro-level of cultural formation. Finally, these infrastructures are performative; they can 'produce' discourses, narratives, and social movements.

On the Symbolic Infrastructure of Face-to-face Communication in Early Modern Society: Simple Success Media[1]

Rudolf Schlögl

Symbolic Infrastructures

Defining infrastructures as mechanisms that extend or limit the human possibilities of action emphasises a technological conception of infrastructures. The concept of action centres on a pattern of ends and means, which connects it to the mechanics of a strict coupling in technological processes. But the very fact that unintended side effects exist indicates that, in most cases, the development of social processes cannot, in fact, be attributed to intentions and the means employed to realise them.

The concept of communication, on the other hand, takes into account that, for those involved, social structures as well as social meaning are distilled from circular processes of acquiring information and of comprehension through the medium of meaning. Alter and Ego operate as two mental units that are independent of one another; meaning cannot be transferred between them but must be gained and stabilised through communication, selecting from an infinite number of possibilities. Each side must assume that the other side's ability to acquire information and their processes of understanding are unpredictable, and similarly, the interests of the other side can hardly be calculated in unstructured communication. Such a calculation only becomes possible once the interaction has been systemically consolidated and once those involved have developed a shared history. The formation of social structures requires time, not least because structures crystallise through repetition.[2]

---

1   This text incorporates in some small sections from Rudolf Schlögl, "Einfache Erfolgsmedien in der Gesellschaft der Frühen Neuzeit," in *Systemtheorie und antike Gesellschaft*, eds. Alois Winterling et al. (in preparation). This chapter has been translated from the original German by Helen Imhoff (2023).

2   Niklas Luhmann, *Soziale Systeme. Grundriss einer allgemeinen Theorie* (Frankfurt: Suhrkamp, 1984).

As a result, double contingency, which precedes all communication, is not simply an obstacle to be overcome; it is also the engine that guarantees that communication will continue. Every communicative offer can provoke reactions that were not anticipated and that give a new direction to one's own observations of the world and the expectations with which one encounters that world.

For this reason, systems that are stable over time – even if it is only a group of regulars at the local pub – assume constraints. Not everyone can join the group at the pub, and it is clear that only certain topics will serve to create a pleasant and convivial atmosphere among the individuals who are present. Communication amongst the pub-goers is also regulated with regard to time. These demands regarding limitations and constraints become greater as social systems increase in size and as the problems which the systems process in order to derive the impulses and energy necessary for their operative reproduction increase in complexity. The observation of the world must be attuned to reducing complexity in order for social systems to be able to maintain the flow of communication internally in a world in which there is an infinite variety of causes and effects to be discovered. The world shows the system that face which supports the operative reproduction of the system.

Communicative mechanisms that support the processing of double contingency in social systems and that simultaneously aid the reproduction of complexity are known as success media.[3] They thus serve as infrastructures with regard to the differentiation and reproduction of social systems. The functional differentiation of modern societies depends decisively on symbolically generalised success media such as money, power, the law, or truth. The way in which they function corresponds to the dominant communication through technologically supported mass media. In the following, we will highlight pre-modern situations, in which communication mainly occurred as interaction.[4] We will call the mechanisms that are functionally equivalent to modern situations "simple success media."

Success media are not produced by social systems; instead, social systems contribute to their stabilisation because the systems' operative reproduction follows these mechanisms. Differentiated societies like the advanced civilisations of the pre-modern period are confronted with a number of problems in the formation of their social structures. Success media make it possible to process these problems. For example, it is necessary to differentiate and stabilise a hierarchical order with an upper class in such a way that this becomes tangible in interactions in everyday life. Concordant views of the world are necessary without the public of technological media. In order for decisions with a greater reach, both in terms of the specifics

---

3   Niklas Luhmann, *Die Gesellschaft der Gesellschaft* vol. 1 (Frankfurt: Suhrkamp, 1997): IX-XI.

4   Rudolf Schlögl, *Anwesende und Abwesende. Grundriss für eine Gesellschaftsgeschichte der Frühen Neuzeit* (Konstanz: Konstanz University Press, 2014).

of the case and the individuals involved, to be effective, it must be possible to re-move the limitations on influence in such a way that it is no longer dependent on situations or personal constellations. Finally, it is also necessary to regulate and shape access to scarce resources. Success media are therefore a matter for society. Society provides the systems differentiating themselves within it with a symbolic infrastructure.

In order to illustrate the achievement of success media in addressing these prob-lems, let us return to the basic constellation of communication. Double contingency can be transformed in continuous communication if the expectations of Alter and Ego become complementary. The requisite for this is that Alter and Ego's mutual ob-servations are guided by the distinction between action and experience. In this way, the complex process of forming social meaning is reduced to a sensory and cogni-tively comprehensible form for those involved. Success media can establish them-selves if Alter and Ego's actions and experience can be unambiguously related to de-fined problems and to one another. If such a constellation is given symbolic rep-resentation, it can be recalled and brought up to date in the process of communi-cation. Thus, success media are not tools that can be strategically and unilaterally employed but instead they integrate Alter and Ego simultaneously into a view of the world that makes a complementarity of expectations possible. They provide a defi-nition of a given situation that is binding for Alter and Ego and set a communicative mechanism in motion that determines what information is to be detected from a message and how that information should be processed. For communication that is in progress, success media function as an infrastructure that determines what those involved can assume within it, without this being elaborated on further. A simple scheme with four fields may illustrate this. It was employed by Niklas Luhmann in his derivation of symbolically generalised success media. Following him, and with-out any claim to completeness, we identify a series of simple success media that can be observed in the society of Early Modern Europe as an infrastructure for the de-velopment of social order.[5]

---

5   Luhmann. *Die Gesellschaft der Gesellschaft*, vol 1, 336. This matrix (for symbolically generalised success media in the modern age) was first used in Niklas Luhmann's "Einführende Bemer-kungen zu einer Theorie symbolisch generalisierter Kommunikationsmedien," *Zeitschrift für Soziologie* 3 (1974), 236–255; it is reproduced here following Niklas Luhmann's *Ökologische Kom-munikation: Kann die moderne Gesellschaft sich auf ökologische Gefährdungen einstellen?* (Opladen: Westdeutscher Verlag, 1986), 175.

Simple success media: a matrix

		EGO		
		experience	action	
ALTER	experience	1) $A^e \Rightarrow E^e$ (concordant experience) rituals ceremonials rhetoric "truth"	2) $A^e \Rightarrow E^h$ (conditional action) friendship honour "love"	
	action	3) $A^h \Rightarrow E^e$ (conditional experience) property and privileges trust "money"	4) $A^h \Rightarrow E^h$ (concordant action) reciprocity/gift giving morality ruling authority contract "power"	

Simple Success Media

In the following, we provide a cursory and incomplete discussion of the four fields as our main focus is the respective mechanism of symbolisation.

The first field addresses the problem of congruently relating to the world in such a way that Alter and Ego's experience of the world does not become identical but concordant. Up to and into the 18th century, such concordance had to be ensured without recourse to an entirely differentiated and generally accessible system of dissemination media and without the procedures of an academic system of scientific enquiry that is committed to the truth through institutionalised objection.[6] Accordingly, simple success media aimed to have a local effect, that is to say to "convince" those who were present. Authority might come to mind. However, for situations in which such positions of authority, that is, roles that were frequently also external to the system, were absent or had not effect, media were required that eliminated any questions regarding the causes of concordance. Rhetoric relied on the power to persuade, in the first instance focusing on emotions and then on arguments or making use of rhetorical techniques that suppressed or diverted possible objections. In

---

6   Luhmann. *Die Gesellschaft der Gesellschaft*, vol. 1, 339.

any case, rhetoric was to serve its purpose precisely when authority failed or was in doubt. In this context, however, the most effective and therefore most widespread approach was performative stagings, in which orders, hierarchies, and situations were defined, produced, and presented in a way that could be perceived by all. Rituals can be regarded as a special case of this in that their focus was on changes in status and situation, that is on turning points, whereas ceremonial performances were always placed in relation to an order that was assumed to exist, in whatsoever way, and to the reproduction of that order.[7]

The situation described in the second field, to the right of the first, ties Ego's actions to Alter's expectations. Contrary to what one might assume, this model of disinterested sociality could not be taken as a given even for face-to-face communication. Charity proved to be too general to connect to a social reference problem. In its Christian tradition, it was a medium of group formation determined by solidarity. It was not so much associated with different expectations as different motives, although disinterest was required. The person who showed charity to a beggar also expected prayers in return. Charity thus became continuously overburdened, with the result that the entire salvation economy was reorganised during the Reformation.[8] Friendship underwent a more successful development, not least because it had already been connected to usefulness and vested interests in Antiquity. As a result, the concept of friendship had a career that extended beyond the middle of the 17th century, when society was beginning to be regarded as a space in which vested interests circulated.[9] The success medium of honour was central to reproducing the hierarchical order of society. Honour demanded that Ego fulfil Alter's expectations of how the latter should be approached. And it obliged Alter to sanction any disappointment of expectations. In this way, honour not only contributed to the formation of hierarchical order, but it also provided a high degree of rivalry and potential for conflict in the daily life of society.

The third field is determined by constellations in which Alter acts and Ego experiences and ratifies this action. In relation to the scarcity of goods and resources, this can be regarded as the social codification of egotisms, which ensure that such actions are accepted and can thus be used for the formation of structures without leading to violence and anomy. Scarcity and the way in which this was treated socially represented an unambiguous reference problem; in such a case, there were also social attribution constellations that could be interpreted without ambiguity

---

7   Barbara Stollberg-Rilinger's *Rituale*, vol. 16. (Frankfurt: Campus Verlag, 2013) provides an overview of concepts and research (not relating to systems theory).

8   Hans-Joachim Klimkeit, "Zwischen Nil und Kaukasus," *Zeitschrift für Religions-und Geistesgeschichte* 46, no. 3 (1994): 270–275.

9   John Locke, *Some Thoughts Concerning Education* (Printed for A. and J. Churchill at the Black Swan in Paternoster-row: London, 1693): par. 142–145.

and to which the semantic codification of property could reliably connect. Thus, this codification appears to have been very stable and of vital importance socially even before money developed from a measure of value to a commodity. This should not, however, distract from the fact that it was the exception for property to act as a binary code structuring communication in conditions of scarcity in such a way that a money- and price- driven allocation of resources and the circulation of goods should have been set in motion. The property code of the Early Modern period worked differently. It was aimed at resolving the social distribution of scarce resources through the distribution of access rights.[10] Owners therefore always had to assume that there might be co-owners, and so the circulation dynamics of buying and selling could only be established with some difficulty. For this reason, ownership of land as well as rights of use always remained tied to specific individuals and their social status. This was intended to ensure that ownership supported rather than undermined the hierarchical order.

The fourth field summarises symbolically condensed semantics and practices that provide society with possibilities of coordination and communicative connections beyond those that result from the potential interests of Alter and Ego. In the first instance, these are very simple mechanisms of influence, such as the principle of reciprocity. Ego does what it has learnt from Alter, and because Alter can assume that this will be the case, Alter can also expect that its actions will direct those of Ego's correspondingly. However, this applies both in the positive and in the negative sense. Someone who does good can also expect good, and a person who inflicts harm on others must expect vengeance. This is an obvious rule in social relations based on interaction, and it solves the problem of attribution between Alter and Ego unambiguously because the chains of action are straightforward. It is only in very fortunate circumstances that this rule actually achieves the implied reciprocity. Outside such a paradise, it quickly leads to problems because Ego can always also decide not to reciprocate good deeds unless additional means, such as the threat of exclusion or the withdrawal of honour, are employed. Reciprocity has a switch that can easily be turned on or off, which makes conflict more likely than coordination. Reciprocity alone therefore tends to maintain a cycle of harm and vengeance rather than one of good deeds.[11] Gifts provide a way out of this.[12] Gifts are good deeds that are marked as such, and if they are accepted, this establishes a claim to a countergift. Because,

---

10   See *Early Modern Conceptions of Property*, eds. John Brewer and Susan Staves (New York: Routledge, 1996).

11   Niklas Luhmann, *Das Recht der Gesellschaft*. vol. 1183 (Frankfurt: Suhrkamp, 1995): 226–233; Niklas Luhmann, "Das sind Preise. Ein soziologisch-systemtheoretischer Klärungsversuch," *Soziale Welt* 34, no. 2 (1983): 155–158.

12   Harry Liebersohn, *The Return of the Gift: European History of a Global Idea* (Cambridge: Cambridge University Press, 2010).

according to convention, gift exchange allows very different things to be connected, depending on a given constellation and intention, it represents a fundamental principle of communicative coordination in face-to-face social contexts. Votes at diets can be exchanged for wine, decisions for money, positions for political allegiance and intimacy for information.[13] To this extent, gifts are a medium that can be employed universally in the creation of structures and in coordination, and it is found in almost all social fields of the Early Modern period. The limits of this communicative codification are found in its temporal structure. Gifts must be repeated at regular intervals if temporally stable, focused, and case-specific structures of influence are to be established. This assumes a gradient of resources so that such "models of reward" can be used to establish identifiable avoidance alternatives which provide lasting and reliable orientation for Ego's actions. Ruling authority that is based on gift exchange must also always be geared towards accumulating resources in order to stabilise its own influence.

On the Dynamics of Social Infrastructures

Early Modern society encountered comparable structural problems to modern society. It developed simple media of communication which could address double contingency and the environmental complexity in the operative reproduction of social systems in a case-specific way (and thus in relation to a particular problem). An infrastructure based on simple success media did, of course, also differ from one based on modern, symbolically generalised success media. Its inability to be generalised across the three dimensions of meaning was particularly consequential. Rituals must be tailored to specific situations, and they are only binding for those that are present. Ruling authority was also only able to bind a small number of individuals as long as there was no shift to negative avoidance alternatives. It was obliged to regenerate itself through continuously repeated gift giving, which considerably restricted the reach and controlling effect of such power.

However, it is clear that such structural deficits in the communication infrastructures served as an incentive to improve them. Making use of writing and printing was one way of doing so. On the one hand, the new media exacerbated the problem of double contingency because they removed context and they also meant that systems were confronted with a more complex environment. However, the developing media system could also be employed to theorise about simple success media, to refine their semantics and thus to strengthen their functionality. Ceremonials,

---

13   Natalie Zemon Davis, *The Gift in Sixteenth-Century France* (Madison: The University of Wisconsin Press, 2000).

rhetoric, and honour, too, were among the success media that were strongly theorised. This shows that they were important for the reproduction of the hierarchical order of society. Contracts and trust, however, had also been a significant focus of attention since the middle of the 17th century.[14] This indicates that the social formation of structure had already moved from presence-based constellations in many social contexts. Written theorisation regarding simple success media was attended by their legal standardisation. This can be observed in the cases of honour, ceremonials, and contracts. Here, the law and all the institutions of legal practice exerted an influence on society's symbolic infrastructure in a way that helped to reduce conflicts or arbitrate them without violence. This extended the productive treatment of "no" in communication considerably.

The effect of law in particular indicates another aspect of the developmental dynamics of symbolic infrastructures. Many of the simple success media lost their key function in modern society, were pushed aside into niches, such as rituals and ceremonials, and survived there as folklore. Contracts and property had to be fundamentally restructured in order to fit into the modern order. This supports an observation put forward here only as a hypothesis: much like technological infrastructures, symbolic infrastructures are resistant to reorganisation through evolutionary processes. Evolution assumes variation and the system-internal compatibility of variation, but infrastructures must reject these aspects precisely in order to be reliable and thus fungible. Infrastructures can be refined and improved, but they always adhere to their basic logic and thus lose any function in the context of a society developing by evolution. In the symbolic order of a society, the new is also constructed alongside the old.

---

14   Patrick S. Atiyah, *The Rise and Fall of Freedom of Contract* (Oxford: Oxford University Press, 1979); Ute Frevert, *Vertrauensfragen. Eine Obsession der Moderne.* Vol. 6104. (München: C. H. Beck, 2013).

Section III: Infrastructures and Sociality

Command and Consilium: On Infrastructures of Decision-Making in Roman Culture[1]

Ulrich Gotter

The aim of the following considerations is to demonstrate why decision-making processes can profitably be understood as infrastructures of political space. This is not self-evident, and we should not, without distinction, label every formation of political opinion an infrastructure. However, what forms decision-making processes according to culturally modelled understandings, by virtue of their defining the decision-making spaces, modalities, and participants, might be called infrastructure, indeed. Those decision-making processes are not due to chance, but manifestations of the regular and repeatable within the framework of a specific political culture. Ancient Rome is a particularly rewarding test-case because Roman decision-making processes appear to have been characterised by contradictory principles. In the following, I will argue that this supposed paradox was in fact none, as those contradictory principles were mediated by the interplay of visibility and concealment. Visibility therefore emerges as a category that should be central to our thinking about infrastructures.

In the following, I will first characterise the essential elements of the Roman decision-making regime before outlining, in a second section, the returns that I believe can be derived from applying the framework of "infrastructure."

A Roman Paradox?

There is probably no other political culture in the ancient world that would have been so concerned, at all levels, about holding individuals accountable for their actions. Every action required authorisation, which assigned it to a specific person. This strict model of representation was not only a deliberative setting that followed the logic of the political sphere; it was, moreover, a fundamental cultural disposition that applied in other segments of society as well. According to the Roman conception, every group, and every organisation needed a representative, an *auctor*, so to

---

1   For helpful discussions of the text, I like to thank Andreas Bendlin (University of Toronto).

speak, who could act on behalf of the group—and who afterwards stood for the success or failure of his action. Under these circumstances, the ability to act effectively was limited to comparatively few people, each of whom was granted an almost uncanny decision-making authority. This began with the father and ended with the civil servant. The *paterfamilias*, the oldest member of the agnatic line, not only had the authority of a clan elder often observed in the Mediterranean; at least nominally, he also held near to absolute power over the other members of his family.[2] Curiously, his powers extended least of all to his wife, who was, over the course of the middle and late Republic, less and less frequently transferred from her original family to that of her husband (by means of the so-called *manus*-marriage) but remained formally under the *potestas* of her father.[3] Over his children, however, the *paterfamilias* could claim almost unlimited power. As long as he lived, he remained the sole owner and only person entitled to dispose of the family property. This applied even to sons who had long since grown up and were Roman office holders. The fact that he was formally authorised to have his children killed (the so-called *ius vitae necisque*) completes this picture, even if this last decision was apparently only taken when state matters were at stake and any examples of this right seem to have been paradigmatic stories of exemplary behaviour rather than lived reality. All the same, the father's authority was often recounted precisely because it signalled personal power in Roman culture unlike anything else.[4]

This scenario is confirmed by the political arena: It is *communis opinio* among scholars that no Greek magistrate was granted the scope of action a Roman *consul* or *proconsul* had. In the Greek perception, Roman magistrates were compared more to monarchs than to political officials.[5] They could act outwardly with extreme forms of violence, start wars, conclude treaties, decree naturalisations, while at home their competence was more than considerable as well. Without them, as heads of the executive, little was possible: neither the people's assembly nor the senate could meet,

---

2   Cf. with a wider scope Jochen Martin, "Zwei Alte Geschichten. Vergleichende historisch-anthropologische Betrachtungen zu Griechenland und Rom," *Saeculum* 48 (1997): 2–3.

3   Jochen Martin, "Die Bedeutung der Familie als eines Rahmens für Geschlechterbeziehungen," in *Bedingungen menschlichen Handelns in der Antike*, ed. Winfried Schmitz (Stuttgart: Steiner 2009), 343–344; Beryl Rawson, "Adult-Child Relationships in Roman Society," in *Marriage, Divorce, and Children in Ancient Rome*, ed. Beryl Rawson (Oxford: Oxford University Press, 1991), 18.

4   Jochen Martin "Die Stellung des Vaters in antiken Gesellschaften," in *Bedingungen menschlichen Handelns in der Antike*, ed. Winfried Schmitz (Stuttgart: Steiner, 2009), 94–97; Jochen Martin, "Familie, Verwandtschaft und Staat," in *Bedingungen menschlichen Handelns in der Antike*, ed. Winfried Schmitz (Stuttgart: Steiner 2009), 368–370; for the representation of the *patria potestas* in Roman discourse see Ute Lucarelli, *Exemplarische Vergangenheit. Valerius Maximus und die Konstruktion des sozialen Raumes in der frühen Kaiserzeit*, (Göttingen: Vandenhoeck & Ruprecht, 2007) with further literature.

5   See, for example, Polybios 6, 11, 12–16, 12, 9.

nor could laws be passed.[6] From this perspective, it seems quite understandable that Theodor Mommsen placed the magistracy at the beginning of his "Staatsrecht," far ahead of the "advisory body," the Senate.[7] In Rome (*domi*), Roman officials could in many places communicate with their fellow citizens in the mode of command; outside Roman territory (*militae*), this was the rule.[8] To the development of law below the level of statutes, which was decisive for the practical Roman normative landscape, the magistrate was also instrumental. One of the Roman praetors (the *praetor urbanus*) announced at the beginning of his term of office the way in which he would dispense justice and was subsequently able to modify the Roman system of rules through individual decisions.[9] Such a thing would have been tyranny in the context of any other polis constitution, whether Greek or Phoenician. In middle and late republican Rome (4th–1st century BCE), no one seems to ever have raised fundamental objections.

The most charismatic display of the individual's power to act in Roman culture was the triumph.[10] After the victory of an army, its commander – the magistrate with *imperium*: *consul, proconsul, praetor* or *propraetor* – was elevated above all other citizens and officials. For a one-day (or, in rare cases, three-day) ceremony the triumphator rode his triumphal chariot in the midst of his spoils and his soldiers, wrapped in the robe of the highest Roman god, his face dyed in the colour of the god's statue. Thus, he paraded through the city before everyone's eyes; thus, he ascended to the temple of Jupiter on the Capitol; there he redeemed the *votum* of the Roman citizenry that he had previously pledged for a victory. He was first *imperator*, then God for a day.[11]

It has previously been noticed that the isolation and monumental exaltation of the individual general after a collective victory of the Roman people is odd.[12] The

---

6   For the notions of authority in Rome see Jochen Bleicken, *Zum Begriff der römischen Amtsgewalt. auspicium – potestas – imperium* (Göttingen: Vandenhoeck & Ruprecht, 1981).

7   Theodor Mommsen, *Römisches Staatsrecht*, (Leipzig: Hirzel, 1876–1877); deals with the magistracies in volume I and II, with the senate in volume III.

8   Cf. Ulrich Gotter, "Cultural Differences and Cross-Cultural Contact: Greek and Roman Concepts of Power," *Harvard Studies in Classical Philology* 104 (2008): 179–230, 199–204.

9   Mommsen, *Staatsrecht* II.1, 185–218.

10   For the different aspects of the Roman triumph see Hendrik S. Versnel, *Triumphus: An Inquiry into the Origin, Development and Meaning of the Roman Triumph* (Leiden: Brill, 1970); Ernst Künzl, *Der römische Triumph. Siegesfeiern im antiken Rom* (München: Beck, 1981); Mary Beard, *The Roman Triumph* (Cambridge: Harvard University Press, 2007).

11   See Jörg Rüpke, *Domi Militae. Die religiöse Konstruktion des Krieges in Rom* (Stuttgart: Steiner, 1990), 230–233.

12   Egon Flaig, "Warum die Triumphe die römische Republik ruiniert haben – oder: Kann ein politisches System an zu viel Sinn zugrunde gehen?" in *Sinn (in) der Antike. Orientierungssysteme, Leitbilder und Wertkonzepte im Altertum*, ed. Karl-Joachim Hölkeskamp, et al. (Mainz: von Zabern, 2003): 299–300.

scene on the Capitol makes it clear where at least the discursive legitimisation for the concentration of agency in Roman culture is to be located. Indeed, the conclusion of the greatest day of a Roman aristocrat is the resolution of the *votum* vis-à-vis Iupiter Optimus Maximus; thereafter, the triumphator becomes a citizen again. By analogy, his term of office begins with an inaugural *auspicium* (i.e., divination) and sacrifice, and only when this has been successful is he capable of acting for the community.[13] Even before every important official act—the people's assembly or senate meeting—he convenes, he must perform the sacrifice that legitimises the event and, on the other hand, stops the event if the sacrifice was not successful. The inevitable sacrifice before a military campaign and before each battle also heaps enormous responsibility on the commander. In this way, he concludes a contract with the gods for all to see. In extremis, even his own sacrifice to the gods (*devotio*) came not entirely unexpected, correcting as it does any potentially negative result of his inquiring of the gods.[14] What applies on a large scale also applies on a small scale. Just as the general binds the Roman people through his actions, the *paterfamilias* binds his family. He performs the sacrifices for the well-being of all and vows or redeems the *votum* for divine support.[15] One could thus formulate that the extreme agency of individuals in Roman culture was legitimised by the personal capacity to act towards the gods.

Under these circumstances, Roman decision-making should have been autocratic in the extreme, mitigated at best by the regular change of office holders. The fact that this is by no means the case becomes apparent only at a closer look. Taking solitary decisions in Rome was not in conformity with the norms, or to put it differently: decisions, especially those of great consequence, were secured by an intensive collective consultation process (*consilium*). To understand the significance of this phenomenon, one must first note its ubiquity. *Consilia* are present in almost all areas since the beginning of documented evidence. They were involved in the decisions of private citizens, in those of magistrates in internal politics, and in decisions in the external (military) sphere.[16] The *paterfamilias* discussed with his confidants not only rigid punitive measures against his sons, but also marriages, divorces, dona-

---

13   Rüpke, *Domi militiae*, 44–47.

14   Andreas Bendlin, "Anstelle der anderen sterben. Zur Bedeutungsvielfalt eines Modells in der griechischen und römischen Religion," in *Stellvertretung. Theologische, philosophische und kulturelle Aspekte*, eds. J. Christine Janowski, Bernd Janowski, and Hans P. Lichtenberger (Neukirchen-Vluyn: Neukirchener-Verl., 2006): vol. 1, 25–30.

15   John Scheid, *An Introduction to Roman Religion* (Edinburgh: Edinburgh University Press 2003), 165–170.

16   Cristina Rosillo-Lopez, "The Consilium as Advisory Board of the Magistrates at Rome during the Republic," *Historia* 70 (2021): 396–436.

tions, and bequests.[17] The *praetor urbanus* discussed the changes he introduced in his edict, especially if they had some weight, with confidants who had a understanding of the matter—if only to make sure that the norms proclaimed by him were acceptable and not reversed by his successor.[18] The *consilium* was of particular importance in the military field,[19] of course, where human lives and, in extreme cases, the existence of the state were at stake. This phenomenon of a consultative superstructure did not change during the principate. It was particularly prominent at the level of rotating provincial commanders and procurators,[20] but imperial action and what we commonly refer to as the imperial central administration were also inconceivable without advisory councils.[21]

At this point another characteristic of the Roman consultative process (and a pertinent research problem) becomes obvious. Not even for the most prominent of all advisory councils, that of the emperor (*consilium principis*), we are well informed about its composition, meeting modalities, and formats of communication. The *consilia* of the Roman Republican and Imperial period are a black box not only because for a long time they have not been adequately studied, but also because as institutions they have very limited visibility in our sources. Although we know just enough to realise that the consultative structures were of fundamental importance to the Roman decision-making regime, we know far too little about how these structures worked in practice. And there is a system in our ignorance. For the *consilia* were and remained institutionally underdetermined. Scholarship on Roman law in particular has seen this as a childhood disease of the republican and early imperial state (4th century BCE–1st century CE), which was increasingly replaced, in a somewhat teleological process, by a more desirable institutionality. Thus, it was assumed that in the second century CE, under Hadrian or Marcus Aurelius, the *consilium principis* was consolidated in terms of personnel and formalised in its function.[22] Something

---

17   See Lucarelli, *Exemplarische Vergangenheit*, 46, 59, 79–80, 86, 163, 204–205, 212, 281; Susan Treggiari, *Terentia, Tullia, Publilia: The Women of Cicero's Family* (New York: Routledge 2007), 83–95, 118–142.

18   See Olga E. Tellegen-Couperus, "The So-Called Consilium of the Praetor and the Development of Roman Law," *Tijdschrift voor Rechtsgeschiedenis* 11 (2001): 11–20.

19   See Pamela Delia Johnston, *The Military Consilium in Republican Rome* (Piscataway: Gorgias Press, 2013).

20   See for example Eckhard Meyer-Zwiffelhoffer, *Politikos archein. Zum Regierungsstil der senatorischen Statthalter in den kaiserzeitlichen griechischen Provinzen* (Stuttgart: Steiner, 2002), 223–267.

21   John A. Crook, *Consilium Principis. Imperial Counsellors from Augustus to Diocletian* (Cambridge: Cambridge University Press, 1955); Francesco Amarelli, *Consilia principum*, (Napoli: E. Jovene, 1983); Werner Eck, "The Emperor and His Advisers," in *The Cambridge Ancient History vol. 11: The High Empire, AD 70–192*, eds. Alan K. Bowman, Richard Garnsey, and Dominic Rathbone (Cambridge: Cambridge University Press, 2000).

22   For the discussion cf. Crook, *Consilium principis*, 56–76.

similar has been proposed for the legal *consilium* of the *praetor urbanus*. However, as recent research has found, neither assumption is supported by our sources.[23] On the contrary, most data fail to suggest a standardised affiliation of certain positions or ranks to *consilia*.[24] This is arguably so where the evidence is best: in the military *consilia* of the Republican period. While there is isolated evidence that quaestors, prefects, and tribunes could belong to the commander's *consilium*, the nature of the evidence contradicts the idea that they did so automatically and regularly.[25] The circle of participants in a *consilium* was apparently not ritually prefigured. The few records of *consilia* we have make at least one thing very clear: members did not have to be peers. In the *consilia* of governors we find not only the *quaestor* and senatorial friends (*amici*) of the governor, but also Roman knights and other Roman citizens and, which is particularly surprising, local provincials.[26] Centurions (mostly *primipilares*, the highest-ranking centurions of a legion) were always present in the military *consilia* of the Republic and the imperial period, and there are also indications of the participation of non-Romans.[27] What is interesting for our question is that these centurions were usually careerists from within the army, i.e., they were definitely not knights or senators.

In summary, consultative processes in Roman culture had the following characteristics: they were ubiquitous but remained largely invisible and weakly institutionalised; participation and debate behaviour were not standardised; it was not rank but expertise and the relationship of trust with the decision maker that determined their composition.

"Infrastructures" as a Means of Cross-Cultural Comparison

In contrast to "structure" as a central category of analysis, "infrastructure" directs the attention to what is concealed or seems self-evident. This is particularly attractive when one examines cultural differences since they, especially the attribution of meaning and social perception by those involved, usually lie beyond perception or discourse. Thus, examining infrastructures contours cultural fingerprints, which can be compared to each other in a second step. Comparing infrastructures operates pragmatically at an intermediate level between comparing holistic cultures on the one hand and individual cultural patterns on the other.

---

23   Telegen-Couperius, "Consilium of the Praetor," 12–18.

24   Rosillo-Lopez, "The Consilium as Advisory Board," 421, 427–28.

25   Cf. Johnston, *Military Consilium*, 6–19.

26   Rosillo-Lopez, "The Consilium as Advisory Board," 421.

27   Johnston, *Military Consilium*, 17–18.

I will try to demonstrate the potential benefits of this approach with my sketched example. If one does not concentrate on the individual aspects of Roman decision-making management (i.e., the *consilium* or the role of the *paterfamilias*, etc.), as research has done until now, but shifts the focus to the infrastructures of decision-making as a whole, a new configuration emerges; the task is then to relate the seemingly divergent patterns (utmost concentration of decision-making power vs. expectation of collective deliberation) to each other and integrate them into a comprehensive model. That consultation is not part of the decision (as Cristina Rosillo Lopez argues[28]) because it is not the advisory board that decides but the individual who convened it, is in my opinion formalistic eyewash: for if the *consilium* had played no role in the decision, the magistrate would not have convened it. And the social expectation that the one representing the decision should consult with others beforehand would also be inexplicable. Therefore, the *consilium* is undoubtedly an important part of the decision-making process. In my opinion, the continuous oscillation between sole responsibility and inevitable collective consultation can be best explained by the distinct levels of visibility of the two. While the formal decision by the public official is visible, attributable, and demonstrative, the collective body of consultation disappears behind a screen. There is clearly a method to the fact that we learn so little about the techniques of deliberation in the *consilium*. My explanation would not be that this mirrored a deficient level of institutionality, but that it was part of a complex exchange of gifts. What the emperor, magistrate, commander, or governor gave to the members of his council was open discussion of his actions, and participation in important decisions. This is particularly remarkable since it also concerned persons (such as centurions) who could not usually claim to participate on the public stage. Their *gratia* for this *beneficium* (i.e., their retribution for the privilege granted) was, in my opinion, twofold: first, they accepted that all honours and public profits were legitimately taken by the official representative, and secondly, they kept silent about their shares in the successful decisions of the incumbent. Both sides of the gift exchange required a considerable degree of self-restraint on the part of those involved, as well as a thorough reflection of the cultural script that underpinned the decision-making regime in Rome.

This solution entails further questions. If the cost of negotiation was so high, in communicative terms, why did the Roman élite cling to it for centuries? This question immediately opens another horizon of perspectives. One could formulate it as follows: only *consilia* made a strong and successful executive à la Rome possible, because a strong executive was only acceptable if it remained limited in time. In this respect, the annual or biennial rotation of offices was a sacred cow, and justly so. Little changed in the imperial period (after 27 BCE): beyond the stable position of the emperor, elite officeholders continued to rotate. However, this necessarily meant that

---

key positions were filled by functionaries who were not or not sufficiently trained for the job. One could almost say that until late antiquity political decisions, and thus also all administrative acts, tended to be carried out and answered for by high-ranking amateurs. Officials often had to make far-reaching decisions under great time pressure and in a state of personal ignorance. This was almost always the case for Roman provincial governors, who ruled unknown territories almost omnipotently with a minimal core of administrative personnel. The same was true, and particularly problematic, for military commands, which were held predominantly, and not only in imperial times, by inexperienced senatorial commanders.[29] That someone without decades of military training should be entrusted with the command of several thousand, occasionally several tens of thousands of men, seems at first sight absurd and is not a particularly safe path to success. It was precisely at this point that *consilia* ensured that the inexperience of the State's omnipotent representatives caused as little damage as possible: hence the enormous pressure on officeholders to practice consultative procedures, hence the agreement that persons of whatever social status with experience should be appointed to a *consilium*. A military professional of centurion rank could thus ensure that the aristocratic amateur would not carelessly put the lives of those under his command at risk. At the same time, the *consilium* functioned as a training program for the senatorial novice, so that his competence grew for the next challenges. Above all, however, the *consilium*, as a standardised prerequisite for decision-making, carved out the social distribution of roles in this process and imparted to Roman leaders the need to listen to subordinates and not to treat lower-ranking expertise with arrogance.[30] The virtuosity of the commander to collect and handle his *consilium* paved the way to his individual success.

At the same time, the consultative processes made it possible to cope with failure, and this is another important observation revealed by focusing on the infrastructures of decision-making. In contrast to what might happen at Carthage or in a Greek polis, a Roman commander could be reintegrated into the community after military defeat,[31] at least if he adhered to the mechanism of consultation. If decision-making was collectivised, he was able to survive even a serious defeat

---

29   See Egon Flaig, *Den Kaiser herausfordern. Die Usurpationen im Römischen Reich* (Frankfurt: Campus 1992), 144–152.

30   This socially rehearsed mindset has been convincingly explored by Martin Jehne, "Jovialität und Freiheit. Zur Institutionalität der Beziehungen zwischen Ober- und Unterschichten in der römischen Republik," in *Mos maiorum. Untersuchungen zu den Formen der Identitätsstiftung und Stabilisierung in der römischen Republik*, eds. Bernhard Linke and Michael Stemmler (Stuttgart: Steiner, 2000), 207–235.

31   Nathan Rosenstein, *Imperatores Victi. Military Defeat and Aristocratic Competition in the Middle and Late Republic* (Berkeley: University of California Press, 1990), 179–203, has the impressive list of Roman magistrates who suffered defeat and returned to Rome; his explanation for this evidence (esp. 170–78) differs from mine.

with many casualties. On the other hand, in the tension between decision and consultation, a different and more dramatic option was possible: A commander could decide either not to consult a council or to disregard the council's advice in a sovereign manner. According to what has been established above, he thereby took a considerable risk, which was not desirable within the framework of the Roman political order. However, the acceptance of this risk was also a source of charismatic leadership. The individual, whose insight was greater than that of the collective, could claim an exceptional position for himself if he was successful. It is therefore probably no coincidence that C. Julius Caesar, who of all Romans of the last generation of the Roman Republic played most penetratingly on the keyboard of charisma, in his narratives constantly belittles the benefits of *consilia* in contrast to his own expertise.[32] In the same vein, Augustus claimed in his *Res Gestae* (of 13 CE) that he had decided *privato consilio*, i.e., without the intervention of others, to take up arms to free the Republic from Antony and his followers.[33] The lonely decision thus became the cornerstone of his charismatic authority.

Examining Roman decision-making processes from an infrastructural perspective offers innovative options for culturally sensitive plots: If one radically exploits its benefits, even the Roman "administration" as a whole might be reconceptualised.[34] The starting point would be to reconsider the lack of institutionality discussed above. If you decide not to understand it in the modern sense, i.e., as a deficiency that hinders rational administrative action, but as a programmatic epiphenomenon of Roman decision-making processes, Roman governance gains a different contour. For institutionality in the modern sense would have prevented two things: first, the radical freedom in composing the consultative bodies, which allowed for the integration of non-peers and thus for an unrivalled aggregation of competence; and second, the enormous personalisation of decision-making, which guaranteed pyramidal hierarchy and centrality, both elementary to the Roman Republic as well as the Empire.

---

32   In his two Commentaries on the Gallic War and on the Civil War, Caesar transmits very few of his own *consilia* (see Johnston, *Military Consilium*, 5–6), not even where they would necessarily have been expected, as after the lost battle of Dyrrhachium. The Caesar of the text essentially decides alone; his *consilium*, on the other hand, when it conflicts with his authority, is openly criticised by him (Caes. bell. Gall. 1, 40); war councils of his subordinate generals and especially the *consilia* of his opponents in civil war appear essentially dysfunctional and lead to catastrophes (bell. Gall. 5, 28–34; bell. civ. 1, 19; 3, 82–83; 3, 86–87; 3, 104).

33   Augustus res gest. 1; Nicolaus of Damascus (18) supports this interpretation of *privato consilio* by narrating, most probably in reference to Augustus' first memoirs, that the young Octavian acted against the advice of those closest to him.

34   It is striking, indeed, that while massive doubts have been voiced against the notion of statehood in antiquity, the key feature of the modern state, administration, continued to be enormously popular in research, especially on the Roman Empire.

Governance à la Rome obviously consisted of alternating zones of de-personalisation (within the framework of the *consilium*) and subsequent re-personalisation by the officeholder. Administration in this sense was not an autonomous process, but a carefully balanced sequence of changing visibilities of authorship. This alternative explanation for the low administrative institutionality of the Roman Empire should then call for a macro-level theory of the emergence of cultural preferences.

Couple Apps as Relationship Infrastructures

Anne Ganzert

A contemporary interdisciplinary approach to infrastructures should consider aspects beyond material structures and include among other things social media interactions in order to fully understand how media practices emerge from infrastructures. And how, maybe more importantly, infrastructures emerge within media practices. Transforming the approach to infrastructures crucially needs to take contemporary digital, smart, and connected devices seriously, as mediated human relationships and "connectivity has grown into a matter of infrastructure reminiscent of electricity, gas, water supply or heating."[1] The specific genre of couple apps for example, when discussed within the framework of this collection's main aspects, demonstrates how generativity, regularity, relationality and maintenance productively intertwine. These apps will be the focal point of this chapter, in which I will first explain the genre of couple apps in distinction to dating apps, before discussing their infrastructuring properties, and lastly examining their impact on the wider discourse on infrastructures. I will show how couple apps create the framework for their own upkeep by the users through media practice within the logic of relationship management. Discussing this necessarily includes different broader, cultural aspects, such as the underlying idea of continual self-optimization and different socio-political aspects of (hetero-)normativity and emphasizes the importance of alternative infrastructural concepts such as 'infrastructures of intimacy' that assume a cultural and media studies perspective.

'Couple Apps' are rooted in the idiom that 'successful relationships need work' and claim to be this work's infrastructure, promising to make it easier on the users in that they are transparent in their infrastructural status and users consciously engage in both the upkeep of their relationship and maintaining the app as its infrastructure. Importantly, relationship apps can also create new relationship forms, which means as infrastructure they generate new social forms. Based on the idea

---

1   Susanna Paasonen, "Infrastructures of Intimacy," in *Mediated Intimacies: Connectivities, Relationalities and Proximities*, eds. Rikke Andreassen et al. (New York: Routledge, 2017): 103–116, 103.

that any technologies, such as these apps, are not simply 'channels' for communication but affordances that curb human relations, this chapter emphasizes that apps, and especially couple apps, afford both emotional and social relational presence.[2] Understanding couple apps as infrastructure is hence insightful for a more general discussion, as they strongly enforce regular and daily use for the sake of stabilizing relationality and ensuring their continued usefulness.[3]

Infrastructures are generally understood as "the vast network that makes possible the movement of people, goods, and information over time and space."[4] Smartphone apps, in combination with underlying infrastructures such as the internet, 'move' information, data, images, and texts while also being essential in the creation of this information. Many of these apps have distinct infrastructural properties as they purposefully communicate their existence, demand users to interact with them, and thus raise "the user's awareness about properties of an infrastructure."[5] Contrary to notions of the 'underlying,' 'invisible' properties of infrastructures, the apps' language, aesthetic properties, push-messages, and nudges make infrastructural properties and processes distinctly visible and specify maintenance as part of their functionality. Marking the apps' technological properties and programming with automated communication and facilitated social interaction and their general appearance is hence an important first step when analysing couple apps as relationship infrastructure.

Generally speaking, couple apps as infrastructures of relationships have not been discussed in depth even though some of the tech-journalistic discourse has called *Pair* (2012), *Avocado* (2012) or similar apps the 'smallest possible social network.'[6] The two nodes of such a network are the couple, two users and their phones, while the app (plus the necessary other technological conditions) is the infrastructure upon which this network unfolds. Researchers from different academic fields have explicitly written about the "infrastructure of intimacy,"[7] which closely relates

2   Larissa Hjorth and Sun Lim, "Mobile Intimacy in an Age of Affective Mobile Media," *Feminist Media Studies* 12, no. 4 (December 2012): 477–484, 478.

3   And in turn generate income, as many of the apps in question collect data or bill their users for specific services. As are all infrastructures, they are embedded within socio-capitalist contexts that intersectionally shape their designs, functionalities, and cultural contents and implications.

4   Barney Warf, "Infrastructure," in *Encyclopedia of Human Geography*, eds. Rob Kitchin and Nigel Thrift (Thousand Oaks: SAGE, 2006): 259.

5   Juan David Hincapie-Ramos, "Infrastructure Awareness," in *Proceedings of the 12th ACM International Conference Adjunct Papers on Ubiquitous Computing: Ubicomp '10* (Copenhagen: ACM Press, 2010): 1–4, 1.

6   Randall Stross, "Social Networks, Small and Smaller," *The New York Times* (14 April 2021); Sarah Kessler, "Pair, the Social Network for Two, Launches an Android App," *Mashable* (8 May 2012).

7   Ara Wilson, "The Infrastructure of Intimacy," *Signs: Journal of Women in Culture and Society* 41, no. 2 (January 2016): 247–280; Paasonen, "Infrastructures of Intimacy."

to debates around mobile and social media and 'networked intimacy' or 'mobilized intimacy'[8] and infrastructures of connectivity in the modern city-scape.[9] Couple apps are structurally different from dating or "Hook Up" apps like *Tinder* (2012), *Badoo* (2006) or *Hinge* (2013), as they do not aim to facilitate a first encounter between somehow matched users, but they address people who are already in a somewhat committed relationship with each other. This relationship, according to the apps' creators, needs a smartphone-based infrastructure to flourish. Most of the apps promise to create or increase intimacy, which is, as Berlant put it, a matter of "connections that *impact* on people, and on which they depend for living."[10] And this is where apps such as *Between* (2012), *Without* (2015), *Couply* (2020), or *Lasting* (2017) come in. They insert themselves between two users, or rather between two phones, and offer to hold open the socio-technical space for the couple to interact in with. In doing so they inherently shape the interaction and consequential human connection they facilitate. They also transport normative frameworks as most couple apps are geared toward heterosexual, monogamous relationships (children are not part of the picture) and implicitly exclude LGBTQIA+ users, as well as alternative types of relationships through wordings, and promotional images enforcing a specific kind of 'successful relationship.' Their target audience can be described as generally professional, digital natives who subscribe to a busy lifestyle that includes certain activities such as workouts, dinner dates etc. Couple apps are hence programmed to create an exclusive space for two smartphone users—their purpose is the stabilization of the existing relationship as well as the creation of new forms of relation.

They promise to help plan a couple's everyday life, somehow enhance their dating or sex life, or organize menial tasks such as grocery shopping. In studying such apps as infrastructures, their surface design, functions, texts, and language have an influence on and are influenced by the respective relationship. Taking discursive sources into account (such as advertisements, product videos, homepage, or app store texts), as well as other artefacts collected from social media platforms or journalistic sources, allows for condensing the apps' missions and branding. By adding

---

8   Charlotte Launder, "Location: Tinder. Locative Social Media as a Dating Tool," *Meco6936* (blog), (28 May 2015), https://meco6936.wordpress.com/2015/05/28/location-tinder-locative-social-media-as-a-dating-tool/; Nichi Hodgson, *The Curious History of Dating: From Jane Austen to Tinder* (London: Robinson, 2017); Martin Stempfhuber and Michael Liegl, "Intimacy Mobilized: Hook-Up Practices in the Location-Based Social Network *Grindr*," *Österreichische Zeitschrift für Soziologie* 41, no. 1 (March 2016): 51–70.

9   Steve Graham and Simon Marvin, *Splintering Urbanism: Networked Infrastructures, Technological Mobilities and the Urban Condition* (London: Routledge, 2001); Ash Amin, "Lively Infrastructure," *Theory, Culture & Society* 31, no. 7–8 (December 2014): 137–161.

10   Lauren Berlant, "Intimacy: A Special Issue", *Critical Inquiry* 24, no. 2 (Winter 1998): 281–288, 284; orig. emph.

observations obtained from the 'walkthrough method,'[11] I can extrapolate which demands these apps aim to fulfil for their coupled-up users and thus discuss couple apps as relationship infrastructures. These demands include closeness through time spent together, games, quizzes, or shared habits such as working out together. The app *Love Nudge* for example is described as a "habit-forming app that helps you intentionally express love in ways that are more meaningful to your partner."[12] It is important to note that the habits mentioned here are all carried out within the apps itself: daily posts or questions, sending pictures every morning, etc. In doing so, the apps promise their users to help time-proof their relationships. By making themselves out to be critical infrastructures for the couple, *Raft* (2016) wants users to "spend more time together and have things to look *forward* to," *Couply* asks them to "*Futureproof* your relationship," and *Lasting* promises to help them "Build a relationship that lasts for a lifetime"—all while simply using an app, ideally multiple times every day. The apps demand that users' behaviour be predictable, consistent, and stable. These traits are what the apps in turn make out to be the necessary foundation for a 'successful' or 'healthy' relationship—which shines a light on the fact that couple apps first and foremost facilitate a stable relationship between a user and their phone. Meanwhile, the marketing texts primarily stress the user-to-user connection they promise to be the interface and infrastructure for, i.e. "The purpose behind our app became *connection*."[13] The short advertorial text seems to emphasize how the relational interaction facilitated by couple apps is inherently multi-faceted. On a human-to-human level, the applications are aimed at "relationship making and maintenance."[14]

Structured on broad strokes, it can be said that couple apps address different types of relationship settings: couples who live together or at least in the same place, couples who are spatially distant, and couples who are spatially distant and must deal with vastly different time zones. *Without*, for example, "displays your partner's

---

11   This means "to systematically and forensically step through the various stages of app registration and entry, everyday use, and discontinuation of use." I specifically focused on the aspects of "vision," "operating model," and "governance" and documented my findings with screenshots and noted "mediator characteristics" such as copy and sound, interface arrangements, button designs, etc. (Ben Light, Jean Burgess, and Stefanie Duguay, "The Walkthrough Method: An Approach to the Study of Apps," *New Media & Society* 20, no. 3 (March 2018): 881–900, 891f.).

12   Moody Publishers Limited, *Love Nudge*, Apple App Store, Version 5.1.7 (2023). https://apps.apple.com/us/app/lovenudge/id495326842. Date accessed: September 2022.

13   Franklin Innovations LLC, *Kindu for Couples*, Apple App Store, Version 3.9.6 (2022). https://apps.apple.com/ie/app/kindu-for-couples/id346524753. Date accessed: October 2022.

14   Rikke Andreassen, Michael Nebeling Petersen, Katherine Harrison, Tobias Raun, eds., *Mediated Intimacies: Connectivities, Relationalities, and Proximities* (New York/London: Routledge, 2018).

neighbourhood and details like the weather."[15] Some couple apps ask their users to be online at the same time to parallelly stream a movie (i.e., *Kast* (2019) or *Tuned* (2021)) or answer sets of quiz questions about the relationship each day (*iPassion* (2015) or *Honi* (2017)).

Other apps fall under an app category that has been discussed in wider technological discourse as "teledildonics."[16] Their purpose is a corporeal connection, the simulation or triggering of touch and/or sexual pleasure through smartphone applications and additional 'hardware' in the form of "Hug Shirts," buzzing bracelets or sex toys that can be triggered by a partner touching their phone screen. In their default settings, many of these apps are very heteronormative, typically linking a male-female set of devices to each other, while those which allow one user to control the other's physical experience are less so. Especially with additional hardware, the couple apps as infrastructure are a prominent part of the relationship, and in this genre the implied relationship is less structured and tame than in the more management-oriented couple apps. Teledildonic couple apps are most obviously infrastructures for new forms of connection and social interaction. The mediated relationship created by and within the apps is typically somehow visualized or archived. This aspect is also essential for the apps' important narrative function: one of their innate effects is to become storages or albums of the relationship and thereby being infrastructures of the mediated versions of a relationship.

Aside from the physical connection, couples can choose from a wide range of infrastructural apps that organize their day-to-day and that specifically address the 'work' aspect of the relationship they imply: shared grocery lists, to-do-lists, calendars, photo storage spaces, and other purposes are common functions that promise to elevate some of the menial tasks that mandate human-to-human connection. These apps synchronize and linearize the relation by synchronizing content and screens. Their promise is that users through the apps' optimized time management will have more 'quality time' with each other once their everyday tasks are successfully completed. By using the app, these 'successes' can be tracked and are even rewarded. The gamification of relationship work and the workification of relationships are hence two central effects of the couple apps as relationship infrastructures. Naturally many couples use different means of communication, not least face-to-face. But within the realm of couple apps, there is no relationship

---

15   Pointless Technology LLC, *Without*, Apple App Store, Version 1.6.3 (2017). Appstore description available via: https ://appadvice.com/app/without-an-app-for-couples-who-like-each-other /868456885. Date accessed: May 2023.

16   Mitchell Hobbs, Stephen Owen, and Livia Gerber, "Liquid Love? Dating Apps, Sex, Relationships and the Digital Transformation of Intimacy," *Journal of Sociology* 53, no 2 (September 2016): 1–14; Sherry Turkle, *Alone Together: Why We Expect More from Technology and Less from Each Other* (New York: Basic Books, 2011).

outside of them; in fact, in the logic of the couple apps, there is no such relationship without them as infrastructure.

***

By taking a closer look at one of the genre's main players, I want to further explore and exemplify how couple apps "keep intimate relations together and bind them with more force while extending their spaces, shapes and rhythms."[17] *Between* was first released in 2011 by a South Korean Company (VCNC) and is available for all smartphone devices. Potential users are first addressed with the question "Are you currently in a relationship?," which is followed by the app's promise to help them "to communicate more lovingly and for storing precious memories easily."[18] The most obvious way this is realized is through the fact that all functions of the app can only be used when coupled with another device and a specific user. As an article in *The New Yorker* describes it, "You can have only one contact on Between—your significant other. If Facebook is a high-school reunion and Twitter is a cocktail party, Between is staying home with a boxed set and ordering pizza."[19] By coupling the apps to each other, the messenger or chat function becomes a two-way-street, which is its only distinctive feature as it is otherwise pretty standard with text, images and emojis. The app rewards repetitive, at least daily use. Notably, *Between* emphasizes the importance of dates—in a twofold sense: it encourages users to remember significant milestones, such as their first kiss or vacation, by putting the dates into the archive and adding images or other digital memorabilia to them. It also urges them to plan ahead and add future date nights to their shared calendar. Two things then happen automatically: firstly, the app calculates the duration until the event takes place: i.e. "27 days until Sushi night." And secondly, once the sushi night comes around, *Between* instantly turns the upcoming event into a memory. In the app's "story" tab all memories and past events are turned into a linear progression of memorable pictures and texts. The infrastructuring is thus ongoing, from planning and anticipation to storing and remembering. Additionally, the app actively creates a mediated version of the couple's history, thus in fact producing said relationship.

Any small thing becomes a milestone within the app's version of the relationship, including countdowns, push messages, congratulations etc. The app quite literally nestles itself *between* the users and creates a version of their relationship that

---

17   Paasonen, "Infrastructures of Intimacy," 107.

18   thingsflow, Inc., *Between*, Apple App Store, Version 1.3.1 (2023). https://apps.apple.com/de/app/between-the-app-couples-love/id458035189. Date accessed: May 2023.

19   Lauren Collins, "The Love App: Romance in the World's Most Wired City," *The New Yorker* (25 November 2013).

appears on the smartphones' screens. It is the infrastructure of user-device-app-relationships and users who want to be, and remain, coupled up through the app.

**

Couple Apps are therefore infrastructures through which a couple's relationship can be structured, reinforced, visualized, organized, remediated, archived, and shaped. Through these infrastructures respective devices and apps are related and synchronized, data is shared, and practices and habits are formed and repeated. Generally speaking, "infrastructures are largely responsible for the sense of stability of life in the developed world, the feeling that things work, and will go on working."[20] Couple apps promise and facilitate such stability – in fact, this is their main aim and user motivation. Through regular use, they keep both users in the relationship connected within the application, while being in turn kept relevant by their use. Generally, couple apps distinctly shape their users' behaviours towards their phones, the application, and each other. Users may transport their routines or specific needs into the app and shape it to fit their needs, but only within the limits of the apps' functionalities. As with all infrastructures, couple apps "exert a huge influence over economic and social activity and are hence distinctly political."[21] They not only transport ideological or culturally tinted content regarding 'successful' or 'good' relationships, but they shape user behaviour, value perception, and social interactions—making them relevant sights for media and cultural studies and a rethinking of infrastructures as a theoretical framework.

---

20   Paul N. Edwards, "Infrastructure and Modernity: Force, Time, and Social Organization in the History of Sociotechnical Systems," in *Modernity and Technology,* eds. Thomas J. Misa, Philip Brey, and Andrew Feenberg (Cambridge: MIT Press, 2003), 185–225, 189.
21   Warf, "Infrastructure," 259.

Infrastructures of Democracy: Lewinian Group Dynamics and the Management of Social Change (1930s-1940s)

Nora Binder

1. Introduction[1]

A conventional understanding of infrastructure conceives of it as "a broad range of systems and services that support or sustain the function of the economy and society, including roads, railways, utility grids, and telecommunication networks."[2] Contrary to a broader understanding that may also take into account language, media, standards, and the like as infrastructure shaping and shaped by our daily lives, this narrow definition highlights its material and technical aspects: Infrastructure is understood as "an ensemble of tangible institutions designed for the anonymous population at large and around which an everyday practice has established itself."[3] However, including the less tangible, and taking up AbdouMaliq Simone's notion of "people as infrastructure,"[4] in this article I explore an aspect of infrastructure ignored by a classical approach, namely infrastructures of sociality that are built and conceived not by technical but by social engineers. More particularly, I will consider the social configuration of the small group as explored by the social psychology of the 1930s and 1940s as an infrastructure of democracy.

In his seminal paper, Simone extends the notion of infrastructure to "people's activities" and the "economic collaboration" of the seemingly marginalized inhabitants in what appear to be the urban ruins of Johannesburg. By engaging with "complex combinations of objects, spaces, persons, and practices," Simone suggests, the resident's activities create "conjunctions" that turn into an infrastructure—"a

---

1   This paper draws on Nora Binder, *Kurt Lewin und die Psychologie des Feldes. Zur Genese der Gruppendynamik* (Tübingen: Mohr Siebeck, 2023 forthcoming).

2   Dirk van Laak, "Infrastructures," *Docupedia-Zeitgeschichte*, 20.05.2021: 2.

3   Van Laak, "Infrastructures," 5.

4   AbdouMaliq Simone, "People as Infrastructure: Intersecting Fragments in Johannesburg," *Public Culture* 16, no. 3 (2004): 407–429, 407.

platform providing and reproducing life in the city."[5] In this historiographic article on the invention of group dynamics by renowned German-Jewish social psychologist Kurt Lewin (1890–1947) during the 1930s and 1940s in the US,[6] I want to trace how the small face-to-face-group was made productive as a similar sort of infrastructure conjunction. Instigated by experimental techniques of social psychologists and characterized by the interactions of group members in specific settings, the small group was discovered as a means of establishing a "democratic" pattern of behaviour, as well as allowing for a genuinely "democratic" management of social change. The small group was found to be the perfect starting point for "re-educating human behaviour and social relationships"[7] in accordance with democratic values and can thus be qualified, as I argue, as an infrastructure of democracy.[8]

Recently, Jan-Werner Müller has pointed out the role of intermediary institutions—like political parties and the free press—as liberal democracy's critical infrastructure that assure that citizens can use their democratic rights and reach out to each other.[9] In the 1930s and against the backdrop of rising authoritarianism and the threat of Nazism, Lewin and his allies identified another dimension critical to a functioning democracy: the behavioural patterns of its citizens as displayed in daily interactions. Lewin had witnessed that democratic institutions alone were not able to guarantee the persistence of the Weimar Republic. Hence, after immigrating to the US, and fully in line with Deweyan thought prevailing there, he stressed that society should not be classified as democratic by only considering "isolated elements of conduct, rules or institutions." More importantly, Lewin's highly influential group

---

5   Simone, "People as Infrastructure," 408.

6   On the work of Lewin and his field-theoretical approach, cf. Binder, *Psychologie des Feldes*.

7   Leland Bradford, Jack R. Gibb, and Kenneth D. Benne, "Preface," in *T-Group Theory and Laboratory Method: Innovation in Re-education*, eds. Leland Bradford, Jack R. Gibb, and Kenneth D. Benne (New York: John Wiley & Sons, 1964): vii–x, vii.

8   The terms "democratic" and "autocratic" are adopted here, but are also clearly identified as designations employed by the historical actors. In retrospect, Lewin's students have been critical of their use of the terms, which seemed so "natural and appropriate" to them at the time. Decades later, the "colorless" terms of "role 1" and "role 2" appeared more scientifically correct to Lippitt and White than "democratic" and "autocratic" in order to describe the behavior of the group leader. However, the "vagueness" of the concepts "with so many different meanings attached to them, and so many values" had prompted them to find at least "one concrete meaning of democracy." Ralph K. White and Ronald Lippitt, *Autocracy and Democracy. An Experimental Inquiry* (New York: Harper, 1960): 8–12. Because of its conspicuous reference to democracy and its values, Nikolas Rose has convincingly called early social psychology a *Science of Democracy*, cf. Nikolas Rose, "Social Psychology as a Science of Democracy," in *Inventing Our Selves: Psychology, Power, and Personhood*, ed. Nikolas Rose (Cambridge: Cambridge University Press, 1998): 116–149.

9   Cf. Jan-Werner Müller, "Liberal Democracy's Critical Infrastructure. How to think about Intermediary Powers," *SCRIPT'S WORKING PAPER* 16 (2022): 3–24.

psychology, which led to the foundation of the *National Training Laboratories* in 1947, defined democracy by its corresponding "larger *pattern* of group life and the group *atmosphere*," concluding that "it is the actual *group dynamics* that counts."[10]

These critical dynamics of the "democratic group" were first explored by Lewin and his team in their famous Democracy Experiments (1936–1940). Conceptualized as an educational infrastructure of democracy, the "group setting" was found to lend itself particularly well to enabling and reproducing forms of what they termed "democratic" patterns of behaviour. Such crucial forms of "democratic interaction" like objective discussion, participative decision-making processes, and cooperative action could be experienced and practiced here. While the experiments found that autocracy could be imposed upon the group that adapted to it quickly, democratic behavioural patterns had to be actively learned "by a process of voluntary and responsible participation."[11] Furthermore, changes in perceptions, habits, or attitudes that were deemed necessary to the survival of democratic societies could be brought about especially well within the democratic group. In the spirit of a *science of democracy* (Rose), as a science in the service of democracy, Lewinian social psychology set out to efficiently steer and make resilient a democratic society at war.[12]

By carefully leading "democratic" groups, Lewin and his allies intended not only to bring about German re-education after the war and to ensure a resilient homefront during wartime, but also to reduce alcoholism and to alleviate intra- and inter-group conflicts in a US-American society still affected by the Great Depression and struggling with racial discrimination[13] Or, in Lewin's words: "There is no hope for creating a better world without a deeper scientific insight into the function of leadership, of culture, and of the other essentials of group life. Social life will have to be managed much more consciously than before if man shall not destroy man."[14] While Simone's study of "people as infrastructure" in inner-city Johannesburg seeks to point out the "unregulated encounters" and "the conjunction

---

10   Kurt Lewin, Ronald Lippitt, and Charles E.Hendry, "The Practicality of Democracy," in *Human Nature and Enduring Peace*, ed. Gardner Murphy (Boston: Houghton Mifflin, 1945): 295–347, here 302 f.

11   Cf. Kurt Lewin, "Cultural Reconstruction," *Journal of Abnormal and Social Psychology* 38, no. 2 (1943): 166–173, 169.

12   On the qualification of early social psychology as a science of democracy, see Rose, "Social Psychology as a Science of Democracy."

13   Cf. Kurt Lewin, *Resolving Social Conflicts: Selected Papers on Group Dynamics* (New York: Harper, 1948) and Kurt Lewin, "Forces Behind Food Habits and Methods of Change," in *The Problem of Changing Food Habits* (Washington D.C.: Bulletin of the National Research Council, 108, 1943), 35–65.

14   Kurt Lewin, "Psychology and the Process of Group Living," *The Journal of Social Psychology* 17 (1943): 113–131, 114.

of heterogenous activities" emanating from and bearing on "flexibly configured landscapes,"[15] early group psychology and the "educational technology"[16] of group dynamics were particularly influential proponents of democratic social engineering. Reaching its zenith between 1918 and 1947, and grounded in late 19th-century progressive education, pragmatic philosophy (both of which are exemplified in the works of John Dewey), and the emerging social sciences, democratic social engineers sought to reconcile social control and planning with the involvement and democratic participation of its subjects.[17] The need of elaborate forms of social steering seemed even more pressing to Lewin after World War II and the use of atomic bombs. If society wanted to win the race against "the destructive capacities set free by man's use of the natural sciences,"[18] the social sciences urgently needed to be applied to practical issues. Accordingly, the social sciences needed to start their own infrastructuring work to counterbalance the effects of the technical and military infrastructures from the realm of the natural sciences. In Lewin's eyes, it was a question of human survival.

2. The Democratic Group in the Laboratory

In its effort to preserve an efficient democracy and secure its robust functioning, Lewinian social psychology carried out pioneering work. In their influential Democracy Experiments (1936–1940) carried out with school children at the *Child Welfare Research Station* at the *University of Iowa*,[19] Lewin and his student Ronald Lippitt brought the social figuration of the group into the psychological laboratory for the first time and treated it as an object of experimental manipulation. Wholes such as the group and the complex relationships of the person to his/her environment—previously rejected as mysticism and banished from the laboratory by prevailing behaviourist ex-

---

15   Cf. Simone, "People as Infrastructure," 409.

16   Leland Bradford, Jack R. Gibb, and Kenneth D. Benne, "Two Educational Innovations," in *T-Group Theory and Laboratory Method. Innovation in Re-education*, eds. Leland Bradford, Jack R. Gibb, and Kenneth D. Benne (New York: John Wiley & Sons, 1964): 1–14, 1.

17   Cf. William Graebner, "The Small Group and Democratic Social Engineering, 1900–1950," *The Society for the Psychological Study of Social Issues* 42 (1986): 137–154.

18   Kurt Lewin, "Frontiers in Group Dynamics: Concept, Method and Reality in Social Science; Social Equilibria and Social Change," *Human Relations* 1 (1947): 5–41, 5.

19   On those groundbreaking experiments, see Kurt Lewin, "Preliminary Note," *Sociometry* 1, no 3 & 4 (1938): 292–300; Ronald Lippitt, *An Experimental Study of the Effect of Democratic and Authoritarian Group Atmospheres upon the Group and the Individual* (MA Thesis: Iowa City, 1938); Ronald Lippitt, "Field Theory and Experiment in Social Psychology: Autocratic and Democratic Group Atmospheres," *American Journal of Sociology* 45, no. 1 (1939): 26–49; and Ronald Lippitt, *An Analysis of Group Reaction to Three Types of Experimentally Created Social Climate* (PhD Thesis: Iowa City, 1940).

perimental social psychology, which held on to methodological individualism—were now elevated to the status of legitimate objects of investigation.[20] Only Lewin and his team made the sustained attempt to establish the group as an autonomous phenomenon that can't simply be investigated in terms of individual psychology, while simultaneously opening up the atmosphere and dynamics of the group as a field of intervention.

The small group was discovered as early as the late 1910s for democratic social engineering and conquered the social sciences in the 1930s.[21] It promised to be a genuinely democratic social figuration: As a "miniature society,"[22] as a mediation between the individual and society, between personal freedom and adaptation, the small group was predestined for decidedly democratic techniques of governing individuals *"in terms of their freedom"*—a form of government characteristic to liberal democracies.[23] In contrast to its predecessor in the history of ideas, the concept of the amorphous and irrational mass, the social figuration of the group opened up new possibilities of steering due to its supraindividual, but nevertheless manageable, social structure. Thus, not long after immigrating to the US, the Jewish psychologist evolved into one of the most important founding figures of social psychology. Laying the foundation of many emerging fields, including organization development and the new managerial approaches of the human relations movement, as well as processes of planned change, the infrastructure of the democratic group still resonates today, and its direct successors like the "team" are with us up until now.[24]

---

20   Cf. Floyd Henry Allport, *Social Psychology* (Boston: Houghton Mifflin Company, 1924). Allport's powerful formulation of experimental social psychology had subscribed to methodological individualism, according to which individual psychology provided the means to study social psychological phenomena. Consequently, it was not the group but the individual that was "real" and to be studied in experiment.

21   Cf. Graebner, "The Small Group and Democratic Social Engineering, 1900–1950," and Nikolas Rose, "Social Psychology as a Science of Democracy."

22   Bradford, Gibb, and Benne, "Two Educational Innovations," 1.

23   Cf. Nikolas Rose, "Introduction," in *Inventing Our Selves: Psychology, Power, and Personhood*, ed. Nikolas Rose (Cambridge: Cambridge University Press, 1998): 1–21, 16. Building on Foucault's studies in governmentality, Nikolas Rose showed how Lewinian group psychology sought for ways "[...] of making democracy operable through procedures that could govern the citizen in ways consonant with the ideals of liberty, equality, and legitimate power." Rose, "Social Psychology as a Science of Democracy," 118.

24   Following Burnes and Cooke, the original core components of OD are T-groups, action research and participative management. All have strong ties to the work of Lewin and his colleagues, cf. Bernard Burnes and Bill Cooke, "Review Article: The Past, Present and Future of Organization Development: Taking the Long View," *Human Relations* 65, no. 11 (2012), 1395–1429; Gilmore Crosby, *Planned Change: Why Kurt Lewin's Social Science is Still Best Practice for Business Results, Change Management, and Human Progress* (New York: Productivity Press, 2020); Klaus Antons and Monika Stützle-Hebel, *Feldkräfte im Hier und Jetzt. Antworten von Lewins Feldtheorie auf aktuelle Fragestellungen in Führung, Beratung und Therapie* (Heidelberg:

Starting in 1936, Lewin and Lippitt investigated the functioning of group life under experimental conditions. By leading two recreational groups of six school children, Lippitt sought to explore "democratic" and "autocratic" group dynamics. In
accordance with the holistic field-theoretical approach developed by Lewin since
the 1920s,[25] the children's group in the Democracy Experiments was considered "as
a whole, existing in a larger social field with many overlapping dynamic relationships."[26] It was not defined by the criterion of the similarity of its members, but,
according to the relational epistemology of Lewinian social psychology, by the criterion of the interdependence of its components. As with a Gestalt approach, each part
proved to be dependent on the other parts; if one part changed, the overall structure
changed accordingly.[27]

In the experiment, the members of each group came together for a 30-minute
session to make masks twice a week over a period of six weeks. Lippitt 'acted' as
the leader in both groups. In his dual role as experimenter and embodiment of the
leader, it was up to Lippitt to create two significantly distinct atmospheres in the
two children's groups through two different leadership styles—an autocratic and a
democratic one.[28] Depending on the atmosphere as stimulated by a specific leadership style, the group member's behavior varied strongly: In the "democratic" group
(D-group), the children's interactions were observed to be cooperative, objective,
friendly, motivated, and responsible; in the "autocratic" group (A-group), children
tended to be aggressive, less accessible to instructions from the leader, less independent in their work, and more competitive. In this group, there was also an incident
in which the children took out their pent-up aggression due to their own powerlessness vis-à-vis the autocratic leader on one child, who was treated as a scapegoat
and soon left the group during the series of experiments. The difference in atmosphere, the corresponding patterns of interaction, and the "relations of interdepen-

---

Carl-Auer Verlag, 2015); and Bernard Burnes, "Kurt Lewin and the Harwood Studies: The
Foundations of OD," *The Journal of Applied Behavioral Science* 43, no. 2 (2007): 213–231.

25   On Lewinian Field Theory, see Kurt Lewin, *Grundzüge der topologischen Psychologie*, eds. Ray-
mund Falk and Friedrich Winnefeld (Bern: Hans Huber, 1969 [1936]) and Binder, *Kurt Lewin
und die Psychologie des Feldes.*

26   Lippitt, "Field Theory and Experiment in Social Psychology," 27.

27   On the Berlin school of Gestalt Theory, see Mitchell G. Ash, *Gestalt Psychology in German Culture, 1890–1967: Holism and the Quest for Objectivity* (Cambridge: Cambridge University Press,
1995).

28   The sociotechnical set up of experimental groups and their respective pattern of human interrelations in the Lewinian laboratory rests not only upon the leadership, but also upon the
careful design of the group's environment: namely the stage and the props. Cf. Nora Binder, "Künstliche Fälle. Inszenierungen in der Sozialpsychologie Kurt Lewins," *Mittelweg* 36, no.
28/29 (2020): 68–91.

dence" (Interdependenzverhältnisse) in the children's groups were soon understood as their specific group dynamics.

Figure 1: Picture of the Club Setting.

Lippitt, *An Analysis of Group Reaction to Three Types of Experimentally Created Social Climate*, 26.

In the course of the experiment, the democratic group not only proved to be clearly superior in terms of the satisfaction of its members. Contrary to all concerns about the efficiency of a less directive guidance of children, the members of the democratic group were just as productive as the children in the autocratic group, and their masks were even strikingly creative in design. The children in this group were motivated and enjoyed their work, which they kept on doing even when the group leader left the room. On the contrary, the members of the "autocratic group" immediately stopped working on their masks when let alone. They even tended to destroy their work products, fully in line with the aggressive atmosphere observed there.

Having argued that the "democratic group" had been made productive by Lewinian social psychology as an infrastructure of democracy, an infrastructure in the broader sense—which transcends a classical definition concentrating on its technical and material features—I now want to raise the question of its workings as an educational infrastructure. What is this infrastructure of sociality made of? How does it operate? By what means does it form a specific conjunction providing, reproducing, and altering human behaviour and social relationships? In order to do this, I briefly turn to present definitions of infrastructure and show how the use and understanding of the small "democratic" group by Lewinian group dynamics relied on central features that are commonly associated with the workings of infrastructure, especially infrastructure's relationality or connectivity and its generativity.

3. The Democratic Group as Infrastructure

Current research on infrastructure agrees that "given the heterogeneous character of systems and institutions referenced by the term," it is difficult to provide a singular definition of infrastructure. "Perhaps," as Paul Edwards suggests, infrastructure "is best defined negatively, as those systems without which contemporary societies cannot function."[29] However, there is also agreement that infrastructures are the "connective tissues" and the "circulatory systems" of modernity.[30] As such, infrastructures continuously produce and structure social relations, enabling certain activities and inhibiting others. Meanwhile, they also display a double relationality: An infrastructure brings together various elements that form its internal multiplicity while simultaneously displaying "connective capacities *outwards*."[31] Finally, and unless they break down, infrastructures "reside in a naturalized background"[32]—their seamless functioning is taken for granted.

In what follows, I take up the above-mentioned characteristic traits—*relationality* and *generativity*—and see how they apply to the workings of the democratic group in Lewinian social psychology. I argue that in the case of Lewinian group dynamics it is the interplay of the group's relational features (the group as Gestalt as well as an interface between the individual and the larger social structure) and its generative capacity (regulating interactions within the group, reinforcing certain behavioural patterns, inhibiting others, re-adjusting the relationships of the individual group member to itself, to other members, and to a larger social context) that account for its exploitation as a powerful infrastructure of democracy from the 1930s on.

---

29   Paul N. Edwards, "Infrastructure and Modernity: Scales of Force, Time, and Social Organization in the History of Sociotechnical Systems," in *Modernity and Technology*, eds. Thomas J. Misa et al. (Cambridge: MIT Press, 2002), 185–225, 187.

30   Cf. Edwards, "Infrastructure and Modernity," 185.

31   Penelope Harvey et al. "Introduction: Infrastructural Complications," in *Infrastructures and Social Complexity: A Companion*, eds. Penelope Harvey et al. (London: Routledge, 2017), 1–22, 5.

32   Edwards, "Infrastructure and Modernity," 185.

Generativity: Democratic Re-education and Processes of Planned Change

In the Democracy Experiments the atmosphere and the existing group dynamics proved to be markedly relevant to action. They sustained and transformed the activities of children within it. As one episode during the first experiment showed, the atmosphere exerted a highly "contagious" effect on them, so that newcomers soon adapted to the prevailing dynamics. In order to study the conditions of political change, the experimental set up had planned that two children would switch from one group to the other during the course of the experiment. When Sarah went from the A-group to the D-group she was unaccustomed to the democratic group dynamics and a little irritated at first. However, Lewin soon realized that her behaviour "mirrored very quickly the atmosphere of the group."[33] No one had explicitly taught Sarah how to acquire a democratic attitude or how to display a democratic form of interaction. Rather, Lewin insisted, the change took place "*deeper* than the verbal level"[34]—it happened below the level of reflection by "the growing of the child into a cultural atmosphere."[35] Accordingly, the atmosphere and dynamics of the group were characterized by their affective and unconscious effects on the group members.[36] Despite being highly effective, the democratic atmosphere went largely unnoticed by Sarah and the other children.

The atmosphere's invisibility can be understood as an essential quality of infrastructure. Susan Leigh Star has stressed the fact that infrastructure is "part of the background for other kinds of work."[37] It is in line with this observation that group dynamics as an infrastructure hardly comes to light, though it deeply affects the acting, feeling, and thinking of subjects in it. Following Star, infrastructures often become visible upon breaking down or when they constitute a barrier to someone. The latter was true in the case of Sue, who was "transplanted" from the D-group to the A-group. She fundamentally disliked the restricted space of free movement in the autocratic atmosphere and decided to rebel against its leader.[38]

Lewinian social psychology profited from the atmosphere's contagious effect. Unlike propaganda or psychological methods, which address the person either in

---

33   Kurt Lewin, "Experiments in Social Space," in *Resolving Social Conflicts: Selected Papers on Group Dynamics*, ed. Gertrud Weiss Lewin (New York: Harper, 1948 [1939]), 71–83, 80.

34   Kurt Lewin, "The Special Case of Germany," in *Resolving Social Conflicts: Selected Papers on Group Dynamics*, ed. Gertrud Weiss Lewin (New York: Harper, 1948 [1943]), 43–55, 49 (emphasis mine).

35   Kurt Lewin, *Psychological Conditioning of Children* (Manuscript), Bentley Historical Library, ISR RCGD Director's Files, Box 26, 2.

36   Cf. Lewin, "The Special Case of Germany."

37   Susan Leigh Star, "The Ethnography of Infrastructure," *American Behavioral Scientist* 43, no. 3 (1999): 355–492, 380.

38   Cf. Lippitt, *An Experimental Study*, 93–95.

an anonymous or in a personal way as an individual, the sociotechnical procedures of group dynamics approach their experimental subjects as members of a democratic group, in a social situation. By addressing the individual as part of a "social field" of interpersonal relations, the techniques of group dynamics promised efficiency in two ways: On the one hand, the group approach benefited from the assumed enhancing effects within groups, in which the contagion logic of mass psychology found its continuation. In other words, the Democracy Experiments made an early use of group pressure. Lewin had observed that the standards and values of the group acquire an independent value, begin exerting a pressure of conformity, and in this way function as a central force field that keeps the individual "in line with the standards of the group."[39] Thus, not every single individual needed to be personally re-educated, the group's own pressure towards conformity would reinforce the change carefully planned and initiated by the group's leader. Or, as Lewin put it in 1943: "[I]t is easier to affect deeply the personality of 10 people if they can be melted into a group than to affect the personality of any one individual treated separately."[40]

On the other hand, the group method held out the prospect of rapid transformation: By addressing the individual person as a member of a small group, Lewinian social psychology hoped to reach and mobilize "large masses" in a short time.[41] Be it the re-education of Nazi Germany after the war or the nutrition education of American housewives during war time, it was through democratic leadership in small groups that altering patterns of behaviour were envisioned. Might not all of Nazi Germany be culturally reconstructed by reproducing democratic leaders? This model was proposed by Lewin in 1943 for his post-fascist former homeland: "It seems to be possible by training democratic leaders and leaders of leaders to build up a pyramid which could reach large masses relatively quickly."[42] Societies should be reformed from the bottom up, supported by many small leaders raising new leaders via the democratic group's educational infrastructure. Accordingly, the group was soon tapped by the Lewinians as a "cultural island," as an infrastructure of sociality in which behavioural changes could be brought about, instigated, and controlled particularly well and quickly.[43]

Finally, Lewinian experiments with democratic groups brought forth the notorious three-phase model of change that informs processes of planned change, even up until today.[44] It rests upon two distinct but interrelated features of the group that are

---

39   Lewin, "Frontiers in Group Dynamics," 14.

40   Kurt Lewin, "Psychology and the Process of Group Living," 113.

41   Cf. Kurt Lewin, "Cultural Reconstruction," *Journal of Abnormal and Social Psychology* 38, no. 2 (1943): 166–173, 172.

42   Lewin, "Cultural Reconstruction," 172.

43   Cf. Lewin, "Psychology and the Process of Group Living."

44   Cf. Bernard Burnes, "Kurt Lewin and the Planned Approach to Change: A Re-appraisal," *Journal of Management Studies* 41, no. 6 (2004): 977–1002.

crucial to its central and generative role in processes of planned change: The social figuration of the group can serve as an amplifier, and thus provide stability, while at the same time being in constant movement, an almost imperceptible but continuous transformation, a "quasi-stationary equilibrium" as Lewin called it, following Gestalt theorist Wolfgang Köhler.[45] If human interaction was to be successfully changed, Lewin's three step model of planned change prescribed the following field-theoretical procedures: The existing force field had to be loosened up by "(a) transferring a quasi-stationary equilibrium into a fluid situation; (b) changing the strength or direction of the forces so that a new level is reached where the intended processes result; (c) establishing circumstances which keep the constellation of forces at that new level. Otherwise, the group will not retain its new mold."[46] As this model makes clear, despite its democratic ethos and the participatory involvement of group members, the Lewinian management of change rests upon well-trained and experienced leaders. Group leaders are in charge of arranging the constellation of psychological forces in the field that are decisive for a successful procedure. Hence, the group remains a carefully planned infrastructure of democracy managed by the social engineer who is in charge of setting up a democratic atmosphere critical to processes of planned change.

Relationality: The Group as "Miniature Society" and Ecological Environment

The small face-to-face group is so prominent in the context of procedures of democratic social engineering not least because it promises to create new relations that are directed *outwards*, namely a specific relationship between the individual and society: As a "miniature society," the small face-to-face group was meant to serve as an interface between the micro- and the macro-levels of society. As the group dynamics pioneers of the *National Training Laboratories* recall:

> The founders of the first laboratory saw the group as the link between the individual person and the larger social structure. They saw the group, therefore, as a medium for serving two sets of interrelated functions: the re-education of the individual toward greater integrity, greater understanding of himself and of the social conditions of his life, greater behavioural planning and achieving changes

---

45   The concurrence of stability and continuous movement that characterizes the organization of the group as a social field may also count as an important characteristic of infrastructure in general, which only at first glance may appear solid and stable, but is instead continuously transforming, adapted, in decay, etc.

46   Kurt Lewin, "Constructs in Psychology and Psychological Ecology," in *Authority and Frustration. Studies in Topological and Vector Psychology III*, eds. Kurt Lewin, Charles E. Meyers, and Joan Kalhorn (Iowa City: Iowa University Press, 1944): 3–29, 20.

both in himself and in his social environment; and the facilitation of changes in the larger social structure upon which individual lives depend.[47]

Figure 2: *Classroom Interpersonal Relations of Club Members.*

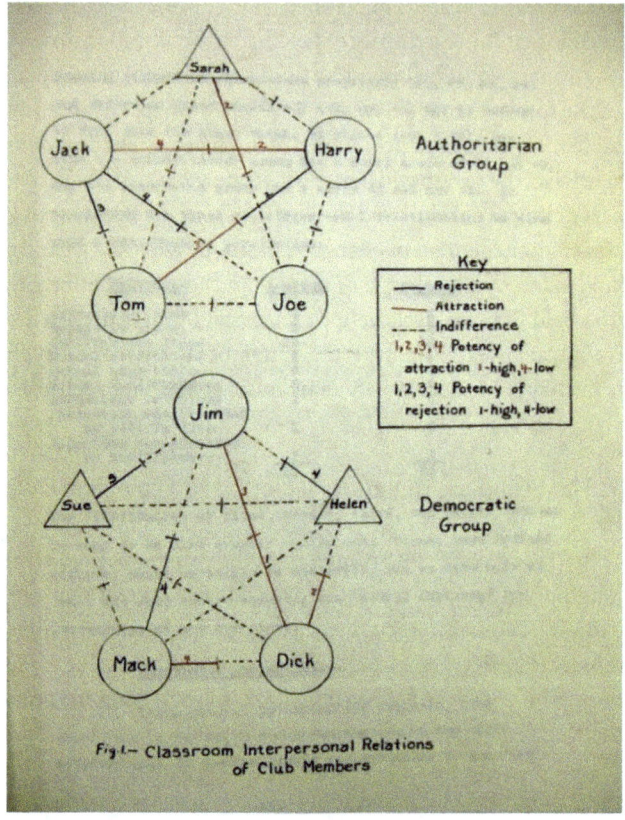

Lippitt, *Democratic and Authoritarian Group Atmospheres*, 28.

But more important still, the sociotechnically-built group creates new *internal* relationships between the group members and the leader. As a result, it produces a new and distinct holistic overall pattern of human interrelations (which Lippitt attempted to grasp with the means of sociometry, cf. Lippitt's diagram, Figure 2). Within Lewinian social psychology, the group is conceived of as a Gestalt, a structure or system of interdependent parts. This suprasummative feature of the experimental group—seized by the terms of "democratic" or "autocratic" atmosphere and

---

47   Bradford, Gibb, and Benne, "Two Educational Innovations," 5.

group dynamics—opened up new spaces for indirect democratic government. According to the prevailing group dynamics, the quality and structure of the human interrelations within the group differed strongly—either facilitating or exacerbating processes of planned change. In the laboratory, Lewin had discovered and explored the greater "openness" of the person in the "democratic" group. While an autocratic atmosphere tended to elicit resistance towards the leader, the democratic group fostered cooperation between its members and with the leader. Thus, integrating a person into a "democratic" group enabled the prospect of reaching the person's "deeper layers."[48] As a result, the group as a re-educational infrastructure was not only operating in a certain environment, but was itself conceived of as an ecological environment for the individual, a "social field."[49]

In order to "improve social practice in the spirit of science and democracy,"[50] Lewinian group dynamics subsequently linked the individual's acting, thinking, and feeling to the environment of the group. Lewin implemented what one could call an infrastructural regime of the self by closely intertwining the self and the social environment of the group. Contrary to the turn-of-the-century regime where the self related to itself in terms of an "autonomous subjectivity"[51] and in which the inner life was thought of as removed from outside influence, the subject of group dynamics is opened up and becomes interconnected. In the re-educational practices of group dynamics, the self and its inner reality get inextricably linked to the environment and to the mutual relations with other members of the group. The individual becomes an integral part in the Gestalt sense of the infrastructure of sociality named "group."

Shortly before Lewin's premature death, his attempt to explore the "democratic" group as an infrastructure for engineering social change culminated in the invention of the so-called Training-, or T-group. The T-group was formed and tested as an even more refined infrastructure of democracy, or more precisely, as a "basic method of laboratory learning about self, group, and interpersonal relations."[52] This powerful tool of "self-re-education" remains relevant today,[53] since the Training-group systemically links the relationship its members have to themselves and to the social world with the other group members' perception and reality. Having transferred the cybernetic concept of feedback from the realm of control engineering to the social sciences, *Macy Conferences* member Lewin devised a technique we have come to call

---

48   Lippitt, *Democratic and Authoritarian Group Atmospheres*, 209.

49   The group and its setting are explicitly named as a "social field" in Lewin, "Frontiers in Group Dynamics," 14.

50   Bradford, Gibb, and Benne, "Preface," vii.

51   Cf. Dominik Schrage, *Psychotechnik und Radiophonie. Subjektkonstruktionen in artifiziellen Wirklichkeiten 1918–1932* (Fink: München, 2001), 8.

52   Kenneth D. Benne, "The Process of Re-education. An Assessment of Kurt Lewin's Views," *Group & Organization Studies* 1, no. 1 (1976): 26–42, 30.

53   Benne, "The Process of Re-education," 30.

"feedback" as a means of communication in the T-group.[54] By implementing a process of giving and receiving feedback in groups, it seemed possible to align people's actions with the needs of the group or the prevailing group standards as instigated by a leader. The T-group was supposed to make people aware of how their behaviour affected others and how their behaviour was reflected by others, as well as to become better sensitized to human interrelations in general. By realizing the discrepancy between self-evaluation and the assessment from the group, the group members were prompted to adjust their conduct accordingly. It was through feedback from the environment that trainees were called to observe themselves continuously and to evaluate and optimize their own actions. This method of experiential learning has had a lasting impact, and has constituted intersubjectivity as an object for rational management, up until today. It marks the dawning of a "cybernetic anthropology" (Rieger) characterized by extensive mechanisms of self-reflexiveness and self-regulation ascribed to humans as its object.[55]

4. Concluding Remarks

After its heydays in the 1930s and 1940s, the small group continued to serve as an infrastructure of democracy beyond the 1950s. It was during the 1960s that the T-group came to use in Germany for the purposes of democratic self-re-education.[56] It was in the same decade that famous humanistic psychologist Carl Rogers qualified the intensive group experience as pioneered by Lewin and then flourishing in the United

---

54   Under the auspices of the Josiah Macy Jr. Foundation, the epoch-making Macy Conferences continued the cross-disciplinary collaboration started during World War II, and extended it into the Cold War era. With the help of such new terms like "information" and "feedback," an interdisciplinary group of physicists, mathematicians, psychologists, psychiatrists, anthropologists, sociologists, and engineers had begun in 1946 to discuss a universal theory of regulation and control. On the famous Macy Conferences, cf. Steve J. Heims, *The Cybernetics Group* (Cambridge: MIT Press, 1991) and Claus Pias (ed.), *Cybernetics: The Macy Conferences 1946–1953*, *Vol. 1 & 2* (Diaphanes: Zürich, 2004); on Feedback, cf. Ulrich Bröckling, "Über Feedback. Anatomie einer kommunikativen Schlüsseltechnologie," in *Die Transformation des Humanen. Beiträge zur Kulturgeschichte der Kybernetik*, eds. Michael Hagner and Erich Hörl (Frankfurt: Suhrkamp, 2008): 326–347.

55   Cf. Stefan Rieger, *Kybernetische Anthropologie. Eine Geschichte der Virtualität* (Suhrkamp: Frankfurt am Main, 2003).

56   Cf. Maik Tändler, "Therapeutische Vergemeinschaftung. Demokratisierung, Emanzipation und Emotionalisierung in der ‚Gruppe', 1963–1976," in *Das Selbst zwischen Anpassung und Befreiung. Psychowissen und Politik im 20. Jahrhundert*, eds. Maik Tändler and Uffa Jensen (Göttingen: Wallstein, 2012): 141–167.

States "as perhaps the most important social invention of this century."[57] But more and more the interest in the small group as a genuine infrastructure of democracy started to fade. Instead, with the T-group model as promulgated by the *National Training Laboratories* from the 1940s on, as well as with so-called encounter groups, the emphasis shifted from the urgent need of democratic social engineering prevalent during the 1930s and 1940s to an interest in personal growth and emotional expression in the 1960s. The same was true for the democratic leadership style that had come out of the Democracy Experiments: It began to lose its direct reference to democracy and became the model for a participatory leadership in industry instead that was meant to reconcile worker's satisfaction with industrial efficiency.

Back in the psychological laboratory, Lewin and Lippitt had discovered the small group as an infrastructure of democracy because small groups allowed for an indirect and participatory approach to elicit individual and social change. By playing an autocratic and a democratic leader, they created a specific connectivity between the group members as well as between the members and the leader. In the case of the democratic group, this newly established pattern of human interrelations was especially favourable to processes of planned change that could be enhanced via the group's standards and norms. The group leader did not have to state the objectives in a direct manner or lecture the group members on their purposefulness. Instead, the democratic group leader started a discussion, secured the participation and involvement of all group members, and steered the group's processes carefully in the right direction—always paying attention to the forces in the group's field and their wanted or unwanted effects. Meanwhile, the democratic group's friendly atmosphere, the cooperative and appreciative quality of its human interrelations, were crucial to the process of democratic re-education that took place on a less conscious and more affective level and profited from the "openness" of the democratic group's members. By creating a democratic pattern of human interrelations in groups that could be drawn upon in order to bring about behavioural change, Lewinian group dynamics explored the small group as a genuine infrastructure of democracy. Merely visible, the dynamics of the small democratic group—its affective atmosphere, the specific pattern of human relations—established new connections inwards and outwards, thus generating social, cultural, and individual change. A thoroughly relational concept, much like the concept of infrastructure,[58] the small group in the Lewinian Gestalt sense can indeed be understood as an infrastructure of sociality.

This specifically indirect form of social steering is one of the reasons why critiques were soon levied against Lewinian group psychology. Max Horkheimer, head of the Frankfurt School in exile, feared that the latter had given up on the idea that

---

57   Carl R. Rogers, "Interpersonal Relationships: U.S.A. 2000," *Journal of Applied Behavioral Science* 4, no. 3 (1968): 265–280.

58   Cf. Star, "The Ethnography of Infrastructure."

the subject played a role in history and suspected that he was merely aiming at manipulating individuals with the help of "psychological methods of administration."[59] After carrying out a successful change experiment with housewives in 1942, Lewin, too, felt compelled to state that their increased consumption of hitherto rejected innards was in no way the result of "manipulat[ing] the group by high-pressure sales talk."[60] Instead, he insisted, it was out of their own motivations that the housewives had decided to adjust their food habits to the potential rationing of meat while ensuring a continuous supply of protein by integrating entrails into their diet.[61]

Not surprisingly, group dynamic's afterlife took place less in the context of a genuinely democratic re-education than in the consulting industry and in organisation development. The small group and democratic leadership evolved into an infrastructure of participatory management. Democratic leadership, as it had emerged from the Democracy Experiments and was made fruitful for Action Research, gradually discarded the adjective "democratic" in the context of industrial psychology. In the famous management theory of Lewin's colleague and collaborator at the *Massachusetts Institute of Technology*—Douglas McGregor's classic *The Human Side of Enterprise* from 1960[62]—democratic leadership eventually merged into a participatory management style. Fully in line with the ideals of the human relations movement, it was supposed to perform its useful services in industry and business, promising to meet the challenge to both boost productivity and ensure worker satisfaction.

---

59   Max Horkheimer, "Letter to Theodor W. Adorno, November 24, 1944," in *Gesammelte Werke. Briefwechsel 1914–1948* (Bd. 17), eds. Alfred Schmidt and Gunzelin Schmid Noerr (Frankfurt am Main: Suhrkamp, 1996): 606–607.

60   Lewin, "Forces Behind Food Habits and Methods of Change," 63.

61   Cf. Lewin, "Forces Behind Food Habits and Methods of Change."

62   Cf. Douglas McGregor, *The Human Side of Enterprise* (New York: McGraw-Hill, 1960).

Conflicting Infrastructures: Ideological vs Social Infrastructures in Transmediterranean Communications of the Twelfth and Thirteenth Centuries

Daniel G. König

Infrastructures are not isolated phenomena that stand on their own. As organised, and maintained phenomena, which are routinely in use, infrastructures interact with their surroundings, generate activity, and consequently have an enormous impact on their environment, including other infrastructures. In the following pages, I would like to analyse the interplay of two infrastructures, one of which will be described as an "ideological," the other as a "social" infrastructure.

By "ideological infrastructure," I mean a frame of mind that is prevalent in a particular collective for a longer period of time and has a decisive impact on this collective by generating different kinds of activity, thus considerably affecting social relations maintained by the collective internally and externally. This frame of mind emerges from a set of interrelated ideas, which stabilise by acquiring a coherent compound form with systemic qualities and are then routinely diffused through propaganda and/or education. Constant repetition, albeit in different variants, ensures that this frame of mind becomes an integral part of collective thought and behaviour both in the activities and counter- reactions it generates.

By "social infrastructure," I mean a form of institutionalised, partly materialised form of human organization that enables a human collective to carry out certain activities within a particular environment. A social infrastructure can either emerge as a result of repeated, increasingly routinised interaction, or it can come into being thanks to a conscious agreement between groups of actors fulfilling a particular function to achieve a common objective. As soon as it is in place, a social infrastructure provides a social, normative, and often physical framework that is kept intact by regular affirmation, normative adjustment, and physical repairs or modifications. This framework provides stability and regular services, thus facilitating activities that are regarded as the infrastructure's objectives. These activities relate the social infrastructure to surrounding actors with whom it engages in routinised forms of interaction.

In this contribution, I will be dealing with the interaction of an ideological and a social infrastructure in the wider Mediterranean of the twelfth and thirteenth centuries. Both emerged around the same period and first coexisted side by side. Soon, however, both infrastructures clashed with each other and consequently obstructed and partly prevented the desired effect to be produced by each infrastructure respectively. The two infrastructures that stand in the spotlight here are the crusading ideology on the one hand, and the *fondaco* system on the other. Given that we are obviously dealing with two very different kinds of infrastructure, it makes sense to explain why both should be classified as "infrastructure" and how they fulfil the definitions given above before turning to an analysis of their interaction.

The Crusading Idea—an Ideological Infrastructure

The crusading idea can be described in terms of an ideological infrastructure, i.e. a set of interrelated convictions that were formulated, justified, legitimised, and propagated for several centuries by various members of the Latin-Christian clergy in Western Europe. Scholarship has long discussed the origins of this ideological infrastructure, which obviously clashes with the principally non-violent outlook of Christianity as formulated in the Gospels.

Carl Erdmann, who wrote the most influential monograph on this topic, led the origins of the crusading idea back to the fourth century, when the official toleration and promotion of Christianity by the Roman Empire put imperial means of coercion at the disposal of the organised church. According to Erdmann, the cooperation between Germanic warlords and the clergy in post-Roman Western Europe made the Latin-Christian church an integral part of emerging political and military power structures. During the many attacks on Western European societies between the seventh and the tenth centuries on the part of Muslims, Vikings, and Magyars, the Latin-Christian church began to condone acts of defensive violence, to bless weapons, and to pray for the victory of its flock against non-Christian enemies. In the course of the monastic reform of the tenth century, monasteries such as Cluny and various bishoprics in the Western Frankish realm drew on military aid to protect their possessions and flocks against rampant feudal warfare. Two important initiatives, the "armistice of God" (*treuga Dei*) and the "peace of God" (*pax Dei*), increasingly enlisted military support to protect civilians from looting, destruction, and killing. In particular, the reform papacy of the eleventh century increasingly interfered in local and regional conflicts, began to publicly support certain political parties, built up its own militia, and patronised certain military campaigns such as the Norman conquests of England (1066) and Sicily (1061–1091). From here, it was only a small step for the papacy to create and put itself at the head of a movement aimed at "liberating" Jerusalem from the hands of the "infidel," while diverting destabilising surplus military energy to the non-Christian exterior.[1] Between the late eleventh and the late thirteenth century, if not longer, members of the Latin-Christian clergy formulated, justified, and propagated the necessity of fighting Muslims, of possessing political control over Jerusalem and the so-called Holy Land, and of actively engaging in this fight to be granted the remission of one's sins.[2] As late as the fourteenth century, long after the last crusader stronghold of Acre had been lost in 1291, Latin-Christian thinkers still developed plans for the recovery of the Holy Land.[3]

Against this backdrop, we can claim that crusading ideology fulfils all criteria necessary to be defined as an infrastructure, i.e. an organised, routinised, and maintained phenomenon produced by humans that generates activity. Crusading ideology can be described in these terms as an increasingly organised set of human ideas that was continuously propagated and legitimised over a period of several centuries to make Christians of Western Europe take up arms against different perceived enemies of the faith. Its impact on European-Christian societies[4] and on the societies aggressed[5] was enormous and has repercussions until today.[6]

The *fondaco* System—A Social Infrastructure

The *fondaco* system, in turn, can be described as a social infrastructure of utmost importance for transmediterranean commercial exchange between Christian- and Muslim-ruled societies in the prime period of the crusading ideology, i.e. the twelfth and the thirteenth century.

The history of the *fondaco* goes back very far. Its terminological origins can be sought in ancient Greek inns housing travellers that were called *pandocheion* (πανδοχεῖον). The term retained this general meaning, when it became part of

---

1   Carl Erdmann, *The Origin of the Idea of Crusade*, trans. Walter A. Goffart and Marshall Whithed Baldwin (Princeton: Princeton University Press, 2019).

2   Penny J. Cole, *The Preaching the Crusades to the Holy Land, 1095–1270* (Cambridge: The Medieval Academy of America, 1991).

3   Thomas Ertl, "De Recuperatione Terrae Sanctae. Kreuzzugspläne nach 1291 zwischen Utopie und 'Useful Knowledge,'" in *Zukunft im Mittelalter. Zeitkonzepte und Planungsstrategien*, ed. Klaus Oschema and Bernd Schneidmüller (Ostfildern: Jan Thorbecke Verlag, 2021), 283–310.

4   Peter Feldbauer, ed., *Vom Mittelmeer zum Atlantik: Die mittelalterlichen Anfänge der europäischen Expansion* (Vienna: Verlag für Geschichte und Politik, 2001); Michael Mitterauer, *Why Europe? The Origins of its Special Path*, trans. Gerald Chapple (Chicago: University of Chicago Press, 2010).

5   Carole Hillenbrand, *The Crusades: Islamic Perspectives* (New York: Routledge, 1999); Daniel G. König, *Arabic-Islamic Views of the Latin West: Tracing the Emergence of Medieval Europe* (Oxford: Oxford University Press, 2015), 268–322.

6   Philippe Buc, *Holy War, Martyrdom, and Terror: Christianity, Violence, and the West* (Philadelphia: University of Pennsylvania Press, 2015).

the Arabic language in the wake of the Muslim takeover of Byzantine territory in the seventh century. Documented since the ninth century, the Arabic word *funduq*, etymologically derived from *pandocheion*, still means "hotel" today.[7] As part of transmediterranean commercial interaction between Christian-and Muslim-led societies in the wake of the first crusade (1096–1099), variants of the term first appeared in medieval Latin (*fondacum, fundacum, fundicus*) and Italo-Romance (*fondaco, alfondegam, fontega, fontego*) texts from the mid-twelfth century onwards.[8] In the course of transmediterranean Christian–Muslim interaction, the *fondaco* acquired particular organisational and institutional characteristics. During the twelfth and thirteenth centuries, *fondachi* evolved to become what Olivia Remie Constable called "colonies before colonialism," and eventually displayed a degree of complexity that allows us to speak of a *"fondaco* system."[9]

In this context, a *fondaco* represents a separate quarter in a Muslim-ruled port city, generally enclosed in walls, that was populated by European-Christian foreigners, most of them engaged in transmediterranean trade. As representatives of the larger Christian maritime trading powers, southern Europeans from Venice, Genoa, Pisa, and the Crown of Aragón were numerically dominant and often, e.g. in times of conflict between Pisa and Genoa, claimed a *fondaco* of their own. By treaty agreement with the local Muslim authorities, these European Christians were allowed to live in the *fondaco* according to their own legal norms. From a legal point of view, the *fondaco* thus constituted an extraterritorial space that, at a later stage of development, was headed by a consul as the legal representative of the respective foreign power responsible for the expatriate merchants and their relatives. The *fondaco* thus stands at the origins of our modern system of diplomatic missions abroad.[10]

The rights and obligations of these European Christians in their interaction with the port and customs authority (*al-dīwān*), the local Muslim merchant community, and interpreters serving as intermediaries were spelled out in detail in

---

7   Olivia Remie Constable, *Housing the Stranger in the Mediterranean World: Lodging, Trade, and Travel in Late Antiquity and the Middle Ages* (Cambridge: Cambridge University Press, 2003), 40–67.

8   Raja Tazi, *Arabismen im Deutschen. Lexikalische Transferenzen vom Arabischen ins Deutsche* (Berlin: de Gruyter, 1998), 232; Giovan Battista Pellegrini, *Gli arabismi nelle lingue neolatine con speciale riguardo all'Italia*, 2 vols (Brescia: Paideia Editrice, 1972), vol. 1, 105, 131, 345; vol. 2, 426.

9   Constable, *Housing the Stranger*, 107–157, 266–305.

10   Acknowledged by Friedrich F. Martens, *Das Consularwesen und die Consularjurisdiction im Orient* (Berlin: Weidmann, 1874), although with a strong paternalistic and Orientalist bias analysed by Andreas T. Müller, "Friedrich F. Martens on 'The Office of Consul and Consular Jurisdiction in the East,'" *European Journal of International Law* 25, no. 3 (2014): 871–891. Modern studies of the consulate often tend to ignore the medieval transmediterranean background of this institution, cf. Ferry de Goey, "History of the Consular Institution" in *Consuls and the Institutions of Global Capitalism, 1793–1914* (London: Pickering & Chatto, 2014), 15–16.

various treaties concluded since the middle of the twelfth century between Pisa, Genoa, Venice, the Crown of Aragón, and various Muslim authorities in southern Mediterranean port cities. The legal status of these merchant enclaves was thus repeatedly explained, continuously reformulated, and legally re-enacted in these treaties until it reached a standardised form with few variants, thus pointing to a process of institutionalisation.[11]

Against this backdrop, we can claim that the Mediterranean *fondaco* of the twelfth and thirteenth centuries fulfils all criteria of a social infrastructure. It provided accommodation, a social setting, a legal framework, and protection for European-Christian merchants engaging in transmediterranean trade. Its institutional characteristics were routinely spelled out in dozens of Christian–Muslim treaties concluded in this period. By the thirteenth century, it had become part of the regular facilities of Muslim-ruled port cities in the southern Mediterranean. Enabling foreign European Christian and local Muslim merchants to engage in commercial transactions and to secure their rights in case of conflict, the *fondaco* represented a pillar of transmediterranean trade. It contributed significantly to the latter's intensification as well as to significant processes of cultural exchange between the northern and the southern borders of the Mediterranean.

Two Infrastructures—Co-existing and Interrelated

It does not seem surprising that the crusading idea—a high-impact ideological infrastructure that militarised transmediterranean relations for centuries—eventually clashed with the *fondaco* system—a high-impact social infrastructure facilitating and regularising peaceful commercial relations between Christian and Muslims on both sides of the Mediterranean. We should consider, however, that both infrastructures co-existed side by side for long periods and may have also been interrelated in different ways.

Since the early crusading campaigns only targeted the region of greater Syria, commercial relations maintained by European-Christian merchants in Egyptian Alexandria or in Tunis were not automatically affected by the crusades. Although we can see occasional repercussions, e.g. when Fāṭimid authorities in Egypt accused Pisan merchants coming from one of the crusader strongholds of bringing along

---

11   Dominique Valérian, "Les fondouks, instruments du contrôle sultanien sur les marchands étrangers dans les ports musulmans (XIIᵉ–XVᵉ siècle)?" in: *La mobilité des personnes en Méditerranée de l'Antiquité à l'époque moderne: procédures de contrôle et documents d'identifications*, ed. Claudia Moatti (Rome: École française de Rome, 2004), 677–698.

spies in 1154,[12] we can acknowledge that crusading campaigns and the *fondaco* system could exist side by side as long as they were separated geographically.

Considering that the systematic establishment of European-Christian merchant enclaves with a special legal status in many Muslim-ruled port cities of the southern Mediterranean only began in the wake of the first crusade, we should ask ourselves, however, whether the crusades as such could have given a decisive input to the emergence of the institutionalised *fondaco*-system.[13] Spaces accommodating foreign merchants predated the crusades by centuries, of course, and European-Christian merchants from maritime polities had already participated in transmediterranean commerce long before the crusades.[14] The Italian maritime city of Amalfi, in particular, is said to have maintained rudimentary institutions to accommodate its merchants in North Africa and Palestine already before the crusades.[15] It is interesting to note, however, that the first treaty spelling out rights for European-Christian merchants similar to the rights and privileges listed in Christian–Muslim commercial treaties concluded in series from the mid-twelfth century onwards, hails from a crusader context. The so-called *Pactum Warmundi*, an agreement concluded between the Venetians and the patriarch of Jerusalem in 1123, i.e. in the wake of the first crusade, granted specific rights and privileges to the Venetians, including the right to reside in an enclosed quarter of a city and legal autonomy.[16] If the crusades actually gave rise to the idea of institutionalising and diffusing a particular enclave-like form of commercial and social integration

---

12   Michele Amari, *I Diplomi Arabi del R. Archivio Fiorentino* (Florence: Felice Le Monnier,1863), seconda serie, doc. II, 241–245.

13   Constable, *Housing the Stranger*, 111.

14   Michael McCormick, *Origins of the European Economy* (Cambridge: Cambridge University Press, 2001); Barbara Kreutz, *Before the Normans: Southern Italy in the Ninth and Tenth Centuries* (Philadelphia: University of Pennsylvania Press, 1996), 75–93; Peter Feldbauer and John Morrissey, *Weltmacht mit Ruder und Segel. Geschichte der Republik Venedig* (Essen: Magnus Verlag, 2004), 45–114; Romney David Smith, "Calamity and Transition: Re-Imagining Italian Trade in the Eleventh-Century Mediterranean," *Past and Present* 228 (2015): 15–56.

15   John Morrissey, *Amalfi. Moderne im Mittelalter* (Vienna: Mandelbaum, 2019), 83–158; Armand O. Citarella, "The Relations of Amalfi with the Arab World before the Crusades," *Speculum* 42, no. 2 (1967): 299–312; David Jacoby, "Amalfi nell'XI secolo: commercio e navigazione nei documenti della Ghenizà del Cairo," *Rassegna del Centro di Cultura e Storia Amalfitana Ser. NS* 18, no. 36 (2008): 81–90; Kreutz, *Before the Normans*, 75–93; Constable, *Housing the Stranger*, 113–114.

16   Hans Eberhard Mayer and Jean Richard, eds., *Die Urkunden der lateinischen Könige von Jerusalem, Teil 3*, (Hanover: Hahn, 2010), doc. 764, 1333–1336; William of Tyre, *A History of the Deeds Done Beyond the Sea*, trans. Emily Atwater Babcock (New York: Columbia University Press, 1943), vol. 1, 552–556. The Genoese received similar privileges in Antioch, Jerusalem, and Yaffa. See Carlo Baudi di Vesme, ed., *Liber iurium reipublicae Genuensis* (Augsburg: Regium Typographeum, 1854), vol. I, doc. VIII–IX, 16–17.

into a host society, then one could claim that the crusading idea as an ideological infrastructure actually inspired and thus contributed to the creation of the *fondaco* system as a particular social infrastructure of European-Christian expansionism. This, however, would need further investigation and is not the main issue in an essay investigating the clash of these two infrastructures.

Clash—The Intricacies of Infrastructural Conflict

Turning to this clash, one would suppose that it is possible to distinguish between two different groups of actors supporting the one or the other infrastructure: highly ideological clergy and fighters infused with crusading ideology on the one hand, and more pragmatic, profit-seeking European-Christian and Muslim merchants on the other. That such a bipolar constellation existed could be implied by the many papal calls for commercial boycotts. Issued from the thirteenth century onwards with the aim of preventing the export of strategic material to Muslim polities fighting the crusaders, trade embargos were regularly ignored by different commercial actors.[17]

The example of Genoa shows, however, that the lines between proponents of aggression and proponents of commerce cannot be drawn so clearly if a maritime polity was engaged both in crusading campaigns and in transmediterranean trade. The "Annals of Genoa" (*Annales Ianuenses*) give insight into Genoa's fluctuating enthusiasm for the crusading movement. Its earliest author, Caffaro (d. 1166), presented the Genoese as one of the mainstays of the first crusade without whom Jerusalem would not have been conquered in 1099. Until around the middle of the twelfth century, his tone remains aggressively anti-Muslim. When the "Annals of Genoa" record the first Genoese trading agreement with the Almohads in 1154, the tone changes radically. From this point, Genoese ships are depicted as regularly calling and arriving from North African ports with merchandise. For several decades at least, Genoa's

---

17   Sophia Menache, "Papal attempts at a Commercial Boycott of the Muslims in the Crusader Period," *The Journal of Ecclesiastical History* 63 (2012): 236–259; Arnold Esch, "Der Handel zwischen Christen und Muslimen im Mittelmeer-Raum. Verstöße gegen das päpstliche Embargo geschildert in den Gesuchen an die Apostolische Pönitentiarie (1439–1483)," *Quellen und Forschungen aus italienischen Archiven und Bibliotheken* 92 (2012): 85–140; Stefan K. Stantchev, *Spiritual Rationality: Papal Embargo as Cultural Practice* (Oxford: Oxford University Press, 2014); Georg Christ, "Kreuzzug und Seeherrschaft. Clemens V., Venedig und das Handelsembargo von 1308," in *Maritimes Mittelalter. Meere als Kommunikationsräume*, eds. Michael Borgolte and Nikolas Jaspert (Ostfildern: Jan Thorbecke Verlag, 2016), 261–280; Mike Carr, "Policing the Sea: Enforcing the Papal Embargo on Trade with 'Infidels,'" in *Merchants, Pirates, and Smugglers. Criminalization, Economics, and the Transformation of the Maritime World (1200–1600)*, eds. Thomas Heebøll-Holm, Philipp Höhn, and Gregor Rohmann (Frankfurt am Main: Campus, 2019), 329–342.

commercial rival Pisa, not the Muslims, are depicted as the commune's main enemy.[18]

While trading with Muslim port cities in North Africa, the Genoese commune also supported crusading ventures, especially if they were undertaken by the French crown. In February 1190, it signed a contract to transport the French king and his knights to the East on the Third Crusade (1189–1192),[19] avoided all trade with Egypt during the Fifth Crusade (1219–1221) in line with papal demands,[20] and transported Louis IX (r. 1226–1270) from Egypt to Acre when he was released from captivity after his failed crusade against Egypt (1248–1250).[21] Louis's next crusade was eventually directed against the thriving commercial city of Tunis.[22] This created a highly awkward situation: the narrative given in the "Annals of Genoa" attests to the contradictory attitudes held by the Genoese when confronted with a crusading enterprise directed against a city, with which trade amounted to about fifteen percent of Genoa's overall overseas commerce in 1252–1253.[23]

In 1267, Louis IX had already announced his intention of going on crusade and had asked Genoa to make peace with Venice as not to imperil the crusading campaign.[24] In 1269, Louis then rented several ships from the commune of Genoa.[25] When the crusade finally set out to Tunis, the crusading force is said to have incorporated

> over ten thousand Genoese with fifty-five two-deckers (...), and the royal ships were also manned by Genoese. Because there were so many of them, they elected the nobles Ansaldus Auria and Philippus Cavarunchus from among them as consuls, who were to be their rulers and judges until the Genoese community provided them with a leader.[26]

---

18   Luigi Tommaso Belgrano, ed., *Annali Genovesi di Caffaro / Annales Ianuenses* (Genoa: Istituto Sordo-Muti, 1890), vol. 1, a. 1154, 40.

19   Merav Mack, "Genoa and the Crusades," in *A Companion to Medieval Genoa*, ed. Caroline Beneš (Leiden: Brill, 2018): 471–495, 482–484.

20   Mack, "Genoa and the Crusades," 487.

21   Cesare Imperiale di Sant'Angelo, ed., *Annali Genovesi / Annales Ianuenses*, vol. 3 (Fonti per la storia d'Italia 13): 1225–1250 (Rome: Tipografia del Senato, 1923), a. 1249, 187.

22   On the crusade, see Michael Lower, *The Tunis Crusade of 1270: A Mediterranean History* (Oxford: Oxford University Press, 2018).

23   Stephen A. Epstein, *Genoa and the Genoese, 958–1528* (Chapel Hill: University of North Carolina Press, 1996), 142–143.

24   Cesare Imperiale di Sant'Angelo, ed., *Annali Genovesi / Annales Ianuenses*, vol. 4 (Fonti per la storia d'Italia 14): 1251–1279 (Rome: Tipografia del Senato, 1926), a. 1267, p. 102.

25   Cesare Imperiale di Sant'Angelo, ed., *Annales Ianuenses*, vol. 4, a. 1269, 113–114.

26   Cesare Imperiale di Sant'Angelo, ed., *Annales Ianuenses*, vol. 4, a. 1270, 131–132.

When the crusading army arrived on the coast,

> Genoese merchants, who had already come there earlier with goods and were staying there without knowing anything about the imminent arrival of the army, were taken prisoner by order of the king of Tunis [i.e. the Ḥafṣid sultan al-Mustanṣir (r. 647–675/1249–1277)]. They were kept in a beautiful palace by royal order, so that they would not be harmed by anyone. The king did not want to offend these merchants, but to protect them, because he was of the opinion that the army had not come to Tunis according to the advice of the Genoese, but according to that of others.[27]

The Genoese accompanying the French king, however, proved to be full of crusading zeal and were among the first to attack the Muslim defenders:

> The Genoese landed with flying colours and immediately set about storming the fortress of Carthage. (...) When the Catalans and Provencals, who were still on the ships, saw this, they too landed in haste and came over. But before they arrived, the Genoese had stormed and taken the fortress. They had so battered the Saracens with ballistae and lances that the latter, unable to resist, turned to flee, whereupon they climbed the walls and planted the Genoese flag there.[28]

Although the commune of Genoa had rented its ships to the French king and had manned some of the ships while "over ten thousand Genoese with fifty-five two-deckers" participated in the campaign, the commune allegedly did not know the crusade's destination. The annals claim that only

> through the transport ships, which went back and forth to bring provisions, weapons, and other necessities, it was learned in Genoa, to general astonishment and regret, that the fleet had sailed to Tunis. For it was the general wish of all sensible men that the army of the king and of those marked with the cross should sail over for the protection of the Holy Land, and for the recovery of the Holy Sepulchre, which the Saracens had insolently taken possession of, to the shame of the Christians, to whom it belonged by hereditary right. And for this reason they were displeased, because not only the wiser ones, but everyone saw that the army in Tunis could do nothing, or as much as nothing, and accomplish nothing praiseworthy, as later results also showed.[29]

---

27   Cesare Imperiale di Sant'Angelo, ed., *Annales Ianuenses*, vol. 4, a. 1270, 132.
28   Cesare Imperiale di Sant'Angelo, ed., *Annales Ianuenses*, vol. 4, a. 1270, 133.
29   Cesare Imperiale di Sant'Angelo, ed., *Annales Ianuenses*, vol. 4, a. 1270, 133.

This, however, did not deter the commune from participating in the matter:

> Since the municipality of Genoa took into consideration that there were a lot of Genoese in this army and did not want to disregard the welfare of their own, they chose the noble Franceschinus de Camilla and sent him with an armed ship to Tunis as the head of all Genoese in the army, so that he should govern them justly. He arrived at his destination on 7 September.[30]

After the French king's death during the campaign, a peace treaty was negotiated, in which the Ḥafṣid sultan of Tunis promised to pay back certain sums to the Genoese.[31]

To summarise: the commune had agreed to provide transport to the French crusaders, allegedly believing that the crusading force would head to the eastern Mediterranean. In fact, Louis IX is said to have kept the final destination of the crusade secret until a few days before the fleet set out for Tunis, at least according to some sources.[32] Arrived in Tunis, however, masses of Genoese fighters participated zealously in the attack on the Ḥafṣid defences while the Ḥafṣid sultan of Tunis had all Genoese merchants residing in the city confined but treated honourably. When informed about the crusade's true destination, the communal elite in Genoa deplored the attack on Tunis, but immediately sent a person to administrate the Genoese forces. Simultaneously, the commune seems to have participated actively in peace talks. The peace treaty of 1270 contains many elements already known from earlier commercial treaties and thus shows that certain members of the crusading camp were making a conscious effort to return to the pre-crusade status quo in terms of commercial relations with Tunis.[33] Notwithstanding this, Genoa never seems to have returned to this status quo. In the 1260s, it had already begun to focus more and more on Black Sea trade, to the effect that Genoese trade with Tunis does not seem to have resumed after 1270.[34] This may have to do with the fact that the

---

30   Cesare Imperiale di Sant'Angelo, ed., *Annales Ianuenses*, vol. 4, a. 1270, 134.

31   Cesare Imperiale di Sant'Angelo, ed., *Annales Ianuenses*, vol. 4, a. 1270, 135: "Ianuensibus nero illas, quas eisdem debebat, peccunie quantitates ad certum terminum se soluturum spopondit."

32   Lower, *The Tunis Crusade*, 98, 107.

33   Cf. Antoine-Isaac Silvestre de Sacy, ed., "Le Traité de Paix entre le Roi de Tunis et Philippe-le-Hardi 1270," in *Histoire et mémoires de l'Institut royal de France* 9 (1831), 467–471; Louis de Mas Latrie, *Traités de paix et de commerce et documents divers concernant les relations des Chrétiens avec les Arabes de l'Afrique septentrionale au Moyen Âge*, vol. 2 (Paris: Henri Plon, 1872), 93–96; with Louis de Mas Latrie, ed., *Traité de Commerce conclu pour Dix Ans entre Tunis et la République de Gênes 1250*, *Traités de Paix et de Commerce*, vol. 2, 118–121.

34   Epstein, *Genoa and the Genoese*, 142–143.

crusade significantly strengthened the influence of Charles I of Anjou, king of Sicily (r. 1266–1285), on Tunis.[35]

Conclusion

Genoa in 1270 was a city torn between its citizens' crusading zeal on the one hand and their long-standing commercial relations and interests on the other. Between 1250, when Genoa concluded a ten-year peace treaty with Tunis and fifteen percent of its overseas trade involved commerce with this city, and the late 1260s, trading relations with Tunis might have deteriorated to such a degree as to make an attack on Tunis attractive. According to the North African historiographer, Ibn Ḫaldūn (d. 808/1406), European-Christian merchants—and why not Genoese?—had actually instigated the French king to attack the city, allegedly because a Ḥafṣid functionary owed them money and their complaints at the sultan's court had gone unheard.[36] Thus, it may seem too simple to explain the situation of Genoa in 1270 as a clash between crusading ideology and the *fondaco* system, i.e. as a clash between an ideological and a social infrastructure.

It is clear, nonetheless, that Genoa would have never assumed its awkward role in 1270 had it not been an active supporter of both infrastructures. Had it kept aloof of the crusading movement—hardly possible for a city in the Latin West of this period that had brought forward important proponents of the crusading movement such as pope Innocent IV (sed. 1243–1254)—it would have never participated in the attack on Tunis. Had it not invested into the *fondaco* system in and beyond Tunis, its merchants would not have been confined in the city while their compatriots were fighting Muslims on the coast. Two infrastructures and related systems of conduct stood in opposition to each other and were bound to clash at some point in the twelfth- or thirteenth-century Mediterranean. War, with its respective ideological backdrops, has always and will always be a danger to the organisational structures facilitating the flow of goods and people. In this sense, the Genoese predicament of 1270 is not really original. But it can inspire us to think about other instances in which co-existing and interrelated infrastructures clash with or obstruct each other.

35   On this, see the old but still valuable monographs: Georg Caro, *Genua und die Mächte am Mittelmeer 1257–1311. Ein Beitrag zur Geschichte des 13. Jahrhunderts*, vol. 1 (Halle: Max Niemeyer, 1896), 142–382, on Genoa's complex relationship to Charles of Anjou; and Richard Sternfeld, *Ludwigs des Heiligen Kreuzzug nach Tunis und die Politik Karls I. von Sizilien* (Berlin: E. Ebering, 1896), on the role played by Charles of Anjou in this crusade.

36   Ibn Ḫaldūn, *Tārīḫ*, ed. Suhayl Zakkār and Ḫalīl Šaḥāda, 8 vols (Beirut: Dār al-Fikr, 2000–2001), vol. 6, 425–426; Daniel G. König, "1270: Ibn Ḫaldūn über das Vorspiel zum tunesischen Kreuzzug Ludwigs IX.," *Transmediterrane Geschichte* 2, no.1 (2020), DOI: https://doi.org/10.18148/tmh/2020.2.1.27.

Section IV: Infrastructures and Religion

Spiritual Infrastructures

Thomas G. Kirsch

In his recent, posthumously published book *The New Science of the Enchanted Universe: An Anthropology of Most of Humanity*, renowned anthropologist Marshall Sahlins states that "the condition of humanity for the greater part of its history and the majority of its society" has been one in which people are "surrounded by a host of spiritual beings [...] (which) are immanent in human existence," determining almost every aspect their fate.[1] He calls on scholars to explore how these "immanentist societies are actually organized and function in their own cultural terms, their own concepts of what there is, and not as matters 'really are' in our native scheme of things."[2]

Perhaps not surprisingly, one of the fields of inquiry where this perspective has hitherto been notably absent is the study of infrastructure. One can only speculate why this is so. It may be that the technically oriented Modernism associated with much of what 'classical' infrastructure research is focused on—such as roads, railways, and telecommunication systems—as well as the 'dogmatically secularistic' outlook of those pursuing it, has engendered this specific blind spot.[3] Infrastructure scholars are not alone with the latter. As Dipesh Chakrabarty has famously argued, historians "will grant the supernatural a place in somebody's belief system or ritual practices, but to ascribe to it any real agency in historical events will be to go against the rules of evidence that gives historical discourse procedures for settling disputes about the past".[4] As a consequence, according to him, "the historian, as historian [...], cannot invoke the supernatural in explaining/describing an event".[5]

---

1   Marshall Sahlins, *The New Science of the Enchanted Universe: An Anthropology of Most of Humanity* (Princeton: Princeton University Press, 2022), 2.
2   Sahlins, *The New Science of the Enchanted Universe*, 3.
3   For the notion of "dogmatic secularism," see Luke Clossey et al., "The Unbelieved and Historians, Part I: A Challenge," *History Compass* 14 (2016): 594–602.
4   Dipesh Chakrabarty, *Provincializing Europe: Postcolonial Thought and Historical Difference* (Princeton: Princeton University Press, 2000), 104.
5   Chakrabarty, *Provincializing Europe*, 106.

By contrast, starting with Edward E. Evans-Pritchard's *Witchcraft, Oracles and Magic among the Azande*,[6] anthropology has long been interested in investigating the ways in which local understandings of the agency of spiritual beings inform people's practices in the world, giving rise to concepts such as "socio-spiritual communities," that is, "religious communities constituted by human beings and their interactions with spiritual entities."[7]

In this article, I take inspiration from Sahlins' plea to study immanentist societies in their own cultural terms so as to rethink infrastructures from a decisively non-secular vantage point. More particularly, I take the case of Pentecostalism to argue that what is required is to go beyond the focus on *religious* infrastructures, that is, the idea of human-made (secular) infrastructures that serve people's religious aspirations, such as pilgrimage infrastructures. Instead, I aim at developing some preliminary thoughts on what I call *spiritual* infrastructures, which means perceiving the agency of spiritual entities *as* infrastructures.

I do so with a view to Pentecostalism as practiced in a specific region of Africa (Zambia). It remains to be seen whether my findings are also valid for Pentecostals in other parts of the world and/or other religious traditions that build on the immanent agency of spiritual entities. Nonetheless, this article hopes to draw attention to the existence of an infrastructural sphere of life that commonly goes unnoticed in academia yet is pertinent to how religious practitioners throughout the world forge relationships among themselves and with the spiritual domain. In the concluding section, I will contemplate possible wider conclusions from this observation.

Counting the Holy Spirit In

In 1985, the then-president of the African Spiritual Churches Association, Nbumiso Ngada, published a booklet entitled *Speaking for Ourselves* in which he notes, with regard to African-initiated churches: "Anthropologists, sociologists and theologians from foreign churches have been studying us for many years and they have published a whole library of books and articles about us [...] The view from outside [...] tends to distort the picture and to prevent the outsider from seeing the real point about what we believe and what we are doing."[8] But most importantly, Ngada gives his argument a special twist in also pointing out that "there is one enormous omission

---

6   Edward E. Evans-Pritchard, *Witchcraft, Oracles and Magic Among the Azande* (Oxford: Oxford University Press, 1937).

7   Thomas G. Kirsch, "Intangible Motion: Notes on the Morphology and Mobility of the Holy Spirit," in *The Social Life of Spirits*, eds. Ruy L. Blanes and Diana E. Santo (Chicago: University of Chicago Press, 2013): 33–51, 34.

8   Nbumiso Ngada, *Speaking for Ourselves* (Braamfontein: Institute for Contextual Theology, 1985), 5.

throughout the whole history that has been written by outsiders. The work of the Holy Spirit throughout our history has simply been left out. The events of our history have been recorded as if everything could be accounted for simply by sociology and anthropology [...] We would like to write our own history from the point of view of the Holy Spirit."[9]

Written from an agnostic point of view, this article is more modest than Ngada's manifest of a postcolonial-cum-spiritual theology. I ask what happens to conventional scholarly views on religious infrastructures in Pentecostalism when we bring the religious practitioners' perceptions of and (embodied) experiences with the Holy Spirit into the equation. To do so, I draw on my ethnographic fieldwork in Zambia (1993–2023), where I was given the following account of the events leading to a co-production of road infrastructure and religious sociality.

In the early 1950s, when Bishop Rabson of the Spirit Apostolic Church (SAC), a small church of the Pentecostal-Charismatic type, was a child, he and his parents lived in the rugged hills of the escarpment between the Central African Plateau and the Gwembe Valley. At that time, access to the Valley and the thinly populated hills was difficult. Some minor footpaths led through the escarpment, which were used by the Gwembe Tonga in bartering with the Tonga on the Plateau, small-scale trading, and seeking labor in the towns and commercial farms adjacent to the railway line connecting Lusaka with Livingstone and with the mines of Southern Rhodesia (now Zimbabwe), South Africa, and the Copperbelt in Northern Rhodesia (now Zambia). Most of the scattered villages on the escarpment and in the Gwembe Valley were only accessible using such paths.

While the Gwembe Valley had long been one of the remotest parts in this region of south-central Africa, this situation altered drastically when the Kariba Dam was built in the mid-1950s. Constructing the dam, which created what at that time was the largest man-made lake in the world, necessitated the resettlement of about 57,000 people—Rabson's family among them—and led to rapid infrastructural developments. An accelerated influx from the outside world, the increased incorporation of the area into systems of market economy, and the initial stages of urbanization were all aspects of this rapid change, which also caused the disintegration of many customary ways of living. Rabson grew up during this time of marked sociocultural, economic, and religious transformation.

In the 1960s, Rabson became a member and eventually pastor of the Full Gospel Church of Central Africa (FGCCA), an African-initiated Pentecostal-Charismatic church founded by a Tonga migrant who had returned from working in the mines of Southern Rhodesia. At around the same time, he joined the crew of a construction company in the township of Batoka on the Plateau near the escarpment. This company was building a tarmac road from Batoka to Maamba in the Gwembe

---

9   Ngada, *Speaking for Ourselves*, 16.

Valley, where open-cast coalmining had recently begun. While being employed as a construction worker and moving along with the road as it was gradually extended, Rabson learned how to drive and obtained a driving license, subsequently finding employment as a driver with a number of different companies. Wherever he went as a construction worker or driver, Rabson tried to establish new Christian communities. From the 1960s onwards, he thus succeeded in setting up twenty-eight branches of the FGCCA, several of whom followed Rabson when he decided to set up his own church, the SAC, in the early 1990s.

How can we frame our analytical understanding of fascinating empirical cases like these where religious community building went hand in hand with the construction of tarmac roads? Answers to this question depend on how the practice of 'spreading Christianity' is conceptualized. In the history of Christianity, some organizations, such as Bible societies, aim at diffusing the Christian message which is then hoped to stimulate the recipients' faith.[10] For other Christian organizations, such as the FGCCA, the emphasis on propositional content is not sufficient. For them, spreading Christianity implies disseminating some spiritual quality. These organizations, many subsumed under the category of Pentecostalism, consider it their duty to bring people into contact with the Holy Spirit and to make them experience, even embody, its divine power.

There are different views among Pentecostals on how the latter can be accomplished. According to several Gwembe Tonga I spoke with, Rabson had 'physically' brought the Holy Spirit to different locations in the Valley for the spirit to do its divine work there, which, in turn, motivated the newly enrolled local neophytes to construct new religious infrastructures, such as altars and church buildings. Others emphasized that the Holy Spirit had motivated Rabson to become a driver and to contribute to constructing a road infrastructure which it (i.e., the Holy Spirit) could subsequently use for its evangelizing mission. Indeed, the latter was the version of the story the majority of Rabson's followers recounted about his biography. But if this is an instance of how practitioners of Pentecostalism describe their world, how can we conceptualize Pentecostal relationships between infrastructures and spiritual beings?

Spirits as Infrastructures

I have suggested in a previous publication that, when embarking on a study of Pentecostalism, it is important to take account of the multifarious ways in which spiritual

---

10   Matthew Engelke, *God's Agents: Biblical Publicity in Contemporary England* (Berkeley: University of California Press, 2013).

entities are manifesting themselves in the world and are experienced by religious practitioners to locate themselves in and move through space.[11]

Thus, as noted above, a possible Pentecostal way of answering the question above would be to say that the Holy Spirit instigates humans to engage in infrastructuring activities, setting them in motion, energizing them, channelling their activities in particular directions, thus literally making them pave the way for the spirit's diffusion and immanence in the world. The importation of spiritual powers from the 'outside' to the social 'inside' and the interpersonal transmission of these powers from religious experts to members of the laity constitute what I have called the "logistics of the spirit."[12] However, in cases like Rabson's, the latter does not implicate transporting the Holy Spirit as an entity but rather transporting the human channel for it. In other words, in this type of spirit mobility, the spatial radius of the Holy Spirit's mobility is relative to the readiness of religious practitioners to seek spiritual power by setting themselves in motion or by allowing themselves to be affected by others who have moved previously. People's movement thus precedes and premises spiritual movement; wherever humans have failed to go, the Spirit does not go. Spiritual infrastructures are dependent on—and most importantly, basically co-extensive with—certain types of human-made (material) infrastructures.

But there are two other ways how the Holy Spirit manifests itself in the Gwembe Valley, which tell a different story of how infrastructures and spirits can be related to each other. The first is 'spiritual self-multiplication.' In all the Pentecostal-Charismatic church services I attended, the Holy Spirit made its initial appearance by inspiring one of the church elders while he or she was praying, singing, or dancing. In most cases, following this initial appearance of the Holy Spirit other church elders also exhibit such symptoms, occasionally giving rise to an atmosphere of collective effervescence with impassioned dancing and a cacophony of glossolalic voices filling the church building. It is at this point that the Holy Spirit starts manifesting itself among members of the laity. All in all, if the rituals are realized in felicitous ways, the Holy Spirit can thus be said to self-multiply in the course of the ritual, starting out from one of the church elders, then bringing its influence to bear on some of the other co-present elders and eventually on selected members of the laity attending the service. In this process, the Holy Spirit manifests itself not in a contiguous spatial area but in distributed form—that is, here and there throughout the ritual space, with the interstitial spaces remaining unaffected by its spiritual powers.

What is important for us here is that the self-multiplied Holy Spirit is forging spiritual connections between people who otherwise might have no prior social con-

---

11   Kirsch, *Intangible Motion*.

12   Thomas G. Kirsch, "Religious Logistics: African Christians, Spirituality and Transportation," in *On the Margins of Religion*, eds. Joao Pina-Cabral and Francis Pine (Oxford: Berghahn, 2008): 61–80, 62.

nectivity, that is, who might otherwise be strangers to each other. These connections are invisible to the human eye but can eventually evolve and give rise to people's socio-religious interactions and institutionalizations in which the Holy Spirits assumes the role and function of a *spiritual infrastructure* that may run parallel to, but may partly also deviate from, human-made infrastructures.

Similarly, collective efforts by churchgoers can lead to a situation where the Holy Spirit is felt to be present in such an extraordinary intensity that everyone entering the ritual scene is automatically affected by its power. On such occasions, the Holy Spirit also makes its initial appearance by inspiring one of the church elders while he or she is praying, singing, or dancing. Yet, in contrast to spirit mobility by self-multiplication, this initial inspiration does not affect only selected individuals positioned at a spatial distance from each other but leads to a self-expansion of the Holy Spirit, so that its beingness pervades the entirety of the ritual space and sometimes even stretches beyond it. On the other hand, in case the churchgoers' collective efforts to appease the Holy Spirit lose strength, this spiritual entity decreases its 'size' by self-contraction and sometimes even retracts in its entirety from the ritual space. Taken together, while undoubtedly involving a perceptible change of position in space, this type of spirit mobility does not take the form of a movement from A to B. Instead, it represents a spatial pulsation between microscale and macroscale that is accomplished by a self-induced upscaling and downscaling of the *gestalt* of the Holy Spirit and results in a spiritual permeation of space on different (local, regional, transregional) scales that serves as an essential infrastructure of religious practice.

Thoughts in Conclusion

In comparison, the two types of spirit mobility described above give rise to different types of spiritual infrastructures. In the case of self-multiplication, it takes the form of a network; in the case of spiritual scaling, the infrastructure is a socio-spatially bound platform or enclave. What both have in common, however, is that human-made infrastructures (e.g., roads, church buildings, distribution networks of religious texts) are *not* considered sufficient for the Pentecostalist practice to evolve in a divinely ordained way. There also ought to be an infrastructure of the *spiritual* kind.

You find my anthropological interest in the Holy Spirit exotic? Well, with its roughly 650 million adherents worldwide, Pentecostalism is an immensely influential religious movement whose membership base lies predominantly, but of course not exclusively, in the Global South. So, at least in terms of numbers, it is definitely not a minority perspective.

You think that my analytical focus on the agency of the Holy Spirit is misplaced because it appears to grant Beingness to something which (non-Christians would say) does not exist? Please note that, depending on one's point of view, something similar can be said about certain Western notions, such as the 'psyche.' My interlocutors in rural Zambia were at a loss when I tried to explicate to them what a 'psyche' is, and they were thoroughly amused by the suggestion that they themselves should be endowed with one. As a consequence, my account of how, in European common sense, *psycho*logical dynamics are informing people's social lives did not make sense to them.

The point I am trying to make as a concluding thought is the following: Throughout the world, people have different ideas of what exists in the world. Some presume the existence of entities or phenomena which others maintain are inexistent. Nevertheless, for those who base their social practices on the assumption of these entities' or phenomena's agency, the latter can function as infrastructures for the former, and should be studied as such.

Infrastructure of Faith: Some Considerations on Correspondence in Late Antique Christianity

Barbara Feichtinger

The Christian correspondence of late antiquity is in many ways the subject of both ancient studies and theological-patristic research. So far, however, the focus has been primarily on the content and form of the texts, while little attention has been paid to the mobility of the texts, their circulation and migration under the spatial, temporal, cultural and social conditions of late antique writing.[1]

---

1   Consequently, the highly significant examination of the development and dissemination of Christian doctrinal content, ideas, and bodies of knowledge in the research landscape of late antiquity largely takes place within one-sided research parameters, which, if at all, take note of the concrete, i.e. real-life nature of late antique scriptural circulation only sporadically, implicitly, and marginally. The central importance of text migration for a deeper understanding of the religious, social, and political developments and constitution of Christian late antiquity thus remains largely ignored. Questions concerning the availability of texts in the context of different subject areas have so far mostly been touched upon and addressed only implicitly. For example, in the context of biographical studies, the whereabouts of a church scholar and his correspondence partners are placed in relation to one another; cf. e.g., maps of Jerome and his epistolary partners in Alfons Fürst, *Hieronymus. Askese und Wissenschaft in der Spätantike* (Freiburg: Herder, 2003); Stefan Rebenich, *Hieronymus und sein Kreis. Prosopographische und sozialgeschichtliche Untersuchungen* (Stuttgart: Steiner, 1992). Dating issues of works play a role in reconstructing historical processes or chronologies of works. In the context of analysing theological conflicts, questions are also asked about the alliances of different bishops or social networks of influential laymen; cf. Elizabeth A. Clark, *The Origenist Controversy: The Cultural Construction of an Early Christian Debate* (Princeton: Princeton University Press, 1992), esp. 11–41. Occasionally, some attention is also paid to the conditions and (often far-reaching and lasting) consequences of the dissemination of individual writings, such as the impact of Athanasius' *Vita Antonii* in the western part of the Roman Empire and its Latin translation on the development of the ascetic movement. Questions of translation (Greek/Latin/Hebrew/Aramaic) and cultural transfer play a role not only in the context of *Biblica*. Naturally, in the context of source studies, the use of pre-texts is addressed. Often, however, their availability is simply assumed without further consideration of the real-life conditions and prerequisites for it. Sometimes, once the messages about traffic and mobility of writings contained in ancient sources are explicitly perceived, only the metainformation associated with them is of interest. Studies on the networking and exchange of local groups in late antiquity also focus (mostly on the basis of archaeological finds such as

However, the spread and implementation of Christianity in the Mediterranean region is inconceivable without a communicative infrastructure of permanently circulating writings.[2] The supra- regional, even "globalized," Christian correspondence was rooted in the tension between the idea of the *unio ecclesiae* and the permanent striving for *oikumene* founded therein, which distinguished Christians from all other religious communities of antiquity, as well as the pronounced autonomy of highly divergent local churches, which had to be bridged and continuously mastered through the exchange of letters and correspondence.[3] Late antique Christianity ultimately constituted itself without geographical, political or national limitations as a discursive space whose boundaries are the boundaries of the flow of information of Christian messages and thus infinitely shiftable (*totus orbis*)[4]—(long- distance) communication is thus t h e constitutive infrastructure of the Christian faith.

While in the beginning (charismatic) individuals functioned as (mobile) nodes of the communicative networks, after the fading of Christian eschatology at the end of the 1st century, in the process of the differentiation of church structures, the correspondence between bishops also began, which aimed at maintaining the unity of the congregations and the creation of a common identity, while also preserving the personal power ambitions of individual bishops. The Christian self- understanding as a world- spanning community is only rendered concrete through the participation in this exchange of information. Contact with other communities was thus existential. In order to achieve the best possible positioning within the Christian community to consolidate their position of power—and thus also in asserting their positions, bishops (as authorized representatives of their congregations)[5] joined together in partly rivalling communication networks. These networks constituted themselves through

---

pottery shards) predominantly on economic contacts; cf. Christian Nitschke and Christian Rollinger, "Network Analysis is performed: Die Analyse sozialer Netzwerke in den Altertumswissenschaften. Rückschau und aktuelle Forschungen," in *Knoten und Kanten III. Soziale Netzwerkanalyse in Geschichts-und Politikforschung*, eds. Markus Gamper and Linda Reschke and Marten Düring (Bielefeld: transcript Verlag, 2015): 213–259, esp. 225–229.

2   Cf. Guy G. Stroumsa, "On the status of books in early Christianity," in *Being Christian in Late Antiquity: A Festschrift for Gillian Clark*, eds. Carol Harrison and Caroline Humfress and Isabella Sandwell (Oxford: Oxford University Press, 2014): 57–73, 61, who points out that the medial change from writing scrolls to codices, which Christian communities in particular took up briskly, facilitated the circulation of writings and ideas.

3   Cf. Eva Baumkamp, *Kommunikation in der Kirche des 3. Jahrhunderts* (Tübingen: Mohr Siebeck, 2014), 1f.

4   On the great mobility and the global-geographical claim of the Christians Fürst, "Ende der Erde," esp. 273–275.

5   On the correspondence privilege of the bishop Baumkamp, *Kommunikation*, 7.

various elements of information exchange and they themselves defined parameters of membership by forming mechanisms of inclusion and exclusion.[6]

After the Constantinian turn (at the latest), Christianity inscribed itself with complex interferences into the spatial as well as communicative fields of power of the *Imperium Romanum*. This not only signals significant change in the sacral topography of the Mediterranean region (partly caused by the emperor through church buildings), but also a modification of (remote) communicative processes.

On the one hand, the bishops now also competed for (spatial as well as discursive) proximity to and corresponding influence on imperial power (e.g., the increase in importance of the bishoprics of Constantinople or Milan). On the other hand, a centrally structured imperial communication had to interact with ecclesial networks whose reactive "elasticity" was enormous and hardly controllable, or at least difficult to control intentionally. Individual nodes can be destroyed or spatially displaced, but the network is flexible and highly regenerative. This had already been indicated in the times of persecution, when fugitive bishops, for example, were able to continue to operate as (epistolary) communication centres from changed locations. It was confirmed in the case of imperial interventions in internal church disputes: The exile of bishops in the course of the Arianism conflict led to contacts and the establishment of communication links between bishops and congregations that would hardly have come into contact without the bishops' change of location, and thus ultimately led to the expansion and consolidation of the communication network.[7]

Therefore, text migration functioned as an infrastructure of knowledge production and dissemination, of phenomena of intertextuality, of translation processes, and of cultural transfer (cultural hybridization). Text migration was an important tool for exercising and asserting influence/authority/rule in the context of (religious) conflict in that it can cause conflict, but it is also a means of alliance building (inclusion/exclusion), serves as a medium of argument and controversy, and is used in crisis management both for conflict escalation and for conflict containment and resolution. Furthermore, text migration creates an impetus for (and is a consequence of) social change, such as the rise of asceticism movements, which blur the boundaries between intimate/private and public/institutionalized communication.

---

6   Cf. Baumkamp, *Kommunikation*, 5f; on the issue of inclusion and exclusion see Alois Hahn, "Theoretische Ansätze zu Inklusion und Exklusion," *Soziologisches Jahrbuch* 16 (2002/3): 67–88, esp. 70f. Already in pre-Constantinian Christianity, letters as a link between congregations functioned as a platform on which the dogmatic, theological, moral and church-political-practical questions of the time were made visible and also conflicts were fought out, Baumkamp, *Kommunikation*, 45f.

7   Cf. Julia Hillner, Jörg Ulrich, and Jakob Engberg (Hg.), *Clerical Exile in Late Antiquity* (Frankfurt: Lang, 2016;
Carmen Cvetković and Peter Gemeinhardt (Hg.), *Episcopal Networks in Late Antiquity: Connection and Communication Across Boundaries* (Berlin: De Gruyter, 2019).

The observation that the range, frequency, and density of the (indispensable) reciprocity of written communication determine the significance, options for influence, and ultimately the position of power of a bishop and the community he represents, but also of individuals, just as much as and sometimes even more significantly than the geographical location or size of the Christian community underscores the great importance of communication infrastructure for post-Constantinian Christianity: Aurelius of Carthage is the African metropolitan, but Augustine of Hippo is the communicative centre of North Africa! Such a comprehensive view can open up further horizons of knowledge about Christian late antiquity, which a study of textual semantics alone is not able to offer.

Which communication patterns and structures are formed simultaneously and/or successively? Regional, suprarational, long-distance networking? How are nodes, agglomerations, areas of thinning-out, breakoffs, etc. distributed? With which factors do these formations correlate—with geographical conditions, existing material infrastructure, political and economic centers, religious hotspots (episcopal seats, martyrs' tombs, etc.) or intellectual individuals? How do Christian (rather) horizontal communication networks generally inscribe themselves into the centrally and vertically structured communication of imperial power? What is the influence of political crises, military conflicts, environmental catastrophes? Which forms, condensations and abruptions of communication develop through religious conflicts, which role do the lifeworld conditions of space and time play in this? What is the relationship between different formations of scriptural circulation and the generation of (religious) power? Or what role do translations play in the formation of an overall Christian Mediterranean? etc.

The final goal, of course, should be the creation of a database or a digital (and therefore permanently expandable) "Atlas of Christian Scripture Traffic" of the 4th century.[8]

---

8   By inscribing the Christian writings as vectors in (chronologically ordered regional or overview) maps of the Mediterranean region (and linking them to commentary fields), the indispensable importance of communication for the Christian order of faith can be specified, since simultaneities and non-simultaneities of scriptural exchange, regional agglomerations, construction, dismantling and breaking down or shifting of communication boundaries in their location in the Mediterranean region can thus be grasped (at a glance). In addition, the digital form of publication offers the enormous advantage of the possibility of continuous updating, so that new research findings (during the project phase, but also later) can be continuously incorporated. Finally, it offers the possibility of multi-level presentations with which the user can interact. Patristic projects operating in the field of digital humanities, such as "Mapping Persecution and Martyrdom in Early Christianity" (Ohio Wesleyan University, Ohio, USA) or "Late Antique Clerical Exile and Social Network Analysis" (University of Sheffield, Sheffield, UK) will serve as a guide and template. For an example of a digital representation of transport routes, times, and costs cf. http://orbis.stanford.edu/. In

In order to approach this distant goal, we have to deal with two (intermingled) levels of infrastructures, so to speak: On the one hand, scriptural communication itself provides a network-like communicative infrastructure for the process of Christianization in late antiquity. On the other hand, written communication, for its part, relies on the material-technical infrastructure of messengers, horses, and roads, but also paper, ink, scribes, or libraries etc.[9]

To be able to better assess the impact of the economic-communicative framework on dissemination, implementation, and establishment of religious content, and thus the complexity of the Christianization process in the *Imperium Romanum*, more attention should be paid to these material and real-life conditions of ancient scriptural communication.

What was the importance of stable and less stable communication channels between bishops in conflicts of faith? Did the availability and financing of better infrastructure—constant access to scribes, copyists, writing materials, messengers, but also archives and libraries—play a decisive role in schismatic situations? What influence on ecclesiastical-political developments do disruptions of the infrastructure have, for example through warlike conflicts that cut off transport routes or increase the dangers of losing texts on unsecured travel routes? How does the factor of time in ancient written correspondence affect religious conflicts? For example, what happens in a city with rival bishops when responses from fellow bishops asked for support or mediation do not (or cannot) arrive for weeks? What consequences does the fact that the Mediterranean Sea was simply not navigable under ancient sea travel conditions during the winter months (*mare clausum*) have for the rhythms of Christian communication in the ecclesiastical year?[10]

---

the medium term, the creation of a digital atlas of Christian scriptural traffic will probably only be possible as a team effort.

9   On the general conditions of ancient writing and librarianship cf. Janine Desmulliez, Christine Hoet-van Cauwenberghe, and Jean-Christophe Jolivet (Hg.), *L´étude des correspondances dans le monde romain de l´Antiquité classique à l´Antiquité tardive: permanences et mutations* (Lille: Université Charles-de-Gaulle, 2010); Lionel Casson, *Libraries in the Ancient World* (New Haven: Yale University Press, 2001); Bastian van Elderen, "Early Christian libraries," in *The Bible as Book: The Manuscript Tradition*, eds. John Sharpe and Kimberly van Kampen (London: Oak Knoll Press, 1998): 45–59; Hans Carel Teitler, *Notarii and exceptores: An inquiry into role and significance of shorthand writers in the imperial and ecclesiastical bureaucracy of the Roman empire (from the early principate to c. 450 A.D.)* (Amsterdam: Gieben, 1985).

10   On the general conditions of ancient travel and transport cf. Linda Ellis and Frank L. Kidner (Hg.), *Travel, Communication and Geography in Late Antiquity: Sacred and Profane.* (Burlington: Ashgate, 2004); Anne Kolb, *Transport und Nachrichtentransfer im Römischen Reich* (Berlin: Akademie Verlag, 2000); Denys Gorce, *Les voyages, l´hospitalite et le port des lettres das le monde chretien des IV. et V siècle* (Paris: Picard, 1925); Wolfgang Riepl, *Das Nachrichtenwesen des Altertums. Mit besonderer Rücksicht auf die Römer* (Leipzig-Berlin: Teubner, 1913).

A specific focus on the communicative infrastructure will also help to shed light on the power-political origin and reference spaces of the preserved texts. Decisions of synods and councils, which are available today in the form of often rather brief *Canones*, emerge as the extremely concise result of highly complex communicative processes that built on an infrastructure of ecclesiastical correspondence created and established specifically for this purpose. The synods themselves were preceded not only by imperial letters of invitation but certainly also by coordination processes between episcopal sees based on (regular) messenger traffic. After the meetings, the results had to be communicated to the wider public, and the recipient of these letters as well as the person who *accepted them*—again, through written correspondence—was of crucial importance for the politics of faith.

When Ammianus Marcellinus, a late antique (pagan) historian, scoffs at the fact "that crowds of bishops were rushing back and forth across the country by state mail because of their so-called synods,"[11] he not only attests to the Constantinian privilege for bishops to use the *cursus publicus*, the imperial postal service actually reserved for high-ranking military and administrative officials, but also directs attention to the hybrid form of the Christian communication infrastructure.

Christian correspondence on the one hand uses—aside from the well-developed road and street network of the *Imperium Romanum*—existing transport systems such as those of the imperial postal service or of local and long-distance trade for the transport of messengers and/or written documents. On the other hand, however, it also generates connections that were organized and financed completely independently. These could be permanent and regularly used regionally as well as supra-regionally, so that they provided for a continuous flow of information (e.g. between episcopal sees, between monasteries, or between church leadership and imperial administration etc.). In addition, there were also large numbers of occasion-specific and strictly demand-driven "ad hoc transfers," which were then initiated, organized, equipped, and financed not only by Christian congregations or monasteries but also by individuals. Thus, the Christian communication networks exhibit a high degree of flexibility, efficiency, and a relatively favourable cost balance and thus largely correspond to the conditions of ancient private correspondence since hardly any usage-independent permanent transport structures had to be established and maintained.[12] At the same time, they differ fundamentally from

---

11   Ammianus Marcellinus, 21,16,18 in *Ammianus Marcellinus, Res gestae*, vol. 1, ed. Wolfgang Sey-
      farth (Stuttgart: Bibliotheca Teubneriana, 1978): 248–249.

12   The construction and maintenance of libraries and archives (rooms, writing materials,
      scribes, copyists, etc.) can be estimated as fixed costs, but transportation costs (messengers,
      pack animals, wagons, food, lodging, ship passages, etc.) were incurred only on occasion. Re-
      cruiting messengers from clerics of the bishop's seat or monks of a monastery saved costs –
      in analogy to trusted slaves of private persons – and increased confidentiality and chances
      of arrival for a document.

ancient private correspondence, especially in their institutionalized, i.e. supra-individual parts, in their actually "world-spanning" network structure, greater regularity, density of connections, and intended duration of existence.

Against this backdrop, the question of the participation options of authors/senders and readers/recipients of writings, who could be clerics or laymen, women or men, Christians or pagans/Jews, literate or illiterate, collectives or individuals,[13] seems particularly exciting for the analysis of the concrete manifestation of Christian text migration—in materiality, frequency, as well as network structure.

Thus, for example, the Christian ascetic movements that became established in the second half of the 4th century (as a consequence of dwindling expectations of the end times and opportunities for martyrdom) made ascetic individuals—often lay people and, among them even women, who at that time were already largely excluded from the clerical office structure—important nodes in the Christian scriptural traffic.

A particularly striking example of an individual who contributed significantly to the shaping of Christian doctrine in the Latin West by establishing and maintaining a personal long-distance communication network that was, nevertheless, linked to the institutional communication network of the official church is Saint Jerome, the biblical scholar and ascetic. His life and work recommend him as the starting point for an experimental analysis of late antique Christian correspondence.[14]

---

13   On late antique correspondence cf. Sigrid Mratschek, *Der Briefwechsel des Paulinus von Nola. Kommunikation und soziale Kontakte zwischen christlichen Intellektuellen* (Göttingen: Vandenhoeck und Ruprecht, 2002); Frank Morgenstern, *Die Briefpartner des Augustinus von Hippo. Prosopographische, sozial-und ideologiegeschichtliche Untersuchungen* (Bochum: Brockmeyer, 1993); Carsten Drecoll, *Nachrichten in der Römischen Kaiserzeit. Untersuchungen zu den Nachrichteninhalten in Briefen* (Freiburg: Carsten Drecoll Verlag, 2006).

14   His addressee network can thus, for example, be compiled from the letter corpus (which addressees also knew each other? Are there greetings to further persons?), which not only shows the accumulation of addressees (e.g. one addressee written to several times by one author; one addressee in several correspondences), their geographical distribution and their regional agglomeration, and social stratigraphy (e.g. status, gender, age, clergy/laity, Christian/pagan, world Christian/ascetic, etc.), but also insights into the chronology of the letters (incl. reconstruction of the answer), temporal condensations (in the context of certain church-political events, conflicts, heretical processes, etc.), or thematic emphases (which topics were discussed in broad public, etc.). More specifically, one of the main issues would be to collect, analyse, and process the information about textual movements contained in the correspondences, such as mentions of requested or co-sent writings, news about duplication processes, messengers (orality/writing), travel routes and transport routes, transport duration, lost writings, or even attempts to withdraw writings from circulation. Another goal is to reconstruct (taking into account the methodological problems involved) the writings available to the authors, aiming at an approximate reconstruction of (private) libraries and archives as (immobile and at the same time dynamic) nodes of the communicative infrastructure.

Jerome was (at least in the first 40 years of his life) himself a great traveller (Stridon/Pannonia – Rome – Trier – Aquileia – Antioch – Constantinople – Rome – Cyprus – Jerusalem – Egypt – Bethlehem), who had known large parts of the Mediterranean region himself. As an (officially) insignificant priest (ordained by a schismatic bishop), without a congregation, he, as an ascetic teacher and theologian, made the rather peripheral village of Bethlehem next to Jerusalem a theological-exegetical centre, which radiated into the entire Mediterranean region. His correspondence partners were located around the Mediterranean Sea (Italy, Gaul, Spain, North Africa, Syria, Palestine, Egypt, Constantinople, Cyprus). He evolved into a central hub in Christian scriptural traffic without being a bishop and without being in a political or economic centre and thus represents a phenomenon of the Christian spatial order of the 4th century. He was himself a pilgrim and built a pilgrim hospice in Bethlehem with his *patrona* Paula. He was not only involved in controversies about pilgrimage and the question of the "Holy Land," but also contributed through his writings to the theological foundation of Christian pilgrimage. Jerome was also an (actively involved) contemporary witness of the beginnings of a hegemony (established via communicative processes of correspondence!) of the Roman *cathedra Petri*, which also has a lasting impact on the communicative infrastructure. He was proficient in Latin and Greek (as well as Hebrew and probably some Aramaic) and acted as an interpreter, translator, and cultural mediator (on a church-political agenda) between the eastern and western Mediterranean lands. Jerome was involved in numerous inner-church disputes (Arianism dispute, Antiochian schism, heresy of Iovinian, dispute about Origen, Pelaganian dispute), so that his writing is able to give deep insights into the spatial-discursive conditions of these conflict scenarios. Jerome's writings, which are extensive enough to provide insights into all these aspects of discursive shaping of the Christian Mediterranean, but also manageable enough to develop, test, and establish methodological parameters, contain a great deal of meta-information on travel and correspondence in the late antique Mediterranean area. His (extensively preserved) writings are quite well datable (by ancient standards).

Above all, he was fully aware of the need for a viable distribution infrastructure for his writings and worked toward this purposefully: He intensively cultivated contact with clerics and lay people who were to pay for and distribute copies of his works.[15] Not only did he proclaim that his complete œuvre is available for copying in his Bethlehemite monastic library (exorbitant in scope and quality!), but he also

---

15   For example, Hieronymus, ep. 71,5,1 in *Hieronymus, Epistulae*, vol. 2, ed. Isidorus Hilberg (Vienna: Austrian Academy of Sciences Press, 1996, = CSEL 55), 5; Hieronymus, ep. 75,4,1 in *Hieronymus, Epistulae*, vol. 2, 33; Hieronymus, *Epistulae inter epistulas Augustini* 27*, Sanctis Aureli Augustini opera II,6, Epistulae ex duobus codicibus nuper in lucem prolatae recensit J. (Vienna: Johannes Divjak, 1981, = CSEL 88): 132–133.

suggested the libraries of Roman friends as alternative sources. He simply recommended his catalogue of works in *De viris illustribus* as an order catalogue.[16]

His correspondence with bishops, clerics, and monasteries, but also with male and female laymen (ascetics), which (demonstrably)[17] reached Italy, Gaul, Spain, North Africa, Syria, Palestine, Egypt, Constantinople, and Cyprus, ensured a widespread and lasting distribution of his writings, and thus laid the foundation for sufficient manuscripts to survive the centuries.

The fact that Jerome—an insignificant monk on the Bethlehemite periphery—in subsequent centuries, in association with the bishops Ambrose, Augustine, and Gregory, advanced to become a Doctor of the Church in the West as well as an authority on doctrine and faith and was formally canonized by Pope Boniface VIII on September 20, 1295, is, in a way, also the result of his lifelong efforts to provide an adequate communication infrastructure.

---

16   Hieronymus, ep. 47,3,1-2 in *Hieronymus, Epistulae*, vol. 1, ed. Isidorus Hilberg (Vienna: Austrian Academy of Sciences Press, 1996, = CSEL 55): 346.

17   Of course, our knowledge of his correspondence partners is sketchy and the actual distribution quantities of his works remain extremely vague for us.

Religious Infrastructure: The Parish Church

Gabriela Signori

The term infrastructure presupposes planning and a planning authority that has the means and possibilities to realise what has been planned. This planning authority is usually equated with the state and its predecessors, varying in time and space (princes or cities), and infrastructure with traffic or transport routes such as roads, bridges, or canals. What is more, in historical research, nascent statehood is virtually derived from infrastructural projects of this kind.[1] This 'etatist' view, however, obscures a) the central importance that users play in the history of infrastructures, and b) the insight that infrastructures are not limited to transport routes, but ultimately encompass everything that people in the past and present need for their daily necessities.[2] Of course, these needs are historically changing, yet basic religious services are still part of them today. However, in Church History the topic is rarely discussed under the label of infrastructure.

As a concomitant of the progressive urbanisation and commercialisation of the Christian world, the question became more important during the 13th century. Urbanisation and commercialisation required not only safe transport and traffic routes that connected centres as well as centre and surrounding areas, but also schools where the literacy skills necessary for trade and commerce could be acquired, public institutions (courts or notaries) that guaranteed the security of contracts, as well as specialised personnel who were either responsible for people's health or dedicated to pastoral care and accompanied people from birth to death and kept their memory alive.[3]

---

1   Cf. Ulf Dirlmeier et al., eds., *Öffentliches Bauen in Mittelalter und früher Neuzeit. Abrechnungen als Quellen für die Finanz-, Wirtschafts-und Sozialgeschichte des Bauwesens*, Sachüberlieferung und Geschichte 9 (St. Katharinen: Scripta-Mercaturae-Verlag, 1991); Rainer Christoph Schwinges, ed., *Strassen-und Verkehrswesen im hohen und späten Mittelalter*, Vorträge und Forschungen 66 (Ostfildern: Thorbecke, 2007).

2   Guy Geltner, *Roads to Health: Infrastructure and Urban Wellbeing in Later Medieval Italy* (Philadelphia: University of Pennsylvania Press, 2019); Abigail Agresta, *The Keys to Bread and Wine: Faith, Nature, and Infrastructure in Late Medieval Valencia* (Ithaca: Cornell University Press, 2022).

3   Ronald J. Stansbury, ed., *A Companion to Pastoral Care in the Late Middle Ages (1200–1500)*, Brill's Companions to the Christian Tradition 22 (Leiden: Brill, 2010); Peter D. Clarke and

In the history of religious infrastructures, the parish church played the overriding role over the centuries and across confessional boundaries because it was the basic ecclesiastical administrative unit, which was often also used for profane purposes (as a council or court house, public notary's office, as an administrative unit for levying direct taxes, guard services and firefighting, etc.), and because the school system developed in many places along the parish system.[4] The parish church largely completed its spatial dimensions spanning all over Christian Europe in the course of the 13th century.[5] At first, the initiative came from bishops, monasteries, and landlords, who retained the right of patronage, the right to elect the parish priest, in the period that followed. From the perspective of the patronage right, the parish church in town and countryside alike reflects the changeable power relations,[6] while inside the church, society broke through almost everywhere, what leads us to the topic of religious infrastructure.

This intrusion took place in several ways and different forms: While in the 14th century the exclusive altar foundations multiplied in the urban parish churches, as well as the equally exclusive Mass donations on the altars, and the burials of the founders in front of it, in the course of the 15th century the more middle-class oriented brotherhoods tended to multiply, too, as did the praedicature foundations, which carried the spreading of the Word of God from the monastery to the parish church.[7] The initiative usually came from the laity; that is, at the level of the parish

Sarah James, eds., *Pastoral Care in Medieval England: Interdisciplinary Approaches* (Abingdon: Routledge, 2020).

4   Arnd Reitemeier, *Pfarrkirchen in der Stadt des späten Mittelalters. Politik, Wirtschaft und Verwaltung*, Vierteljahrschrift für Sozial- und Wirtschaftsgeschichte, Beihefte 177 (Stuttgart: Steiner, 2005); Enno Bünz, "Die erfolgreichste Institution des Mittelalters. Die Pfarrei," in *"Überall ist Mittelalter": zur Aktualität einer vergangenen Epoche*, eds. Dorothea Klein, Markus Frankl, and Franz Fuchs (Würzburg: Königshausen & Neumann, 2015), 109–138.

5   Martial Staub, *Les paroisses et la cité. Nuremberg du XIIIᵉ siècle à la Réforme*, Civilisations et sociétés 116 (Paris: Édition de l'École des Hautes Études en Sciences Sociales, 2003); Enno Bünz and Gerhard Fouquet, eds., *Die Pfarrei im späten Mittelalter*, Vorträge und Forschungen 77 (Ostfildern: Thorbecke 2013); Michele C. Ferrari and Beat Kümin, eds., *Pfarrei in der Vormoderne. Identität und Kultur im Niederkirchenwesen Europas*, Wolfenbütteler Forschungen 146 (Wiesbaden: Harrassowitz, 2017); Enno Bünz, *Die mittelalterliche Pfarrei. Ausgewählte Studien zum 13.–16. Jahrhundert*, Spätmittelalter, Humanismus, Reformation 96 (Tübingen: Mohr Siebeck, 2017); Pascal Vuillemin, *Parochiae Venetiarum: les paroisses de Venise au Moyen Âge*, Bibliothèque d'histoire médiévale 20 (Paris: Classiques Garnier, 2018).

6   Dietrich Kurze, *Pfarrerwahlen im Mittelalter. Ein Beitrag zur Geschichte der Gemeinde und des Niederkirchenwesens*, Forschungen zur kirchlichen Rechtsgeschichte und zum Kirchenrecht 6 (Cologne-Graz: Böhlau 1966); Wolfgang Petke, "Kirchenpatronate in städtischer Hand: Göttingen," in *Aufsätze zur Pfarreigeschichte in Mittelalter und Früher Neuzeit* (Göttingen: Vandenhoeck & Ruprecht, 2021): 361–399, 364–366.

7   Bernhard Neidiger, *Prädikaturstiftungen in Süddeutschland (1369–1530)*, Veröffentlichungen des Archivs der Stadt Stuttgart 106 (Stuttgart-Leipzig: Hohenheim-Verlag, 2011). The topic

church, it was primarily the laity who gave the religious infrastructure its time- specific shape.

The possibilities for shaping one's church and inscribing oneself into it were manifold. The spectrum ranges from exclusive chapel and altar endowments to the associated liturgical vessels and vestments signed with the coats of arms or letters of the donors. Almost all of these possibilities stood in the service of the commemoration of the dead, brought from the monastery to the parish church through the lay foundations.[8]

In the following, I will focus on the altar and mass endowments as an expression of the increased appreciation of the liturgy of the Mass, since it left a far more lasting mark on the church space and life than many other endowment options.[9] I will concentrate on the three cathedral- like (in the words of Felix Fabri[10]) burgher churches of Breisach, Freiburg im Breisgau, and Ulm, called Minsters.[11] First, I will explore the quantitative dimensions of the phenomenon, and then ask who is responsible for the transformations, as well as how and why. On a large scale the burgher churches show what can be observed in countless smaller parish churches of the time in the city and the countryside: namely the massive influence on liturgy and church by exclusive groups of lay people. Yet, counting mass foundations is a difficult task that

---

of the urban confraternities is broadly discussed, yet seldomly linked to the parish church: *Le mouvement confraternel au moyen âge: France, Italie, Suisse* (Geneva: Droz, 1987); James R. Banker, *Death in the Community; Memorialization and Confraternities in an Italian Commune in the Late Middle Ages* (Athens: University of Georgia Press, 1988); Monika Escher-Apsner, ed., *Mittelalterliche Bruderschaften in europäischen Städten / Medieval Confraternities in European Towns*, Inklusion / Exklusion 12 (Frankfurt: Peter Lang 2009); Konrad Eisenbichler, ed., *A Companion to Medieval and Early Modern Confraternities*, Brill's Companions to the Christian Tradition 83 (Leiden: Brill, 2019).

8   Enno Bünz, "Vikariestiftungen verändern den Kirchenraum. Zum Wandel spätmittelalterlicher Pfarrkirchen im deutschsprachigen Gebiet," in *Die mittelalterliche Pfarrei*, 234–257.

9   Jean-Michel Matz, "Chapellenies et chapelains dans le diocèse d'Angers (1350–1550): éléments d'enquête," *Revue d'histoire ecclésiastique* 91 (1996): 371–397; Clive Burgess, "Chantries in the Parish, or 'Through the Looking-glass'," *Journal of the British Archaeological Association* 164 (2011): 100–129; Vincent Tabbagh, "La messe comme pratique de salut (XIIIᵉ–XVᵉ siècles)," in *Des pots dans la tombe (IXᵉ–XVIIIᵉ siècles). Regards croisés sur une pratique funéraire en Europe de l'Ouest*, eds. Anne Bocquet-Liénard et al., Publications du CRAHAM (Caen: Presses universitaires de Caen, 2017): 431–440.

10   Felix Fabri O.P., *Tractatus de civitate Ulmensi /Traktat über die Stadt Ulm*, ed., transl. and annotated by Folker Reichert (Konstanz: Ed. Isele, 2012), 74.

11   Regarding the difficulties of the term "city" and "burgher church," cf. Hartmut Boockmann, *Bürgerkirchen im späteren Mittelalter. Antrittsvorlesung* (Berlin: Humboldt-Universität zu Berlin, Fachbereich Philosophie und Geisteswissenschaften, 1994); Marc Carel Schurr, "Architektur als politisches Argument. Die Pfarrkirche als Bauaufgabe der mittelalterlichen Städte im Südwesten des Reiches," in *Die Pfarrei im späten Mittelalter*, 259–278.

even contemporaries often failed at.[12] For the churches were in a constant state of change: new chapels, altars, or Mass foundations were added, and old ones were merged because they had not been sufficiently endowed. Nevertheless, it is helpful to start with the numbers in order to make the dimensions of the phenomenon tangible.

The Breisach St. Stephen's Minster received its Gothic appearance in the course of the 13th century, and work on it continued uninterrupted up to the Reformation.[13] At the beginning of the 16th century, the patronage of the church still lay with the lords of Rappolstein on the left bank of the Rhine,[14] but this did not affect the citizens' willingness to endow their parish church, on the contrary.[15] The "Subsidium charitativum" of the diocese of Constance from 1493 lists twelve altars with a total of 16 Mass foundations. Among the founders, the families Brenner, Schmidlin, Schultheiß, Seckler, Veschelin-Münzmeister, von Pforr, and zum Rhein stood out.[16] Accordingly, the prebends (Pfründe) were called the Brenner-, the von Pforr-, the Seckler-, etc. benefices. A similar picture emerges with the Ulm Minster with its more than 50 altars, the only one of the three burgher churches whose patronage rights lay with the city council.[17] In Ulm, however, not only the benefices but also the altars were named after the founders, including four Besserer altars![18] In the Liebfrauenmünster (Our Lady Minster) in Freiburg, according to the "Registrum in levatione caritativi subsidii" from 1497, there were only 21 altars, but most of them were endowed with several benefices at the same time, so that there were 69 benefices for the 21 altars in 1497.[19] The Mass foundations ensured, so to speak, a round-the-clock

---

12   The problems in this regard have already been pointed out by Hermann Tüchle, "Die Münster-altäre des Spätmittelalters. Stifter, Heilige, Patrone und Kapläne," in *600 Jahre Ulmer Münster. Festschrift*, eds. Hans Eugen Specker and Reinhard Wortmann, Forschungen zur Geschichte der Stadt Ulm 19 (Stuttgart: Kohlhammer, 1977): 126–182, 127.

13   *Das Breisacher Münster*, ed. Münsterpfarrei St. Stephan Breisach am Rhein, Große Kunstführer 216 (Regensburg: Schnell & Steiner, 2005).

14   Andreas Lehmann, "Die Entwicklung der Patronatsverhältnisse im Archidiakonat Breisgau," *Freiburger Diözesan-Archiv* 39. NS 12 (1911), 249–317, 255–257.

15   Wolfgang Müller, "Der Wandel des kirchlichen Lebens vom Mittelalter in die Neuzeit, erörtert am Beispiel Breisach," *Freiburger Diözesan-Archiv* 82/83 (1962/63): 227–247.

16   "Das subsidium charitativum im Archidiakonat Breisgau vom Jahre 1493," in "Registra subsidii charitativi im Bisthum Konstanz am Ende des 15. und zu Anfang des 16. Jahrhunderts," eds. Franz Zell and M. Burger, *Freiburger Diözesan-Archiv* 24 (1895), 183–237, 188–189; Karl Joseph Rieder, "Das *Registrum subsidii caritativi der Diözese Konstanz aus dem Jahr 1508*," *Freiburger Diözesan-Archiv* 35 (1907), 1–108, 75–76.

17   Tüchle, "Die Münsteraltäre des Spätmittelalters," passim.

18   Rieder, "Das *Registrum subsidii caritativi der Diözese Konstanz aus dem Jahr 1508*," 59–60.

19   Peter P. Albert, "Zur Geschichte des Freiburger Münsters im Jahre 1497," *Freiburger Münsterblätter* 15 (1919), 19–22. Similar are the results for Lüneburg and Lübeck: Georg Matthaei, *Die Vikariestiftungen der Lüneburger Stadtkirchen in der Kirche des Mittelalters und der Reformation*, Studien zur Kirchengeschichte Niedersachsens 4 (Göttingen: Vandenhoeck & Ruprecht, 1928);

liturgy. Most of them came from the 14th century, with a marked increase in the second half of the century in the years after the outbreak of the plague; about a dozen foundations were added in the 15th century, and three more at the beginning of the 16th century.[20] With more than five Mass benefices, the Corpus Christi altar, the St. John Baptist altar, and the St. Oswald altar were the preferred ones of Freiburg's citizens. As in Breisach, the benefices in Freiburg also bore the names of their benefactors and went down in tradition as Malterer-prebend, Ätscherin-prebend, Tolerin-prebend, etc.[21] Most of them belonged to the exclusive circle of the "younger twenty-four," at this time the leading families of the city.[22]

The images are similar: regardless of the question of church patronage, in the course of the 14th century the laity gradually conquered the interior of the church, the nave as well as the choir, and donated altars and masses for their salvation and that of their ancestors. Often these altars were also the place where their family grave stones were located, as can be seen from the anniversary book of the Freiburg Minster (which registers almost five hundred church burials!).[23] Everywhere these benefices bore the family names of the founders; Ulm went one step further: here the founders replaced the saints in whose honour the altars had been consecrated, i.e. the founder's name swallowed up the altar patrocinium.[24]

Wolfgang Prange, "Die Altäre der Lübecker Marienkirche mit ihren Vikarien und Kommenden," *Zeitschrift des Vereins für Lübeckische Geschichte und Altertumskunde* 78 (1998): 143–163.

20   Andreas Lehmann, "Die Entwicklung der Patronatsverhältnisse im Archidiakonat Breisgau," *Freiburger Diözesan-Archiv* 40 NS 13 (1912): 1–36, here 16, 21, 30; The St. Helena altar, endowed by Beatrix von Munzingen in 1504, the St. Wolfgang altar (1505), an endowment by Peter Sprung, and the Oberriet-benefices (which were endowed in 1503) on the Holy Cross altar. In the years of 1505 until 1536, individual founders decided to establish expensive chapels, named after their families, in the new ambulatory: Thomas Flum, *Der spätgotische Chor des Freiburger Münsters. Baugeschichte und Baugestalt*, Neue Forschungen zur deutschen Kunst 5 (Berlin: Deutscher Verlag für Kunstwissenschaft, 2001), 70–79.

21   Wolfgang Müller, "Mittelalterliche Formen kirchlichen Lebens am Freiburger Münster," in *Freiburg im Mittelalter. Vorträge zum Stadtjubiläum*, ed. Wolgang Müller, Veröffentlichung des Alemannischen Instituts 29 (Bühl/Baden: Verlag Konkordia, 1970), 141–181.

22   Mathias Kälble, *Zwischen Herrschaft und bürgerlicher Freiheit: Stadtgemeinde und städtische Führungsgruppen in Freiburg im 12. und 13. Jahrhundert*, Veröffentlichungen aus dem Archiv der Stadt Freiburg im Breisgau 33 (Freiburg: Archiv der Stadt Freiburg im Breisgau, 2001): 218–233.

23   Erwin Butz, *Das Jahrzeitbuch des Münsters zu Freiburg im Breisgau (um 1455–1723)*, Forschungen zur oberrheinischen Landesgeschichte 31A (Freiburg: Karl Alber, 1983): 167–198.

24   For Freiburg, this same phenomenon is not unknown, but not registered in the *subsidia* list of the diocese: "Urkunden und Regesten zur Geschichte des Freiburger Münsters," ed. Peter P. Albert, *Freiburger Münsterblätter* 4, no. 120 (1908): 34; *der Malerinenaltar*.

The right of presentation, the right to choose the priest to whom the Mass was conferred, was usually attached to the Mass foundation.[25] This gave the founders additional options to impose their values and ideas. The "Subsidium charitativum" from 1493 details the Breisach situation.[26] While the council claimed the rights to two altars, the chapter and dean administrate the benefice of the former dean of the Minster, Johannes Murer—the only mass benefice endowed by a clergyman. All other foundations were managed by lay people.

In Freiburg, too, until the parish church was handed over to the university,[27] only five of the endowments of benefices can be traced back to clergymen.[28] In Freiburg, too, the council was designed responsible but for two benefices;[29] three others are identified in the "Registrum in levatione caritativi subsidii" of 1497, while the burgher prebend on the St. Margaret altar was lent by the church warden.[30] Yet, unlike in Breisach and Ulm, the large number of female founders in Freiburg is striking,[31] as well as several endowments that were made jointly by married couples.[32] In Freiburg, about a third of the documented mass foundations were made

---

25   Markus Walser, "Art. Präsentation, Präsentationsrecht," *Lexikon für Theologie und Kirche* 8 (31999), col. 513.

26   "Das *subsidium charitativum* im Archidiakonat Breisgau vom Jahre 1493," 188–89.

27   In Freiburg, the Duke of Austria handed over the right of patronage in 1456 to the university he founded. Peter P. Albert, ed., "Urkunden und Regesten zur Geschichte des Freiburger Münsters," *Freiburger Münsterblätter* 8 (1912): no. 662, 103; Peter P. Albert, ed., "Urkunden und Regesten zur Geschichte des Freiburger Münsters," *Freiburger Münsterblätter* 9 (1913): no. 776, 79; Cf. Andrea Perlt, "Die Universität Freiburg und das Freiburger Münster im 15. und 16. Jahrhundert. Eine Beziehung zwischen befruchtender Symbiose und innerstädtischen Interessenkonflikten," *Zeitschrift des Breisgau-Geschichtsvereins. Schau-ins-Land* 131 (2012): 31–49.

28   Peter P. Albert, ed., "Urkunden und Regesten zur Geschichte des Freiburger Münsters," *Freiburger Münsterblätter* 6 (1910): no. 254, 35; no. 264, 38; no. 275, 42; Peter P. Albert, ed., "Urkunden und Regesten zur Geschichte des Freiburger Münsters," *Freiburger Münsterblätter* 8 (1913): no. 763, 77; Peter P. Albert, ed., "Urkunden und Regesten zur Geschichte des Freiburger Münsters," *Freiburger Münsterblätter* 10 (1914): no. 956, 85.

29   Peter P. Albert, ed., "Urkunden und Regesten zur Geschichte des Freiburger Münsters," *Freiburger Münsterblätter* 4 (1908): no. 128, 37 (1346); Peter P. Albert, ed., "Urkunden und Regesten zur Geschichte des Freiburger Münsters," *Freiburger Münsterblätter* 5 (1909): no. 142, 26 (1350).

30   Albert, "Zur Geschichte des Freiburger Münsters im Jahre 1497," 20–21.

31   Peter P. Albert, ed., "Urkunden und Regesten zur Geschichte des Freiburger Münsters," *Freiburger Münsterblätter* 3 (1907): no. 70; Peter P. Albert, ed., "Urkunden und Regesten zur Geschichte des Freiburger Münsters," *Freiburger Münsterblätter* 4 (1908): nos. 120, 132; Peter P. Albert, ed., "Urkunden und Regesten zur Geschichte des Freiburger Münsters," *Freiburger Münsterblätter* 5 (1909): nos. 138–140, 157, 189; Peter P. Albert, ed., "Urkunden und Regesten zur Geschichte des Freiburger Münsters," *Freiburger Münsterblätter* 6 (1910): nos. 220, 231, 302, 311, 324, 334.

32   Albert, *Freiburger Münsterblätter* 4 (1908): no. 105, 209: *Johannes von Hagenȯwe, ein burger ze Friburg, und Katerine, sin elichü wirtinne; ibidem* 5 (1909): no. 167, 35: *Jacob Ederli, ritter, und vrouw Elzebet von Wittenhein, sin eliche wirtin, burgere ze Friburg; ibidem* 5 (1909): no. 224, 83: *Cůnrat Rohart, der wechsler, und Agnes, sin eliche wirtin, burgere von Friburg; ibidem* 9 (1913): no. 678, 51:

by women, all but one of whom were addressed as citizens.[33] Their foundations are concentrated on the altar of St. Mary Magdalene, on the altar of St. Margaret, and on the altar of St. Oswald on the north side, the women's side of the church.[34] The altars of St. Martin and St. Catherine on the south side, the men's side, were preferred by male donors.[35]

In the Freiburg foundation charts, various models emerge as to how the right of presentation could be transferred from one generation to the next: 1) Half of the founders wished the right to remain within the family (*sipprechthalb*, i.e. by the law of kinship), including the clergy, who behaved like citizens in this respect; 2) the other half entrusted the office to fabric and/or other church wardens, 3) and/or to the council or the mayor of the city; 4) while the fourth and last group opted for a hybrid solution and combined church policy with family interests. Men and women again set somewhat different accents in this respect.

When it came to the question of who should have the right to appoint the priest after the founder's death, the women tended to favour their relatives and also appointed other women on several occasions as in the case of the widow Elizabeth Kötzin. On 15 May 1363, Elizabeth, with the consent of her daughters, completed a project begun by her late husband and established a benefice on the St. Nicholas altar. As long as she lived, she wanted to decide for herself; after her death, the right of presentation was to go to her eldest daughter Catherine, provided she lived in Freiburg. Otherwise, it would go to her younger sister Elizabeth. After that, the right was to go to the eldest child, if not from her family, then from her late husband's family, always assumed the person in question lived in Freiburg.[36] The designated priest had to celebrate daily, was not allowed to have any other benefices, and was to be present at the daily Main Mass.[37] Other founders added that the priest had to be "experienced in the divine services," that he had to say the masses personally, and

Hans Bernhart Snewlin Im Hoff und Margret von Kilchein, sin elich gemahel; ibidem, no. 696, 57: *Cůnrat Mủntzmeister, genant Frowenberg, und Eils Griesserin, sin eliche froue, sesshaft ze Friburg im Brisgow.*

33   Peter P. Albert, ed., "Urkunden und Regesten zur Geschichte des Freiburger Münsters," *Freiburger Münsterblätter* 5 (1909): 157, 31–32: *Gisel dü Lôffelerin, dü wilont Heintzi Lôffelers seligen elichü wirtinne was, ein ingesessen selderin.*

34   Gabriela Signori, "Links oder rechts? Zum 'Platz der Frau' in der mittelalterlichen Kirche," in *Zwischen Gotteshaus und Taverne. Öffentliche Räume in Spätmittelalter und Früher Neuzeit,* eds. Susanna Rau and Gerd Schwerhoff, Norm und Struktur 21 (Cologne: Böhlau, 2004), 339–382.

35   For the late medieval altars of the Frauenmünster, see Butz, *Das Jahrzeitbuch des Münsters zu Freiburg im Breisgau,* 169–181.

36   Peter P. Albert, ed., "Urkunden und Regesten zur Geschichte des Freiburger Münsters," *Freiburger Münsterblätter* 5 (1909): no. 189, 41–42.

37   Albert, *Freiburger Münsterblätter* 5 (1909): no. 138, 23.

that he reside locally,[38] or they gave preference to the same candidates from their family.[39]

The ecclesiastico-political dimensions of the altar and mass foundations are obvious, not only in Breisach and Ulm, but also in Freiburg, where almost every foundation charter was authenticated with the burgher seal![40] Yet, the foundations should not be reduced to a trial of strength between lordship and community as thought in the older research.[41] The main driving force came from society, as ultimately shown by the massive participation of women and couples. Altar and mass endowments were one way among others of shaping architecture and liturgy and thus of expressing one's belonging to the church under consideration beyond one's death. In order to conceptualise this affiliation, Felix Fabri (d. 1505) uses the word *affectus* in his "Treatise of the City of Ulm."[42] This *affectus* unites common welfare and self-interest, the two main driving forces in the late medieval development of religious infrastructure.

---

38   Peter P. Albert, ed., "Urkunden und Regesten zur Geschichte des Freiburger Münsters," *Freiburger Münsterblätter* 4 (1908): nos. 130, 132–33; Albert, *Freiburger Münsterblätter* 5 (1909): nos. 132, 167, 194, 234; Albert, *Freiburger Münsterblätter* 6 (1910): no. 264.

39   Albert, *Freiburger Münsterblätter* 3 (1907): nos. 80, 91; Albert, *Freiburger Münsterblätter* 4 (1908): nos. 105, 109, 120, 130, 133; Albert, *Freiburger Münsterblätter* 5 (1909): nos. 138–139, 156–57, 167, 211, 224, 234; Albert, *Freiburger Münsterblätter* 6 (1910): no. 236.

40   Already the Early-Morning-Mass-Foundation of Gottfried von Schlettstadt from 1310; Albert, *Freiburger Münsterblätter* 3 (1907): no. 70, 72: *unde durh sine bette mit der burger von Friburg ingesigeln besigelt.* Cf. Albert, *Freiburger Münsterblätter* 3, no. 91; Albert, *Freiburger Münsterblätter* 4 (1908): nos. 108–110, 128, 132; Albert, *Freiburger Münsterblätter* 5 (1909): nos. 138–140, 142, 157, 167, 189, 224.

41   Rolf Kießling, *Bürgerliche Gesellschaft und Kirche in Augsburg im Spätmittelalter. Ein Beitrag zur Strukturanalyse der oberdeutschen Reichsstadt*, Abhandlungen zur Geschichte der Stadt Augsburg 19 (Augsburg: Mühlberger, 1971), 126: "genossenschaftlichen Gegenstück zur herrschaftlichen Auffassung der Kirche."

42   Felix Fabri O.P., *Tractatus de civitate Ulmensi /Traktat über die Stadt Ulm*, 78.

Section V: Infrastructures and Genre

Infrastructural Poetics

Timo Müller

The modern era is characterized by the emergence of pervasive global infrastructures: traffic systems, electrical grids, resource cycles, information channels. Many of these infrastructures are designed to be overlooked. Built underground or often hidden, they are accompanied by discourses that legitimize and normalize them so that they become part of their users' mental routines.[1] Literature has not merely depicted this increasingly infrastructured world but has been shaped by it on several levels. This can best be seen in the paradigmatic genre of the modern era: the novel. The modern novel emerges in the eighteenth century and comes into its own in the age of industrialization, whose infrastructures—urban architecture, railroads, coal mines, alienated labor—are among its main thematic resources.

Numerous scholars have examined the representation of particular infrastructures in particular novels, writers, or periods, while others have traced the infrastructures that sustain the production and distribution of literature. It was not until the early twenty-first century, however, that the concept of infrastructure itself received sustained attention in literary studies.[2] This infrastructural perspective can build on discussions of the "poetic" dimension of infrastructure in the social sciences. The anthropologist Brian Larkin locates this poetic dimension in the symbolic surplus of spectacular infrastructure; Lauren Berlant locates it in the creative capacity infrastructure unfolds in interrelating otherwise disparate elements.[3]

---

1   Brian Larkin, "The Politics and Poetics of Infrastructure," *Annual Review of Anthropology* 42 (2013): 327–343; Susan Leigh Star, "The Ethnography of Infrastructure," *American Behavioral Scientist* 43, no. 3 (1999): 377–391; Dirk van Laak, "Garanten der Beständigkeit. Infrastrukturen als Integrationsmedien des Raumes und der Zeit," in *Strukturmerkmale der deutschen Geschichte des 20. Jahrhunderts*, ed. Anselm Doering-Manteuffel (Munich: Oldenbourg, 2006): 167–180.

2   Steffen Richter, *Infrastruktur. Ein Schlüsselkonzept der Moderne und die deutsche Literatur 1848–1914* (Berlin: Matthes & Seitz, 2018); Bruce Robbins, "The Smell of Infrastructure: Notes Toward an Archive," *boundary 2* 34, no. 1 (2007): 25–33; Michael Rubenstein, Bruce Robbins, and Sophia Beal, "Infrastructuralism: An Introduction," *Modern Fiction Studies* 61, no. 4 (2015): 575–586.

3   Larkin, "The Politics and Poetics of Infrastructure"; Lauren Berlant, "The Commons: Infrastructures for Troubling Times," *Environment and Planning D: Society and Space* 34, no. 3 (2016): 393–419.

This article offers a complementary approach to infrastructural poetics by shifting the perspective from the poetic dimension of infrastructure to the infrastructural dimension of poetics. Grounded in literary studies, the following discussion explores how the pervasive infrastructuration of modern society shaped the poetics of the modern novel. It draws on two interrelated senses of the term 'poetics': the internal organization of a text (for example, by plot structures and narrative modes) and the underlying conception of what literature is and does. Both of these changed as writers were reorganizing their texts to render the scope of modern infrastructure and the experience of living in a world pervaded by it. The article begins with a brief sketch of novelistic modes in the eighteenth and nineteenth centuries to indicate the diachronic dimension of this infrastructural poetics. Zooming in on the early twentieth century, the article argues that the infrastructuration of the novel attained a new level in the high modernist period as avant-garde writers structured their texts with covert, interrelated patterns that were foundational in investing a seemingly disjointed text—and world—with meaning.

From its eighteenth-century beginnings, the modern novel typically traced the development of one or several individual characters over time. As the novel situated these individuals in their social surroundings, it also developed a wider, systemic perspective. In the nineteenth century, 'panoramic' novels such as Dickens's *Bleak House* (1852–53), George Eliot's *Middlemarch* (1870–71), and Zola's *Germinal* (1894) subordinated the individual point of view to this systemic perspective in order to portray an entire community or a cross-section of modern society.[4] This approach can be understood as an attempt to negotiate the increasing infrastructuration of social life. Accelerated mobility systems, new communication channels, mass media, and other infrastructures of the industrial age engendered new modes of sociality and intensified existing ones. To record an individual character's development, the novel thus had to encompass a greater geographical and social range as well as the rapidly increasing amount of information at the character's disposal. Moreover, the individual's actions in an infrastructured society could have a much broader impact in a much shorter time. This presented significant challenges to traditional modes of storytelling and encouraged the emergence of the panoramic novel.

This process of differentiation allowed the panoramic novel to represent both the macro- and the micro-level of infrastructuration by exploring how it affected the individual within modern society. A paradigmatic example is Dickens's *Bleak House*, which alternates between an authorial narrator's sweeping descriptions of the industrial megacity of London and an individual character's account of her adventures within this city. The overarching perspective of the god-like narrator provides epistemological security by suggesting that, for all its ramifications, the modern world

---

4   Gerhard Friesen, *The German Panoramic Novel of the 19th Century* (Berne: Lang, 1972).

can be understood and organized into a coherent whole. Tracing the urban infrastructure and its effects plays an important role in this endeavour, as the opening lines of the novel indicate.

> London. Michaelmas Term lately over, and the Lord Chancellor sitting in Lincoln's Inn Hall. Implacable November weather. [...] Smoke lowering down from chimney-pots, making a soft black drizzle, with flakes of soot in it as big as full-grown snow-flakes—gone into mourning, one might imagine, for the death of the sun. Dogs, undistinguishable in mire. Horses, scarcely better; splashed to their very blinkers. Foot passengers, jostling one another's umbrellas, in a general infection of ill temper, and losing their foot-hold at street-corners, where tens of thousands of other foot passengers have been slipping and sliding since the day broke (if the day ever broke), adding new deposits to the crust upon crust of mud, sticking at those points tenaciously to the pavement, and accumulating at compound interest.[5]

All of these infrastructures—jurisdiction, heating systems, transportation, finance—will have profound effects on the characters. These individuals too can become and remain coherent wholes even if they cannot fully grasp the multiplying interrelations in which their lives unfold. This is confirmed by the alternating first-person report of the protagonist, Esther Summerson, who introduces herself as "not clever" (ch. 3) but becomes increasingly aware of the hidden connections in her social and urban environment as her maturation progresses.

These promises come into doubt as the infrastructuration of society expands. The technological innovations of the nineteenth and early twentieth centuries dramatically widens the mobility of people and information, so that the individual is continually confronted with strangeness. At the same time, it organizes daily life in such a way that existential affordances such as food and water supply, sanitation, and income depend on processes and people outside the individual's range of perception. These complications register in novelistic narration. In the late nineteenth century, writers begin to delimit or abolish the authorial narrator and to question the coherence of the character-narrator. Instead, they explore figural narration, which limits its scope to an individual character's immediate experiences and foregrounds the insecurities this narrowed scope entails. Figural narration merges the macro- and micro-perspectives on infrastructure by curtailing both. It reflects a world whose infrastructuration has expanded to an extent that defies even the overarching perspective of the omniscient narrator. On the micro-level, figural narration replaces the coherent character-narrator with techniques such as free

---

5   Charles Dickens, *Bleak House*, eds. George Ford and Sylvère Monod (New York: Norton, 1977), 5.

indirect speech, interior monologue, and stream of consciousness, which register how the character's perception is channelled and delimited by these infrastructures.

The shift to figural narration was a key factor in the emergence of the modernist novel. It was accompanied by a range of other techniques across literary and artistic genres that disrupted holistic and coherent representation. As the influential poet and critic T. S. Eliot emphasized, however, disruption did not equal arbitrariness or chaos. On the contrary, the purpose of literature was that "of controlling, of ordering, of giving a shape and a significance to the immense panorama of futility and anarchy which is contemporary history."[6] In this sceptical view, which many of Eliot's contemporaries shared, order and significance could no longer credibly be imposed from above. God was dead, political and military leaders were disgraced by the incompetent mass slaughter of the Great War, families and local communities were disintegrating into the anonymity and the newfound freedoms of modern life. Literary representations that were holistic or coherent were no more credible under these circumstances than god-like authorial narrators and linear character development.

What order and significance remained in a world that had "lost all form," Eliot pointed out, must be traced laboriously underneath: in belief systems, social ties, shared narratives, and collective imaginaries that had been broken apart and buried under the onslaught of modern life but which could be traced, unearthed, and recombined by the aesthetic sensibilities and the formal techniques of avant-garde literature.[7] In this view, literature is itself a process of infrastructuration in that it constructs cognitive and aesthetic configurations that underlie and shape modern life in ways that most users (readers) are not fully aware of but need for their wellbeing or even their very existence. "It is difficult / to get the news from poems," the avant-garde poet William Carlos Williams wrote, "yet men die miserably every day / for lack / of what is found there."[8] The most famous—and arguably most influential—example of this covert infrastructuration is the novel on which Eliot based his abovementioned discussion of modernism: James Joyce's *Ulysses* (1922).

Like other novels of the modern metropolis, from John Dos Passos's *Manhattan Transfer* (1925) and Virginia Woolf's *Mrs. Dalloway* (1925) to Alfred Döblin's *Berlin Alexanderplatz* (1929), *Ulysses* situates its characters in material and social environments that are infrastructured to an unprecedented degree. These characters' lives

---

6   T.S. Eliot, "*Ulysses*, Order, and Myth," in *Selected Prose of T.S. Eliot*, ed. Frank Kermode (London: Faber, 1975): 175–178, 177.

7   Cf. Astradur Eysteinsson, *The Concept of Modernism* (Ithaca: Cornell University Press, 1990); Timo Müller, *The Self as Object in Modernist Fiction: James—Joyce—Hemingway* (Würzburg: Königshausen & Neumann, 2010); Daniel Joseph Singal, "Towards a Definition of American Modernism," *American Quarterly* 39, no. 1 (1987): 7–26.

8   William Carlos Williams, *Journey to Love* (New York: Random House, 1955), 56.

and personalities are defined by skyscrapers, bridges, and prisons; by transport, health, and legal systems; by newspapers, advertisements, and movies; by electricity, toilets, and trash cans.[9] Unlike their nineteenth-century predecessors, these novels employ figural narration, stream of consciousness, and other techniques of episte-mological disruption to represent the pervasiveness of modern infrastructuration and its unsettling effects on the individual. This multilayered sensitivity manifests, for example, when Leopold Bloom, the protagonist of *Ulysses*, is watching a ship ex-porting Guinness beer:

> As he set foot on O'Connell bridge a puffball of smoke plumed up from the para-pet. Brewery barge with export stout. England. Sea air sours it, I heard. Be inter-esting some day get a pass through Hancock to see the brewery. Regular world in itself. Vats of porter, wonderful. Rats get in too. Drink themselves bloated as big as a collie floating. Dead drunk on the porter. Drink till they puke again like christians. Imagine drinking that! Rats: vats. Well of course if we knew all the things.[10]

Bloom's stream of consciousness identifies and interrelates many of the infrastruc-tures on which the Guinness brewery relies: trade networks, hygiene regulations, the internal infrastructures of the factory (a "regular" world in more senses than one) and the hidden ones of modern mass-produced nutrition.

As in other novels of the modern metropolis, the surface of *Ulysses* is dominated by anonymity, speed, and information overload. This ensures that readers share the characters' experience of epistemological destabilization. Just as the inhabitants of the city rely on routines to reestablish some degree of order and meaning, however, the novels rely on a variety of covert patterns that help the reader understand how disparate elements of the novel interlink. Bloom can do his errands because he is familiar with the geography of the city and many of its cultural codes and social in-stitutions. The reader can follow his physical and mental wanderings by attending to the subplots, leitmotifs, and other underlying patterns that structure the novel.

The most prominent of these underlying patterns is the Homeric *Odyssey*. The protagonists of Joyce's novel move through the streets and transport systems of Dublin just as Odysseus and his comrades travel through the Mediterranean on their ship and as Odysseus' family negotiates the physical and social infrastructures of Ithaca. Both the myth and the urban geography provide underlying patterns that readers can use to reestablish a degree of order, control, and significance:

---

9   Kate Marshall, "Sewer, Furnace, Air Shaft, Media: Modernity Behind the Walls in *Native Son* and *Manhattan Transfer*," *Studies in American Fiction* 37, no. 1 (2010): 55–80; Richter, *Infras-truktur*; Michael Rubenstein, *Public Works: Infrastructure, Irish Modernism, and the Postcolonial* (Notre Dame: University of Notre Dame Press, 2010).
10   James Joyce, *Ulysses* (London: Penguin, 2000), 191.

to make sense of the novel and of the epistemological confusions of modern life that the novel renders. Eliot describes this as a "method" that allows the novel to incorporate a great range of "living material" and give form to a world that has "lost all form."[11] In more recent terminology, the work these patterns do is best described as infrastructural: they are constructed underneath the surface texture of the novel; they are elemental for the reading experience because they generate meaning by interrelating diverse elements of the novel—and the world it depicts—across time and space; they require some training from the user (reader) but that training quickly subsides into routinized half-awareness.

Some of these textual infrastructures replicate the characters' own experience of the modern world: the characters of *Ulysses* too use their knowledge of Dublin's geography to understand the social texture of the city; they too use their knowledge of old stories—including local legends and literary classics—to make sense of modern life. Others, such as the chapter structure and the Homeric parallels, are added in the diegesis, either by the narrator's voice or the structure of the novel, to provide additional guidance to the reader. This layering recalls the combination of first-person and authorial perspectives in the early panoramic novel, but in modernist novels like *Ulysses* the increasing infrastructuration of the text—made possible by devices such as figural narration—interlaces the characters' perspectives much more closely with the reader's. As characters and readers rely on underlying epistemic patterns for guidance through the modern world, they also share the experience of failure that this approach entails. Both the underlying patterns and the modern world are too comprehensive to grasp as a whole, and they change continually, thus also transforming one another. Like Gatsby's green light that "year by year recedes before us," the ideal of control and understanding remains elusive as everyone needs to develop their individual interpretations of the underlying patterns and of their significance in and for the modern world.

This inherent contingency is another infrastructural dimension of modernist poetics. Eliot's variety of modernism may yearn for the systematic order of a closed world(view)—hence the fascination with fascism that Eliot shared with modernists as diverse as Marinetti, Yeats, Pound, and Jünger. Early scholars of modernism tended to project a similar "unity" on the literature,[12] but such readings were at odds with the ostentatiously fragmented, open-ended nature of modernist literature from the very beginning. The modernists' sense of epistemological instability precludes any poetics of closure. Their writings are at opposite ends of propaganda, where underlying epistemic patterns map neatly on the intra-and extradiegetic worlds the text presents. Even the political conservatives among the modernists

---

11   Eliot, "*Ulysses*, Order, and Myth," 177.
12   Joseph Frank, *The Widening Gyre: Crisis and Mastery in Modern Literature* (New Brunswick: Rutgers University Press, 1963), 13.

break apart closed forms and coherent patterns in their literary works. Their texts enact an ambivalence that, as Tung-Hui Hu points out, characterizes technological infrastructure as well. Designed to preempt its own collapse, Hu argues, infrastructure is a necessarily contingent "way of translating future capacity into the present."[13] It is a planned system that aims to absorb the greatest possible extent of unplanned usage and unplannable circumstances.

Joyce, for one, envisioned a very similar kind of generative permanence for *Ulysses*. Two of his best-known statements about the novel are that if Dublin "suddenly disappeared from the earth it could be reconstructed out of my book," and that he designed the book to "keep the professors busy for centuries."[14] Both statements indicate that Joyce designed the textual infrastructure of the novel to function indefinitely by leaving it open to interpretation, that is, to usage under circumstances that elude the planner's control. As a result, this infrastructure is necessarily contingent. No individual reader, including Joyce himself, can fully understand and systematize it, as is attested by the ongoing speculations about structural elements such as the anonymous narrator of the Cyclops episode or the "man in the mackintosh" whom characters perceive at several points in the novel. By keeping the reading experience from completion, such loose ends ensure that the novel remains as epistemologically unstable as the world itself.

The infrastructural poetics of modernism thus extends beyond thematic representations of specific infrastructures. It seeks to render the epistemic shifts caused by the pervasive infrastructuration of society as a whole. For this purpose, it adopts infrastructuration as an organizing principle of the literary text, developing an increasingly complex, relational, and generative conception of how literature works and how it affects society. The ambivalent meaning of the Greek *poiesis*, which in Plato as well as Aristotle encompasses both intellectual and physical creation, points to the implications this reorganization of literature has for the *techne* of material infrastructure. By providing patterns of perception and representation attuned to the complicated infrastructure underlying the modern world, literature affects readers' attitudes toward specific infrastructures as well as the infrastructuration of society as a period-defining phenomenon. By facilitating new ideas about infrastructure—its appearance, function, and effect, its ethics and politics, and its alternatives—these epistemic patterns influence contemporaneous discourses about its construction and usage in daily life. By creating textual infrastructures, modernist literature helps create material ones.

---

13   Tung-Hui Hu, "Black Boxes and Green Lights: Media, Infrastructure, and the Future at Any Cost," *English Language Notes* 55, no. 1–2 (2017): 81–88, 83.

14   James Budgen, *Joyce and the Making of* Ulysses (Bloomington: Indiana University Press, 1960), 67; Richard Ellmann, *James Joyce* (New York: Oxford University Press, 1982), 521.

Queering Infrastructures of Romance

Anja Hartl, Jonas Kellermann, and Christina Wald

Drawing on recent research in both infrastructure and queer studies, this article proposes to rethink romantic love as a mental, social, and cultural infrastructure that has been built and rebuilt over centuries and that continues to shape the ways in which we conceptualise love, relate to each other romantically, and assess our own lives and those of others. This infrastructure of romance consists of abstract concepts and archetypal narratives which frame and determine how we intellectually conceptualise and emotionally experience love, and which shape the principles according to which we lead our lives. It has both material and immaterial aspects, as it is formed by and in turn forms conceptions and dramaturgies of love as distributed in various discourses, genres, and media. This sociocultural and mental infrastructure of romance works in conjunction with established infrastructures in film production, TV networks, literary publishing, and digital communication.

The infrastructure of romance has been under construction for as long as it has existed, and is currently being updated for a number of reasons, including the trend of mathematical, algorithmic matchmaking[1] and forms of 'posthuman romance' between humans and machines as well as attention to the "logistical aesthetics" of desire in late capitalism.[2] This article will focus on a different ongoing

---

[1]   For this, see for instance Christina Wald, "Matchmaking and the Infrastructure of Romance: *The One* or *What You Will?*" in *Figures of Pathos / Figuren des Pathos. Festschrift in Honor of Elisabeth Bronfen*, eds. Frauke Berndt, Isabel Karremann, and Klaus Müller-Wille (Würzburg: Königshausen & Neumann, 2023): 293–305, on which this article partly draws. Wald compares Shakespeare's romantic comedy *Twelfth Night* to its unmarked adaptation in the 2021 Netflix TV series *The One* from an infrastructural point of view. Set in a future in which everyone can identify their one perfect match via DNA data and digital technology, *The One* in a speculative manner interferes in traditional dramaturgies of romance plots marked by confusions, misrecognitions, and obstacles, thus pointing towards a potential future rebuilding of romance's infrastructures.

[2]   Sam McBean, "Circulating Desire: Queer Logistical Aesthetics," *Feminist Media Studies* (2022): 1–15, 6. This logistical aesthetic connects the capitalist circulation of goods to the circulation of desire and builds on the premise that "the material, infrastructural, and logistical condition the kinds of social structures that can be built, and integrally, dictate what can circulate" (McBean, "Circulating Desire," 7). Desire thus becomes an entity of logistical circulation. In

process with its own considerable history, namely the queer rebuilding of romance's infrastructures. Queering the infrastructure of romance enables an engagement with non-normative expressions and narratives of desire without perpetuating the exclusionary norms of the ideology of romantic love. In a brief case study of how a recent novel has intervened in the sociocultural afterlife of William Shakespeare's *Romeo and Juliet*, we will argue that adaptation offers a powerful cultural practice for rewriting iconic literary narratives and reconceptualising popular notions of romantic love.

Romance and/as Infrastructure

In its broadest sense, romance can, as proposed by literary scholar and cultural theorist Lauren Berlant, be understood as "a particular version of the story of love."[3] Berlant's definition not only establishes love as a key emotional experience at the heart of romance, but also draws attention to its discursive quality and the close interaction between social and literary forms to narrate love. Above all, culturally specific notions of romantic love provide a scaffolding for social interaction, a script which our intersubjective relations follow, whether consciously or unconsciously. As literary and cultural historians have shown, the forms and meanings of romance as a European discourse have shifted considerably since the late Middle Ages.[4] Sociologists like Niklas Luhmann have theorised romantic love as a historically evolving "code, a set of rules according to which emotions can be expressed and which is already elaborated before one enters the game of love."[5] For Luhmann, love is not only a powerful emotion but also a medium of intimate communication which has changed with the growing individualisation and complexity of modernity. In his perspective, the European semantics of romantic love shifted around 1800, when European Romanticism idealised love to paradoxically "unify a duality," a union of two individualised lovers primarily based on their mutual, identity-forming love.[6]

---

the Netflix series *Sense8* (2015–2018), this circulation is represented as "an imagined global network of connection that looks akin to the supply chains of late capitalism (even runs on them) but that is suffused with sex, desire, and queer utopian possibility" (3).

3   Lauren Berlant, *Desire/Love* (Brooklyn: Punctum Books, 2012), 6.

4   See for example David Shumway, "What's Love Got to Do With It? Romance and Intimacy in an Age of Hooking Up," in *The Routledge Companion to Romantic Love*, ed. Ann Brooks (Abingdon-on-Thames: Routledge, 2022): 15–25, 15.

5   Korbinian Stöckl, *Love in Contemporary British Drama: Traditions and Transformations of a Cultural Emotion* (Berlin: De Gruyter, 2021), 74.

6   Niklas Luhmann, *Love as Passion: The Codification of Intimacy* (Cambridge: Harvard University Press, 1986), 136.

This also marks the moment when the idea of passionate romance as part of hetero-sexual marriage became the new norm which shapes Western societies until today.

Having developed into well-rehearsed clichés, the discursive expressions, cultural narratives, as well as individual experiences of romantic love have acquired normative status. As such, romance has become implicated in the socio-political negotiations of our time in a paradoxical manner: it has not only served as "a tool for heteronormative" and "patriarchal [...] power structures"[7] but has also been turned into a consumerist good through what sociologist Eva Illouz has described as a reciprocal process of "the romanticization of commodities and the commodification of romance" in late capitalism.[8] Against such functions that support the status quo, romance has also been employed to distort and transform social conventions. Critically dismantling and rebuilding the infrastructure of romance can pave the way to new social imaginaries and realities. For instance, inspired by the work of bell hooks, who has conceptualised love not as a script for reproduction and consumption but as an "active and transformative practice," a feminist strand of critical love studies has explored romance as a means of challenging social structures and cultural conventions.[9] Within this context, Berlant has called for a queer perspective on love, which she describes as "a site that has perhaps not yet been queered enough,"[10] as we will show below in greater detail.

Crucially, the power of notions of romantic love is tied to their interdependency with "fantasy" and the imagination.[11] Building on these insights into the social and cultural mechanisms of romance, we argue that processes of constructing, perpetuating, and interrogating romantic love are tied to and dependent on fictional narratives: romance fiction is capable not only of representing, but, more importantly, also of actively shaping sociocultural romantic scripts. Therefore, romance fiction can both reinforce and diversify romance conventions. This intersection between romance as fictional genre and romance as social discourse has contributed to the creation of a complex infrastructure that shapes our social behaviour and forms psychological expectations.

---

7   Jennifer Leetsch, *Love and Space in Contemporary African Diasporic Women's Writing: Making Love, Making Worlds* (London: Palgrave Macmillan, 2021), 8.

8   Eva Illouz, *Consuming the Romantic Utopia: Love and the Cultural Contradictions of Capitalism* (Oakland: University of California Press, 1997), 26. Lauren Berlant, too, connects "[t]he installation of romantic love as the fundamental attachment of humans" to "the normalization of heterosexuality and femininity in consumer culture" in "Love, a Queer Feeling," in *Homosexuality and Psychoanalysis*, eds. Tim Dean and Christopher Lane (Chicago: University of Chicago Press, 2001): 432–451, 440.

9   Leetsch, *Love and Space*, 9.

10   Berlant, "Love, a Queer Feeling," 433.

11   Lauren Berlant, *Desire/Love*, 69.

Recent research in interdisciplinary infrastructure studies has provided a useful framework for understanding the emergence and negotiation of social relations. Anthropologist Ara Wilson has drawn attention to the interconnection between infrastructures and intimacy, arguing that specific urban material infrastructures are not only "involved in" but also "shape the conditions for relational life."[12] Building on Illouz's sociological and Berlant's cultural analysis, empirical studies by media scholars like Sander de Ridder have elucidated how the algorithms of dating apps shape current patterns of intimacy and romantic love. They belong to "a widely adopted, technologically and commercially driven mathematical mindset to dating" that is characterised by a desire for predictability, controllability, and convenience in romantic and sexual encounters.[13] Urban material infrastructures and digital infrastructures thus shape and are in turn shaped by conventions and narratives of romantic love, which we propose to regard as mental, cultural, and social infrastructures. Just like their architectural and digital counterparts, these individual and collective mental infrastructures are often taken for granted and employed habitually. Regarding this infrastructural quality of romance, Susan Leigh Star's notion of infrastructure as "an embedded strangeness, a second-order one, that of the forgotten, the background, the frozen in place" can explain why lovers are often unaware that they seek and enact a romantic script rather than spontaneous, individual emotions.[14]

One of the most prevalent tacitly accepted scripts on which infrastructures of romantic love hinge is heteronormativity. As Wilson has put it, "[i]nfrastructure involves the very norms that queer and feminist scholarship excavates so ably. It aims for the invisible, taken-for-granted status of the best ideology: when infrastructure works as it should, we often stop seeing it."[15] Yet, if maintenance of infrastructure fails, the invisible suddenly becomes visible and what we have long taken for granted is laid bare to critical re-examination and possibly even repurposing of its original functions. Drawing on literary, filmic, medial, cultural, and technological infrastructures that have shaped our understanding of romance, we argue that paying close attention to these infrastructural mechanisms—to "how [love] actually works

---

12   Ara Wilson, "The Infrastructures of Intimacy," *Signs: Journal of Women in Culture and Society* 41, no. 2 (Winter 2016): 247–280, 247.

13   Sander de Ridder, "The Datafication of Intimacy: Mobile Dating Apps, Dependency, and Everyday Life," in *Television & New Media* (2021): 1–17, 2. See also Thorsten Peetz, "Digitalisierte intime Bewertung. Möglichkeiten sozialer Beobachtung auf *Tinder*," *Kölner Zeitschrift für Soziologie und Sozialpsychologie* 73 (2021): 425–450.

14   Susan Leigh Star, "The Ethnography of Infrastructure," *American Behavioral Scientist* 43, no. 3 (1999): 377–391, 379.

15   Wilson, "Infrastructures," 248.

as a principle of living"—may also untap a radical potential for 'queering' common notions of romantic love.[16]

The question of whether romantic love can be 'queered' at all has been fiercely debated in queer theory. In his influential critique of reproductive futurism, Lee Edelman has attacked love as a "totalizing fantasy, always a fantasy of totalization"[17] that compels us into normative commitments towards futurity and sociality. It is this totalizing commitment that Edelman's queer figure of the "sinthomosexual"[18] defies: "In breaking our hold on the future, the sinthomosexual [...] forsakes all causes, all social action, all responsibility for a better tomorrow or for the perfection of social forms."[19] Unsurprisingly, this critical stance towards love as a compulsory social form also pertains to its institutionalization in marriage. Accordingly, many queer theorists have scrutinized activism for the legalization of same-sex marriage as assimilation into an inherently oppressive system, rather than celebrating it as liberation therefrom. In their view, expecting social inclusion and political change via marriage rights means participating in the "cruel optimism" analysed by Berlant,[20] as queer activists hope "that the heteronormative, patriarchal, and state-controlled institution of marriage will somehow make up for the legacies of gay and lesbian abjection."[21] While these critiques of gay marriage are important, we argue that a conception of romance as infrastructure will help us engage with romantic love without automatically turning it into a confining ideology which, in the case of non-heterosexual relationships, simply replaces one oppressive normativity, such as heteronormativity, with another, such as the homonormativity of state-sanctioned monogamy in marriage. Instead, by shedding light on the infrastructures that facilitate how we experience and think about love, including queer love, we may uncover ways to rebuild those very infrastructures and thereby allow for a non-normative optimism that is neither cruel nor based on abjection. If "[t]he prefix infra [...] flags the intended purpose of conventional infrastructural projects

---

16   Berlant, "Love, a Queer Feeling," 443.

17   Lee Edelman, *No Future: Queer Theory and the Death Drive* (Durham: Duke University Press, 2004), 73.

18   "Sinthomosexuality" is Edelman's neologism that blends homosexuality with the Lacanian "sinthome", which denotes the "psychotic kernel that can neither be interpreted (as symptom) nor 'traversed' (as fantasy)" and thereby "represents the final limit of the psychoanalytic process." Slavoj Žižek, *Looking Awry: An Introduction to Jacques Lacan Through Popular Culture* (Cambridge: MIT Press, 1991), 137. Sinthomosexuality thus embodies the death drive in that its self-shattering jouissance rejects any notion of futurity.

19   Edelman, *No Future*, 101.

20   Lauren Berlant, *Cruel Optimism* (Durham: Duke University Press, 2011).

21   Mari Ruti, *The Ethics of Opting Out: Queer Theory's Defiant Subject* (New York: Columbia University Press, 2017), 16.

to end up hidden from the view of most users,"[22] then a consideration of queer infrastructures of romance will foreground those expressions of love that have long since laid hidden from view in the shadows of heteronormativity. As our case study exemplifies, "queer romance," which "remains peripheral to most academic accounts of the genre,"[23] provides an important testing ground for such reparative re-figurations of infrastructure, as it offers narrative space to create fantasies of queer love that counter Edelman's debilitating fantasy of totalization.[24]

An infrastructural approach to romance therefore illuminates how the dynamics with which cultural ideals as perpetuated by specific works and discourses can be universalized to the point of obscurity, or rather of infrastructural invisibility. It reveals how, as Berlant puts it, the "the formalism of love is exploited and expressed by the repetitions of intimate conventionality" while also demonstrating that "to change the aesthetic of love, its archive of reference, inevitably animates discourses of instability from anxiety through revolution."[25] In the following brief case study, we will elaborate on the potential of such an infrastructural approach to romance by examining one of the culturally most influential literary stories of romantic love, William Shakespeare's tragedy *Romeo and Juliet*, and its queer adaptation in Douglas Stuart's novel *Young Mungo* (2022).

Queering *Romeo and Juliet* in Douglas Stuart's *Young Mungo* (2022)

Arguably, few artistic works emblematize the tension in romantic love between normative perpetuation and subversion as powerfully as William Shakespeare's dramatization of the tragic love story of *Romeo and Juliet*, first performed around 1597. In his 2017 Norton Critical Edition, Gordon McMullan suggests that "*Romeo and Juliet* has become, over time, the absolute embodiment, the tragic paradigm, of romantic

---

22   Wilson, "Infrastructures," 270.

23   Andrea Wood and Jonathan A. Allan, "Special Issue: Queering Popular Romance (Editors' Introduction)," *Journal of Popular Romance Studies* 5, no. 2 (2016): 1–5, 1.

24   As Jayashree Kamble has showcased, these reparative counter fantasies include "the re-definition of ideal masculinity and 'good' sexual orientation undertaken in popular discourse" in the wake of the gay rights movement and the rise of queer romance publishing. Jayashree Kamble, *Making Meaning in Popular Romance Fiction: An Epistemology* (London: Palgrave Macmillan, 2014), 88, 125. The publishing industry in itself can therefore be considered an infrastructure that conditions the proliferation of queer romance writing. See Len Barot, "Queer Romance in Twentieth-and Twenty-First-Century America: Snapshots of a Revolution," in *Romance Fiction and American Culture: Love as the Practice of Freedom?*, eds. William A. Gleason and Eric Murphy Selinger (Abingdon-on-Thames: Routledge, 2015): 389–404.

25   Berlant, "Love, a Queer Feeling," 438.

love."[26] McMullan's reference to the long-term nature of that process is telling, considering that the story of the Veronese lovers did not yet occupy its current status in Shakespeare's lifetime. By contrast to other literary couples, the protagonists of Shakespeare's first tragedy of love were relative unknowns, and it was this obscurity and transposability that paved the way for the play to become the cultural icon that it is today.[27]

Just as *Romeo and Juliet* was gradually consolidated as a cultural icon of romantic love, so were the ideological implications which were drawn from it. According to Dympna Callaghan, "*Romeo and Juliet* consolidates the ideology of romantic love" and "has been used to perpetuate" that very ideology ever since.[28] In negotiating different forms of desire, that process of consolidation is faced with love as both a universal and a particular experience. *Romeo and Juliet* straddles the line between being "an apparently benign, lyrical document of universal love" and the idealization of a specifically heteronormative manifestation of love as defined by patriarchal discourses.[29] Callaghan notes that this very idealization positions the tragedy in close generic proximity to comedy and "the possibility of a happy conclusion," indicating that as a dramatic plot, romantic love is entangled as much with the comedic as with the tragic realm.[30]

This generic flexibility is certainly one of the reasons why *Romeo and Juliet* has enjoyed an unprecedented creative afterlife, transcending generic and geographic boundaries. The cultural imprint of Shakespeare's play ranges from opera and ballet to Hollywood films like James Cameron's *Titanic* to Japanese anime series and video games to fan-made web series.[31] Whether direct or indirect, all of these various engagements with Shakespeare's play add to its status as "the iconic text of romantic love."[32] An infrastructural approach can reveal the overt and covert processes

---

26   Gordon McMullan, "Introduction," in *Romeo and Juliet*, by William Shakespeare (New York: Norton, 2017): ix–xxiii, xvi.

27   Marjorie Garber, *Shakespeare and Modern Culture* (New York: Anchor Books, 2008), 46.

28   Dympna Callaghan, "The Ideology of Romantic Love: The Case of *Romeo and Juliet*," in *The Weyward Sisters: Shakespeare and Feminist Politics*, eds. Dympna Callaghan, Lorraine Helms, and Jyotsna Singh (Hoboken: Blackwell, 1994): 59–101, 62, 60.

29   Callaghan, "Ideology of Romantic Love," 88.

30   Callaghan, "Ideology of Romantic Love," 81.

31   Jonas Kellermann, *Dramaturgies of Love in* Romeo and Juliet: *Word, Music, and Dance* (Abingdon-on-Thames: Routledge, 2021); Eric S. Mallin, *Reading Shakespeare in the Movies: Non-Adaptations and Their Meaning* (London: Palgrave Macmillan, 2019), 85–138; Ryuta Minami, "What's in a Name? Shakespeare and Japanese Pop Culture," in *The Routledge Handbook of Shakespeare and Global Appropriation*, eds. Christy Desmet, Sujata Iyengar, and Miriam Jacobson (Abingdon-on-Thames: Routledge, 2020): 290–303, 295–299; Ariane M. Balizet, *Shakespeare and Girls' Studies* (Abingdon-on-Thames: Routledge, 2019), 144–146.

32   Callaghan, "Ideology of Romantic Love," 88.

through which such cultural icons are constructed and the (subliminal) influence that they exude on our individual and collective imagination.

As Wilson notes, the term "infrastructure" originally referred to "the understructure of railways (land, embankments, bridges) as opposed to their superstructure (rails, stations, and any type of overhead structures)."[33] Considering the influence of artistic productions like *Romeo and Juliet* on our cultural imagination of romantic love, we may likewise consider these productions as the infrastructure upon which that imagination is built—or vice versa. Depending on our interpretative practice of infrastructural foregrounding, we can consider cultural notions of love as the understructure that enables specific literary texts, theatrical performances, and films. This cultural imagination as formed by, and in turn forming, specific artistic productions provides the understructure that shapes our social interactions. The influence of this infrastructure of romance becomes so pervasive that they are effectively rendered 'invisible,' universalizing something normatively specific like heterosexual love to the point where we simply take it for granted, without wasting a second thought where that ideal may have originated from. According to Berlant, "love's function is to mark the subject's binding to the scenes to which s/he must always return;"[34] an infrastructural approach to romance may help us get a better hold onto the origin and maintenance of those scenes and prevent them from falling into the shadowy background of ideological unreflectedness. Using the influential term proposed by computer scientist Geoffrey C. Bowker, we can perform an "infrastructural inversion" that foregrounds the background and focuses on the infrastructure itself;[35] as Bowker points out, this also means that each decision to examine a phenomenon as the ground for something else is an interpretative act of infrastructuring, of turning something into an infrastructure. Understanding romance as infrastructure, even a seemingly unshakable icon of heteronormativity like *Romeo and Juliet* may thereby be appropriated to queer and destabilize the very infrastructures that it consolidated in the first place.

Douglas Stuart's sophomore novel *Young Mungo* (2022), for example, relocates the early modern feud between the Capulets and Montagues to the confessional conflict in 1980s Glasgow. Against all odds, the Protestant Mungo falls in love with the Catholic James; together, the two boys try to keep their relationship a secret from Mungo's alcoholic mother, his violent Tybalt-esque brother Hamish, and James's homophobic father. The novel affirms its obvious thematic indebtedness to Shakespeare halfway through when Mungo's sister Jodie confronts her visibly enamoured

---

33   Wilson, "Infrastructures of Intimacy," 267.

34   Berlant, "Love, a Queer Feeling," 439.

35   Geoffrey C. Bowker, "Information Mythology and Infrastructure," in *Information Acumen: The Understanding and Use of Knowledge in Modern Business*, ed. L. Bud-Frierman (Abingdon-on-Thames: Routledge, 1994): 231–247, 235–236.

brother with the words "But, soft!, what light through yonder window breaks," directly alluding to the perhaps most famous love scene of all time, and even calling him "Romeo" moments later.[36] The novel thus forms part of a larger spectrum of global adaptations that "illuminate[] *Romeo and Juliet*'s queer and transcultural possibilities."[37] More specifically, it self-reflectively sheds light on its Shakespearean intertext and raises expectant questions whether the star-crossed love of Mungo and James will automatically meet the same tragic fate in the violent setting of working-class Glasgow as their Veronese counterparts. Stuart thus makes visible and explicit the cultural understructure upon which his novel and its representation of queer love are built, highlighting the Shakespearean myth of star-crossed love as an infrastructural script with a potential for subversively creative license.

Furthermore, *Young Mungo* also emphasizes the degree to which infrastructures themselves facilitate intimate encounters and relationships. On the one hand, James talks about his experience of calling a hotline that connects him with other anonymous gay men in a time prior to digital dating platforms like the appositely titled *Romeo* (previously *Gay Romeo* and *Planet Romeo*).[38] Ironically, the hotline that was intended to grant James secret intimacies with other men eventually leads to the reveal of his sexuality to his homophobic father who receives an unusually high phone bill.

On the other hand, when Mungo and James decide to leave their tenements to spend an afternoon together that eventually culminates in their first kiss, Stuart emphasizes the infrastructures that they pass on their way out of the city:

> They debated whether to cross a bridge over the roaring motorway. Mungo had a distrust of bridges, it was only an overpass that separated the Protestant Billies from the Catholic Bhoyston. On the far side he could see another housing scheme, but beyond that was a low line of trees, and there were no tower blocks, nor gasworks, to spoil the horizon.[39]

The bridge fulfils several functions in the novel. It not only connects the Protestant and Catholic housing schemes—and serves as location for the catastrophic gang fight towards the end of the novel; it also promises access to a seemingly pastoral sanctuary beyond the city where Mungo and James can live out their love undisturbed, exemplifying how infrastructures as potential sites of intimacy eschew conventional demarcations of the public and the private.[40] Paradoxically even, then, the novel's urban material infrastructures point towards a utopian existence *without* any

---

36   Douglas Stuart, *Young Mungo* (London: Picador, 2022), 246–247.
37   Ja Young Jeon, "Romeo at the Girls' School: *Fantasy of the Girls*' Queer Teen Adaptation of Shakespeare," *Adaptation* (2022): 1–21, 3; cf. Balizet, *Shakespeare and Girls' Studies*, 144–146.
38   Stuart, *Young Mungo*, 230–234.
39   Stuart, *Young Mungo*, 225.
40   See Wilson, "Infrastructures of Intimacy."

infrastructures and religious division. Yet, this infrastructure-less utopia is simultaneously subverted by the novel's second plot. After Mungo's relationship to James becomes known, two men that his mother met in an AA meeting force him to go on a fishing trip with them to the Highlands. In the deserted wilderness of the north, Mungo is sexually abused and eventually has to kill his tormentors to find a way back into civilized, 'infrastructured' life. In the end, both Mungo and James survive, unlike their Shakespearean predecessors, yet whether or not the boys will possibly have a future together beyond their wordless greeting that concludes the novel remains open. If "[f]iction provides models of the relation between love's utopian prospects and its lived experience," then *Young Mungo* uses its intertextual and intratextual infrastructures to showcase the fragility but also the hopefulness of that relation and the extent to which our ideological scripts of romantic love may be rewritten after all.[41]

In conclusion, this article has suggested an infrastructural approach towards romance that highlights how our mental, social, and cultural understandings of romantic love persistently inform (in often subliminal ways) our contemporary experience of love. These understandings provide the infrastructural foundation upon which both our romantic interactions in everyday life and artistic representations thereof rest and build. Yet, the required use and maintenance of infrastructure also leaves space for its subversive re-purposing. In the current moment of diversifying sexualities and gender identities, infrastructures of romance are once again reconstructed. Heteronormative ideologies of love as perpetuated by iconic narratives like *Romeo and Juliet* are 'queered,' showcasing the exemplary potential of adaptation as a cultural instance of infrastructural inversion and transformation.

---

41   Berlant, *Desire/Love*, 97.

Counting the Impacts in the Solar Off Grid Sector

Eva Riedke

Solar off grid entrepreneurs dream of doing their meaningful share towards ending global energy poverty by delivering clean, reliable, and sustainable electricity to the millions of people who live with no or only partial connection to the grid. At the same time, and in line with the pro-business rhetoric of philanthrocapitalist foundations, the selling of solar power to people living 'off' or 'under' the grid also represents an opportunity to pursue the untapped commercial value of new and expanding markets in Africa and Asia.[1] Initially, it was a sector defined by the mass production and marketing of simple solar lanterns that came to represent a 'minimal technology for living.'[2] The solar lanterns came to serve, as Cross[3] puts it, "as a benchmark of whether or not people have access to the most basic level of clean, efficient energy deemed necessary for human life." Today, the sector has grown to incorporate the sale of a wide array of other ingenious other solar-powered devices and systems, of different size and scale. In turn, lanterns, as the once iconic product, have largely come to be replaced by so-called solar home systems—sufficient, in the smaller formats, to power lights, mobile phone chargers, and in many cases a radio. The larger solar home systems provide enough energy to also power TVs, fans, and refrigerators. It is the latter kind of solar off grid products that this chapter will engage with. More specifically, my concern is here with the 'impact metrics' that are fashioned in

---

1   Eva Riedke, "A solar off-grid software: The making of infrastructures, markets and consumers 'beyond energy,'" in *Digitisation and Low-Carbon Energy Transition*, ed. Siddharth Sareen and Katja Müller (Basingstoke: Palgrave Macmillan, 2023): 31–52; Eva Riedke and Catherine Adelmann, "The good payers: Exploring notions of ownership in the sale of pay-as-you-go solar home systems," *Energy Research & Social Science* 92, no. 102773 (2022): 1–8; Jamie Cross, "The Solar Good: Energy Ethics in Poor Markets," *Journal of the Royal Anthropological Institute* 25, no. S1 (2019): 47–66; Jamie Cross, "Capturing Crisis: Solar Power and Humanitarian Energy Markets in Africa," *The Cambridge Journal of Anthropology* 38, no. 2 (2020): 105–124; Tom Neumark, "Leapfrogging the Grid: Off-grid Solar, Self-reliance and the Market in Tanzania," *Social Anthropology/Anthropologie sociale* 30, no. 2 (2022): 140–160.
2   Peter Redfield, "Bioexpectations: Life Technologies as Humanitarian Goods," *Public Culture* 24, no. 1 (2012): 157–184.
3   Jamie Cross, "Solar Basics," *Limn. Issue 9* (2018), https://limn.it/articles/solar-basics.

relation to these solar off grid products—metrics that are meant to give quantifiable insights into the results, effects and ultimately 'impacts' that solar companies are having in places that remain formally unelectrified.

By exploring metrics and what 'metrics do' in the solar off grid sector, the aim of this chapter is to draw attention to the relationality between what initially appears to be a series of heterogeneous and distinct infrastructures. The aim is namely to illustrate how impact metrics, being fashioned in response to the roll-out of solar off grid products, engender relations between solar off grid infrastructures and particular fiscal architectures. The chapter hereby engages with the sale of solar off grid products as representative of an 'infrastructure in the making' that readily aligns with our normative understanding of the term, i.e., as an infrastructure with a concrete material form. It also goes on to explore the wider constitutive relations which emerge therefrom. Solar off-grid infrastructures are made to produce certain metrics and these metrics, in turn, also come to serve as a tool to attract and incentivize investment, generating relations to wider economic infrastructures. Exploring the use of metrics in this manner, so my proposition, works to unsettle and extend our understanding of how material and immaterial infrastructures can hang together, overlap, and allows us to retheorize their mutual embeddedness.

Making sense of these developments allows us to generally explore how the provision of basic forms of solar electrification—a sector in which philanthropic, altruistic claims and high notions of 'common good' are commonplace—is being tethered to market logics and the ongoing rise of neoliberalism.[4] More specifically, exploring the sutures made between these different infrastructures, enables us to begin exploring ethnographically what is often presented and experienced as the more benign side effects in a sector that is out to sell solar products to people living with or using off-grid solar energy—namely the significance of forecasting investment opportunities 'off the grid.' Focusing on the infrastructure sutures at hand, draws our attention to what Crane[5] has, in the context of global health humanitarianism, described as the 'valuable inequalities' that create opportunities for investment, yet that also demand the creation of data and stories to document and justify them.[6]

Let me begin with recounting a meeting I had with solar entrepreneurs in April 2021. It is over zoom that I sat together with three founders of a small solar energy start-up, who I will here refer to as Jua Power, that initially sought to produce and market solar home systems in rural Kenya but who then—after being a few years on the market—reoriented towards software development. They were now in the

---

4   Cross, "The Solar Good"; Neumark, "Leapfrogging the Grid."

5   Johanna Tayloe Crane, *Scrambling for Africa: AIDS, Expertise, and the Rise of American Global Health Science* (London: Cornell University Press, 2013).

6   Lilly Walkover, "When Good Works Count," in *Metrics: What Counts in Global Health*, ed. Vincanne Adams (London: Duke University Press, 2016): 163–178.

business of developing digital services for other solar companies, including digital platforms through which the latter could then manage sales operations, track payments as well as generate performance and impact metrics—i.e., numbers, enumerations, and quantifications to account for the money spent, to gauge sales impact, and to evaluate electrification outcomes. They sought my opinion on a series of impact metrics that they were hoping to integrate that would be equally meaningful for their clients (namely other solar firms) and the investors that stand behind these clients. We discussed the common indicators that solar off grid companies regularly reported on, to what degree the data for these were readily collectable, and the range of phenomena that they worked to push inside and outside of visibility. We concentrated our discussion on the example of a solar-powered street food cart in Nairobi—a solar 'product' for which they were currently programming a template in their software. What were legitimate impacts to measure and report on? They suggested indicators directly linked to the product, such as: 'Amount of CO_2 saved,' 'Quantities of charcoal saved,' 'Amount of clean cooking hours enabled.' In addition, they also sought to highlight financial and social impacts, which included 'Income generated,' 'Jobs created,' 'Lives affected,' and 'Women empowered'—indicators for which, as they readily admitted, numbers were a bit more difficult to find.[7]

A few days later, I discussed these last three metrics with an investment advisor in Nairobi. I remarked: "How do companies realistically go about estimating the number of jobs created, lives affected, and women empowered when it comes to a solar powered street food cart? Or even the 'simpler' products like solar powered lanterns?" The answer she gave was straightforward: "The numbers are far-fetched, that is clear." She laughed. "Off grid populations are, by definition, more difficult to speak to and to count." "But this [these numbers/ metrics] is what social impact investing is about and what everyone in the sector needs to appeal to when selling to investors." She added: "Significant is that these [numbers/ metrics] are also less about evaluating the impact *made*. Attached to them are also stories about the future. So, the *future worth* of such food carts if one invests."[8] Herein, as Erikson[9] has similarly illustrated for the field global health, metrics that initially served to ensure accountability for money invested, are now undergoing a shift towards becoming 'value' metrics—defining a prospective future-centric value of a potential investment. Accountability metrics are tethered to market logics, Eriksen elaborates,

---

7   All indicators are linked to the global indicator framework established for the sustainable development goals (SDGs). Since 2015 the sector has, also in relation to the SDGs, established a series standardized impact metrics specifically for lighting products (see https://www.gogla.org/impact/gogla-impact-metrics).

8   Interview, 12 October 2022, emphasis added.

9   Susan L Erikson, "Metrics: What Counts in Global Health," in *Metrics*, ed. Vincanne Adams (London: Duke University Press, 2016): 225–230.

and in the process, these become suffused for investors with a sense of anticipatory forward-looking excitement, for they become suggestive of how much money is likely to be made.

One Solar Lantern = One Kerosene Lamp

The significance of metrics to ensure accountability for money spent is not new. However, with the rise of private-sector non-profits, a new emphasis on metrics has taken shape, including a significant rise in requests that numbers produced also function to tell 'future values.' This includes using metrics as *anticipatory praxis*. A development, if we follow others,[10] that is ascribable to the unique character of many developers of humanitarian goods, like solar off grid startups, that, following the promise often sold by financial advisors of the Gates Foundation, seek to 'make money by doing good.' These philanthrocapitalist players do not envision their objects only as stop-gap solutions or 'band-aids' for entrenched systemic failures,[11] but rather "envisage their technologies as the building blocks for new kinds of universal infrastructures" and envision markets as the most effective mechanism for realizing scale.[12] There is a repeated commitment to the "market's vocabulary, as well as its values and assumptions of growth", as the only viable engine of infrastructure development and social change.[13] This, in turn, has an effect on the pressure to produce particular kinds of metrics and works to define notions of what the complex grafting together of numbers and stories is supposed to do—effects already reflected in the documents that start-up companies sign with investors.

The three solar entrepreneurs concerned with defining impact indicators for a solar powered food cart in Nairobi emphasized in our conversation that the commitment of investors is always newly dependent on the numbers produced. "Even if aspects like jobs created and women empowered is difficult to measure," Ruby B., one of the co-founders of the start-up explains, "solar companies stand in competition with one another and those who sell more impact attract more investment."[14] Despite describing new pressures that have arisen in the context 'selling of impact' in recent years (in particular, the emphasis on shorter time frames), Ruby emphasizes

---

10   Cross, "The Solar Good"; Peter Redfield, "Shacktopia: The Meantime Future of Humanitarian Design," *Social Anthropology/Anthropologie sociale* 30, no. 2 (2022): 16–33; Erikson, "Metrics: What Counts in Global Health."

11   Peter Redfield, "On Band-Aids and Magic Bullets," *Limn. Issue 9* (2017), https://limn.it/articles/on-band-aids-and-magic-bullets/.

12   Jamie Cross and Alice Street, "To Fail at Scale!: Minimalism and Maximalism in Humanitarian Entrepreneurship," *Social Anthropology/Anthropologie sociale* 30, no. 2 (2022): 101–109, 104.

13   Cross and Street, "To Fail at Scale!," 116.

14   Zoom meeting with the author, 23 April 2022.

that "the problem with the indicators has always been there, ever since the sector emerged and sold simple solar lanterns."

A good example for the problem being an 'old one' in the sector is the calculation of 'number of people electrified per solar lantern sold.' Instead of companies calculating the impact on the basis of the number of mobile lanterns sold and the number of people who may *actually* use each lantern (at the same time)—a calculation which takes into consideration that a 25 lumen lantern has less of an impact than a 300 lumen lantern—solar off grid companies progressively moved on to define the impact in terms of the number of people who could *potentially* use the lantern available in a household. Different producers of solar lanterns, in turn, went on to define 'households' in very different terms—with the average number of people per household ranging from 2.8 people to 6 people. As an (incomplete) overview by Schützeichel[15] suggests with reference to different producers of solar lanterns:

- 2.8 people/lantern: Lighting Africa
- 3.4 people/lantern: Little Sun
- 4.5 people/lantern: SolarAid / Sunny Money
- 5–6 people/lantern: D.light

The companies listed here have in common that they did not consider the brightness (in lumen) of the actual lanterns sold. As a senior industry consultant based in Johannesburg, Esther B. remarks with reference to this list: "Another funny thing is, that these metrics about the 'number of people electrified' are then also translated into 'the number of kerosene lamps replaced' and in turn 'the amount CO_2 saved.'"[16] She adds, "[b]ut, when we look closely, we often find that the solar lantern is only really used for a very short period in the evenings, to find the kerosene lamps and to light them." As she explains, at the end of the day, most solar lanterns, if only one is bought, simply do not provide enough light for a household with multiple persons and therefore do not replace the kerosene lamp.

In the last few years, as mentioned, the sector has rapidly diversified from solar lanterns to also include in their portfolios the marketing and sale of other products, such as TVs, fans and refrigerators (amongst others), that are then powered through so-called solar home systems. The latter are frequently technically designed in a manner that allows for the monitoring of the customer's energy usage data in real time—making it possible to zoom in, at a distance, and analyse individual cus-

---

15   "How to measure social impact of a solar lantern?," *Sun Connect: Sub-Saharan Africa News*, 2014, accessed 19 January 2022, https://sun-connect.org/how-to-measure-social-impact-of-a-solar-lantern/.

16   Interview, 26 January 2022.

tomer's energy consumption patterns.[17] "We can already go online in the evenings and see how many times that fridge door was opened and closed on that day [...]," I am told by Julius D., the CEO of a Berlin-based start-up.[18] He goes on to explain that on the basis of this data, similar predictions can be made about 'CO2 saved,' for the solar unit providing power for the fridge is likely to have replaced a diesel-powered generator. "For companies dependent on capital from private investors, this data will also need to be translated into a series of other indicators such as 'Jobs created' or 'Income generated'. There are no capacities to do surveys with off-grid customers to determine whether in fact, a kiosk was established or whether income was factually generated, he goes on to explain.

Sutured Infrastructures

Metrics as the "translation of (assumed) realities into numbers" have for decades been the standard means of evaluating processes and phenomena as a form of creating and ensuring accountability and transparency.[19] Modern governments succeed or fail, as James Scott illustrated compellingly in his book, on the basis of their ability to measure or evaluate complex social phenomena through numbers and thereby render these comparable and countable.[20] "Yet there is little doubt" as Beer suggests, "that these systems of measurement have escalated and intensified over recent years," particularly through the cultivation of forms of neoliberalism. In addition, the growth of IoT technologies and products in the sector have intensified and incentivized the reliance on metrics further.[21]

In the solar off grid sector, as in other fields, the production of metrics today is as troubled by imperfection as were the efforts in previous times.[22] This does not however, as Adams underlines, "get in the way of efforts to produce them, nor does it impede efforts to rely on their empirical products as if they were indelibly factual."[23]

---

17   Riedke and Adelmann, "The good payers."

18   Interview, 10 October 2021.

19   Richard Rottenburg et al., *The World of Indicators: The Making of Governmental Knowledge Through Quantification* (Cambridge: Cambridge University Press, 2015), 2.

20   James C Scott, *Seeing Like a State* (New Haven: Yale University Press, 1999); see also: Vincanne Adams, *Metrics: What Counts in Global Health* (London: Duke University Press, 2016), 7.

21   David Beer, *Metric Power* (London: Palgrave Macmillan, 2016), 4.

22   Adams, *Metrics: What Counts in Global Health*, 8.

23   Adams, *Metrics: What Counts in Global Health*, 8.

Metrics acquire an authority that makes it difficult to imagine other forms of creating transparency and accountability.[24]

Convincing investors to invest in solar off grid electrification as a 'thing,' as an 'asset class,' means using metrics to elaborate on (future) value. Few numbers are available and yet these need to serve as the basis for more elaborate stories about on the ground, complex social phenomena and need to sell 'solar' as an investment from which to expect attractive annual returns. As one scans through the evaluations in 2022 that concern the potential of the solar off grid sector, commentators highlight that market leaders are increasingly 'gaining investors' trust' as they are going 'beyond energy' and diversifying into energy-adjacent products such as mobile phones and digital finance.[25] "This shows that the infrastructure built by off-grid solar companies has a great potential to be maximized to respond to new consumer needs."[26] The aim of the sector has been, so the point also in this evaluation, to deliver clean energy access to the so-called 'unelectrified poor,' but beyond that has also been to catalyse and expand markets for goods and services that go beyond energy and establish new consumer subjects for these very markets.[27] In order for the market to grow, Koen Peters, the head of the global association for the off-grid solar energy industry (GOGLA) underscores in a guest commentary on the *NextBillion* website, "[t]he sector needs to find a way to tell its story compellingly, highlighting the fact that there will be profits in the long term, along with other positive human and climate impacts, and those future profits and impact should play a more important role in the narrative."[28]

What an engagement with metrics in the solar off grid sector allows us to explore are the new linkages being sutured between policy and finance, between philanthropic aims to provide basic access to electricity and international investment portfolios, between ambitious utopian quests and opportunities for profiteering. Metrics in this case work to connect the roll out of electrical infrastructure that we

---

24   Beer, *Metric Power*, 5; Wendy Nelson Espeland and Michael Sauder, "Rankings and Reactivity: How Public Measures Recreate Social Worlds," *American Journal of Sociology* 113, no. 1 (2007): 5.

25   GET.invest, "New Investment Data: Global Off-Grid Solar Investments at a Record Sum in 2021," *GET.invest* (16 June 2022), https://www.get-invest.eu/new-investment-data-global-off-grid-solar-investments-at-a-record-sum-in-2021/.

26   GET.invest, "New Investment Data."

27   Cross, "Capturing Crisis"; Riedke and Adelmann, "The good payers"; Riedke, "A Solar Off-Grid Software."

28   Koen Peters, "The Growing Urgency of Funding Off-Grid Solar: Exploring the Multi-Billion Dollar Investment Opportunity in Achieving Climate and Energy Access Goals," *NextBillion*, 2 Feburary 2022, accessed 18 April 2022, https://nextbillion.net/off-grid-solar-investment-opportunity-funding-climate-energy-access/.

readily think of in big material terms with the less tangible financial investment infrastructures. These are hybrid and the sutures are prone to escape our 'infrastructural gaze' for while we are positioned to readily adopt definitions of infrastructure as socio-technical, so Lemanski and Massey have also argued, "our critical exploration of the ways in which infrastructure networks are also socio-technical is more limited."[29] As hybrid and heterogeneous infrastructure configurations are sutured together, the larger whole that comes fully into view runs the risk of losing something of its infrastructural force and thereby evading the 'infrastructural lens.'

The study of a sutured configuration of hybrid, heterogenous infrastructures, in the context of the solar off grid allows us to trace old and new paths of capture and extraction,[30] and to ethnographically illuminate what people, through the purchase of these solar products, become enmeshed in—including, not least, the rapidly emerging digital data 'grids.' Further, it allows us to shed light on the emergence of infrastructure as a global asset and the new forms of speculation that are increasingly coming to characterize experiments in infrastructure finance.[31] Put differently, taking metrics as one of many vantage points to explore the relationality between these different infrastructures, in turn, works to draw our attention further to the kinds of accumulation that infrastructure has become associated with, the postcolonial practices of valuation, as well as the "apparently 'anomalous,' 'peripheral,' or 'frontier' sites" so central to global capitalism.[32]

---

29   Charlotte Lemanski and Ruth Massey, "Is the Grid People or Product? Relational Infrastructure Networks in Cape Town's Energy-Housing Nexus," *Urban Geography* (2022): 1–25, 2. Lemanski and Massey speak of the physical-material and the human-relational as a heuristic binary that, when acknowledging their overlaps, effectively allows us to explore what makes "infrastructure." They refer throughout their text to the notion of 'infrastructural networks', highlighting that the lexicon of 'networks,' still "represents a primary discourse and practice through which infrastructures are imagined, planned, and delivered" (4).

30   Michael Degani, Brenda Chalfin, and Jamie Cross, "Introduction: Fuelling Capture: Africa's Energy Frontiers," *The Cambridge Journal of Anthropology* 38, no. 2 (2020): 1–18, 2.

31   Laura Bear, "Speculations on Infrastructure: From Colonial Public Works to a Post-Colonial Global Asset Class on the Indian Railways 1840–2017," *Economy and Society* 49, no. 1 (2020): 1–26.

32   Bear, "Speculations on Infrastructure," 19.

Section VI: Infrastructures and the Environment

Water for a Good Government: Andean Infrastructures in Guaman Poma de Ayala's Chronicle (1615)

Kirsten Mahlke

Recently, pre-Incaic water infrastructures in the Andean highlands have become the focus of policy makers and conservators, as water security is severely threatened under conditions of global warming.[1] The art of keeping water available for fields, livestock, and people during long droughts has a millennia-long tradition in the Andes. Water as a scarce resource determines the Andean societies in such a great scale that one could call the water infrastructure, a la Marcel Mauss, a *fait total social*. It is certainly interesting to examine Andean water infrastructure and its usability today through the lens of technological history—and is perhaps even essential for its survival. However, such an approach is insufficient for understanding "Indigenous infrastructure" as a complex interaction of various immaterial and material elements. The transmission of this infrastructural knowledge in the literal sense of a "culture" (lat. colere: to cultivate, maintain, preserve) is a part of this infrastructure, which I show in this paper by considering a Peruvian colonial-era text from the 17th century.

In 1615, Guaman Poma de Ayala, an Indigenous scholar from Huamanca[2] in the then Viceroyalty of Peru finished his chronicle and treaty of good governance for

---

1 The conclusion of the authors regarding the efficiency of the Indigenous infrastructure for today's demands is positive: "We combined hydrological monitoring and tracer experiments to characterize the hydrological functioning of a 1,400-year-old infiltration enhancement system developed by pre-Inca cultures to cope with climate variability in the Peruvian Andes. Our results confirm that the system effectively enhances hillslope infiltration to reach downslope springs. We estimate a mean residence time of 45 d, with a range between 2 weeks and 8 months, which shows that the system can be used to increase water availability at the community scale during the dry season." Boris Ochoa Tocachi, Juan Bardales, et al., "Potential Contributions of Pre-Inca-Infiltration infrastructure to Peruvian water security," *Nature Sustainability* 2 (July 2019): 584–593, 590.

2 Guaman Poma de Ayala, an Indigenous scholar in colonial service, claims to be of noble Andean descent: On his father's side from the dynasty of the Yarovilca Allauca Huánuco, on his mother's side from the Inca dynasty. Cf. Rolena Adorno, "Waman Puma: El autor y su obra," in *Felipe Guamán Poma de Ayala: Nueva crónica y buen gobierno*, eds. John V. Murra, Rolena Adorno, and Jorge L. Urioste (Madrid: Historia-16, 1987): XVII–XLVII.

the Spanish King Felipe III, *El Primer nueva corónica i Buen Gobierno.*[3] The explicit goal of the chronicle, conceived as a letter, is to fundamentally reform colonial government, including all of its institutions from state administration to the provisioning of household communities, in order to guarantee the survival and good life in an Andean understanding of the concept of individuals and communities in the colonial sphere. The reform that the king is suggested to set in motion includes the transformation of infrastructures in a near-modern understanding of the term: water supply, communication routes, transportation infrastructure, food supply, mining, and welfare. A good Andean government, announced by the title, differs from the Spanish colonial government, precisely and decisively, in terms of its infrastructures.

I would like to examine this Indigenous text published in Spanish as a complex demand for infrastructural restitution. From a literary studies' perspective, such an investigation cannot be complete without considering the nature of the text and its meaning-bearing structures as part of infrastructural knowledge. The guiding questions of this paper then are: How do textual infrastructures (in the broadest sense)—grammars, semiotics, logics—connect to imaginaries of material infrastructure? This question leads to related questions like whether textual substructures that are normative or meaning-making can usefully be studied as infrastructures, and what would be the added analytical value of such a conceptual extension to textual structures. Since the immaterial codes of texts form the infrastructure for understanding material infrastructures yet to be built, both concepts are equally significant parts of a fundamental sociocultural concern, namely imagining infrastructures of a good life in the midst of a decades-long experience of catastrophe during the early Spanish colonial period. Heuristically, this article assumes a notion of infrastructure that is not preconceived as modern. Thus, it does not ask, for example, how "irrigation infrastructure" (a modern term) is described, but rather by what means water reaches people, animals, and fields at the necessary rate. In this regard, the infrastructure question becomes open-ended: what elements need to be considered, how do they interact, or how do things favour or hinder each other when it comes to water supply? What are the cultural foundations (writing systems, spiritual texts, legislation) that turn the natural element of water into a culturally diverse and complex phenomenon for human and social life?

This paper is exploratory in both theoretical and interpretive terms and therefore cannot yet offer an infrastructural analysis of the entire text by Guaman Poma.

---

3   I use the facsimile online edition of Guaman Poma de Ayala, *El Primer nueva corónica I buen Gobierno*, Lima 1615, provided by the Danish Royal Library with a critical apparatus by Rolena Adorno, John Murra and Jorge L. Urioste Macchi: http://www5.kb.dk/permalink/2006/poma/ (last accessed 11 July 2022). English translation by Roland Hamilton: *Guaman Poma de Ayala, First New Chronicle and Good Government, 1615* (Austin: University of Texas Press, 2010).

In the first part I outline the particular temporality and socio-cosmic sphere of water in the Andes that Guaman Poma portrays in his claim for the restitution of irrigation culture. He refers to hybrid cultural registers and epistemes that, roughly speaking, combine pre-Columbian-Andean and colonial-Spanish notions of infrastructure in terms of a complex symbolic-material substructure for living well.[4] The Andean water infrastructure stands paradigmatically for a decentralized common good economy that is built, maintained, and used autonomously by household communities (ayllus) against a centralized power, be it an Inca or a Spanish usurper.

The Large Temporal and Cultural Scale of Water Infrastructure

The practical and theoretical knowledge of artificial irrigation, which is at least 1500 years old, has been preserved materially and immaterially to some extent until today in the driest and highest regions of the Andes. Drawing canals that route springs into many paths over the mountain slopes, much like the digging of ridges for agriculture, is a very early cultural achievement in the history of mankind, which Guaman Poma situates in his chronicle in 'the second age of humans' and in a time even before the invention of weaving and house building.[5] The Inca calendar, described in detail, is ordered according to the economic cycles of water (rainy seasons, maintenance of canals and irrigation of plantations), the central element of Andean cosmology.[6] Half of the year has abundant rainfall and in the other half, peaking in November, drought prevails. These water cycles are also reflected in the night sky, forming the astronomical part of what Sherbondy calls the Andean "hydrology of the universe."[7] The Milky Way, visible in the Andes from the southern hemisphere, is called "mayú," meaning "river." From this "river" a "llama," a dark-cloud constellation, drinks during the watery season and disappears behind the horizon during the dry season. Water is a precious and scarce commodity, humanly manipulated in many rites and invocations, that must be channelled, cleaned, distributed, and

---

4   "Living well" is a current translation of the Andean and Amazonian concepts of "buen vivir" (*sumaq kawsay* in Quechua), which have recently returned to medial awareness with occurrence of Indigenous environmental and other resistance movements in South America. Cf. Alberto Acosta and Mateo Martínez Abarca, "Buen Vivir: An Alternative Perspective from the Peoples of the Global South to the Crisis of Capitalist Modernity," *The Climate Crisis: South African and Global Democratic Eco-Socialist Alternatives*, ed. Vishwas Satgar (Johannesburg: Wits University Press, 2018): 131–147.

5   The second human age is the period of the "Huari runa," as Guaman Puma classifies them. See *Nueva corónica*, 54.

6   Jeannette Sherbondy, *Agua, Riego y Árboles: Ancestros y Poder en el Cuzco de los Incas*, (Lima: Sociedad Geográfica, 2017) 47.

7   Sherbondy, *Agua, Riego, y Árboles*, 47.

kept available even during dry seasons, not least by means of offerings and techno-logical irrigation channels. The dry months of October and November in Guaman Poma's chapter on the annual time count can therefore be read as an instruction for the preservation of this conjoined immaterial-material and sacred-worldly infras-tructure complex.

The great detail and wide space in the chronicle devoted to water management contrasts with the Spaniards' harmful misuse of this precious resource of life. Dur-ing and after the conquest, it becomes clear to Indigenous observers cited in the *Nueva corónica* that the Spaniards do not know how to handle water, nor do they un-derstand its value. Only those who can dig and redistribute watercourses are consid-ered cultural heroes, even divinities. When Francisco Pizarro was observed carrying water in jars and canisters with his soldiers it became obvious that the Spaniards were neither gods nor leaders.[8] To the great displeasure of the Indigenous people, they diverted water for their *encomiendas*[9] without respecting water rights, cleaning and maintenance practices, or seasonal rhythms. Sherbondy's ethno-archaeological research on pre-Incaic hydrology has shown how social structure is produced, regu-lated, and stabilized by irrigation infrastructure: A household community, *ayllu*,[10] is defined as a water and sewer stewardship community whose ancestry passed down in myths. As the common good of an *ayllu*, its construction, maintenance, cleanup, and use rely on proportionate and rotating community services called "minka." The infra- and supra-structural social system implied here is responsible for and condi-tioned by the *asequias*, stone irrigation canals fed by rivers, wells, ponds, and lagoons from which they are diverted. Guaman Poma reports that they had been built at the dawn of humanity, "con tanto travajo." The irrigation system is not the canals alone, but an ensemble of *pata* (passage), *chacra* (field), and *larca* (irrigation canal).

---

8   "They perform no miracles nor do they [...] produce rivers and springs in areas, that need water. When they travel through arid regions, they carry water with them in jars and gourds." Juan de Betanzos, *Narrative of the Inca*, trans. and eds. Roland Hamilton and Dana Buchanan, from the *Palma de Mallorca* Manuscript [1550s] (Austin: University of Texas Press), 248.

9   *Encomienda* is a Spanish colonial juridical term referring to the privilege awarded by the king to colonists for military achievements. It includes the right to collect labor and tribute from up to 200 Indigenous people. In return, the king obliged the *encomenderos* to guarantee the Christian mission among the laborers. Although the privilege did not include a title to land property, it was *de facto* interpreted as such within a very short time.

10   The smallest household units are called ayllus, "grupos que comparten un sentido de paren-tesco, de compartir antepasados comunes y de originarse en las mismas fuentes de aguas. Esta es la unidad que da al individuo andino su identidad étnica principal" ("groups that share a sense of kinship, of sharing common ancestors and originating from the same water sources. This is the unity that gives the Andean individual his or her primary ethnic identity." (Author's translation)). Sherbondy, *Agua, Riego, y Árboles*, 44.

Figure 1: *"Work: zara carpai iaco mucchoy rupay pacha": "Watering corn, lack of water, heating the earth" (Author's translation). The caption indicates the climatic conditions of water shortage and heat, and the ritual and technical tasks that must be performed during this time. In the text on the following page, Guaman Poma explains that the young woman is in charge of the communal fields, which she irrigates with water from the lagoon, collected in a container made of stones and distributed to the irrigation channels through an opening.*

Guaman Poma: *Nueva corónica y buen gobierno* (c. 1615) Zara Carpai p. 1162 [1172] [11]

---

11   Royal Danish Library, GKS 2232 kvart: Guaman Poma, Nueva corónica y buen gobierno (c. 1615), p. 1162 [1172]], URL digital facsimile: https://poma.kb.dk/permalink/2006/poma/1172/en/text/.

The times and rhythms, the responsibilities, and rights and duties for maintaining the *asequias* are so indispensable to the functioning of this infrastructure that this assemblage can be understood as intangible infrastructure of irrigation, including the unwritten or knotted laws and customs. Legally derived from pre-Inca customary law, water and land use rights and duties are inherited together, never alone as in Spanish law. The handling of water is regulated in the *"ordenanzas,"* which are older than the Inca Empire. As Guaman Poma writes,

> mandó los señores rreys Yngas guardar el costumbre y ley de que no meneasen todas las dichas secyas, agua de rregar. Las dichas sementeras hasta los pastos de ganados rregauan en los altos y quebrados, sauiendo que no auían de poder aquella que tanta gente la edeficaron.[12]

> Thereupon the Inca kings ordered the custom and the law to be upheld, that one must not touch all said water ditches and the water for irrigation. The said seed fields, even the pastures for the cattle, were irrigated on the heights and in the ravines, for they knew that they had no power over them, for so many people had built them. (Author's translation)

The sacredness and commonality of irrigation infrastructures is derived from the immeasurable labor of so many people over whom not even the Inca ruler can "claim power" ("no auían de poder"). In a sense, construction and maintenance are located temporarily and epistemically as a popular megaproject beyond individual systems of governance or even ownership. Built and preserved by uncountable numbers of people since time immemorial, the Inca—and as Poma argues, the Spanish king as a successor—are only humble custodians of the decentralized and autonomous maintenance[13] of this complex infrastructure, which is for the benefit of all in times past, present and future. Sustainability, as presented here, is bound to a myth of a collective origin and unalienable communitarian autonomy. Above all, the supply of water for the poorest must be guaranteed: A "silquiwa," water judge, is employed to guard the canals, drive away the cattle and watch over the fair distribution of water to the poor. No cattle and no human being, it is said, may touch the canals. In case of transgression, correspondingly heavy penalties without appeal are due: "Y ací puso una pena cin apelación sentencia que ninguna persona lo dañe ni menee ninguna piedra y que ningún ganado entre en las dichas asecyas." ("And so he passed a judgment

---

12   Guaman Poma, *Nueva corónica*, 944 [958].

13   A central hydraulic administration did not exist in the Inca Empire, much less before. Sherbondy points out that water supply was the core of self-sufficiency and autonomy of the individual villages and ayllús. See Sherbondy, *Agua, Riego, y Árboles*, 117.

against which no appeal was possible, and a sentence that no man should damage it, nor move a stone, that no herd-animal should enter the said water ditches").[14]

The Spaniards asserted their loyalty to the Andean water management rules. Guaman Poma notes, however, that Francisco de Toledo and the Spanish king both, at first, accepted these rules and then broke them. From the disruption of one element in the water infrastructure, the text, like a chain, unfurls a litany of paratactically linked events, which Guaman translates into entangled Spanish-Indigenous loss and decay on every level of existential conditions:

> Y así no se a guardado esta ley. Y así se pierde todas las sementeras por falta de agua. Desto pierde los yndios sus haziendas y pierde su quinto rreal su Magestad y pierde la santa madre yglecia el diesmo que le deue. Y así en este tienpo los españoles sueltan sus bestias y rreguas de mula o ganados y pasen las cabras, obejas y hazen grandes daños. Y se sacan las dichas aguas y se quiebran las asecyas que no se pueden aderesar con nengún dinero. Y la poca agua sólo quitan a los yndios pobres. Y así se ausentan los yndios de sus pueblos.[15]

> And so, this law has not been followed. And therefore, all the seed fields are lost for lack of water. Thus the Indians lose their possessions, and His Majesty loses the royal fifth, and the Holy Mother Church loses the tithes that are owed to her. And so, at this present time, the Spaniards are letting their domestic animals and mules or herds of cattle roam free, and the goats and sheep are grazing and causing great damage. And the said waters dry up, and the ditches decay, that no sum of money can put them in order. And the little water is taken away from the poor Indians. And that is why they move away from their villages. (Author's translation)

The customary legal infrastructure of water management underlies and preconditions every single element of the communities' survival—the Andean one as well as the Spanish church and aristocracy, both rich or poor—because of their interdependencies. The disrupted order brings about social stress, including the whole ecological system like fields, cattle, sheep, and goats. The temporal, demographic, spatial and functional large scale of the infrastructure, as can be seen here, cannot be restored monetarily, since simply everything depends on it and the dimensions of the dependent elements are incommensurable. It is therefore no wonder that the transgressors of this law are located in the chapter on hell, a hell populated by "man-eating" priests, *encomenderos*, and thieves. The "City of Hell" illustrates the atmosphere down there.

---

14   Guaman Poma, *Nueva corónica*, 944 [958].
15   Guaman Poma, *Nueva corónica*, 944 [958].

Figure 2: *The "City of Hell."*

Guaman Poma Nueva corónica y buen gobierno (c. 1615) Ciudad del
Infierno p. 941 [955][16]

The impact of the colonization of the former Inca Empire (*Tawantinsuyu*) by the
Spanish was devastating, especially in terms of water supply. In the second part of
the *Nueva corónica*, "La Conquista," Guaman Poma exposes the dysfunctional effects
on coexistence, and indeed on the very survival of the entire colonial society in all
its segments. The problems of the colonial government become legible as problems
of its understanding of infrastructures: violence, negligence, material destruction,

---

16   Royal Danish Library, GKS 2232 kvart: Guaman Poma, Nueva corónica y buen gobierno
      (c. 1615), p.941 [955], URL digital facsimile: https://poma.kb.dk/permalink/2006/poma/955/e
      n/text/.

exploitation, dispossession, abuse, enslavement through economic and political administrative structures that serve solely to increase the wealth of the crown, leading to the flight, loss of identity, suicide, and mass dying of the Indigenous population.

The book on the Conquest (pp. 370–437), in which all these grievances are listed, is framed in the text by the chapters on the pre-Columbian Inca government (pp. 342–369) and the "good government" after the Conquest (pp. 438–490). It is thus embedded in the order of the text between the report on the good Andean order, which for Guaman Poma had been paradigmatically realized during the reign of Tupac Inca Yupanqui (1471–1490). Tupac Inca Yupanqui supplies a model for the Spanish king regarding the areas of responsibility that are incumbent upon him and the means and functions that are available to him among the officials. The chapter on the Inca government is accordingly divided into the areas of the following infrastructures: the jurisdiction in the *Tawantinsuyu*, the provincial administrators, the post runners on the Inca roads, the surveyors, measurers and boundary stone setters, the administrators of the Inca roads, the bridge administrators, the bookkeepers, tax collectors and accountants, and finally the 16-member council of the Inca in Cusco. The ultimate goal is to establish material and moral justice throughout the empire and in each community, down to each *ayllu*. Guaman Poma reports that the highly respected surveyors and boundary setters (*sayua ch'iqta suyuyoq*[17]) had to divide the fields, irrigation canals, plantations, pastures, livestock, and mineral resources among the inhabitants, especially with regards to the care of the poor (sick, old, widows, orphans, travellers) in such a way that each individual would be granted equal resources for housing, clothing, food, and feasts. The listing of these basics in relation to a description of the functions of government is not arbitrary in its order. Guaman Poma emphasizes that the order of tasks and things follows an ancient ancestral classification order that underlies the coding and recording systems of the knotted cords (*quipú*) and calculating machine (*yupana*). The quechua verb "kamay," to order things (in knots, calendars, communities), means "to provide life."

---

17   Guaman Poma , *Nueva Corónica*, 353 [355].

Spatial and Temporal Coding Systems: Knotted Cords and Water Lines

Figures 3 + 4: The typography (left) of the manuscript, dedicated to the social order in the Inca state, imitates the coding system of the quipú (right) with its horizontally and vertically aligned text lines. Guaman Poma points out that the counting and writing systems of the Latin script and the knotted cords are to be considered equivalent to each other. Social order, counting, measuring, and equitable distribution of resources are linked in this texture. The extent to which this texture also denotes a water infrastructure knowledge will be explored in this final part.

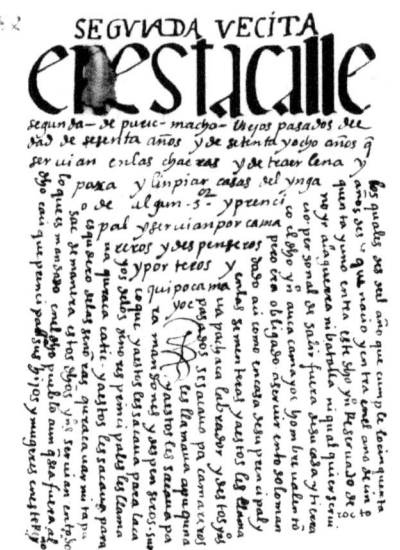 

Guaman Poma Nueva corónica y buen gobierno (c. 1615), Escritura quipú, p. 195 [19] and Quipu-camayoc, p. 360 [362][18]

---

18   Royal Danish Library, GKS 2232 kvart: Guaman Poma, Nueva corónica y buen gobierno (c. 1615), p.196 [197], URL digital facsimile: https://poma.kb.dk/permalink/2006/poma/19 7/en/text/ ; Royal Danish Library, GKS 2232 kvart: Guaman Poma, Nueva corónica y buen gobierno (c. 1615), p.360 [362], URL digital facsimile: https://poma.kb.dk/permalink/2006/p oma/362/en/text/.

The basis of living well, according to Guaman Poma, lies in the precision of data collection and knowledge transmission. The main accountant, shown above, brings together all available data[19] of the entire Andean region in Cusco. All Andean peoples tell their origin from Lake Titicaca, thus both a cultural and cosmic founding history have their origins in the water. The foundation of the political node of Cusco is also linked to water: Cinche Roca is remembered as the founder of Cusco because he created the drainage canals that made the entire valley of Cusco cultivable and protected from floods: "Era él quién drenó las aguas del lago o pantano que ocupaba la zona central del Cuzco, permitiendo la construcción de la plaza Aucaypata, hoy día plaza de armas." ("It was he who drained the waters of the lake or swamp that occupied the central area of Cuzco, allowing the construction of the Aucaypata square, today the Plaza de Armas.")[20] He also channeled the Huatanay River, which allowed cultivation of the area and better control of floods. The territorial order of the Tawantinsuyu and the social, political and economic division is based, as Zuidema, Rostworowski and Sherbondy have shown, on "*ceques*," subterranean water lines radiating towards the Cusco node and on which 41 sacred places ("*huacas*") are topologically recorded, springs that function as if "nodes" on a circularly laid out *quipu*.

The diagonals imaginarily drawn by two water lines "Ceques" divide the "Four Realms" *Tawantinsuyu* into its four regions Chinchaysuyu, Andesuyu, Contisuyu and Collasuyu. The Inca nobility divides along the lines and binary division into upper and lower moiety (*Hanan* and *Hurin*, mountain and water) their obligations and claims to water and territories. This radial collective mental infrastructure of water lines and *quipu* serves as orientation for the political, social, religious, and economic order, whose material basis is in turn the equitable distribution of water resources.

---

19   This includes demographic, legal, military data, crop products, resources, labor services, and
      more. To the order of node counting from left to right and top to bottom: The most valuable
      agricultural products, weapons are placed on top. In the census, on the first thread were the
      men over sixty years old, on the second mature men from fifty, the third over forty years old,
      always ten-year-old groups to still children. In the same order they counted women of all
      ages. Thinner threads on the same strand indicated the number of widows. Garcilaso de la
      Vega El Inca, *Comentarios reales de los Incas* (Lisbon : Pedro Crasbeeck Printshop, 1609): Chap.
      VIII, 136.

20   Sherbondy, *Agua, Riego y Árboles*, 123.

Figure 5: Ceques del Cusco, 1964.

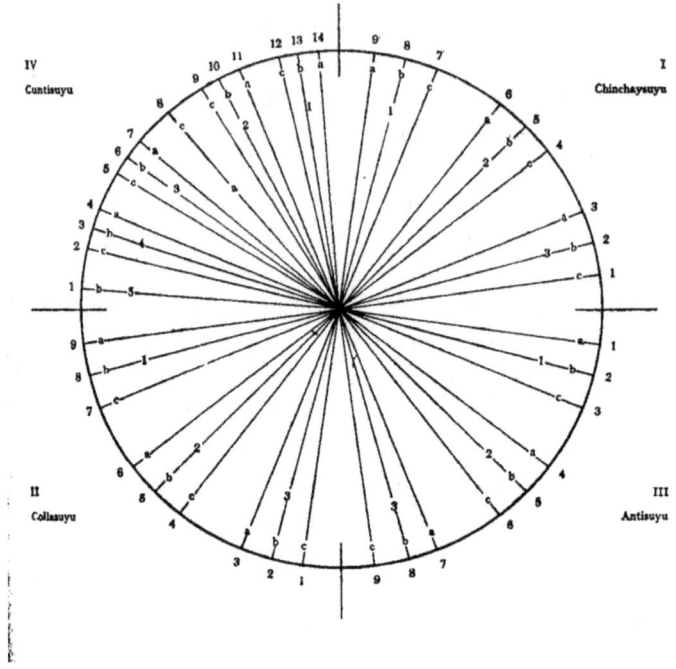

Tom Zuidema.[21]

---

21   Tom Zuidema, 1964. *The Ceque System of Cuzco. The Social Organisation of the Capital of the Inca* (Leiden: Brill), 2.

Figure 6: The 41 ceques and huacas represent imaginary cords and knots that run through the entire valley of Cusco and whose extension also divides the administration of the entire empire. The 41 ceques correspond to the 41 weeks in the Inca calendar, which Guaman Poma, however, no longer lists.

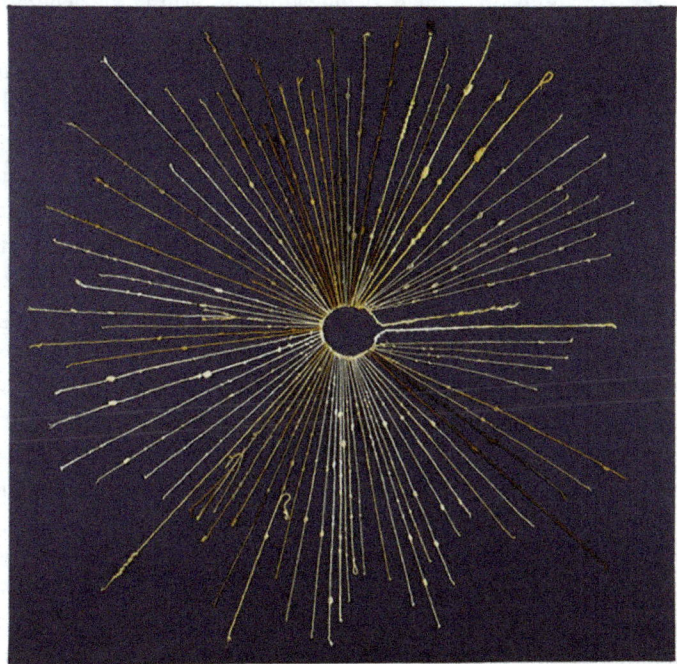

Imaged by Heritage Auctions, HA.com

Quipú circular, © Heritage Auction.[22]

Conclusion

In this article I aimed to test if "infrastructure" can serve as a key term to understand what the inter-cultural confrontation during conquest and colonial times entailed in the Viceroyalty of Peru. Indeed, it allows for insights into the articulations and interfaces, the frictions and catalysts between such different material and immaterial cultural systems like customary law, cosmology, scripture, irrigation systems, communication, and spirituality. "Infrastructure" turns out to be thought provoking, even if—or maybe because—it is a term heavily charged with assumptions

---

22   Heritage Auction Fine Art, Quipú circular, https://fineart.ha.com/itm/textiles/quipu-inca-a d-1430-1530-cotton-camelid-fibers-diameter-34-1-2-in-at-break-point-the-present-exampl e-has-been-di/a/643-47254.s?ic4=GalleryView-Thumbnail-071515.

about "modernity." The idea that colonization was technically civilizing the American Indigenous population came up as early as the Spanish implemented their administrative headquarters and ruled over the distribution of all resources. Guaman Poma asks, how "civilizing" this administration really is, if it leads to the destruction of fields, animals, and people. The basic question concerning the generative function of infrastructure, "What is it good for?" is answered in opposite ways by Guaman Poma and the Spanish crown, as his texts shows. For the Andean population it meant for "buen vivir" of all the communities independently of individual governments and rulers. For the Spanish, any exploitation of resources, including water, was to augment the wealth of the Spanish crown. Value systems, myths, ritual calendar rhythms, rights and duties, are strongly tied to the different outcomes, including or excluding parts of the population, which become visible during the conquest. The typographic design of the text written in Latin letters as if they were knotted cords is already a representation of Andean infrastructure knowledge and coding, which, analogous to the political-economic order in its radial and knotting systematics, refers to imaginary water lines.[23] The concern for precision in the counting and measuring system, forming physical and mental irrigation landscapes as *quipu* knots, serves the concern for distributive justice, which, as has been shown in Guaman Poma's lore, produces and sustains a water infrastructure knowledge that is decentralized, communal and intangible, as it dates back to unthinkable times in human history (the second age of man) and is based on innumerable labor contributions by the population. This large-scale dimension in construction, ownership, management, and maintenance has precisely the consequence that the dominion over the water can never be withdrawn from common ownership and use. The punishments to be expected are painted (to Christian ears) in hellish scenarios that bloom for anyone who so much as touches the sacred water rights, the water calendar order, or the material water infrastructure. The detailed description of the consequences of destruction, which occurred everywhere as a result of the conquest, makes clear how little Guaman Poma trusts the king's cultural understanding of the importance of water to good government. The centrality of irrigation systems can thus not be understood without its cultural environments, informing and granting the communitarian purpose of water infrastructure. The hope to make use of Andean irrigation

---

23   "Este complejo sistema de organización compuesto por ceques y huacas, hacía las veces de un gran quipu que con sus 'cuerdas y nudos' cubría toda la ciudad. El culto de cada uno de los 348 lugares se encontraba a cargo de un grupo social, el cual debía ser practicado según el calendario ritual. Estas líneas también fueron referencias para delimitar la propiedad de las tierras de los ayllus cusqueños." María Rostworowski, *Los Incas. Obras Completas*, Vol. IX, (Lima: Instituto de Estudios Peruanos, 2001), 113. See further: Pedro de Villagómez (1585–1617), "La naturaleza Pan-Andina del Sistema de Ceques," in *Batan Grande y la Unidad Cosmológica en los Andes Centrales Prehistóricos* 21, ed. Emilio Choy (2001): 31–45.

knowledge for future droughts might be fruitful only in this holistic understanding of infrastructure.

The Dangers of Infrastructure Byproducts and What We Can Learn From Muriel Rukeyser's "The Book of the Dead"

Aaron Pinnix

In December 2020, the journal *Science* published an article proving that the chemical 6PPD, which is used worldwide in car tires as a means of impeding rubber oxidation, causes extreme morbidity among U.S. Pacific Northwest coho salmon.[1] Up to 90% of a returning salmon population may die from exposure to 6PPD, which gets delivered to streams via tire wear and road runoff. As the authors note, it is unlikely that salmon are uniquely sensitive to this chemical, and as such 6PPD is probably killing fish around the world.[2] Part of the challenge of addressing 6PPD is that not only is it so small as to almost escape awareness, it is also a substance with a specific purpose in the larger infrastructure of roads and cars, and through the fulfilment of this purpose becomes subsumed within the smooth functioning of road infrastructure. Often infrastructure byproducts like 6PPD only gain our attention once they have accumulated to the point that significant disruptions occur to the processes of life itself. For instance, the scientists who discovered 6PPD's toxicity worked backward from acute mortality events to discern the root chemical cause.[3] This sort of scalar shift, in which miniscule byproducts are discovered to have outsized effects, is part of the work that both science and literature do—to make visible that which might otherwise remain invisible.

In 1930, work began on a 3.75 mile long tunnel to divert the New River to a hydroelectric plant in Gauley Junction, West Virginia that would, in turn, produce electricity for a metallurgical plant. The hydroelectric project, the tunnel, and the metallurgical plant were all, through legalistic sleight-of-hand, owned by Union Carbide and Carbon Corporation. The tunnel was discovered to have very high concentrations of

---

1   Zhenyu Tian et al., "A Ubiquitous Tire Rubber–Derived Chemical Induces Acute Mortality in Coho Salmon," *Science* 371, no. 6525 (December 3, 2020): 185–189.
2   Tian et al., "Ubiquitous," 189.
3   Tian et al., "Ubiquitous," 185.

valuable silica and was expanded into a mine.[4] 4,887 men, many of whom were migrants and/or Black, worked on this project, and at least 2,982 men worked in the tunnel. For the sake of expediency and profit, safety measures like using masks and wetting the silica were ignored. As a result, airborne silica caused significant health problems for the miners, and an estimated 764 miners died from silicosis, in which silica accumulates within and cuts up the lungs, causing scaring and ultimately suffocation.[5]

In 1936, the poet Muriel Rukeyser drove to West Virginia to report on the Gauley Tunnel disaster. By this point Rukeyser, although only 22, was already an established poet—her first poetry collection, *Theory of Flight*, had been selected to receive the Yale Younger Poets Prize in 1935.[6] In 1938, she published the documentary poem series "The Book of the Dead" in her collection *U.S 1*, named after the East Coast highway she took from New York City to West Virginia. "The Book of the Dead" turned out to be an early entry in a lifetime of socially-attentive works about America. The first line of "The Book of the Dead" is "These are roads to take when you think of your country," a line that unifies thinking of one's country, here America, with the road infrastructure that makes this country accessible, and perhaps in some way constitutes it.[7] In other words, critical consideration, location, and infrastructure overlap. Later in the text, after readers have encountered the mortal dangers of silica and its uses in steel and concrete, a version of this line returns as "this is the road to take when you think of your country,/ between the dam and the furnace, terminal," unifying thinking of one's country with the infrastructure projects of the hydroelectric dam and steel furnace, while also emphasizing with the word "terminal" how such projects can entail mortal costs.[8] Here, infrastructure projects and the country they create can be dangerously intertwined.

Significant attention in "The Book of the Dead" is paid to the greed that underlay such dangerous working conditions.[9] As Rukeyser points out, the contractors organizing the tunnel "neglected to provide the workmen with any safety device."[10] The effect was that "Almost as soon as work was begun in the tunnel/ men began to die

---

4   Tim Dayton, *Muriel Rukeyser's The Book of the Dead* (Columbia: University of Missouri Press, 2003), 16.

5   Dayton, *The Book of the Dead*, 17.

6   Dayton, *The Book of the Dead*, 13.

7   Muriel Rukeyser, "The Book of the Dead," in *The Collected Poems of Muriel Rukeyser*, eds. Janet E. Kaufman and Anne F. Herzog (Pittsburgh: University of Pittsburgh Press, 2005), 73.

8   Rukeyser, "The Book of the Dead," 97.

9   Here and throughout, I refer to the poetry series as a whole, rather than identifying individual poems, though it is worth noting that twenty poems make up the series, and while each poem touches upon different aspects of the disaster, they also work in conjunction with each other, with themes reappearing and developing over the course of the text.

10   Rukeyser, "The Book of the Dead," 75, 76.

among dry drills. No masks."[11] The motivation for this was profit: "A fellow could drill three holes dry for one hole wet."[12] Mitigating or ignoring standard safety protocols meant the silica could be drilled faster, and thanks to the Great Depression, laborers were numerous and deemed replaceable. Thus, "The ambulance was going day and night."[13] Sick workers were misdiagnosed as having "pneumonia" or "fever," and Union Carbide would fire workers as soon as they said they felt ill.[14] Similarly, Union Carbide utilized the legal system to styme accountability.[15] Altogether, "The Book of the Dead" shows how workers were sacrificed for profit.

The privatization of public utilities, an issue infrastructure projects face today, is also discussed in "The Book of the Dead." As Rukeyser points out, the project was originally licensed "to develop power for public sale," but instead sold all power to the metallurgical plant.[16] As Bruce Robbins notes in "The Smell of Infrastructure," public utilities "are required by law to render adequate service at reasonable prices to all who apply [...]. It is because these services are deemed essential to the public welfare that they are regulated directly by the government."[17] That the project wholly benefited Union Carbide speaks to the mendacity of the project, but it also implicates governmental acceptance of such privatization. As Rukeyser points out, after the disaster Congress failed to pass "A bill to prevent industrial silicosis."[18] Instead, "Bill blocked; investigation blocked," implicating a degree of governmental complicity in the ability of businesses to place profit over workers' health.[19]

Generally (though perhaps incorrectly), infrastructure is understood as invisible, except for when it falters. As Adam Rothstein points out, "Visibility, or lack thereof, is [a] common theme in infrastructural research [...]. The infrastructure itself is designed to be kept out of sight." In response to the question of "why do we go to the effort to make [infrastructure] visible?," Rothstein replies: "Perhaps because of the lengths those in power will go to control the visibility of infrastructure."[20] The Gauley Tunnel project became visible due to the large number of workers that died, but Union Carbide worked hard to obfuscate these deaths, for instance by quickly

---

11   Rukeyser, "The Book of the Dead," 79.

12   Rukeyser, "The Book of the Dead," 105.

13   Rukeyser, "The Book of the Dead," 80.

14   Rukeyser, "The Book of the Dead," 85, 87.

15   Rukeyser, "The Book of the Dead," 92.

16   Rukeyser, "The Book of the Dead," 76. See also Dayton, *The Book of the Dead*, 18.

17   Bruce Robbins, "The Smell of Infrastructure: Notes Toward an Archive," *Boundary 2: An International Journal of Literature and Culture* 34, no. 1 (Spring 2007): 26.

18   Rukeyser, "The Book of the Dead," 102.

19   Rukeyser, "The Book of the Dead," 104.

20   Adam Rothstein, "How to See Infrastructure: A Guide for Seven Billion Primates," *Rhizome*, July 2, 2015, https://rhizome.org/editorial/2015/jul/02/how-see-infrastructure-guide-seven-billion-primate/.

burying the dead.[21] Rukeyser is undertaking this task of making visible what was hidden, but this task is also the same of the scientists who discovered 6PPD as being the root cause of acute mortality events in coho salmon. In both instances, the normative invisibility of infrastructure is overturned in favour of showing the broader negative effects of infrastructure on life itself.

Part of what I think we can learn from "The Book of the Dead" lies in the text's attention to how something as small as silica can undergird infrastructure projects. Silica (silicon dioxide, SiO_2), sometimes referred to as quartz, is a hard mineral used to make concrete, bricks, and tiles more robust. The popularly available Portland cement contains about 25% silica, though concrete may contain up to 70% silica.[22] Even a short amount of exposure to airborne silica, for instance in breathing in dust while mixing concrete, can cause irreversible lung tissue damage. This becomes even more notable when we consider concrete's importance to infrastructure projects. Every year, three new tons of concrete are laid per each person on Earth. It is the second most consumed material, next to water.[23] Concrete production creates 4 to 8% of the world's carbon dioxide, with only coal, oil, and natural gas being greater sources of greenhouse gases. An article in *The Guardian* identifies concrete as "The Most Destructive Material on Earth," noting that "If the cement industry were a country, it would be the third largest carbon dioxide emitter in the world with up to 2.8bn tonnes, surpassed only by China and the US."[24] If we consider the effects of silica, concrete becomes even more deadly. As Rukeyser notes, in 1938 "500,000 Americans" had silicosis.[25] More contemporarily, as of 2012 "More than 23 million workers in China and more than 10 million in India are exposed to silica dust," and "1.7 million people in the United States and 3 million in Europe [are] similarly exposed," while "more than 24,000 workers in China die each year from silicosis."[26] Rukeyser was calling attention to a threat that has only grown as our usage of concrete, and thus of silica, has developed.

---

21   Rukeyser, "The Book of the Dead," 93.

22   Veronica Stanley, "A Close Look at Portland Cement," *The Synergist*, February 2018, https://synergist.aiha.org/201802-close-look-at-portland-cement.; Health and Safety Executive, "Control of Exposure to Silica Dust: A Guide for Employees," UK Government, March 2013, https://www.hse.gov.uk/pubns/indg463.pdf.

23   Colin Gagg, "Cement and Concrete as an Engineering Material: An Historic Appraisal and Case Study Analysis," *Engineering Failure Analysis* 40 (May 2014): 114.

24   Jonathan Watts, "Concrete: The Most Destructive Material on Earth," *The Guardian*, February 25, 2019, https://www.theguardian.com/cities/2019/feb/25/concrete-the-most-destructive-material-on-earth.

25   Rukeyser, "The Book of the Dead," 103.

26   Tan Ee Lyn, "China Study Finds Mine Workers at Higher Risk of Cancer, Heart Disease," *Reuters*, April 19, 2012, https://www.reuters.com/article/us-china-mines-disease-idUSBRE83I04S20120419.

Overall, I think we should consider how infrastructure depends on material byproducts that are released throughout the various stages of infrastructure construction, usage, and deterioration. By the term "byproduct" I mean both definitions provided in the *OED*: "A secondary product; a substance of more or less value obtained in the course of a specific process, though not its primary object," as well as something that is "transferred."[27] Silica, for instance, was initially a secondary product of the tunnelling project, while also being transferred into the miners' lungs. 6PPD is a byproduct of car tire wear and is also transferred into streams and waterways. Via the creation and usage of infrastructures such byproducts are transferred to locations where they have negative effects on life.

Central to discovering and attending to infrastructure byproducts is the task of making the invisible visible via processes of scalar shift. For instance, "The Book of the Dead" describes a series of x-rays taken over a ten-month period that track the accumulation of silica in a miner's lungs. By using language to make the silica visible, both through the poem's contraction of ten months to a few stanzas and in representing the piercing vision of x-rays, Rukeyser is calling attention to the cumulative effects of silica.[28] In turn, silica gets connected in the text with a wide range of infrastructures, including roads, mines, dams, and electrical grids, as well as the bodies of knowledge represented in medical reports and judicial and legal proceedings. This process of interconnecting the miniscule and vast aligns with Lynn Keller's discussion in *Recomposing Ecopoetics: North American Poetry of the Self-Conscious Anthropocene* of using scalar shift as a tool for comprehending the Anthropocene, even while "The Book of the Dead" precedes by almost 75 years Keller's examples of works by contemporary poets. As Keller points out, "Fundamental to the concept of the Anthropocene is its bringing together—and even into collision—vastly discrepant scales."[29] In addition to thinking "in scales of deep time and space," we must also "shrink our gaze to attend to the surprisingly grand significance of microbes and microfauna [...] of the health effects of minute amounts of toxic chemicals.[30] While preceding knowledge of the Anthropocene, "The Book of the Dead" attends to how miniscule particulates can have outsized effects. At one point, silica even becomes the speaker of the text, describing "my death upon your lips" and how "Now they are feeding me into a steel mill furnace," supplying silica with a degree of agency and subjecthood

27   *Oxford English Dictionary Online*, "by-product, n.," accessed September 3, 2022, https://www.oed.com/view/Entry/25592?redirectedFrom=byproduct.

28   Rukeyser, "The Book of the Dead," 83.

29   Lynn Keller, *Recomposing Ecopoetics: North American Poetry of the Self-Conscious Anthropocene* (Charlottesville: University of Virginia Press, 2017), 32.

30   Keller, *Recomposing Ecopoetics*, 33.

that threatens the reader.[31] These sorts of scalar shifts help the reader to conceptualize silica's dangerous materiality in ways that move beyond silica's miniscule size.

Byproducts like silica and 6PPD are central to the operations of infrastructure, but because of their small size often remain invisible to us until we consider their large-scale repercussions. We often discuss infrastructure projects in relation to their intended goals, but as silica and 6PPD show, there are also important unintended effects. Michelle Murphy argues that such oversights in our accounting may be purposeful, noting, for instance, that our understanding of industrial chemicals are inherited from "corporate forms of technoscience" that emphasize "discrete molecules" as if such molecules remain isolated and without context.[32] In turn, these constricted models are used in environmental regulations that industrial lobbyists ensure depend on "corporate-produced data" that "structurally will not count side effects, fallouts, or discards."[33] In other words, part of why more attention may not be paid to a dangerous particulate like silica or 6PPD is because of the dominance of corporate-influenced models for understanding and regulating such particulates. Indeed, it may surprise you to learn that about 2,000 times more particle pollution is produced by tires than vehicle exhaust, and though tires introduce 250 different chemicals into the environment, many of which are carcinogenic, there is little regulation on what chemicals tires can contain.[34] These sorts of oversights are beneficial for companies who get to treat the environment, much like Union Carbide treated its workers, as disposable. As Rukeyser notes, after "They poured the concrete," "stocks went up."[35]

I introduced 6PPD and its effects on coho salmon at the start of this article because I want to show how infrastructure byproducts affect more than just humans. Rukeyser excellently attends to how silica adversely affects human life, but we might also consider how infrastructure can have substantial, though perhaps often-overlooked, effects on the creatures around such infrastructures. As Stephanie Wakefield and Glenn Dyer argue, while infrastructure may seemingly appear "immanent to life, banal and commonplace," the study of infrastructure ought to "reorient the way we think about power, life, and revolution, and to set out adequate starting

---

31   Rukeyser, "The Book of the Dead," 95.

32   Michelle Murphy, "Alterlife and Decolonial Chemical Relations," *Cultural Anthropology* 32, no. 4 (November 18, 2017): 495.

33   Murphy, 495–496.

34   Damian Carrington, "Car Tyres Produce Vastly More Particle Pollution than Exhausts, Tests Show," *The Guardian*, June 3, 2022, https://www.theguardian.com/environment/2022/jun/03/car-tyres-produce-more-particle-pollution-than-exhausts-tests-show.

35   Rukeyser, "The Book of the Dead," 101.

points from which to begin rebuilding all three."[36] I think attending to infrastructure byproducts could prove a productive inroad toward reorienting how "we think about power, life, and revolution," since attending to infrastructure byproducts challenges assuming that infrastructure is either immanent to life or banal, and instead focuses attention on how infrastructure can disrupt the operations of life in ways that may initially be difficult to discern. Thus, attending to infrastructure byproducts could prove a robust tool in both infrastructure studies and the environmental humanities by helping us to better comprehend infrastructures' effects and entanglements with the world. Considering the upstream and downstream costs of the construction and operations of infrastructure—the silica poisoning of miners and laborers, the carbon dioxide footprint of concrete, the life-disrupting effects of 6PPD—should be part of our accounting when discussing infrastructure. Much like 6PPD's disruption of the life processes of salmon reveals the entanglement of road infrastructure with aquatic life, considering infrastructure byproducts offers a more expansive understanding of humans' relations with the living world.

---

36   Stephanie Wakefield and Glenn Dyer, "Notes from the Anthropocene #2: Infrastructure," *Brooklyn Rail*, March 5, 2015, https://brooklynrail.org/2015/03/field-notes/notes-from-the-anthropocene-2-infrastructure.

Afrofuturist Infrastructure as Allegory: Picturing Sustainability in Wanuri Kahiu's *Pumzi* (2009)

Katalin Schober

In an interview about her short film *Pumzi*, Kenyan filmmaker Wanuri Kahiu invokes the ancient African tradition of seers and goes on to tell her audience that she wanted to create a hopeful vision of our world in which we as human beings "nurture Mother Nature."[1] By adopting science fiction elements, her acclaimed film directs the audience's gaze to the uses of infrastructure in the human realm, to their operational capacities, as well as to their limits. As a result, it imagines a world in which modern technology is primarily used to preserve a cyclical and sustainable lifestyle, thereby shedding light on the infrastructural workings in our world aimed at the excessive consumption of natural resources.

Infrastructure in *Pumzi*

Set in Eastern Africa some 35 years after World War III, the 'Water War,' *Pumzi* depicts the infrastructural workings of the Maitu community. Its Kikuyu name Maitu refers to 'mother' and could be interpreted as 'Mother Nature,' whose resources have been depleted by humankind.[2] Due to overconsumption and waste, pollution, and radioactive contamination, as well as subsequent distribution battles, Mother Nature has developed into an uninhabitable wasteland.[3]

The only way of guaranteeing the survival of humankind in this dystopian vision is to create an inside world which is self-contained and thus protected from the outside. In this inside world, the infrastructural conditions and mechanisms are con-

---

1   Wanuri Kahiu, "Africa & Science Fiction: Wanuri Kahiu's *Pumzi*, 2009," interview by Oulimata Gueye (2013): 00:00–10:16, 07:43, https://www.youtube.com/watch?v=SWMtgD9O6PU (accessed 13/01/2023).

2   Daniela Fargione, "The Aquatic Turn in Afrofuturism: Women and Other Critters in Nnedi Okorafor's *Lagoon* (2014) and Wanuri Kahiu's *Pumzi* (2010)," *Le Simplegadi* 19, no. 21 (2021): 55–66, 61.

3   Lizelle Bisschoff, "African Cyborgs. Females and Feminists in African Science Fiction," *Interventions* 22, no. 5 (2020): 606–623, 619–620.

verted into a cyclical economy aimed at self-sustenance. The community's inhabitants are asked, for instance, to purify their bodily fluids, like urine and sweat, and transform them into drinking water, which, in turn, represents the community's new currency.[4] What is more, everyone is expected to act as a self-power generator and to contribute his or her share to renewable energies by way of physical exercise on the treadmill.[5]

The community's infrastructural workings are, however, not always directed at ecological outcomes. In order to ensure the intactness of the inside world, all members are asked to take dream suppressants.[6] They limit their imagination, that is their capacity to picture something which does not exist in reality. To put it differently, their imagination might lead to wishful thinking, a deviation that needs to be contained according to the patterns of the fictional world depicted in the short film. Hence, an authoritarian regime resorts to medication and digital communication as tools of control.[7]

Thematically speaking, infrastructural mechanisms are foregrounded in this science fiction storyworld, which speculates about humankind's future. As sketched above, the routines they enable set the pace of the protagonist's daily responsibilities. At the same time, they point to another world prior to the Maitu community: newspaper headlines stored at the natural history museum, for example, bear witness to the greenhouse effect, climate change, and migration due to famine and devastation.[8] This preceding world, which then ushered in a collapse, strikingly resembles the world of our own experience with its current multiple crises.[9]

The film's double fictional world puts our world's infrastructure into perspective; it raises questions about infrastructural limits and possible disturbances; but it also alludes to alternative systems which might solve some of today's environmental problems. The depiction of infrastructure is thus turned into an allegory, which allows for the imagination of another world, of one existing prior to the Maitu community, but also of multiple others set in the distant future.

Interestingly, these possible alternatives result from an infrastructural failure within the confined world of Asha's existence: at one point, she is shown as a female seer whose visions of a magnificent tree in the outside world cannot be contained by

---

4   Wanuri Kahiu, *Pumzi* (Kenya: Inspired Minority Pictures, 2009): 00:00–22:09, 02:20–03:20, https://www.youtube.com/watch?v=iPD-mvR6C-M (accessed 13/01/2023).

5   Wanuri Kahiu, *Pumzi*, 01:50.

6   Wanuri Kahiu, *Pumzi*, 01:22.

7   Jane Bryce, "African Futurism: Speculative Fictions and 'Rewriting the Great Book,'" *Research in African Literatures* 50, no. 1 (2019): 1–19, 5.

8   Wanuri Kahiu, *Pumzi*, 00:35.

9   Marie-Paule Macdonald and Sheila Petty, "Afrofuture ecosystems," *International Journal of Francophone Studies* 23, no. 3–4 (2020): 331–340, 335.

dream suppressants.[10] When she receives a soil sample from an unknown sender, she transgresses her community's restrictions another time: she benefits from her access to the natural history museum, analyses the soil sample, which seems to be free of radioactive radiation, and additionally, finds traces of water.[11] Mother Nature seems to have restored herself, at least at the particular spot where the soil sample was taken.

An excursion to the outside world is, however, refused, so Asha needs to find another way of breaking free from her community. She finally succeeds, by the help of another female employee,[12] takes the soil sample from the natural history museum with her, mixed with water and a seed, and begins her long march through the desert.[13] Another vision of a tree tells her to stop at one place where she plants the seedling, cultivates it with the last drops from her water bottle, and protects it from the burning sun.[14]

The film ends with a final fade-out in which Asha's frame merges with and then changes into the tree of her imagination.[15] Her self-sacrifice allows for the renewal of life on earth, which is indicated by the film's title *Pumzi* referring to 'breath.'[16] The fictional world's collapsing infrastructure, i.e., Asha's visions as well as her transgressions, lay the groundwork for renewed infrastructural systems in an alternative world to come.

Afrofuturist Allegories

Reluctant to revert to negative stereotypes often associated with the African continent, like starvation, environmental devastation, and war,[17] filmmaker Wanuri Kahiu alludes to these images in the first place only to transform them into a positive vision indicated at the end of the film. Her speculative fiction has been repeatedly termed Afrofuturist in this respect.[18] Even if Wanuri Kahiu is skeptical towards particular labels associated with African storytelling traditions,[19] her short film

---

10   Wanuri Kahiu, *Pumzi*, 01:10.

11   Wanuri Kahiu, *Pumzi*, 05:15.

12   Wanuri Kahiu, *Pumzi*, 11:18.

13   Wanuri Kahiu, *Pumzi*, 11:55.

14   Wanuri Kahiu, *Pumzi*, 19:30.

15   Wanuri Kahiu, *Pumzi*, 19:52.

16   Beti Ellerson, "Teaching African Women in Cinema: Part Two," *Black Camera* 7, no. 2 (2016): 217–233, 227.

17   Kahiu, "Africa & Science Fiction," 06:38.

18   Fargione, "The Aquatic Turn in Afrofuturism," 63.

19   Wanuri Kahiu, "No More Labels," *TEDxEuston* (2014): 00:00–15:41, 01:05, https://www.youtube.com/watch?v=4--BIlZE_78 (accessed 13/01/2023).

Pumzi blends various generic conventions, such as the ancient African tradition of seers[20] or elements steeped in popular culture, like science fiction and modern technology.[21] Accordingly, it shows the aesthetic hybridity typical of Afrofuturist works. As famously stated by Ytasha L. Womack, "[b]oth an artistic aesthetic and a framework for critical theory, Afrofuturism combines elements of science fiction, historical fiction, speculative fiction, fantasy, Afrocentricity, and magic realism with non-Western beliefs."[22]

Hence, the short film's fictional world, turned into an extended allegory, exposes a "reenvisioning of the past and speculation about the future rife with cultural critiques"[23] by pointing to alternative environments.[24] Such a vision shifts the focus away from the overexploitation of natural resources to a cyclical economy, which is sustainable and actively promoted by everybody in society.[25] Every member of the Maitu community, for instance, is asked to use resources with moderation in order to contribute to renewables. Asha's self-sacrifice, in the end, might be seen as the epitome of a heightened sense of responsibility towards her community.[26]

Obedience towards authoritarian regimes, however, does not belong to the vision of a true alternative, as shown in the film: Asha follows her personal wisdom for a higher good when analysing the soil sample and escaping to the desert in the outside world. Her common sense combined with courage tell her to speak up for herself and transgress the boundaries that are in place to safeguard the inside world of the Maitu community.

If moderation and common sense laid the groundwork for an alternative world, a balanced resource allocation could finally be achieved. Even more so, the sensible view that human beings truly form an integral part of the earth's ecosystem could become reality.[27]

---

20   Kahiu, "Africa & Science Fiction," 03:48.

21   Kahiu, "Afrofuturism in Popular Culture," *TEDxNairobi* (2012): 00:00–15:12, 11:04, https://www.youtube.com/watch?v=PvxOLVaV2YY (accessed 13/01/2023).

22   Ytasha L. Womack, *Afrofuturism. The World of Black Sci-Fi and Fantasy Culture* (Chicago: Chicago Review Press, 2013), 9.

23   Womack, *Afrofuturism*, 9.

24   Tobias van Veen, "Vessels of Transfer: Allegories of Afrofuturism in Jeff Mills and Janelle Monáe," *Dancecult* 5, no. 2 (2013): 7–41, 10.

25   Sofia Samatar, "Toward a Planetary History of Afrofuturism," *Research in African Literatures* 48, no. 4 (2017): 175–191, 184.

26   Allison Mackey, "Guilty Speculations: The Affective Climate of Global Anthropocene Fictions," *Science Fiction Studies* 45 (2018): 530–544, 536–537.

27   Fargione, "The Aquatic Turn in Afrofuturism," 60–64.

Infrastructure as Allegory

Aesthetically speaking, thinking about infrastructures, their capacities, and their limits, puts those works into perspective in which infrastructures are accentuated, for example in *Pumzi*. In this case, the film's science fiction storyworld— with its detailed illustration of infrastructures— is formed into an extended allegory pointing to multiple worlds with infrastructural capacities and shortcomings while indicating futuristic alternatives at the same time. Interestingly, the failure of the world similar to the one of humankind's daily existence constitutes the prerequisite for the imagination of the Maitu community's contained regimes aimed at self-sustenance and rigid control, which show signs of disruptions and of an imminent breakdown as well.

The looming collapse of the Maitu community, initiated by Asha's visions and her subsequent escape, eventually amounts to a metapoetic argument, as it foregrounds the protagonist's imagination, that is her faculty for generating images and presenting them in her mind's eye. Asha's imagination is, in turn, guided by a structuring principle akin to that of allegory, which evokes images and associations by appealing to the audience's mind's eye in the same way.[28] To put it differently, both, imagination and allegory make the invisible visible by concealing their underlying structures and disclosing them simultaneously.

As a result, *Pumzi's* possible world to come, indicated by Asha's visions and ultimate self-sacrifice, suggests a truly sustainable way of life, thereby encouraging further discussions about posthumanist conceptions of co-living with nature after the Anthropocene. This possible world thus allows the film's audience to take a fresh look at their own experiential world with its infrastructural workings and shortcomings. To put it differently, the film's basic structuring principle, that is its depiction of infrastructures turned into an extended allegory, serves as a means of defamiliarization which breaks with the audience's expectations and patterns of seeing.

Viewed from an aesthetic or, more broadly speaking, cultural angle, infrastructures within our world may be perceived as complex systems open to interpretation, which do not conceal their own mechanisms per se.[29] On the contrary, their spectators' patterns of seeing and experiencing them rather amount to processes of familiarization, which, in turn, make infrastructures seem invisible. An aesthetic perspective, however, may add to their defamiliarization, thereby making the seemingly invisible visible again.

---

28   Verena Olejniczak Lobsien and Eckhard Lobsien, *Die unsichtbare Imagination. Literarisches Denken im 16. Jahrhundert* (München: Fink, 2003), 62–86.

29   Brian Larkin, "The Politics and Poetics of Infrastructure," *Annual Review of Anthropology* 42 (2013): 327–343, 336.

It is precisely this line of thought which is developed in *Pumzi*. And it is this idea which allows its audience to see infrastructures in their aesthetic duplicity similar to allegorical structures: as something, which is visible, and as something else, only hinted at, which might be possible.

Section VII: Infrastructures and Colonialism

Canals & Clans: Mediterranean Infrastructures[1]

Manuel Borutta

Infrastructures made the modern and contemporary Mediterranean. This chapter highlights their impact on the imagination and transformation of the region, their appropriation by local actors, and also sheds a light on the resilience of cultural practices and structures. Questions of relationality, generativity, and agency are crucial: How were imaginaries, transformations, and appropriations of infrastructures related? In what ways did infrastructures enable the emergence of political and economic configurations such as empire, capitalism, and organized crime? To what extent did they contribute to the transformation of Mediterranean societies? How did local groups in turn use them for their own interests? What served as infrastructure for what? In the following, I will first illuminate an early nineteenth century vision of infrastructural connectivity and transformation of the Mediterranean, then, using Marseille as an example, shed light on the material and cultural impact of the implementation of this vision, and finally focus on Corsican appropriations of French infrastructures in the (post)imperial age.

Infrastructuralist Vision: Chevalier's *Système de la Méditerranée*

Infrastructures have been defined as "material forms that allow for the possibility of exchange over space. They are the physical networks through which goods, ideas, waste, power, people, and finance are trafficked."[2] Yet before they can be built, they must be conceived. French Saint-Simonians were key 'infrastructuralists' of the early and mid-nineteenth century, in theory and practice. Even though the term "infrastructure" was coined later,[3] they were among the keen observers, active lobbyists

---

1   Section 1–2 are based on my forthcoming book *Mediterrane Verflechtungen. Algerien und Frankreich zwischen Kolonisierung und Dekolonisierung*, while section 3 outlines a new research project on *French Connections: A Global History of Corsica*.

2   Brian Larkin, "The Politics and Poetics of Infrastructure," *Annual Review of Anthropology* 42, no. 1 (2013): 327–343.

3   Dirk van Laak, "Der Begriff ‚Infrastruktur' und was er vor seiner Erfindung besagte," *Archiv für Begriffsgeschichte* 41 (1999): 280–99, 280.

and determined entrepreneurs of infrastructural connectivity and transformation. Underlying their infrastructure projects were new utopian forms of social organization and human cohabitation, which were tested in shared housing experiments and projected onto entire societies such as Algeria, Egypt and France.[4] At the same time, large-scale Saint-Simonian projects such as the Suez Canal and the Panama Canal directed and intensified global flows of goods, ideas, and people, reinforcing the perception of 'time-space compression.'[5] In this way, they contributed to the project and process of 'globalization.'[6]

The Mediterranean played a key role in the Saint-Simonian project to transform the world by building new infrastructures. In 1832, the *polytechnicien*, mining engineer and economist Michel Chevalier developed his *système de la Méditerranée* in the journal *Le Globe*: The vision of an integrated Euro-Mediterranean system consisting of canals, railways, steam ships and telegraph lines that would pacify the world. According to Chevalier, the age of war which had devastated Europe in the wake of the French Revolution was over. A new age of "universal association" had begun: "the organization of a system of industrial works that embraces the entire globe." In his view, "industry" had a pacifying effect because it created mutual interdependencies between formerly hostile societies. It was composed of production centres joined together by "a relatively material" and "a relatively spiritual bond," i.e., by transport routes and banks. A tightly interconnected industrial network would enable the "best exploitation of the globe."[7]

The new imperial order of the Mediterranean determined by European powers formed the geopolitical context of Chevalier's intervention: While Britain controlled the sea and France conquered Algeria, Russia supported Orthodox Christian movements for autonomy and secession within the Ottoman Empire. At this point, Muslim rulers in Cairo, Istanbul and Tunis adapted Western ideas and technologies to initiate ambitious projects of imperial self-strengthening. Under the rule of Muhammad Ali, the "industrial pasha," Egypt became a laboratory of infrastructural modernization and social change: Here the expansion of the irrigation canal system with the help of French engineers and forced labour enabled the rise of an export-oriented cotton industry and a capitalist state monopoly economy. Chevalier wanted to use this momentum to turn the Mediterranean into a laboratory of universal association where a joint infrastructure policy would pacify formerly hostile societies.

4   Pamela M. Pilbeam, *Saint-Simonians in Nineteenth-Century France: From Free Love to Algeria* (Basingstoke: Palgrave Macmillan, 2014).

5   David Harvey, *The Condition of Postmodernity: An Enquiry into the Origins of Cultural Change* (Malden, Mass.: Blackwell, 1989).

6   Jürgen Osterhammel and Niels P. Petersson, *Globalization: A Short History* (Princeton: Princeton University Press, 2005).

7   Michel Chevalier, *Religion Saint-Simonienne: Politique industrielle et système de la méditerranée* (Paris, 1832), 32–33, 107, 131.

Since the dawn of history, he argued, the region had been a "battlefield" between Orient and Occident. Now it was to become the "wedding bed" of East and West, "a vast forum on all points of which the hitherto divided peoples will commune." A "peaceful policy" of association around the Mediterranean "of peoples who for three thousand years have been clashing" would be the first step towards universal association. The region would become "the center of a political system which will rally all the peoples of the old continent, and would allow them to harmonize their relations between themselves and with the new world."[8]

Chevalier's 'Mediterranean system' was also aimed at transforming a region which he saw as falling into lethargy. To awaken the Mediterranean from its slumber, it was to be linked by faster means of communication to the dynamic northwestern European financial and industrial production centres. Capital and technology would be transferred through these channels creating an industrial mentality within the region, driving cultural change and economic development. A dense network of canals and rivers, railways, steamships, and telegraph lines, jointly funded by banks and governments stood at the heart of his project. According to Chevalier, this integrated network of fluvial, maritime, and terrestrial connections would not only multiply and intensify relations between former enemies, but also enable a "political revolution": the "uniformity" and "instantaneousness" of these faster means of communication would make it easier to "govern" these areas.[9]

Within a few decades Chevalier's vision was largely realized. In 1876, the geographer Élisée Reclus depicted the Mediterranean Sea as a "sea of junction" and "great mediator" of cultural and economic exchange. Since the opening of the Suez Canal (1869) it had become a "highway" of steam navigation between Western Europe, India, and Australia. Within the region, the "regularity" and "speed" of steamships, railroads, and telegraphs had made trade grow in the region and had even promoted visions of its "unification."[10] This was, of course, a harmonizing view that ignored intra-European rivalry and growing asymmetries between Christians and Muslims. While native Muslims were repressed and discriminated in French Algeria, the Muslim regimes in Cairo, Istanbul and Tunis had to pay tribute to their expensive infrastructure policies which had been pursued as projects of westernization: In the 1870s they all went bankrupt and had to submit to an international debt regime. The 'spiritual networks' established by banks were not cut, but the balance of power shifted: Tunisia and Egypt became (official) French and (veiled) British protectorates, while the Ottoman Empire allied itself with the German Empire to undertake infrastructure projects such as the Baghdad and the Hejaz Railway.

8   Chevalier, *Religion*, 122–124, 126, 131.
9   Chevalier, *Religion*, 133.
10   Élisée Reclus, *Nouvelle géographie universelle: La terre et les hommes*, vol. 1: *L'Europe méridionale (Grèce, Turquie, Roumanie, Serbie, Italie, Espagne et Portugal)* (Paris: Hachette, 1876), 33, 48.

In this sense, the infrastructural revolution of the nineteenth century contributed to a Europeanization of the Muslim Mediterranean: to the partial adaptation of Western models and lifestyles; the opening of markets and land for European products, merchants, and settlers; and the loss of financial and political autonomy. In the interwar period, after the violent dissolution of the Ottoman Empire, the Mediterranean seemed to have become a European *mare nostrum*. This immediately fuelled new infrastructural fantasies to merge Europe and Africa into one continent: *Pan(eu)ropa, Atlantropa, Eurafrica*. In these visions, infrastructures were assigned the task of providing Europe with African *Lebensraum*, energy and raw materials enabling Europe to survive in the alleged global power struggle with America and Asia. As in the 1830s, infrastructural transformation again took its departure from cultural imaginaries and ideas of gender and race. The Mediterranean was understood as both a medium and an object of colonization.[11]

Transforming Marseille: The Politics of Infrastructure

Infrastructures also transformed Southern Europe. Chevalier's 'Mediterranean system' envisioned ports as nodes of terrestrial, fluvial, and maritime connections. In Marseille, he saw the key to French domination of the Mediterranean. In the 1830s, he promoted an infrastructural modernization and linking of the city. Since the old port was overburdened by the swelling maritime trade and the well-organized corporation of the *portefaix* kept slowing down the flow of goods, a new port with docks and machinery was to be built and connected to other seas and rivers via canals and the regulated Rhône. The construction of a direct railroad to Paris would give France direct access to its colonies Algeria and Corsica, which still had to be wrested from "barbarism," and allow domination of the Mediterranean.[12]

Supported by the grand merchants of Marseille, Chevalier's plan was largely implemented in the 1840s and 50s: The direct steamship connection with Algiers accelerated the transport of information, goods, troops and settlers and closely intertwined the local with the colonial economy: a new port was built at *La Joliette*, docks opened where the *portefaix* were replaced by immigrant workers and machines, and the Paris-Lyon-Méditerranée (PLM) express train service connected the capital with the Mediterranean sea. As Marseille became a major hub for the movement of goods

---

11   Peo Hansen and Stefan Jonsson, *Eurafrica: The Untold History of European Integration and Colonialism* (London: Bloomsbury, 2015); Philipp N. Lehmann, "Infinite Power to Change the World: Hydroelectricity and Engineered Climate Change in the Atlantropa Project," *American Historical Review* 121, no. 1 (2016): 70–100.

12   Michel Chevalier, *Des intérêts matériels en France: Travaux publics. Routes. Canaux. Chemins de fer* (Paris: Gosselin et Coquebert, 1838), 42; Michel Chevalier, "Lettres du Midi," *Journal des débats politiques et littéraires*, November 9 and December 10, 1838; February 5, 1839.

and people between the Mediterranean, the Indian and Pacific Ocean, and the Chinese Sea, the city moved from the margin of the nation to the centre of the empire: the first national colonial exhibition took place in Marseille in 1906.[13]

A driving force and great profiteer of Marseille's infrastructural transformation was the Saint-Simonian Paulin Talabot, who as founding director of the PLM and the dock company not only controlled the new port and the rail connection to Paris, but also trans-Mediterranean traffic by running and financing steamships, railways, forests, mines, and infrastructural works in Algeria. Talabot's logistics empire personified the integration of terrestrial and maritime transport systems that Chevalier had called for. And as envisaged, this 'Mediterranean system' of connectivity drove the re-globalization of Marseille and thus of France: In the 1850s, Marseilles steamships began crossing the oceans to destinations in Africa, the Americas, and Asia. Mediterranean connections were followed by global ones, and Marseille became their nodal point.[14]

Yet one problem with this centring was Marseille's simultaneous colonization by Paris. The headquarters of the banks and companies controlling the local infrastructure and movement of capital, people, and goods were located in Paris. In the course of its infrastructural connection, Marseille was degraded to a place of transit and became an object of investment and speculation for Parisian capital: it was transformed from a *subject* to an *object* of colonization.[15] Another problem was the strong population growth, mainly by immigrants, first hired from Italy and Corsica, then from Africa and Asia. As these immigrants competed with natives for jobs and housing, socioeconomic conflicts became increasingly violent and expressed in a language of cultural and racial difference.[16]

In addition, conflicts arose over Marseille's cultural identity. On the one hand the city's new diversity was celebrated at the 2,500th anniversary (1899), the second national colonial exhibition (1922), and the cosmopolitan magazine *Cahiers du Sud*. Gabriel Audisio depicted Marseille as the capital of a "liquid continent" that did not belong to any single nation or race, but rather merged them.[17] On the other hand, external observers such as Joseph Roth and Albert Londres described the

---

13   Paul Masson, *Marseille et la colonisation française: Essai d'Histoire coloniale* (Marseille: Barlatier, 1906).

14   Jean Lenoble, *Les frères Talabot: Une grande famille d'entrepreneurs au XIXe siècle*, (Limoges: Souny, 1989).

15   Marcel Roncayolo, *L'Imaginaire de Marseille: Port, ville, pôle* (Lyon: ENS, 2014).

16   Laurent Dornel, "Cosmopolitisme et xénophobie: Les luttes entre français et italiens dans les ports et docks marseillais, 1870–1914," *Cahiers de la Méditerranée* 67 (2003): 245–267; Céline Regnard-Drouot, *Marseille la violente: Criminalité, industrialisation et société, 1851–1914* (Rennes: Presses universitaires de Rennes, 2009).

17   Gabriel Audisio, *Jeunesse De La Méditerranée* (Paris: Gallimard, 1935).

city as a Moloch of globalization or as a part of North Africa.[18] Marcel Pagnol, who was born in nearby Aubagne, portrayed the town's transformation as a threat to its Provençal tradition. In his bestseller theatre play Marius (1929), he juxtaposed the cultural traditions of the old port and the modern infrastructures of the new port. While César's bar in the *Vieux Port* seems to be located in a Provençal fishing village untouched by change, the sirens of the steamships of *La Joliette* threaten to separate the wanderlust-stricken Marius from the love of his life Fanny, because he wants to sign on an ocean liner. Pagnol staged modern infrastructure as a threat to happiness and origins.[19]

Cultural Infrastructures: Corsican Networks

Due to the rise of the local mobsters Paul Bonnaventure Carbone and François Spirito, interwar Marseille gained the reputation of a 'French Chicago.' While Spirito's family was of Italian origin, Carbone was born in the Corsican port town Propriano and had grown up in Marseille's *Le Panier* district at the old port where most Corsicans lived.[20] He had first sailed on steamships to the Middle and Far East and then opened a brothel in Cairo with Spirito. Upon their return to Marseille, they took control of the local and Parisian underworld and used their 'material' and 'spiritual' infrastructures—the port of Marseille and their friends and compatriots aboard ocean liners—to smuggle women (white slave trade), weapons, and opium between the Mediterranean, South America, and East Asia. It was a precursor of the postwar *French Connection*, which would monopolize the US heroin market until the 1970s. The rise of Carbone and Spirito was only possible because of a close alliance with right-wing populist politician Simon Sabiani. Like Carbone, Sabiani was from southwestern Corsica. As deputy mayor of Marseille (1931–35), he acted as a patron to the 60,000 Corsicans living in the city, who formed his loyal electorate and who in return received posts in the administration. Carbone's and Spirito's henchmen were given access to the prefecture, and thus exempt from prosecution.[21] This mix of clientelism and gangsterism made Marseille a European capital of organized

---

18   Joseph Roth, "Marseille [1925]," in *Orte. Ausgewählte Texte*, ed. Heinz Czechowski (Leipzig: Reclam, 1990): 199–205; Albert Londres, *Marseille, port du sud* (Paris: Les éditions de France, 1927).

19   Marcel Pagnol, *Marius: Pièce en quatre actes* (Paris: Éditions de Fallois, 2009).

20   Marie-Françoise Attard-Maraninchi, *Le Panier, village corse à Marseille* (Paris: Autrement, 1997).

21   Paul Jankowski, *Communism and Collaboration: Simon Sabiani and Politics in Marseille, 1919–1944* (New Haven: Yale University Press, 1989); Jacques Follorou and Vincent Nouzille, *Les Parrains Corses* (Paris: Fayard, 2004); Grégory Auda, *Bandits corses: des bandits d'honneur au grand banditisme* (Paris: Éditions Michalon, 2005).

crime. The case illustrates not only another 'dark side' of globalization, but also the virtuoso appropriation of infrastructures by subaltern Mediterranean actors, as well as the resilience and flexibility of supposedly 'backward' cultural structures and practices such as clans and patronage.

The same dialectic can be observed on Corsica itself. The island had been annexed and conquered by France in 1768, but not fully integrated until the Second Empire (1852–70). Napoleon III, who staged himself as the father of the Corsican 'family,' provided Corsican elites with important offices in Paris and drove the infrastructural modernization of the island. As a result, however, Corsica was flooded with industrial foodstuffs from Marseille, so that local agriculture collapsed. Due to strong population growth and failed industrialization, young Corsicans were forced to emigrate. Some signed on with steamship companies, most settled in Marseille, Algeria, and the French overseas colonies, where they took on posts in the army and administration. In a way, they formed a human infrastructure of the empire, which struggled to mobilize people from the mainland.[22] Yet they also imposed their own cultural logic on the empire which ran counter to the French 'civilizing mission' and the Republican imperative to 'assimilate' settler colonies like Algeria. By using the resources of the colonial state to distribute land and labor to compatriots, Corsicans flexibly adapted cultural practices of the island to a new context. Instead of mixing with other French overseas, they preserved their linguistic and cultural identity. They founded newspapers and associations that cultivated Corsican traditions, represented Corsican interests in the colonies, and lobbied for the island's infrastructural connectivity. In 1958, pro-colonial Corsicans used their contacts and connections to prevent the secession of Algeria and overthrow the Fourth Republic.[23] After decolonization, when France tried to develop Corsica in terms of infrastructure,[24] clan chiefs tried to redirect these resources to their clientele on the island. In France's former colonies in sub-Saharan Africa, Corsicans played a central role in *Françafrique* (sometimes called *Corsafrique*) networks. By maintaining good relations with postcolonial African elites, they helped the French state, the Gaullist party, and oil companies such as *Elf Aquitaine* to develop cheap energy sources and launder money.[25] Whereas the French state had colonized Corsica, Corsicans colonized the latter's (post-)colonial infrastructures and repurposed them to their own avail.

22 Antoine-Marie Graziani, ed., *Histoire de la Corse des révolutions à nos jours: permanences et évolutions* (Ajaccio: Éditions Alain Piazzola, 2019).

23 Francis Pomponi and Ange Rovere, "1958. La Corse à l'heure des événements d'Algérie," in *Le mémorial des Corses*, vol. 5, *De l'histoire à l'actualité 1945–1980*, ed. Francis Pomponi (Ajaccio, 1982), 42–65.

24 Raymond Lazzarotti, *SOMIVAC et développement économique de la Corse: L'apport d'une société d'équipement a l'essor d'une région* (Bastia: SOMIVAC, 1982).

25 Thomas Borrel et al., eds., *L' Empire qui ne veut pas mourir: Une histoire de la Francafrique* (Paris: Seuil, 2021).

Conversely, their networks served the French state and business as a cultural infrastructure whose informal channels and personal contacts could be activated to achieve subversive political goals or to facilitate illicit business. In this way, canals and clans served as complementary infrastructures in/of the modern and contemporary Mediterranean.

Imagined Infrastructures: Eurafrica and Worldmaking in the Mid-Twentieth Century

Martin Rempe

Infrastructures of great scale have fuelled the imaginations of humankind in various ways. Think of the mythical tower of Babel as a human attempt of community building to reach God in heaven which ultimately resulted in the Babylonian confusion and scattering of humankind all over the world. The *long durée* of the Suez Canal, whose precursors go back to the second millennium BC, and which saw several construction attempts before its eventual opening in 1867, is another infrastructural project that was both fraught with imaginary power and entailed double-edged social effects. As Valeska Huber has shown, the realization of the canal did not simply connect Europe with Asia, it also acted as an infrastructural chokepoint that created new ethnic and spatial demarcations.[1]

Since the late nineteenth century, many infrastructural projects have been large-scale utopian blueprints to improve human living conditions that could gain a lot of public attention but never turned into reality. Later on, dubbed by development experts as "white elephants," they symbolized the technological hubris widespread among engineers, technocrats, and politicians from the mid-twentieth century western world onward.[2]

Over the second third of this century, numerous imagined infrastructures, which ultimately turned into white elephants, clustered around the concept of "Eurafrica." The term, which can be traced back to the years around 1900, basically denotes a vague idea of close political and economic ties between Europe and Africa. During the interwar period, thanks to Count Richard Coudenhove-Kalergi and his Pan-European movement, the idea of Eurafrica gained currency among intellectuals, politicians, and colonial business circles. Whereas Coudenhove-Kalergi and his fellows sought to use Eurafrica as a geopolitical argument and economic incentive for European reconciliation, integration, and community building, other

---

1   Valeska Huber, *Channelling Mobilities: Migration and Globalisation in the Suez Canal Region and Beyond, 1869–1914* (Cambridge: Cambridge University Press, 2013).

2   Dirk van Laak, *Weiße Elefanten. Anspruch und Scheitern technischer Großprojekte im 20. Jahrhundert* (Stuttgart: Deutsche Verlags-Anstalt, 1999), 9, 13.

blueprints of Eurafrica such as architect Herman Sörgel's famous *Atlantropa* project, launched in 1932, took a decidedly infrastructural approach to reach these goals. The construction of a gigantic dam at the Strait of Gibraltar was supposed to control and substantially lower the level of the Mediterranean in order to gain fertile land, territorial connectivity to Africa, and energy through several hydroelectric power plants to be placed at the shores of the imagined inland sea. After the turmoil of the Second World War, these political-economic and infrastructural ideas of Eurafrica experienced a second heyday during the 1950s and peaked in the so-called association of European member states' overseas territories in Africa to the European Economic Community, the forerunner of today's EU founded in 1957. However, disillusion about this alignment on many sides was not a long time coming.[3]

Both the political-economic and the infrastructural variants of Eurafrica have been subject to detailed historical investigation. Whereas Peo Hansen and Stefan Jonsson use political visions of Eurafrica to reveal the colonial roots of European integration, Dirk van Laak highlights German engineers' and technocrats' infrastructural visions for Africa to trace the career of the very concept of infrastructure and to point to the crucial role of these figures as worldmaking public intellectuals.[4] Following in their footsteps, this essay argues that imagined infrastructures of Eurafrica transcended the political realm and reached society at large. Their imaginary power mattered because they transported distinct geopolitical visions of an African continent in transformation. By highlighting technical feasibility and economic advantages, these visions carried strong notions of European community building. At the same time, they largely concealed possible societal repercussions for African people and thus helped to preserve well-established ideas of "traditional" African societies.

The emphasis on the popularization of imagined infrastructures has several purposes. First, it aims to bring immaterial dimensions (back) into the study of infrastructures which, particularly in the colonial context, has in recent years been shaped by a focus on built infrastructures, including their materiality, various uses, and social as well as political consequences.[5] Second, by focusing on ways of dissemination and reception within society at large, the cultural significance of imagined in-

3   Sven Beckert, "American Danger: United States Empire, Eurafrica, and the Territorialization of Industrial Capitalism, 1870–1950," *The American Historical Review* 122, no. 4 (2017): 1137–1170; Thomas Moser, *Europäische Integration, Dekolonisation, Eurafrika. Eine historische Analyse über Entstehungsbedingungen der Eurafrikanischen Gemeinschaft von der Weltwirtschaftskrise bis zum Jaunde-Vertrag, 1929–1963* (Baden-Baden: Nomos, 2000).

4   Peo Hansen and Stefan Jonsson, *Eurafrica: The Untold History of European Integration and Colonialism* (London: Bloomsbury, 2014), 1–5; Dirk van Laak, *Imperiale Infrastrukturen. Deutsche Planungen für eine Erschließung Afrikas 1880 bis 1960* (Paderborn: Schöningh, 2004), 12–13.

5   See, e.g. Brian Larkin, "The Politics and Poetics of Infrastructure," *Annual Review of Anthropology* 42 (2013): 327–343; Deborah Cowen, "Following the Infrastructures of Empire: Notes on Cities, Settler Colonialism, and Method," *Urban Geography* 41, no. 4 (2020): 469–486; Julia

frastructures and the distinct worldviews aligned to them come to the forefront.[6] Overall, these Eurafrican dreams are a case in point for taking imagined infrastructures—past and present—seriously because they both stabilize and transform society's ability for "worldmaking," to borrow and widen Adom Getachew's catchy phrase. Whereas Getachew contrasts worldmaking with nation-building in order to highlight the global aspirations of anticolonial nationalists in the age of decolonization, I use it here to coin the activity of ordering and envisioning the world more generally.[7]

To elaborate on my argument, it is necessary to go back to Herman Sörgel's *Atlantropa* project. Among the infrastructural Eurafrican dreams, it has no doubt attracted the greatest attention just because of its infrastructural boldness. 3.5 million square kilometres of arable land were supposed to be generated by the construction of several dams and the irrigation of the Sahara, and 150 million horsepower of energy would be produced by the hydropower plants—an amount which at that time equalled all existing powerhouses in Europe.[8] However, Sörgel's concept was not a solely technological project. On the contrary, *Atlantropa* was imagined as a solution to perceived economic and geopolitical challenges of the time. As the Munich architect put it in his 1932 project description, "the final aim of Atlantropa is the transformation of Europe with Africa into a strong and healthy continent between Pan-America and Pan-Asia," with the effect of "multiplying Europe's strength and dimension, ultimately turning it into a unified power."[9] Hence, the great utopian surplus of *Atlantropa* attracted interest among politicians and engineers as well as among architects and writers.

As Alexander Gall in his pioneering study of the project points out, nothing served the dissemination of *Atlantropa* more than (science-)fiction books which put the construction of a dam centre stage. The most successful novel, *Amadeus*, published by the Swiss author John Knittel in 1939, quickly sold up to 200,000 copies in Germany, Switzerland, England, and the United States. After the Second World War, translations into Italian, French, and Spanish followed, while the German

Tischler, *Light and Power for a Multiracial Nation: The Kariba Dam Scheme in the Central African Federation* (Basingstoke: Palgrave Macmillan, 2013).

6   A similar argument is made by Ashley Carse and David Kneas in "Unbuilt and Unfinished: The Temporalities of Infrastructure," *Environment and Society* 10 (2019): 9–28, here 15–16; see also the essays of the online project "Coloniality of Infrastructure," eds.Nick Axel, Kenny Cupers, and Nikolaus Hirsch, https://www.e-flux.com/architecture/coloniality-infrastructure /.

7   Adom Getachew, *Worldmaking after Empire: The Rise and Fall of Self-Determination* (Princeton: Princeton University Press, 2019), 1–5.

8   Alexander Gall, *Das Atlantropa-Projekt. Die Geschichte einer gescheiterten Vision. Herman Sörgel und die Absenkung des Mittelmeers* (Frankfurt: Campus, 1998), 21–24.

9   Herman Sörgel, *Atlantropa* (Zürich: Fretz & Wasmuth A.G., 1932), 115.

version experienced several reissues. Altogether, Gall estimates around 1 million copies of *Amadeus*, which uses a trivial love affair as a background story to explicitly promote Sörgel's vision and to spread the idea of European community building through joint work on the infrastructural extension to Africa, were published.[10]

Next to Knittel's bestseller, Gall identified eight science fiction novels published between 1930 and 1956 that, more or less prominently, featured the construction of the projected Gibraltar dam.[11] The German engineer and author Titus Taeschner wrote two books in a row, entitled *Atlantropa* (1935) and *Eurofrika: Die Macht der Zukunft*, (*Eurofrica: The Power of the Future*) which was published three years later. Whereas the former highlights the realization of Sörgel's vision under German leadership and against both French rivalry and indigenous resistance, the latter places the plot decades into the future: thanks to the construction of the Gibraltar dam, Europe and Africa have been joined for a long time, whereas the Jews have been ousted from Europe and banned to the Asian part of Russia, now a "Jewish-Bolshevik refuge."[12] "Eurofrika" is now in European hands under German leadership and the task the infrastructural penetration of the African inland. By damming the Congo River at several points, a huge new "Congo Sea" was to be created and Lake Chad to be considerably increased. These tasks had to be implemented against the "barbarian" locals, for which respect was out of the place in the eyes of the German central character Sörrensen (the phonetic proximity to Sörgel is of course no coincidence).[13] Overall, the completion of the infrastructural penetration of the African continent would serve the self-assertion of German-dominated Europe against communist and Jewish threats. Taeschner's books harmonized Eurafrican dreams with Nazi ideology and fascist visions of the future. Even though his story went against the official party line—the Bavaria Film studios actually produced a very successful movie entitled *Ein Meer versinkt* (*A Sunken Sea*) in 1935 which featured *Atlantropa* as a gigantic failure—it provided a basis for individuals' worldmaking through imagining Eurafrican infrastructures.[14]

Another great fan of Sörgel was the successful Austrian journalist, energy expert and nonfiction writer Anton Zischka (1904–1997). In his first book entitled *Le monde en folie* (*The World in Madness*) published in 1933, Zischka depicted *Atlantropa* in detail as a solution to the political and economic crisis in Europe and praised Sörgelas a

10   See John Knittel, *Amadeus* (Berlin: Büchergilde Gutenberg, 1940); Gall, *Atlantropa*, 151–152.

11   Gall, *Atlantropa*, 153.

12   Titus Taeschner, *Eurofrika. Die Macht der Zukunft* (Berlin: Buchwarte, 1938), 9. Cf. Titus Taeschner, *Atlantropa* (Bern: Goldmann, 1935).

13   Taeschner, *Eurofrika*, 17–20.

14   Cf. Gall, *Atlantropa*, 40, 155–157; on Taeschner in the context of other fascist visions in science-fiction novels, see Jost Hermand, "Zwischen Superhirn und grüner Siedlung. Faschistische Zukunftsvisionen," *Zeitschrift für Religions-und Geistesgeschichte* 40, no. 2 (1988): 134–50, here 146–150.

"prophet": "I don't know whether he is a good prophet, but at least he has a vision."[15] The book became a bestseller and sold over 200,000 copies, allowing Zischka to become self-employed and to settle in Mallorca in 1935, where he lived until his death. All in all, his literary oeuvre includes more than 50 books, some of which have been translated into up to 18 languages, as well as countless articles in magazines and newspapers worldwide.[16]

While Sörgel was very active (albeit not very successful) to win political and societal support for his project after the Second World War until his sudden death in December 1952, Zischka became another, and perhaps the most important, advocate of Eurafrica during the 1950s. This was mainly due to his book *Afrika: Europas Gemeinschaftsaufgabe Nr. 1* (*Africa: Europe's no. 1 Community Task*), published in 1951. Again, Zischka's imaginations of Eurafrican exploitation were based on well-known infrastructural projects, from the Gibraltar dam and the Congo Sea to the Chad Sea and many more large-scale undertakings. To give but one more example, Zischka dreamt of the continental connection of Africa's railways, including the construction of the so-called Trans-Sahara railroad, the idea of which dates back to the last third of the nineteenth century. Zischka claimed that technical feasibility was beyond any doubt, and he dreamt of massive deposits of coal, phosphates, copper, and zinc, not to mention the estimated 300,000 tons of cotton to be transported from freshly irrigated and cultivated land in the Niger region, between Timbuktu and Ségou. In a nutshell, following Zischka, Africa was Europe's rosy future and infrastructures were key to its realization.[17]

Admittedly, the sales figures of Zischka's book were by no means exhilarating. The first edition was to have 14,000 copies printed, and only 6,000 sold after about a year. Nonetheless, the book was quickly translated into Dutch, Italian, and French. In addition, it was widely and predominantly positively reviewed in European academic media like the *Geographical Journal* as well as in political weeklies like *Der Spiegel*, which is reflective of how serious Zischka's ideas were taken. Following a review in the *Wochenend*, Zischka even turned into a regular guest writer for this German penny press. Hence, as I argue elsewhere in more detail, Zischka's book was attractive for many different audiences just because his book depicted

15   Anton Zischka, *Le monde en folie* (Paris: Les Editions de France, 1933), 240–244, quote 240.

16   On Zischka see in detail Dirk van Laak, "Energie von A bis Z. Anton Zischka erschließt die Welt," *Non Fiktion. Arsenal der anderen Gattungen* 2, no. 1 (2007): 79–93; on his positioning towards the Nazi regime, see Heike Weber, "Technikkonzeptionen in der populären Sachbuchliteratur des Nationalsozialismus. Die Werke von Anton Zischka," *Technikgeschichte* 66 (1999): 205–236.

17   Anton Zischka, *Afrika. Europas Gemeinschaftsaufgabe Nr. 1* (Oldenburg: Gerhard Stalling Verlag, 1951), 70–71. On the history of the Trans-Saharan Railroad, see Daniel R. Headrick, *The Tools of Empire: Technology and European Imperialism in the Nineteenth Century* (Oxford: Oxford University Press, 1981), 199–202.

Eurafrica as a crude mixture of a technocratic development project, an apology of colonial politics, and a German large-scale fantasy. Ultimately, Zischka blended all the dominant conceptions of the relationship between the two continents that had unfolded since the interwar period into a grand Eurafrican peace project under European leadership.[18] In doing so, he created an intellectual space for individual worldmaking.

At the same time, Zischka's imagined infrastructures omitted any true reflection of the actual future of African societies. Consequences of his infrastructural dreams for the local populations were hardly mentioned in the book. As a staunch defender of racial hierarchies, Zischka argued for the separation of living and working environments between Whites and Blacks. While he acknowledged that modernization was under way and that Africans had in principle the right to benefit from it, he was at the same time convinced that "peasant activities remain the norm for native Africans."[19] Zischka's intention to disseminate stereotypical images of "traditional" African societies became crystal clear in one of his follow-up articles in the penny press *Wochenend*. Entitled *Ur-Afrika lebt weiter...* (*Primordial Africa is Alive...*), Zischka explicitly juxtaposed the most vulgar clichés of uncivilized, wild, and even cannibalistic Africans with modern infrastructure built by European colonial powers for a White population.[20]

These Eurafrican visions of the mid-twentieth century and their popularization have shown that imagined infrastructures mattered. They mattered because they offered multiple possibilities to both consolidate and transform the worldmaking of a broad German and European readership of fiction and nonfiction literature as well as of highbrow to lowbrow print media. Thus, imagined infrastructures raised the possibility of envisioning the world and of intellectually arranging spatial belonging and demarcation.

Relating this practice to Benedict Anderson's famous *Imagined Communities*, imagined infrastructures can and should be studied as one mechanism or "style," as Anderson puts it, to create community.[21] In the case of Eurafrica, Knittel and Zischka even explicitly pinned their hopes in the practical infrastructural work to create a European community. However, imagined (as well as realized) infrastructures might also entail destructive effects for communities, as the introductory examples of the Babel Tower and the Suez Canal have already indicated, and the

---

18   Martin Rempe, "Think Global: Anton Zischka, Eurafrica and His Followers," in *France, Allemagne, Afrique: représentations, transferts, relations / Frankreich, Deutschland, Afrika. Repräsentationen, Transfers, Beziehungen*, eds. Emmanuel Droit, Anne Kwaschik, and Silke Mende (Stuttgart: Steiner, 2023 forthcoming).

19   Zischka, *Afrika*, 254–256, quote 255.

20   See Anton Zischka, "Ur-Afrika lebt weiter..." *Wochenend* no. 3 (14 January 1953): 3.

21   Benedict Anderson, *Imagined Communities: Reflections on the Origin and Spread of Nationalism* (London: Verso, 2006 [1983]), 5–7, quote 6.

Eurafrican dreams prove in detail. Worldmaking through Eurafrican infrastructure concerned primarily imagining only Europe's geopolitical and economic future, first under Nazi domination and later, during the early Cold War, as a third force between the superpowers, leaving Africa and its populations out of the picture.

Another slight difference of imagined infrastructures to Anderson's framing concerns their temporality. Of course, the practice of imagining has its reference point in the past present. However, while Anderson's nations are thought of as immortal, fusing past, present, and future, imagined infrastructures were specifically focused on one of these temporalities. They were either oriented to the remote past, as in the case of the Tower of Babel, to the past present, as in the case of the Suez Canal, or to the past future, as in the case of Eurafrica. To what extent these specific temporalities affected the imaginary power might be an interesting question to follow up.[22] Finally, in the light of China's Belt and Road Initiative, which was launched in 2013 and includes the African continent as well and is perhaps the biggest infrastructural vision the world has ever seen, research interest in imagined infrastructures should not be relegated to the past. On the contrary, the new "Silk Road" not only testifies to the continuity (or return) of large-scale infrastructural projects till now, but should also make us keep track of both the realized and the imagined parts of the initiative.[23] In the end, as this brief essay has sketched out, studying infrastructures in all its consequences can only work by reflecting on both dimensions at once.

---

22   Anderson, *Imagined Communities*, 11–12, 36.

23   Seth Schindler, Simin Fadaee, and Dan Brockington, "Contemporary Megaprojects: An Intro-
        duction," *Environment and Society* 10 (2019): 1–8; on the African dimension of this initiative,
        see Yunnan Chen, "Silk Road to the Sahel: African Ambitions in China's Belt and Road Ini-
        tiative," *Policy Brief*, no. 23 (2018): 1–4.

Imperial Roads and the Fascist Culture of Total Mobilization

Fernando Esposito

Infrastructures have a cultural dimension. In fact, railroads, roads, electric grids, or telegraphic cables only become *infrastructure* by way of the practices and discourses that inform them. Infrastructures are what Bruno Latour and Donna Haraway call "monsters," "cyborgs," or "tricksters."[1] They are "techno-social-semiotic hybrids" that transcend common categorical classifications.[2] Thus, infrastructures are complex chimeras consisting of technology, society, and nature, of signs, institutions, and people, of knowledge and power. This chapter takes a cursory look at the close nexus between the fascist culture of total mobilization and Fascist imperial roads at the Horn of Africa.[3]

Tracks—Berlin 1930

The view from his room was of the tangle of tracks of the Stadt-and Reichsbahn, children were noisy in the house and it smelled of cabbage. The room was not very bright, crammed with books, decorated with masks and strange wood-carved figures, on the desk stood a microscope, beetle collections and jars full of odd intertwined pale green substances stood on the shelves.[4]

---

1   Cf. Bruno Latour, *We Have Never Been Modern* (Cambridge: Harvard University Press, 1993), 47, and Donna Haraway, *Simians, Cyborgs, and Women: The Reinvention of Nature* (New York: Routledge, 1991), 1 et seq.

2   Andréa Belliger and David J. Krieger, "Einführung in die Akteur-Netzwerk Theorie," in *ANThology. Ein einführendes Handbuch zur Akteur-Netzwerk-Theorie*, eds. Andréa Belliger and David J. Krieger (Bielefeld: transcript Verlag, 2006): 13–50, 23.

3   As is common within fascism studies, fascism with a lower-case "f" refers to the generic phenomenon, Fascism with a capital "F" refers to Italian Fascism.

4   Ernst von Salomon, *Der Fragebogen* (Hamburg: Rowohlt Verlag, 1951), 292. Cf. Helmuth Kiesel, *Ernst Jünger. Die Biographie* (Munich: Siedler Verlag, 2007), 320.

According to the national revolutionary Ernst von Salomon, it was in this Berlin room in the Stralauer Allee 36, and in view of the "tangle of tracks," that the kindred spirit Ernst Jünger wrote his influential essay *Total Mobilization*. Published in 1930 in an anthology edited by Jünger and titled *Krieg und Krieger (War and Warrior)*, the essay was a call to Weimar Germany's right: if it wanted to win the longed-for future war, it would have to embrace modern technology and come to terms with the turbulent new world of the third estate. However, the essay was also an astute description of the spirit of modernity which had reared its ugly head in the First World War. According to Jünger, the "dawn of the age of labor [*Arbeitszeitalter*]" went hand in hand with "the growing conversion of life into energy, the increasingly fleeting content of all binding ties in deference to mobility". And he continues:

> It suffices simply to consider our daily life, with its inexorability and merciless discipline, its smoking, glowing districts, the physics and metaphysics of its commerce, its motors, airplanes, and burgeoning cities. With a pleasure-tinged horror, we sense that here, not a single atom is not in motion—that we are profoundly inscribed in this raging process.[5]

The war had heralded this new age and revealed its nature as a culture of "total mobilization." Like a modern day Hercalitus, Jünger understood war as the father of all and saw everything in movement—πάντα χωρεῖ.[6]

The culture of radicalized and incessant movement was, and is, intimately connected with tracks, roads, and telegraph cables for they were, and are, "the connective tissues and the circulatory systems of modernity" and "the built networks that facilitate the flow of goods, people, or ideas and allow for their exchange over space."[7] These technological systems lie at the root of the "growing conversion of life into energy."[8] At the same time, however, it is the culture of total mobilization—specific concepts, patterns of meaning, and practices—inscribed into these technological systems which makes them into the *infrastructure* of modernity. It is no coincidence that the example which clarifies the intrinsic nexus of modern infrastructure and the culture of total mobilization also stems from the context of fascism, for Fascism

---

5   Ernst Jünger, "Total Mobilization," in *The Heidegger Controversy: A Critical Reader*, ed. Richard Wolin (Cambridge: MIT Press, 1998), 119–139, 126 et seqq.

6   DK 22 B 53; Plato, Crat. 402 a.

7   Paul N. Edwards, "Infrastructure and Modernity: Scales of Force, Time, and Social Organization in the History of Sociotechnical Systems," in *Modernity and Technology*, eds. Thomas J. Misa et al. (Cambridge: MIT Press, 2002), 185–225, 185; Brian Larkin, "The Politics and Poetics of Infrastructure," *Annual Review of Anthropology* 42, no. 1 (2013): 327–43, 328.

8   Jünger, "Total Mobilization," 126.

was not only an ideology of movement, the Fascists were also restless revolutionaries.[9]

Roads—Horn of Africa, 1935–1936

Tortuous paths, roads that follow the indolent curves of rivers, or that hug the irregular backs and stomachs of mountains—these are the laws of the earth. Never a straight line; always zigzags and arabesques. Velocity has finally given human life one of the attributes of divinity: the straight line. [...] We have to persecute, whip, and torture all who sin against speed.[10]

Figure 1: The street from Nefasit to Dekemhare in Eritrea—as straight and "divine" as the Futurist and Fascist Filippo Tommaso Marinetti praised.

Unknown photographer, picture in: Giuseppe Pini, "Le Strade dell'Africa Orientale Italiana," *Le Strade* 20, no. 6 (1938): 318–336, 325.

In the forefront of the invasion of Haile Selassie's Ethiopian Empire on October 2, 1935, the Italian Fascists put in motion "a gigantic labor process" closely resem-

---

9   Cf. Fernando Esposito and Sven Reichardt, "Revolution and Eternity: Introductory Remarks on Fascist Temporalities," *Journal of Modern European History* 13, no. 1 (2015): 24–43.

10   Filippo Tommaso Marinetti, "The New Religion-Morality of Speed," in *Futurism: An Anthology*, eds. Lawrence Rainey, Christine Poggi, and Laura Wittman (New Haven: Yale University Press 2009): 224–229, 224 et seq.

bling the one described by Jünger.[11] Waging war some 4,000 kilometres from home in the Ethiopian Highlands as well as the Somalian steppe and desert was firstly an enormous logistical challenge. Desperate to avoid a further disgraceful defeat like the one suffered at the Battle of Adwa in 1896, the Italian military assembled a massive force at the Horn of Africa. On the eve of war 134,000 Italian officers and soldiers and 82,500 Askaris stood ready for battle in Eritrea and Somalia. By May 1936, the troops had grown to 330,000 Italians and 87,000 Askaris which had 10,000 machine guns, 1,100 pieces of artillery, 350 airplanes, 250 tanks, 90,000 mules and horses, and 14,000 motor vehicles at their disposal.[12] Men and material had to not only pass through the British controlled Suez Canal, but the ports of Massawa and Mogadishu had to be expanded and reliable transportation routes built to the deployment areas of the troops and then subsequently to the Ethiopian interior.

As Emilio De Bono, former Minister of Colonies, in 1935 both High Commissioner for Italian Africa, and Governor of Eritrea stated in the aftermath of the Italian victory:

> Conditions in Eritrea were certainly not such as to facilitate the movement thither of great bodies of troops, and all that is involved by an extraordinary massing of armed forces. Even less did they permit of the logistic and strategical movement of armed forces.[13]

The Fascist dromocrats knew not only that, to quote Sun Tzu, "speed is the essence of war," but also that infrastructure was the necessary condition for a *"guerra rapida e decisiva,"* that is the Italian variant of a *blitzkrieg*.[14] The most urgent problem they had to solve was the "Cyclopean task" of building roads suitable to the demands of the Fascist war-machine—for its military advance as well as its supply.[15] Thus, De Bono

---

11   Jünger, "Total Mobilization," 126.

12   Giorgio Rochat, *Guerre italiane in Libia e in Etiopia. Studi militari 1921–1939* (Paese: Pagus edizioni, 1991), 105.

13   Emilio De Bono, *Anno XIIII* [sic]: *The Conquest of an Empire* (London: Cresset Press, 1937), 18.

14   Sun Tzu, *The Art of War* (Oxford: Oxford University Press, 1963), 134 (XI.29). On dromocrats cf.: Paul Virilio, *Speed and Politics* (Los Angeles: Semiotext(e), 2006); on the Italian *blitzkrieg* avant la lettre cf. Daniel Hedinger, *Die Achse. Berlin-Rom-Tokio 1919–1946* (Munich: C.H. Beck, 2021), 286–92 and Giulia Brogini Künzi, *Italien und der Abessinienkrieg 1935/36. Kolonialkrieg oder totaler Krieg?* (Paderborn: Schöningh, 2006), 234–238.

15   De Bono, *Anno XIIII*, 63. On this and the following cf. Richard Pankhurst, "Road-Building During the Italian Fascist Occupation of Ethiopia (1936–1941)," *Africa Quarterly* 15 (1976): 21–63; as well as Marco Antonsich, "Addis Abeba 'Caput Viarium'. Le strade del Duce in Abissinia," *Limes* 13, no. 3 (2006): 133–44; Aram Mattioli, "Unterwegs zu einer imperialen Raumordnung in Italienisch-Ostafrika," in *Für den Faschismus bauen. Architektur und Städtebau im Italien Mussolinis. Kultur–Philosophie–Geschichte*, eds. Aram Mattioli and Gerald Steinacher (Zurich: Orell Füssli, 2009): 327–352.

deployed a steadily growing army of Italian workers: in the run-up to the attack, between February and October 1935, their numbers grew from 10,000 to 50,000.[16] Shortly before entering Addis Ababa on May 5, 1936, Marshal Pietro Badoglio was deploying 170,000 men to build roads on the northern front, while in the south General Rodolfo Graziani had to make do with 30,000.[17] As Giulia Brogini Künzi has shown, this massive labor force produced extraordinary results: between October 1935 and May 1936 it built 1,800 km of new roads, and mended 900 km of existing roads on the northern front alone, including 1,570 bridges.[18] Yet Mussolini's plans for the newly conquered *spazio vitale/Lebensraum* were even grander.

On May 19—ten days after the declaration of the Italian Empire—il Duce decreed that 2,850 km of roads be built connecting Massawa with the Ethiopian capital via Asmara and Dessie (*Strada della Vittoria*) and the latter to the port of Assab (*Strada imperiale*).[19] In June 1937, the astronomical sum of 7.73 billion lire was allotted to road construction. A few more figures may illustrate the gigantomania that underlay the Fascist infrastructure project: between December 1936 and December 1937, 596,000 tons of cement, 3,630 tons of iron, and 616 tons of dynamite were shipped to *Africa Orientale Italiana* (A.O.I.) where—as of the beginning of June 1937—63,530 Italian, 43,720 indigenous, and 10,680 Yemenite and Sudanese workers used them to materialize the network of imperial roads.[20] Until the Fascists were ousted from the Horn of Africa in the course of 1941, the colonies were to consume twenty percent of the state budget.[21] It is fascist imperial infrastructure's cultural dimension which allows us to grasp why this gigantic labor process was set in motion.[22]

---

16   De Bono, *Anno XIIII*, 67. Cf. Pankhurst, "Road-Building," 26.
17   Pankhurst, "Road-Building," 33.
18   Brogini Künzi, *Italien und der Abessinienkrieg*, 253.
19   Pankhurst, "Road-Building," 34; Angelo Del Boca, *Gli Italiani in Africa Orientale. Vol. 3, La caduta dell'impero* (Rome: Laterza, 1982), 159. Cf. Mattioli, "Unterwegs zu einer imperialen Raumordnung," 334 et seqq.
20   Del Boca, *Gli Italiani in Africa Orientale*, 159, 162.
21   Giuseppe Maione, "I costi delle imprese coloniali," in *Le guerre coloniali del fascismo*, ed. Angelo Del Boca (Rome: Laterza, 1991): 400–20, 401.
22   On imperial infrastructure cf. Dirk van Laak, *Imperiale Infrastruktur. Deutsche Planungen für eine Erschließung Afrikas 1880 bis 1960* (Paderborn: Ferdinand Schöningh, 2004).

Imaginaries—Rome, Anno XIV

> Everyone knows that I have a kind of Roman passion for roads, in which I see one of the fundamental elements of the well-being and unity of the people.[23]

As mentioned, infrastructure is best conceived as a hybrid, as a composite consisting of signs and things, knowledge and power, nature and society, humans and non-humans.[24] It was the symbols, narratives, and imaginaries which transformed the steel, gravel, and cement into a fascist imperial infrastructure—and Rome was Fascism's most potent symbol. Rome lay at the heart of the Fascist imaginary and functioned as foundational narrative. Rome defined the Fascist style and aesthetics, it underlay the vision of the New Man and of the bellicose and orderly society which the Fascists aimed to bring forth. Consequently, the myth of Rome also informed the infrastructure which the Fascists built at the Horn of Africa. As Giuseppe Pini, the chief engineer of the roads works in eastern Africa, stated in 1939:

> The first works that the Romans imposed in the conquered regions were the roads for the valorization of the lands, for the development of trade and for the welfare of the peoples: roads, which, with their routes and bridges, still testify after millennia not only to the skill and genius of the builders, but also and above all, to the humane and civilizing purpose of the conquest. After our troops entered Addis Ababa, the first order given by the Duce to H.E. Badoglio for the enhancement of the Empire bears the words: roads, roads, roads.[25]

The imperial roads connected not only the ports, cities and towns of *Africa Orientale Italiana*, they also linked an imaginary past with both the present and future of the empire. Rome was inscribed into the imperial roads and transformed them into symbols of the supposed benevolence of the Fascist presence in eastern Africa. Here, as in Libya and elsewhere around the Fascist Mediterranean, Rome legitimized the Fascist empire and disguised the murderous imperial undertaking as Fascism's universal civilizing mission.

---

23   Benito Mussolini, "Al Gran Rapporto del Fascismo," in *Opera Omnia di Benito Mussolini Vol. XXIV*, eds. Edoardo Susmel and Dulio Susmel (Florence: La Fenice, 1964): 132–46, 134.

24   Cf. Latour, *We Have Never Been Modern*, 100 et seqq.

25   Giuseppe Pini, "Il piano del Duce," in *L'industria in A.O.I.*, ed. Confederazione fascista degli industriali (Rome: U.S.I.L.A., 1939): 51–75, 51.

Figure 2: An illustration from the book L'industria in A.O.I. shows the close nexus between Rome and roads. The caption reads: "I have a kind of Roman passion for roads, in which I see one of the fundamental elements of the well-being and unity of the people."

Confederazione fascista degli industriali, ed., *L'industria in A.O.I.* (Rome: U.S.I.L.A., 1939), n.p. Courtesy of The Wolfsonian–Florida International University, Miami Beach, Florida, The Mitchell Wolfson, Jr. Collection, XB1990.587. Photo: David Almeida.

But it was not Rome alone and the eternal, motionless order it stood for, that informed the imperial roads. It was also the concept of movement, of total mobilization itself. Movement was central to the modern understanding of territoriality that spurred Fascism's imperial conquest: space needed to be conquered and penetrated, subjugated, divided, and enclosed. But it also needed to be saturated by the state, and in the 1930s roads were the means of choice to allow for the necessary flow of statal energies.[26] But the imperial roads and the war they enabled served not only to 'energize' the vast new imperial space. Rather, they also served to revitalize, Fascism itself.

Figure 3: A further illustration from the book L'industria in A.O.I. captures the spirit of the age of total mobilization. The caption reads: "The word that sums up and gives unmistakable character to our century is 'movement'.

Confederazione fascista degli industriali, ed., L'industria in A.O.I., n.p. Courtesy of The Wolfsonian–Florida International University, Miami Beach, Florida, The Mitchell Wolfson, Jr. Collection, XB1990.587. Photo: David Almeida.

---

26   Cf. Charles S. Maier, "Consigning the Twentieth Century to History: Alternative Narratives for the Modern Era," *American Historical Review* 105, no. 3 (2000): 807–831, 819 et seqq.

The war in Ethiopia was to revive the original spirit of fascism, that is, the spirit of *squadrismo*. As Arturo Marpicati, former vice-secretary of the PNF, stated in 1938:

> Fascism remains a movement of action, a deed, a total commitment of our personality thrown forward. It is in vain to declare oneself a fascist, where this spirit, in which Fascism—yesterday as today—most properly consists, is lacking. Otherwise, the revolution would no longer go forward. Instead, it is on the march. [...] In movement is life.[27]

Fascism was *movement* and war was both its impetus and end. Violence and warfare stood not only at the beginning of the Fascist movement, they were also its lifeblood. After thirteen years in power the Fascists' *élan vital*, their destructive, revolutionary urge, had waned. The Fascist movement was in danger of coming to a standstill. The war in Abyssinia and the violence it unleashed served to put the Fascists back on the revolutionary track. Now they were on the road again and the empire served, as Alexander De Grand notes, as a "testing ground for a Fascism that sought to free itself from any constraints. What had not been done in Italy for some years or could not be done at all, now could be experimented with in Africa."[28]

While the Fascists had conquered the capital of the Ethiopian empire with a *blitzkrieg* in 1936, they were never able to truly 'pacify' the enormous territory—not to mention failing to 'saturate' it with the institutions and representatives of the fascist colonial state. The brutal war against guerrilla forces and the civilian population raged on for another five years.[29] In light of the bombardment of civilians, the use of poison gas and the death of between 350,000 to 760,000 of the ten million Ethiopians, Aram Mattioli rightly sees the Italo-Ethiopian War not only as a laboratory of violence but also as the first fascist war of annihilation—a war with an underlying genocidal tendency.[30] The imperial roads set the fascist war machine in motion. Yet, they not only enabled the new fascist warfare, but they were also materializations of the culture of "total mobilization."[31] As Jünger, with whom this piece began, stated,

27   Arturo Marpicati, *Il Partito Fascista. Origine – sviluppo – funzioni* (Milan: Mondadori, 1938), 35.

28   Alexander De Grand, "Mussolini's Follies: Fascism in its Imperial and Racist Phase, 1935–1940," *Contemporary European History* 13, no. 2 (2004): 127–47, 138.

29   Aram Mattioli, "Ein Schlüsselereignis der Weltkriegsepoche," in *Der erste faschistische Vernichtungskrieg. Die italienische Aggression gegen Äthiopien 1935–1941*, eds. Asfa-Wossen Asserate and Aram Mattioli (Cologne: SH-Verlag, 2006): 9–25, 9.

30   Mattioli, "Ein Schlüsselereignis," 9. Cf. also Aram Mattioli, "Entgrenzte Kriegsgewalt. Der italienische Giftgaseinsatz in Abessinien 1935–1936," *Vierteljahrshefte für Zeitgeschichte* 51 (2003): 311–37; Aram Mattioli, *Experimentierfeld der Gewalt. Der Abessinienkrieg und seine internationale Bedeutung 1935–1941* (Zürich: Orell Füssli Verlag, 2005).

31   Cf. Miguel Alonso, Alan Kramer, and Javier Rodrigo, eds., *Fascist Warfare, 1922–1945: Aggression, Occupation, Annihilation* (Cham: Palgrave Macmillan, 2019).

the latter's "technical side is not decisive. Its basis—like that of all technology—lies deeper."[32] The same could be said for infrastructure in general.

---

32   Jünger, "Total Mobilization," 129.

Authors

Nora Binder is a postdoctoral researcher in the history of the human and social sciences at Universität Konstanz. Her current project investigates the epistemology of human interrelations within applied psychology and its ties with the concept of social competence (1930–1970). In her doctoral thesis *Kurt Lewin und die Psychologie des Feldes* (2023) she scrutinizes early experimental social psychology and the beginnings of group dynamics.

Manuel Borutta is Professor of Modern and Contemporary History at the University of Konstanz. His research focuses on European culture wars and nation-building, colonialism and decolonization. His publications include *Antikatholizismus. Deutschland und Italien im Zeitalter der europäischen Kulturkämpfe* (Vandenhoeck & Ruprecht 2011), *A Colonial Sea: The Mediterranean, 1798–1956* (edited with Sakis Gekas, Routledge 2012), *Braudel in Algier: Die kolonialen Wurzeln der Méditerranée und der Spatial Turn* (Historische Zeitschrift 2016) and *Vertriebene und Pieds-Noirs in Postwar Germany and France* (edited with Jan C. Jansen, Palgrave 2016). He is currently completing a monograph on (post)colonial entanglements and interactions of Algeria and France.

Bettina Braun completed her PhD in Phonetics/Phonology at Saarland University in 2004. After Postdoc positions at the Phonetics Laboratory at the University of Oxford and the Max-Planck-Institute (MPI) for Psycholinguistics in Nijmegen, she has been appointed Professor of General Linguistics at the University of Konstanz in 2009. She regularly publishes in the areas of phonetics, phonology, psycholinguistics and language acquisition. She currently is Associate Editor for Laboratory Phonology and a member of the Scientific Advisory Boards of the MPI for Empirical Aesthetics in Frankfurt and the Austrian Academy of Sciences.

Bernhard Brehmer received his PhD in Slavic Linguistics from the University of Tübingen in 2004. From 2006 to 2013 he worked as an assistant professor of Polish and Serbocroatian Linguistics at the University of Hamburg before he was appointed Professor of Slavic Linguistics at the University of Greifswald. In 2020 he joined the University of Konstanz. His research interests include individual and so-cietal bi- and multilingualism, language acquisition and attrition, language contact, language policies, and sociolinguistics. He conducted several large scale projects on heritage speakers of Russian and Polish in Germany, partly in collaboration with colleagues from Poland and Russia.

Jochen Briesen is a Heisenberg Fellow at the University of Konstanz's Department of Philosophy. Prior to his acceptance into the prestigious Heisenberg Program by the German Research Foundation, he worked as an assistant (wissenschaftlicher Mitar-beiter) at the University of Bonn, the University of Konstanz, and Freie Universität Berlin. He also held positions as a visiting professor at Humboldt University Berlin and the University of Cologne, as well as a visiting scholar at Harvard University, Universitet Uppsala, and New York University. Briesen's research focuses on epis-temology, the philosophy of language, and aesthetics. He has authored two books in German, oversees two research series, and has made significant contributions to renowned international philosophical journals including *Synthese*, *Philosophical Studies*, *British Journal of Aesthetics*, *British Journal for the Philosophy of Science*, and *Australasian Journal of Philosophy*.

Fernando Esposito is assistant professor at the Department of Modern History at the Universität Konstanz. His book *Fascism, Aviation and Mythical Modernity* (2015) scrutinizes the aviation discourse in Italy and Germany, reading it as a blueprint for a fascist mythical modernity. His second book (habilitation) deals with the trans-formation of European understandings of time and history and the chronopolitics that arose from modern temporality.

Barbara Feichtinger is Professor of Latin Literature at the University of Konstanz. Her research interests include (Christian) Late Antiquity, Augustean literature, lit-erary theory, and Gender studies. She is currently leading a DFG project on citations as literary sites of negotiation of cultural hybridity using digital methods of analysis.

Anne Ganzert is coordinator for the CRC initiative "Serious Gaming or: Taking Gaming Seriously" and a postdoctoral researcher in media studies at Universität Konstanz. She has done successful research in the projects "Dynamics of social ex-clusion in social media platforms. International and transnational perspectives on fragmented publics" and "Smartphone-Communities: Participation as Promise and Imposition." Her book *Serial Pinboarding in Contemporary Television* (Palgrave 2020) focuses on TV series and their pin boards as dispositives of seriality. Recent publica-tions include the entry on "Participation" in the *Handbuch Televisuelle Serialität* (eds.: O. Moskatova and S. Grampp, Springer 2022) and "(Nach-)Denken und (Ver-)Folgen – Verschwörungserzählungen, Pinnwände und ihre Gefolgschaften" in *Following*.

Medien der Gefolgschaft und Prozesse des Folgens (eds.: A. Ganzert, P. Hauser and I. Otto, de Gruyter 2023).

Ulrich Gotter is Professor for Ancient History at the University of Konstanz since 2004. He received his PhD from the University of Freiburg/Br. in 1992 where he worked till 1998 on the political culture of the Later Roman Republic and on processes of cultural transfer in the Mediterranean. At the University of Münster he studied the religious transformations in Late Antiquity. He is interested in the comparative history of civil wars and in the impact of empires on the organisation of space and power.

Anja Hartl is Assistant Professor at the Department of English at the University of Innsbruck, Austria. Her research interests include contemporary British theatre, Bertolt Brecht, Shakespearean drama, adaptation studies, affect theory, and Victorian fiction. She is currently working on a postdoctoral research project on shame in the Victorian novel. Her first monograph, *Brecht and Post-1990s British Drama: Dialectical Theatre Today*, was published in 2021 as part of Bloomsbury's Methuen Drama Engage series. She is the editor of *The Threepenny Opera* by Bertolt Brecht (Bloomsbury Methuen Drama Student Editions, 2022) and co-edits the Methuen Drama Agitations series.

Jonas Kellermann is Assistant Professor of British Studies at the University of Konstanz. He studied English Philology and Theatre Studies at Freie Universität Berlin and the University of Edinburgh, and received his Ph.D. from the University of Konstanz in 2020. He is the author of *Dramaturgies of Love in Romeo and Juliet: Word, Music, and Dance* (Routledge 2021) and a recipient of the Martin Lehnert Prize by the German Shakespeare Association. Aside from the early modern period, his research focuses on the anglophone novel of the 20th and 21st century and queer studies. His work has appeared in journals including *Cahiers Élisabéthains*, *Shakespeare Jahrbuch*, *Critique*, and *Adaptation*.

Thomas G. Kirsch is Professor of Social and Cultural Anthropology at the University of Konstanz. He has published two monographs and articles in some of the major refereed anthropology journals (e.g., Africa; American Anthropologist; American Ethnologist; Visual Anthropology). Among the books (co)edited by him are *Domesticating Vigilantism in Africa* (James Currey, 2010, with Tilo Grätz), *Regimes of Ignorance: Anthropological Perspectives on the Production and Reproduction of Non-Knowledge* (Berghahn Books, 2015, with Roy Dilley), *Ethical Fields in Africa* (special issue Africa, 2017, with Astrid Bochow and Rijk van Dijk) and *Religiopolitical Activism in Southern Africa* (special issue Journal of Religion in Africa, 2021, with Franziska Duarte dos Santos and Rijk van Dijk).

Steffen Koch is an assistant professor (wissenschaftlicher Mitarbeiter) at Bielefeld University's Department of Philosophy. Before joining the department in 2021, he worked as a doctoral researcher in the Emmy Noether group "Experimental philosophy and the method of cases" at Ruhr University Bochum. Koch's research focuses on philosophy of language, metaphilosophy, and experimental philosophy. He has edited several books and special issues on conceptual engineering and philosophical methodology. His research on these and related topics has been published in leading philosophy journals, including *Analysis, Ergo, Erkenntnis, Inquiry, Philosophical Studies*, and *Synthese*. He is a founding member of the Conceptual Engineering Network (CEN), which hosts regular talks and discussions, and oversees the philpapers.org entry on "conceptual engineering."

Daniel G. König is Professor for the History of Religions at the University of Konstanz. After his PhD-thesis on motivations to convert to Christianity in the Western Roman Empire of Late Antiquity and its Romano-Germanic successors (*Bekehrungsmotive*, Husum: Mathiesen, 2008), he re-evaluated the Arabic-Islamic documentation of medieval Christian Europe in *Arabic-Islamic Views of the Latin West* (Oxford: OUP, 2015). Since the publication of *Latin and Arabic: Entangled Histories* (Heidelberg: HeiUP, 2019), an edited volume on the interaction of Latin and Arabic as linguistic systems, he has been working on various facets of Christian–Muslim interaction and communication in the wider Mediterranean.

Steffen Krämer is postdoctoral researcher at the Konstanz section of the Research Institute Social Cohesion at the University of Konstanz. He received his PhD in media studies from the University of Hamburg with a dissertation about diagrammatic media in the field of epidemiology. Currently, his research focuses on the communication of ignorance and withdrawal in digital social networks.

Kirsten Mahlke is Professor of Cultural Theory at the department of Literature, Arts and Media Studies at the University of Konstanz. She received her PhD in Romance literature and her Master's degree in Ethnology, Russian, French and Hispanic Literatures at the Goethe University of Frankfurt/Main. In 2009 and 2017 she received grants from the European Research Council for research and transfer projects on Narratives of Terror and Disappearence in the aftermath of the Argentine dictatorship. Her current research is focused on early modern literature and infrastructures of conquest and early colonialism in America, both from European and Indigenous perspectives. Among her publications are books and articles on Franco-Brazilian, Mexican, Andean, and Caribbean conquest accounts and violent histories in the Southern Cone: *Offenbarung im Westen*, 2005, *Auf den Spuren der Konstanzer Kolonialzeit*, 2021.

Christian Meyer is a professor of Sociology at the Department of History and Sociology of the University of Konstanz, Germany, where he is also chairman of the Social Science Archive (Alfred Schutz Memorial Archive). Before, he was a professor of sociology at the University of Würzburg and of communication at the University of Duisburg-Essen. His research interests include social and cultural theory, phenomenological sociology, sociology of embodied interaction, studies in comparative sociality, and qualitative methods of social research. Recent publication include *Ethnomethodologie reloaded* (Bielefeld 2021, co-edited), "The Phenomenological Foundations of Ethnomethodology's Conceptions of Sequentiality and Indexicality. Harold Garfinkel's References to Aron Gurwitsch's 'Field of Consciousness'" in *Gesprächsforschung* 23 (2022): 111–144, and *Culture, Practice, and the Body* (Stuttgart 2018).

Timo Müller is Professor of American Studies at the University of Konstanz, Germany. His research focuses on modernism, African American literature, and the environmental humanities. His work has appeared in journals including *American Literature*, *Arizona Quarterly*, and *Twentieth-Century Literature*. He has edited several textbooks and written two monographs, *The Self as Object in Modernist Fiction* (2010) and *The African American Sonnet: A Literary History* (2018), which is now available in paperback from the University of Mississippi Press. He has held visiting fellowships at the British Library, Harvard, and Yale. He currently serves as president of the German Association of Anglophone Postcolonial Studies (GAPS). From 2023 to 2027 he is directing the ERC-funded research project "Off the Road: The Environmental Aesthetics of Early Automobility."

Isabell Otto is Professor of Media Studies at the University of Konstanz. She leads a sub-project on the topic of "Smartphone Communities" in the research group "Media and Participation" and a project on the topic of "Dynamics of Social Closure in Social Media Platforms" in the Konstanz sub-institute of the Research Institute for Social Cohesion. Her research focuses on media and the history of knowledge, film and television cultures, media participation in digital cultures, as well as media theory and temporality. Her recent publications include: *Prozess und Zeitordnung. Temporalität unter der Bedingung digitaler Vernetzung* (Göttingen: Konstanz University Press 2020).

Aaron Pinnix is a Postdoctoral Researcher in American Studies at the University of Konstanz in Germany. Recent publications include articles in *JCMS: Journal of Cinema and Media Studies*, *Atlantic Studies*, *ZAA: A Quarterly of Language, Literature, and Culture*, *Shima*, and forthcoming in *The Routledge Companion to Ecopoetics*. His research is on ocean-focused poetry that conjoins ecological and social justice, and he is currently working on a monograph, titled *Poetry of the Submerged Anthropocene*, that examines how contemporary poetry addresses humanity's effects on underwater life.

Martin Rempe is a historian of modern European and global history at the University of Konstanz and currently fellow of the DFG Heisenberg Program. He specializes in the history of development, the social history of music and cultural work as well as the history of European-African relations. Rempe is author of *Entwicklung im Konflikt. Die EWG und der Senegal, 1957–1975* (Köln: Böhlau, 2012) and of *Art, Play, Labour: the Music Profession in Germany 1850–1960* (Leiden: Brill 2023). Research articles have been published in *Itinerario, Humanity, European Review of History, Geschichte und Gesellschaft*, and other journals. Together with Klaus Nathaus, Rempe has co-edited the handbook *Musicking in Twentieth Century Europe* (Berlin: de Gruyter, 2021).

Eva Riedke is post-doc researcher in the Division of Social and Cultural Anthropology at the University of Konstanz. Her current research focuses on energy anthropology, on issues of energy and climate change, on infrastructures and the formation of publics around them, and on questions of energy ethics. Pursuing ethnographic fieldwork in both Germany and Kenya, she is concerned with solar devices that are being marketed to those living without reliable access to the electricity grid. "Following the product," she engages with their design in Germany to their use in rural Kenya, exploring the energy futures that solar entrepreneurs envision for themselves and others.

Katalin Schober is Junior Professor of Language Education at the University of Konstanz, Germany. She received her Ph.D. in English Literature and Culture from Humboldt University, Berlin. Her research interests focus on questions of literary and media literacies, transculturality, and Human Rights Education. Her publications include a monograph on eighteenth-century travelers touring Greece and the Levant as well as articles about Language Education.

Rudolf Schlögl, geb. 1955, wurde 1986 in Erlangen mit einer Arbeit zum Verhältnis von bäuerlicher Wirtschaft und Staatsbildung im 17. Jahrhundert promoviert. 1992 habilitierte er sich in Münster mit einer Studie zu Prozessen der Säkularisierung im Übergang vom 18. zum 19. Jahrhundert. Von 1995 bis 2021 hatte er den Lehrstuhl für Neuere und Neueste Geschichte an der Universität Konstanz inne. In den Jahren von 2009 bis 2016 war er zum Sprecher des Exzellenzclusters Kulturelle Grundlagen von Integration bestellt. Er forscht und publiziert zu einer Geschichte der europäischen Gesellschaft der Frühen Neuzeit auf systemtheoretischen Grundlagen.

Gabriela Signori, from 2001 to 2006 Professor of the History of the Late Middle Ages and Historical Auxiliary Sciences at the Westfaelische Wilhelms University of Muenster, since 2006 Professor of the History of the Middle Ages at the University of Konstanz, mbW (significantly involved researcher) in the Cluster of Excellence "Cultural

Foundations of Integration," researches mainly on the fields of social history, urban history, cultures of economy, monasticism and church history, gender history, family and kinship (childless couples, old people, "singles", adoption, fosterage).

Axel Volmar is a currently a Guest Professor at the Institute of Music and Media at the Humboldt-University in Berlin. Previously, he was a Research Associate in the research initiative "Transforming Infrastructure" at the University of Konstanz (2022–2023) and in the Collaborative Research Center "Media of Cooperation" at the University of Siegen (2016–2022). From 2014 to 2016, he was a Postdoctoral Fellow of the Andrew W. Mellon Foundation in the Department of Art History and Communication Studies at McGill University. His research is in the areas of media history, media theory, and the praxeology of media, intersecting with the history of science, infrastructure studies, format studies, and disability studies. Volmar is author of *Klang-Experimente. Die auditive Kultur der Naturwissenschaften 1761–1961* (2015) and co-editor of various edited volumes, including *Format Matters: Standards, Practices, and Politics in Media Cultures* (2020); *Media Infrastructures and the Politics of Digital Time: Essays on Hardwired Temporalities* (2021); *Interrogating Datafication: Towards a Praxeology of Data* (2022); and *Video Conferencing: Infrastructure, Practices, Aesthetics* (2023).

Christina Wald is Professor of English Literature and Literary Theory and director of the Centre for Cultural Inquiry at the University of Konstanz. Her research focuses on contemporary drama, performance, film, and TV series as well as on early modern drama and prose fiction. She is the author of *Hysteria, Trauma and Melancholia: Performative Maladies in Contemporary Anglophone Drama* (2007), *The Reformation of Romance: The Eucharist, Disguise and Foreign Fashion in Early Modern Prose Fiction* (2014), and *Shakespeare's Serial Returns in Complex TV* (2020). She has co-edited several books, among them *The Literature of Melancholia: Early Modern to Postmodern* (2011). Her work has appeared in journals including *Shakespeare Survey, Shakespeare, Shakespeare Bulletin, Modern Drama, South African Theatre Journal, Adaptation, The Journal of Commonwealth Literature*, and *Classical Receptions Journal*.

[transcript]

PUBLISHING. KNOWLEDGE. TOGETHER.

transcript publishing stands for a multilingual transdisciplinary programme in the social sciences and humanities. Showcasing the latest academic research in various fields and providing cutting-edge diagnoses on current affairs and future perspectives, we pride ourselves in the promotion of modern educational media beyond traditional print and e-publishing. We facilitate digital and open publication formats that can be tailored to the specific needs of our publication partners.

OUR SERVICES INCLUDE

- partnership-based publishing models
- Open Access publishing
- innovative digital formats: HTML, Living Handbooks, and more
- sustainable digital publishing with XML
- digital educational media
- diverse social media linking of all our publications

Visit us online: www.transcript-publishing.com

Find our latest catalogue at www.transcript-publishing.com/newbookspdf